Rube Waddell

RUBE WADDELL

The Zany, Brilliant Life of a Strikeout Artist

by

ALAN H. LEVY

McFarland & Company, Inc., Publishers
Jefferson, North Carolina, and London

Acknowledgments: I am indebted to several people for their generous assistance in my research. Mr. Bruce S. Markusen of the National Baseball Hall of Fame and Museum kindly provided me with all the materials on Rube Waddell in the files at Cooperstown. Mr. David Kelly of the Library of Congress was most kind and helpful in steering me to the many pertinent sources in that most grand facility. The staff of the Library of Congress Microfilm Reading Room were always courteous and prompt in hunting up the many obscure reels I requested. Mr. Eric Duchess of Evans City, Pennsylvania, who has done some of his own digging on Waddell, took the time to converse with me on a few occasions, and I thank him for exchanging some thoughts and bits of information with me. I would also like to thank Mr. Bruce Irwin who provided some useful thoughts and invaluable help in proofreading and indexing.

Less directly, but no less importantly, I owe a debt to Mr. Drew Craig, the son of one of my colleagues at Slippery Rock University. One afternoon, while telling Drew a few Rube tales, I noticed a certain spiritual communion occurring between these two strong and unique characters. The animation which the Waddell fables sparked in my young friend left me with the notion that a biography of the Rube would make a nice present for Drew's then upcoming tenth birthday. When I searched for a biography, however, I discovered none existed. It was at that point that I decided to embark upon the penning of a biography of a ballplayer who has certainly long deserved one. So Drew, this one's for you.

On the cover: Rube Waddell on the practice field with the
Philadelphia Athletics in 1904. (National Baseball Hall of Fame
Library, Cooperstown, N.Y.)

Library of Congress Cataloguing-in-Publication Data

Levy, Alan H.
    Rube Waddell : the zany, brilliant life of a strikeout artist / by
Alan H. Levy.
        p.   cm.
    Includes bibliographical references (p.) and index.
    ISBN 0-7864-0786-7 (softcover : 50# alkaline paper) ∞
    1. Waddell, Rube, 1876–1914.   2. Baseball players — United
States — Biography.   I. Title.
    GV865.W23   2000
    796.357'092 — dc21   00-30474
    [B]

British Library cataloguing data are available

Manufactured in the United States of America

McFarland & Company, Inc., Publishers
  Box 611, Jefferson, North Carolina 28640
    www.mcfarlandpub.com

Contents

Pregame

Rube Waddell. Just by itself, his name stands as a sentence for fans of old time baseball, from the days before Babe Ruth and before "new" stadiums like Wrigley Field and Fenway Park. Rube's name brings both a grin and a sad shake of the head. Part-time political commentator and full-time baseball fan George Will hailed Waddell as "the strangest man ever to play baseball."[1] The great pitcher Walter Johnson once reflected that Rube Waddell "had more sheer pitching ability than any man I ever saw."[2] Both Johnson and Will were right, and there lies the combination of ingredients that makes Rube Waddell so intriguing a figure. Were it just for his personality, Waddell would be a fascinating figure. His ability alone also merits the attention of every baseball fan. Combined, the two points were and remain irresistible.

As an artist of the pitcher's mound, Waddell had it all. Pitching great Cy Young called Waddell the greatest left-hander of all time. Connie Mack declared Rube and Christy Mathewson the greatest pitchers ever. Rube was an absolute terror to hitters. He was a very large man, about six foot two, and he usually weighed around 225 pounds. He could throw with the velocity of any man who ever played the game. When he played with the Pittsburgh Pirates, Rube took part in a throwing contest with teammate Honus Wagner, and both threw the ball nearly 400 feet (the Dutchman beat him by a foot). Waddell's fastball was the equal of any pitcher he faced, including Christy Mathewson, Cy Young, and Walter Johnson, a fact each freely admitted. And Rube's fastball was quite a riser. Left-handed hitters were often startled when they would reach for a fastball on the outside corner, only to find it suddenly about to graze their nose. Many a hitter swung at the letters as a Waddell blazer whizzed by them at eye level.

Then there was the Waddell curve, or more accurately the curves. Waddell had unusually large hands (and feet) even for his size, features of giantism. His shoe size was 13. As for his hands, John McGraw noted that Waddell could "encircle a baseball with his fingers as the ordinary man could a billiard ball."[3] Waddell could nearly touch his middle finger with his thumb

1

around a ball's diameter. In the 1990s, Seattle pitcher Randy Johnson imposed the kind of towering presence on the mound which Waddell held in the American League in the first decade of the twentieth century. With his huge hands, maybe Rube could have been a concert pianist (doubtful, though he could play). What Waddell learned like no other was to use his great left paw to make a baseball spin in any number of controlled ways. He could curve it out or down, of course, like a normal curve ball, but with a severity that was remarkable. Waddell's curve could explode from the shoulder to the ankle and do so at the speed of his fastball. Many was the time that as great a hitter as Ty Cobb or Nap Lajoie would be swinging belt high while the catcher was digging Rube's pitch out of the dirt. Connie Mack said Rube's curve often broke more than two feet, and, he emphasized, it came at incredible speed.[4]

Rube could also curve it the other way, away from a right hander, into a lefty. Today we call that a screwball; others have called it fadeaway. Christy Mathewson was famous for it, but Rube could throw it, too.

Rube also had two kinds of "puzzlers," off-speed change-ups, one of which, some reporters mused, a hitter could swing at three times before it got to the plate. The other slow one Rube called his "wobbler," which today would be called a knuckleball. Rube had quite the arsenal, as complete as anyone's then or since. The Rube could summon any part of it at will, and he usually did at just the right times. Although a complete head case off the field, on the field Rube was all savvy, with skill and "stuff" heightened by speed that was truly frightening.

In 1903 Rube struck out 301 batters while no other pitcher in the league topped 175. In 1904 he struck out an incredible 349, walking just 81. Rube never walked 100 in any season; even Christy Mathewson broke triple figures once. Rube's 349 strikeout mark would not be broken until 1965, and then only after the season had been lengthened. (Baseball officials never "Roger Maris'ed" that record.) In September of 1904 Rube also missed about eight starts due to an injury while on a real hot streak, so his mark of 349 might actually have approached 400. Rube's strikeout feats need to be considered in context, too. In 1903-4 players tended to swing not for the fences but just to make contact, so strikeouts were less frequent. Here Rube was a phenomenon, far beyond the normal play of his day. The 349 he struck out in 1904 bettered half the total of any other *team* that year.

As a boy, I went to a Dodgers-Phillies game in old Connie Mack Stadium, a stadium which could indeed be termed "the house that Rube built." That day Sandy Koufax, the man who broke Waddell's single-season strikeout record, was slated to pitch. During the pregame warmups I situated myself at the railing alongside the field as close to catcher John Roseboro as I could get. I stood within two feet of where the right-handed batters' box would

have been and experienced as much as possible what it is like to stand and
face a pitcher like Koufax. It would actually be inaccurate to say that from
there I saw Koufax pitch. Rather, I *heard* him pitch, for I never really saw the
ball. I could only hear, and feel, the whoosh of the ball and the shotgun-like
pop his pitches made into Roseboro's mitt. I did the same thing on other occasions in other parks with various pitchers, including Jim Palmer and Tom
Seaver. It was not the same, though Cleveland's Sam McDowell came close.

My memory of Koufax, while anything but scientific, gives me some
appreciation of how the pitching of someone like Waddell must have appeared
to the players, and the adoring young fans, of his era. The parallel of Rube
with Koufax involves more than my own little experience, however. The two
were quite similar as players on the field. Off the field they could not have
been more different. Koufax was as stable a pitcher as ever played. The only
off-field link between them could be that a rabbi happened to preside at Waddell's funeral. (No, unlike Jim Palmer, Rube was not Jewish, but a rabbi happened to be on hand in San Antonio, Texas, where Rube died penniless in
1914.)

The similarity *on* the field between Koufax and Waddell lies not only in
the totally dominating presence each exerted in their respective heydays but,
as well, in their relatively short times of absolute perfection. Koufax took several years to find himself as a pitcher. He came up with all the raves about
his speed, but his control was problematic, though many forget that in some
of his early years the left-handed Koufax was pitching half his games in the
L.A. Coliseum, which had an absurdly short left field line that damaged the
ERA of many southpaws. Still, when Koufax gained a full mastery over the
location of his shoots he went on to six years of pitching during which he was
virtually unhittable. Indeed, when Casey Stengel saw Koufax he remarked,
"You can forget about Rube Waddell and the other guy [Walter Johnson],
this guy's the best." Maybe Koufax was the best, but it is noteworthy that of
all the greats, Stengel turned to Waddell as a touchstone of comparison.

For very different reasons, Rube Waddell also had several inconsistent
years when he first arrived in the majors. He showed some brilliance but much
eccentricity, and on numerous occasions it looked like he would never stick
in the majors. Then came a string of seasons from the middle of 1902, when
he first played for Connie Mack and the Philadelphia Athletics, through 1908,
when he nearly pitched the St. Louis Browns to a pennant. (The Brownies
didn't always finish last; almost always.) For those six and a half seasons Rube
was the best; some would argue, as they do with Koufax, the best ever. In
1902, for example, Rube arrived with the A's in late June. He won his first
game on July 1, and ended his season about ten days early since the A's had
wrapped up the pennant. During that short stretch Rube compiled 24 wins

and topped the league in strikeouts for the year — all this in slightly more than *half* a season! Koufax and Waddell were as fast or faster than any pitcher of their own day. And both had curves that were actually better than their fastballs. That cannot be said about any other Hall of Famer. When they were "on," the hitters did not have a chance — Willy Mays, Ty Cobb, it didn't matter.

Data on ballplayers of old are sometimes difficult to assess. Charles "Old Hoss" Radbourne won 60 games in the 1870 season, for example — but before 1892 pitchers threw from 45 feet, not 60, and they could "run up" their delivery like a cricket bowler. It was in 1890 that the rules for baseball pitchers jelled into those of the current game — pitching from the rubber, from 60 feet, no balking. (The spitball and other foreign substance rules which began in the 1920s ended or curbed practices that were not discovered and perfected until Rube's era, though Rube never cared to throw a wet one. Connie Mack actually did not want him to, fearing one could sail off his hand and conk a fan, leaving the team's management financially liable.) Certainly conditions have changed since the early twentieth century, but conditions were at least comparable, while they were not in earlier eras.

It is in regard to players of one era versus another that endless arguments emerge. There are no clear distinctions as to quality of players between eras. Naturalist and baseball writer Stephen Jay Gould has pointed out, in regard to hitters, that while the best players' batting averages were higher in earlier times, the worst averages were also lower, and that the average batting average has not changed much one era to the next. More generally, Gould has written about society's misunderstandings, and misapplications, of Darwinian evolution. Evolution is change, but it is not necessarily improvement. Applying this to his beloved baseball, he and others note that the skills of players have not really improved or deteriorated. Conditioning and equipment may be better, but, as with other sports, such improvements help middling talent. Second-rate players remain second-rate. And the stars' brilliance continues to emanate from wellsprings which have little or nothing to do with technology. Bad carpenters and poor chefs still produce unsightly cabinetry and inedible food, no matter the improvements in shop and kitchen paraphernalia. Shakespeare had a pen, Hemingway had a typewriter, and today's writer has a word processor. But was Hemingway better than Shakespeare? Are today's writers superior to Hemingway? Even if the answer is "yes," it is not due to any improvement in the mere means by which words can be placed on paper.

In such sports as golf or track and field, where achievements can be quantified, modern scores have certainly bettered those of prior generations. Some of this is due to better equipment, techniques, and training. The runners and golfers of yore would likely be better than they were had modern breakthroughs been available to them. As with the quality of writers, though, the essential matters of quality in these endeavors remain within the realm of the inexplicable. Golfer Jack Nicklaus once commented, for example, that while the players' scores of his time surpassed those of prior greats like Bobby Jones and Ben Hogan, the fact remains that if you put someone like Hogan into a situation with better play around him he would, as Nicklaus said, "likely rise to the occasion." That "rising" factor is present is all areas of physical and mental achievement. It cannot be quantified, and it is at the heart of what makes a few truly great.

With most sports there are no data which can compare the stars of different eras. The question of one generation's best versus another's usually results in endless debate. How many barbershop and saloon arguments have there been over who would win if Joe Louis had fought Jack Dempsey? Resolutions to such impossible debates have come, at worst with violence, at best with humor. In the 1950s retired Detroit Tiger second baseman Charlie Gehringer was asked to reflect on how Ty Cobb would fare in baseball today. Gehringer thoughtfully nodded and opined that "if Cobb were playing today he would probably hit about .320." The reporter snapped at the bait and energetically asked, "Well, then, why do people make such a fuss over his achievements if the game has so eclipsed that of his day?" "Now, do remember," Geringher softly interrupted, "the man is 73 years old."

Such jokes are better than a bar fight, but the point is that the questions of "the best ever" in sports and most other fields of endeavor cannot be resolved, for there is always context as well as content. Context cannot deconstruct all notions of talent, of course, no matter the silly efforts from some academic circles. I played ball, for example, but the quality of my playing would render me mediocre in my era or in any other. The limits of technology and know-how in my era were not revealed in my middling sort of athleticism. Only where there is excellence can the nature and limits of context appear. Thus when we get to the questions of who was the best ever at baseball or any other endeavor, there is first a qualitative line to be drawn. Sandy Koufax is in. Billy O'Dell, an OK pitcher of the late 1950s, is out. Among those who are in, context muddies the distinctions. After the fights and jokes, there are only ties. When the National Basketball Association celebrated its 50th anniversary in 1996, it fittingly named not the best player ever, only the best *players* (Russell, Chamberlain, Baylor, West, Erving, Bird, Johnson, Jordan — and they left Bob Lanier off the list!).

When discussions turn to who was the best pitcher in the history of baseball there can then only be a question of who belongs on the list. Eppa Rixey may be in the Hall of Fame, but he does not belong on the list. Don Larsen may have had a perfect World Series day in 1956, but he does not belong there, either. Joe Wood may have had one of the best single seasons any pitcher ever had (34 and 5 in 1912), but an injury quickly put him out of the box at age 24, and he, like Cleveland's Herb Score, remains one of the game's ultimate "might have beens." Hal Newhouser may have had three incredible seasons, but it was not enough for true immortality.

The list of immortal pitchers involves those about whose greatness there is no doubt — Cy Young, Christy Mathewson, Grover Alexander, Walter Johnson, Lefty Grove, Carl Hubbell, Satchel Paige, Bob Feller, Warren Spahn, Bob Gibson, Nolan Ryan. Doubtlessly, others could bring up more nominees, and again, within reason there are only ties. That's the group in which Sandy Koufax is commonly placed, and Rube Waddell belongs there, too. Koufax and Waddell were arguably better than the 11 greats listed above. Each was the fastest of his day, with the best curveballs, to boot. Each was, however, the greatest of his day for a relatively short time.

Were the issue of Waddell's legacy merely that of his artistry as a pitcher, there would be every reason to pen a biography of the man. He was that great a pitcher, and an all-around athlete as well. Rube was a top-notch football player. He was a marksman who competed with and beat some of the champion riflemen of his day. His boxing impressed heavyweight champ Jim Jeffries. Rube played golf, and without practice he could beat club champions on their courses with borrowed clubs. He was also a fisherman who could magically pull trout and bass out of streams which local fanatics had long deemed dead. He may not have been Jim Thorpe, but Rube was quite the athlete, a natural in every way.

In regard to his suitability for biographical study, Rube's pitching and his general athletic prowess pale before other features of the man. These were the features that made him such an idol in his day, and such a vexing figure to all who worked with him. When asked about Rube and what he could have accomplished under better self-management, the man who knew him best, Connie Mack, could only stare a few moments, smile, shake his head, and sigh with a chuckle, "That Waddell, if only he had ever grown up, my, my, my, my goodness."[5] Psychologists could come up with a lexicon of highfalutin' mumbo jumbo that captures aspects of the Rube — manic depressive, bipolar, personality disorder(s), acting out, narcissism (and alcoholism) — all variations of Connie Mack's simple wisdom. Rube was a looney to the extreme, and he was the first such case about whom newspapermen found the public loved to read.

One evening on the road, Mack was in a hotel lobby talking with the front desk clerk when Rube strode in. Rube pulled out his handkerchief as he walked by, and a pistol dropped out of his pocket. The gun landed on the floor and discharged, leaving a sizable a hole in the wall and a lot of shaken people, including the desk clerk. Rube said nothing and walked upstairs. Ever the small-town New England pharmacist, Mack looked at the dazed clerk and calmly observed, "That man is unpredictable," leaving the incident to resonate in the dazed clerk as it would.

Rube was unpredictable, all right. Many a time when Rube was pitching, a fire truck whizzed by the stadium and Rube ran off the mound to follow it. "Where's Rube?" was a question many managers asked minutes before a key game when Rube was slated to start. Sometimes he was on a vacant lot, umpiring a game with local boys or playing with them. Sometimes he was under the grandstand playing marbles with kids. Often he was off in the wilds hunting or fishing. He could be selling hot dogs in the stands, climbing inside a cage in a local zoo to play with the bears, wrestling alligators at a circus, standing as a mannequin in a local department store window, acting on the vaudeville stage, leading a marching band down main street, or teaching a gaggle of geese how to skip rope. He did it all. Most often he was at or behind a local bar. In early twentieth-century Philadelphia a standard joke asked: "What are the two biggest attractions in the City of Brotherly Love, and what do they have in common?" The answer: "The Liberty Bell and Rube Waddell, and both are a little cracked."

Baseball has had its share of zany characters — Babe Ruth, Bugs Raymond, Dizzy Dean, Satchel Paige, Jimmy Piersall. Rube Waddell was their patron saint. Baseball lore has always held lefthanders to be the nuts of the game. Rube galvanized that legend like no other. Some crazies like Dizzy Dean and Satchel Paige crafted their antics with a watchful eye on the press, knowing, dumb as a fox, both the audience for whom they were performing and the financial rewards they could reap. Rube Waddell was no such calculating posturer. He marched to a drummer trained in a school that saw what it had wrought and immediately closed down for fear of graduating another such percussionist. Rube was the nuttiest, zaniest, most exasperating, unpredictable, fun-loving, troublemaking, hell-raising nut who ever stepped on a ball field. And he was one of the game's finest players. "I have been in this business for a couple of lifetimes," noted Connie Mack. "I have seen them all.... I have seen Wild Bill This and Screwy Sam That, but in his heyday the Rube made them all look like amateur night.... I never suffered a dull moment as long as he was on my payroll.... [But] when he was right I've never had another who could touch him."[6]

"No one ever knew," wrote John McGraw, "exactly the mental process that enabled Waddell to think so clearly and quickly on the field and then do such nonsensical and freakish things off the field. There was never another like him."[7] American legend, theater, cinema, and fiction have given us the likes of Queequeg, Paul Bunyan, Huckleberry Finn, Randle Patrick McMurphy, and Forrest Gump. Elements of their legacies lie all about the life of

Rube Waddell. But the key point about Rube is that his life was not a fiction, nor was it staging or hyperbole. Everything that follows here, dear readers, is true. Rube did all this stuff.

God help us if another such person appears among us, but thank goodness we've had one to experience, if only from afar. Here, then, is the cockeyed, brilliant, tragicomic life of George Edward "Rube" Waddell.

NOTES

1. Quoted in Ken Burns, *Baseball*, Public Broadcasting Series, 1995.
2. Statement dated 1924, Clippings File, National Baseball Hall of Fame and Museum, Cooperstown, New York.
3. John Joseph McGraw, *My Thirty Years in Baseball* (New York: Boni and Liveright, 1923), p. 27.
4. H. G. Salsinger, "Greatest Pitcher? Waddell!" *Detroit News*, reprinted in *Baseball Digest*, vol. 10, no. 9, September 1951, pp. 72–74; Grantland Rice, "Setting the Pace," Clippings File, Cooperstown.
5. Bill Corum, *New York Journal American*, June 27, 1950, Clippings File, Cooperstown.
6. Pete Martin, *Peter Martin Calls On...* (New York: Simon and Schuster [1936], 1962), pp. 45, 59.
7. McGraw, *My Thirty Years*, p. 227.

Chapter 1

Throwing Rocks
at the Crows

"What's my son doing here sleeping in the firehouse?"

"Well, Mr. Waddell," shrugged the Bradford fireman, "he just wandered in a few days ago, and he seemed to like it here."

George Edward Waddell was only three years old when he arrived at the firehouse. He had simply walked away from the home where he was born near Bradford, Pennsylvania, on Friday, October 13, 1876, an unlucky day in a lucky American year. That was always the mixture with the Rube.

Why does a three year old wander off to a fire station? John and Mary Waddell had no idea. They had four other children who handled the rugged farm life of Northwestern Pennsylvania fairly well. But young George Edward showed himself to be a decidedly different sort of child.

Barriers were always something simply to be removed as far as this lad was concerned. It did not matter if a barrier was physical or social, if something was in the way, young George Edward would push through the thickets that would block or at least channel most anyone else. When he was two years old he broke all the bars on his crib. He wanted to be elsewhere, and he simply used what power he had to go where he had the urge to be. When he was seven, Edward spied a fish that was eluding his hook, so he promptly dove into the stream after it (and he grabbed it). The work of firemen seemed to attract him in much the same spirit. Social customs, manners — not only were they irrelevant in such work, it was stupid ever to consider them. Such logic would never cease with Waddell. If he liked someone he always said so, and he was equally blunt if he did not. He liked firemen.

John Waddell, Sr., always harbored the sense that his son had inherited some of his own traits. When Rube once hoped to play for the Pittsburgh Pirates in 1896, then-manager Connie Mack was walking into the office of owner William Kerr. On his way in he passed a man departing Kerr's office, a man he had never seen before. Mack took little notice and walked into

9

George Edward "Rube" Waddell

Kerr's office and found the usually serious owner bemused and chuckling to himself. "Do you know who that was?" asked Kerr. "No idea," responded Mack. "That was the father of a young man who wants to pitch for us. He came in to tell me that if his son acts a little odd at times to please understand, since 'I am a little odd myself.'" Kerr did not know how strangely Rube could act, though he would learn. Connie Mack would see more of it than anyone. He would actually be able to handle the antics. Most couldn't.

George Edward Waddell grew up in the farm country around Bradford. As a nine-year-old he was described as "full of fun and laughter and very good natured."[1] His schooling was unremarkable, but he seldom went anyway. While you could rarely find George Edward in school, you could always find him playing baseball, fishing, or running after a fire engine. If Rube had a "Rosebud," it was a fire engine. Still, Waddell received a basic schooling. And by the standards of late twentieth-century America education, both in general and especially among athletes, young Eddie was literate. But his interests did not lie with books. He attended church with his English/Pennsylvania-Dutch family. As an adult he actually went to church on occasion and bristled at a reporter who joked about the irony of Rube doing such a thing.

Young Eddie could always be counted on to help lend a hand with emergency situations in the community, particularly if a fire broke out. After the family moved to Butler County, some forty miles north of Pittsburgh, Waddell worked in some of the small mines and oil drilling sights in the region. Eddie was also a good farmhand. Weight training or any other sort of athletic training was unknown to him. He rarely trained at any point in his life. But with mining, drilling, and farming, he developed a huge physique. It was all natural, a set of big farmboy muscles and a pair of shoulders that were so wide everyone could not help but notice him. Out on the farm George Edward could plow with two mules by the time he was 13. He liked plowing, and it was here that he learned to throw — mainly rocks. He did not throw rocks at school windows, if only because in those days there were not many windows in the Butler County schoolhouses. The throwing was more than mere casual play; it came during spring plowing. One of the scourges on the land of Western Pennsylvania involved the crows that eagerly devoured the seeds as farmers planted them. Young Eddie learned to plant with a load of rocks in his pocket, and he grew quite adept at hurling the stones, as well as shooting a gun, at flying crows. He could shoot well and throw hard and accurately with either hand. It was never clear whether Rube was a righty or a lefty — he could throw either way. He shot a gun right handed. In baseball he batted right handed but always threw lefty. It was always a bit of a muddle, but this was Rube Waddell; how could it have been otherwise?

After the family had moved to Butler County, young Eddie found himself in the town of Prospect, with easy access to Butler, the county seat and the biggest city in the area. Waddell's hulking size and his skills at throwing made him a natural for baseball, and like all American boys Rube played ball. Locals noted the speed with which Rube could hurl. The only barrier Rube had ever found to playing ball as a child was that many of the other boys would not play with him. He threw so hard it stung their hands.[2] In 1895 Rube's powerful throwing landed him a spot on the local Butler team. This was great for Eddie, as he could still live at home and walk or ride over to the Butler ballfield. He was a big, broad-shouldered, grinning teenager with a throwing arm like no one else in the county. Players and spectators began to notice him. Eddie readily sensed that he was the center of attention, and he loved it like no feeling he had ever had before.

The Butler team did well playing against teams from such surrounding communities as Grove City, Tarentum, and Freeport. Young George Edward pitched well, though he showed a certain rawness both in his playing and in his spirit. He had to be told, on bouncers back to the mound, not to try to hit the batter with the ball as a way of getting him out. "Hit the batter and he's out where I come from," said Eddie.[3] That had not been the rule of the game for over 20 years, though untutored children still played that way. Eddie shrugged, heeded the advice, and stopped whacking the runners.

Often Waddell would be absent from games without notice, usually because he had gone fishing. Once a friend simply pulled up in a buggy along the first base line, held up a fishing pole, and asked Eddie if he wanted to go. Waddell happily obliged, dropped his ball and glove, and walked off the mound in the middle of the game.[4] Priorities were always drawn askew with Rube. In Butler he made a habit of wearing a bright red set of skivvies under his baseball uniform in case a fire broke out so he could strip off and get to the fire in proper dress as quickly as possible. He actually did this on several occasions. In later years some managers tried to curb Waddell's fire chasing and thought they could accomplish this by insisting on team uniform rules that forbade his wearing the red skivvies. This point carried added weight because Rube rarely owned more than one set of under apparel. Rube agreed to the requests, and under his uniform he subsequently wore nothing. Rube logic! One time later in his career Rube was playing and heard a fire bell. He reacted instantly, shedding his uniform as he galloped off the field, forgetting he had obliged his manager's uniform code.

Folks around Butler grew familiar with Eddie and his eccentricities. Most took it all in stride. In an age before any significant media beyond newspapers, American communities' love of baseball focused largely on their local teams. They knew of the big city teams and could read about the results, but they had no way of directly seeing or hearing of their exploits. Local players were thus real heroes. They were paid little, sometimes not at all, but they were treated royally. Eddie grew accustomed to the treatment and made the most of it. He never lost the art of touching up people for a favor or a loan. Yet few found this irritating. Few ever would. Rube was just the kind of person it was impossible not to like.

In 1896 a traveling salesman named Wesley Baker saw Waddell pitch and was impressed with his speed and cunning.[5] Small-town team managers relied on informal networks of information from such "scouts" as salesmen who had trustworthy eyes for talent. Baker had a friend in the town of Franklin, Pennsylvania, and they offered Waddell a job. Franklin, about fifty miles north of Butler, was one of four towns in Pennsylvania and Ohio that had started a new baseball league — the Iron and Oil League, the other towns being Oil City, Titusville, and Warren, Ohio. They played one another and matched clubs in nearby cities like Wheeling, West Virginia, and Youngstown, Ohio. The owners hoped the quality of the team would bring out fans who would fork over a quarter or even fifty cents to watch the game. The players received a few dollars a game, so Waddell was interested, and the level of play was a clear cut above that of the Butler team. Indeed, Butler played Oil City on July 31, 1896, and lost badly. A local newspaper simply reported the score (8–3) and sadly noted "further remarks are superficial and painful."[6]

Waddell arrived in Franklin in June 1896. He went out to warm up. The catcher assigned to him was named Jack Nelson. Nelson put on his mask, crouched, and took a look at this great big kid, clearly right off the farm, and yelled out, "All right, Rube, let's see what you got!" The nickname "Rube" was a common term in late nineteenth-century America for "farm boy," "bumpkin," or "hick." With his big, gangling appearance, broad shoulders, and even broader grin, the name was so perfect for Waddell that everybody instantly warmed to it. The name stayed with Waddell from then on, and all his life Jack Nelson proudly displayed his bent index and middle fingers from catching the Rube's fastball.[7]

There are other stories, about the origin of "Rube." One boyhood friend, Isaac Allen, recalled in 1962 that Eddie was such a big lad and always wore a big straw hat and was generally such a hayseed that "we called him Rube because he was a Rube." In another case (where the reporter cast Waddell pitching for Oil City against Franklin, which was wrong), the story goes that Waddell won the first game of a doubleheader. When the fans saw the boy walking out to pitch the second game, which he also won, they yelled "What a Rube!" Rube himself told yet a third story, that sounded a trifle puffed. He said he was pitching for Franklin and won the first game of a double header. "The man intended to pitch the second game got drunk," recalled Rube,

> so I went in again. In the second inning with the score 2–0 against us, a line ball hit me in the forehead and knocked me unconscious for about five minutes. I was sore and insisted on pitching out the game. We beat them 16–2 and they did not get another man to first base, while I made two home runs, two doubles, and a single. That night the manager of the Oil City team met me on the street and said: "You're a regular robber. No one but a rube could recover from an accident like that and finish the game." That fastened the nickname on me and it has stuck.[8]

Either of the first three stories about the origin of the nickname may be right. (Although the only thing that may be accurate about Rube's own story was the point that at least one pitcher was drunk.)

Waddell did not like the nickname at first. He once knocked a man down a flight of stairs for calling him "Rube," but he came to accept it, though his friends and managers always called him "Eddie" or, in reference to his Pennsylvania-Dutch roots, "Dutchman." The latter was less common, for among baseball players at the turn of the century "the Dutchman" could only mean Honus Wagner.

Franklin had done well in the Iron and Oil League in 1895, but in 1896 they were weak, particularly in the field. Butler, on the other hand, had been poor in 1895 but played well in 1896. Waddell was not the culprit for either turn. It was just his luck, something which would follow him for the next twenty years. Franklin was pitiful indeed. In a game on June 10, they committed twelve errors. Waddell had started the game, and he gave up ten runs, all unearned. A week later, Franklin's shortstop made six errors in one game. On June 25 Franklin lost to Tarentum 16–5, with ten team errors. Two days later they were down to Oil City 8–6, after four errors. Waddell then came in to pitch after the fourth inning. He shut out Oil City from there, but the club could score no more. Even though it was a lower-level league, Franklin's play was so poor that it prompted the *Pittsburg Post* to opine: "Any club that comes along these days can beat Franklin, owing to their stupid playing and poor batting." The previous day, Titusville had beaten Franklin 11 to 10; Franklin's errors: eight. When Franklin actually won a game from Oil City, the *Post* noted the Oil City team "seemed to be hypnotized."[9] Franklin's only other wins came against weaker amateur clubs in Grove City and Youngstown.

Franklin fans were disgruntled, of course. They could be generous about weak hitting or poor pitching. But bad defense simply looks comical and stupid. It prompts a sense in spectators of: "Hell, I could play that well, why am I paying for this?" While 300 or so were regularly coming to see Oil City and Titusville play, Franklin's paid attendance dwindled to the dozens, and after July 8 they fell off the baseball map. With this, away went Waddell's employment.

Waddell had been of little help. He was often absent, off fishing as he had been in Butler. He was also beginning to go off on drinking benders. But no one, not even a young (or sober and dependable) Rube Waddell, could do anything for Franklin. It looked like the young kid's foray into semi-pro baseball was to be a short one. He went home to the farm in Prospect and enjoyed kicking around in Butler, getting into his family's hair and most everyone else's in the community. His future appeared to be strictly that of a local eccentric.

NOTES

1. Donald Honig, *The Greatest Players of All Time* (New York: Crown, 1988), p. 7.

2. J. G. Taylor-Spink, "Rube Waddell — His Life, Laughs, and Laurels," *The Sporting News*, November 12, 1942, p. 4.

3. Clippings File, National Baseball Hall of Fame and Museum, Cooperstown, NY; Jack Newcomb, *Fireballers* (New York: Putnam, 1964), p. 18; Robert Miller Smith, *Heroes of Baseball* (Cleveland: World Publishing, 1952), p. 197.

4. Spink, "Rube Waddell," *The Sporting News*, November 12, 1942, p. 6; and Spink, "Rube Waddell," *Baseball Register*, 1944.

5. Martin Appel and Burt Goldblatt, *Baseball's Best: The Hall of Fame Gallery* (New York: McGraw Hill, 1980), p. 21; A. H. Tarvin, "More About Waddell," *Baseball Magazine*, LXXXI, July, 1948, pp. 270-71.

6. *Pittsburg Post*, August 1, 1896, p. 6.

7. Appel, *Baseball's Best*, p. 21; and Spink, "Rube Waddell," p. 6.

8. John Dell, "Here's the 'Real' Rube Waddell Story," *Philadelphia Inquirer*, May 5, 1962, p. 18; A. H. Tarvin, "More About Waddell," *Baseball Magazine*, LXXXI, July 1948, pp. 270-71; Tim Murmane, *How to Play Baseball*, 1904, Clippings File, Cooperstown.

9. *Pittsburg Post*, June 11, June 18, June 26, June 28, July 1, 1896, p. 6.

Chapter 2

A Cup of Coffee
and Off to College

Waddell spent the winter of 1896-97 home at the farm, and it looked like there would be a typical spring of planting with a little baseball. Rube may have given a little thought to trying out for some other club at the level of Franklin's, prayerfully a better one. But such thinking was idle. Life would go on as it had, working the land and stealing a laugh wherever he could.

Rube applied to play for a team in Youngstown, Ohio, in the Interstate League. They told him he was too slow. He asked again but got no reply.[1] Somewhere in late March or early April came an offer from none other than the Pittsburgh Pirates. Rube had tried to secure a tryout with the Pirates the previous summer but to no avail. Now he had more of a record. The Pirates had also had three decidedly mediocre seasons under catcher/manager Connie Mack. After the '96 season they replaced Mack with a new player/manager, Patsy Donovan. With the team not terribly strong, Donovan naturally felt the Pirates needed some new talent. Scouts saw some potential in Waddell's work with Franklin. Donovan heard about the big kid north of Pittsburgh and was willing to take a risk. He asked Waddell to join the club one morning, have breakfast, and go out for a practice.

The prospect of a free breakfast was enough to get Waddell to come down to Pittsburgh. He loved to eat. He could pack away a quart of ice cream in no time. Several people saw him eat an entire gallon.[2] Rube arrived in Pittsburgh, ready for breakfast and baseball. Donovan asked him to sit next to him. No one knows exactly what Waddell said or did that morning while sitting over breakfast next to Donovan, but it must have been offensive. For immediately after breakfast, before he had even seen Waddell throw a single ball, Donovan released him outright. Baseball people commonly refer to a brief stint in the majors as "a cup of coffee." Never was such an experience more literally so than Rube's touch with the Pittsburgh Pirates in the spring of 1897.[3] Full bellied, but empty handed, Rube trudged back to Butler.

Back home, Rube received an unexpected baseball offer. It was not from a pro or semi-pro team, but from a college. George Edward had supposedly attended school, and he could read and write, but he had no ambitions which required any sort of college-level study. Nearby Volant College (pronounced Vol-ANT) had no such ambitions for young Waddell either, they simply wanted him to play on their baseball team.

Volant College was less than ten years old. It served primarily as a "Normal School," i.e., a teachers college. It was a private school, always in need of students. The State of Pennsylvania had recently created a group of state supported Normal Schools, including one not too far from Volant, so the competition for students and their tuition dollars was stiff or even, as private enterprise supporters would argue, unfair. (And Volant College would go out of business in 25 years.) While struggling to survive, college leaders sought to increase enrollments by advertising the institution. Like many administrators elsewhere, Volant people figured the development of good athletic teams would serve as good publicity. Volant College was located in Lawrence County, just west of Butler, and many people there certainly knew of the prowess of local athletic talent, including one George Edward Waddell. So they made Eddie an offer. They would enroll him in the college. Tuition, room, and board would be free. They would pay him one dollar a game to play ball, and he would be supplied with free chewing tobacco, or as Eddie always called it "Backy."

It all sounded like a good deal to Eddie. He had made little more money than that playing for Franklin. As for the rigors of college, well Eddie apparently never attended class anyway. He did, however, take in some of the band's rehearsals. He was the drum major, of course. (He was not completely unqualified for this, as somewhere along the way Waddell had learned how to play the piano, though he could never actually read a musical score.)

With Rube winging it that spring, the band blared, and the Volant baseball team was unbeatable. Rube was winning two or three games a week, and on off days he was riding up to the town of Greenville and pitching there. In mid season two neighboring colleges, Grove City and Westminster, having learned of Waddell's pitching prowess, suddenly informed Volant's manager, Thomas H. George, that their schedules were full and they would be unable to play Volant that spring.

Volant did lose one game that season. The loss occurred one day when some ruffians from a team in the nearby town of Mercer literally kidnapped Waddell while he was buggy riding from Greenville to Volant. At gunpoint the kidnappers drove the big pitcher up to Mercer and held him there until it was too late to return to Volant for the game. Waddell then agreed to pitch for Mercer. They won easily and paid Waddell a dollar. Rube had a heck of a time convincing Coach George of what had happened to him.[4]

On several occasions at Volant, Waddell called his outfield off the diamond and struck out opponents with no defense behind him and then returned to the bench, either walking on his hands, flip flopping feet to hands, or turning cartwheels. Eddie enjoyed the dollar he dutifully received for each game. Usually he would treat a girl at the town soda fountain. A glass of soda cost a nickel, and Eddie usually drank his dollar's worth. Volant breezed through the season to win their league's championship, with the studious Waddell averaging 15 strikeouts a game (with college games going seven innings not nine).[5]

It is certainly scandalous that a college like Volant would pay an athlete to perform while he never attended class. But it must be noted that American college athletics were then in their infancy. Irregularities had yet to be exposed and were much less effectively regulated with the mature honesty of later eras. By the late twentieth century, as is well known, student athletes attend class at least twice as often as Waddell did, and major university athletic budgets do not allocate anything close to such a scandalous figure as $1 a game per player. They have risen far above all that.

Waddell's college career ended that spring of '97, and he went back home. He did some pitching for Butler and threw well. One day, while mowing down the opposition from Oil City, a detachment of National Guardsmen marched onto the Butler field, hauled Waddell off the mound, and placed him under arrest. Like many children, young Waddell loved uniforms, and his fascination had prompted him to join the Guard one day. The duties which enlistment required were hardly matters Eddie took too seriously. The Guard took them in deadly earnest, of course, and they were not about to excuse any lad being AWOL, especially if he was conspicuously playing baseball. Waddell landed in the stockade, and his pitching prospects for the rest of the summer appeared bleak. With so many tight spots in which he would find himself, Waddell always seemed to have the "Br'er Rabbit" knack for escape. Later in the afternoon while Waddell languished in the stockade, Guardsman outside the building were jolted by a sudden explosion. They discovered that "someone" had tossed a load of ammunition cartridges into a stove. No one could fully identify who could hurl such items with the necessary strength and accuracy. The guards had their suspicions. None of the other prisoners showed any inkling to cooperate with investigators, however, and the Guard officials concluded it best to release Waddell from all further obligations.[6]

That summer in '97 Rube did some more pitching for a local club in Evans City. One story has had it that Waddell had gone down to Evans City with some friends to watch a game, during which Evans City ran out of pitchers and was ready to forfeit. Friends began to yell and brag about their buddy. The Evans City manager relented, and Waddell pitched hitless ball the rest of the way.[7] Waddell continued to pitch for Evans City. On August 7, against the town of Mars, Pennsylvania, he struck out fourteen Martians. On the 14th he beat them again, striking out eight. The *Pittsburg Post* took note of it. "Mars," they simply stated, "could not hit Waddell." Within a few years many in the American League would be saying the same thing. Rube pitched a few more for Evans City, a four-hit shutout of Hilldale on the 17th, and on September 3 he beat his old Butler team. Farmers from miles around began coming to Evans City that summer just to watch this young fireballer. Sometimes before the games, Evans City would stage a parade. Rube would march behind a boy carrying a banner which read: "Come and see Big Rube fan 'em out."[8]

Whether the notoriety came from Butler, Franklin, Volant College, or Evans City in the summer of 1897 (though some say 1898) between stints for Evans City, Waddell apparently took up an offer from an amateur but big-time team in the Pittsburgh area. Homestead, Pennsylvania, was a steel town with a big working population and a growing passion for baseball. All the little blue collar neighborhoods in and around the Steel City had community teams — football in the fall and winter, baseball in the spring and summer. There were often games during the work week, but it was on the weekends especially that the city's blue collar communities turned out *en masse* to root for their boys. (Indeed, "Our Boys" was the name of one of the Pittsburgh area teams.) Throughout towns like Oakmont, Braddock, and Duquesne, community pride bordered on fanaticism, a fanaticism that could get quite hot when rivals met on the baseball diamond at places like Frick and Schenley Park. Teams wanted to win at most any price, and they took to recruiting to do it. Someone in Homestead learned of the big fastballing kid from up Butler way. Other teams might have suspected a "ringer" in their midst, but they were doing the same thing.

The Homestead Athletic Club had been having a good year, and as the season was heating up they were to go up against Duquesne, who was vying with them for bragging rights as the best in the area. There were also several semi-professional teams from Pittsburgh and Philadelphia on Homestead's schedule. Homestead picked up the "Rube," to come down and pitch here and there.* In his appearances the nickname "Rube" resonated ever more

---

*The story of Waddell's work with Homestead is a commonly told tale of Waddell's break into the big time; however, neither of Pittsburgh's newspapers of the era — the Post and the Dispatch — mention any such series of appearances by Waddell. Some have also placed the series in 1898, after Rube's first stint in the National League, and after he had played with notice in Detroit and in Chatham, Ontario. Again, no Pittsburgh newspaper covered the Homestead play in 1898, and with his notoriety from games with Louisville and Detroit, the likelihood of coverage was stronger had the event actually taken place that year. Furthermore, if the Homestead games had taken place in 1898, the whole idea that Rube attained the notice of big league scouts from his work in Homestead does not follow, since by then he had already gained visibility in much faster company. Additionally, Rube

affectionately among the city folk. In a series against the Duquesne Club, Rube won four games and received what was for him an unheard of amount — $100. He had been offered $25 a game, and the manager wanted to pitch him twice in four days. But given such money as he had never seen, Rube went out and pitched all four games. $100! Rube really felt he'd hit the big time.[9]

Homestead also used Rube in a series with a semi-professional team of Pittsburghers and Philadelphians. "The Rube" was again in the box, and his nickname spread rapidly, now not only in the stands but on the opposition bench. The first game went 15 innings, there was no score, and darkness halted the drama, with the Rube having gone the distance. The next week came a rematch. Rube pitched. The game was 2–2 in the 12th when darkness again halted matters. Rube went the distance this time too. Homestead stood toe to toe with a good group of players, and this big country Rube was most impressive. The third game pitted Rube against Sam Leever who would soon pitch for the Pirates. Again it was 2–2 in the 12th, with Rube going the distance. This time, however, the sun was just setting, and there was time for another inning. Rube held the visitors scoreless in his half of the 13th, and in the bottom of the inning Homestead rallied for the winning run. Homestead won the series, and Rube had pitched 39 impressive innings against some real ballplayers.

William R. "Doc" Marshall, who would later play for the St. Louis Cardinals, was Rube's catcher at Homestead. Marshall was also a native of Butler and knew Waddell. Marshall said that it was Waddell's pitching in Homestead that summer against the traveling Philadelphians and Pittsburghers that led big league scouts to notice him.[11] Rube shuttled back to Evans City to beat his old Butler mates on September 3. But then he signed with the Louisville Colonels, a team in the National League. Doc Marshall claimed to have witnessed the signing.[12] Rube received $500. He had never seen such a sum of money. The Louisville agent bought him a train ticket and told the lad to meet the team at a hotel in Washington, D.C., where the Colonels were just finishing a series. The Rube eagerly jumped on the next train. He was off to the majors.

(continued) *had to play another full and very successful season in the minors in 1899 before manager Fred Clarke would give him another shot with the Louisville club in the National League. So if the Homestead stint was in 1898 it was a relatively meaningless point in Rube's career. In 1962, Rube's friend Isaac Allen, at the age of 84, insisted that Rube pitched for Homestead in 1897, right after pitching for Evans City.*[10]

NOTES

1. *Youngstown Telegram*, February 20, 1908.

2. Robert Miller Smith, *Heroes of Baseball* (New York: The World Publishing Company, 1952), p. 179.

3. *Louisville Courier*, September 16, 1897, p. 6.

4. Clippings File, Archives of the National Baseball Hall of Fame and Museum, Cooperstown, N.Y.

5. Thomas F. Collins, M.D., "Waddell as a Collegian," manuscript, September 1947, Clippings File, Cooperstown.

6. "Current Sports," *The Evening Bulletin*, February 8, 1904, p. 13.

7. Told by Isaac Allen, quoted in John Dell, "Here's the 'Real' Rube Waddell Story," *Philadelphia Inquirer*, May 5, 1962, p. 18.

8. *Pittsburg Post*, August 8, August 15, August 18, and September 4, 1897; *Sporting Life*, August 1897.

9. See Myron J. Smith, *Baseball: A Complete Bibliography* (Jefferson, N.C.: McFarland, 1993); Spink, "Rube Waddell," p. 7.

10. *Philadelphia Inquirer*, May 5, 1962, p. 18.

11. Recalled by William R. Marshall, *Philadelphia Inquirer*, May 15, 1906. (That year, Marshall was playing for the Philadelphia Phillies, and Waddell was with the Philadelphia A's.)

12. Ibid.

Chapter 3

Wake Up, Mr. Clarke, I'm Here

Waddell arrived in Washington, D.C., in the early A.M. hours of September 8. He went straight to the hotel where the Louisville Colonels were staying and inquired as to the room number of manager Fred Clarke. The desk clerk explained to Rube that the hour was late and that Mr. Clarke had left explicit instructions not to be disturbed. Clarke was in a bad mood, even for him. He had been playing well that season, but the team was weak. In the previous six days, the Colonels had slipped in the National League standings from 8th to 10th place (of 12). Clarke's batting average hovered around .400 all season, and he would finish third in the league behind only future Hall of Famers Willie Keeler and Ed Delahanty. In June, Colonels president James Pulliam and secretary Barney Dreyfuss had decided to promote their one good player to manager, not unusual in those days. Clarke continued to play well. Outside of John McGraw, there was no more snarling and feisty a player in that era than Fred Clarke.* But Clarke could not light much of a fire under his men. The only gem to appear was a rookie from the Pittsburgh area named Hans Wagner. The team's pitching was especially weak, and in late August several pitchers sustained injuries, including his one good hurler Chick Fraser. This was why the team signed Waddell.

Clarke may have wanted Waddell but not at 2:00 A.M. Rube, meanwhile, was absolutely full of himself and would not take "no" for an answer from the desk clerk. After several pleadings, he wore down the night manager,

---

*One of Clarke's innovations involved picking up second base and running to third with the sack in hand. That way, if called out, he would protest that he was still "on" second. Baseball rules were more amorphous then, and other spirited players of the day like John McGraw were also trying to bend them any way they could, as had Mike Kelly in the previous decade and as would Ty Cobb later on. They were some of the real movers of the game, and that same aggressive spirit they brought to their play made them effective managers as well as star players. Clarke actually got away with his "base holding" stunt in a game against Chicago on July 25, 1897, much to the consternation and protest of the Chicago team.[1]

obtained the room number, and proceeded up to Clarke's room. He knocked on the door. Clarke got up, opened the door and snarled: "Go downstairs and let me sleep." Rube waltzed in anyway and loudly proceeded to spill out a string of braggadocio about what a great pitcher he was, how he was going to turn the team around, and so on. Clarke tried again to get Rube to shut up, let him sleep, and see him in the morning. After several attempts, he concluded that the tactic was useless and decided it best to channel Rube's energies out of his room. He told the eager lad that it would be a good idea if he would go down the halls to each room and introduce himself to *all* his new teammates.

Rube eagerly nodded and obliged and began knocking on doors and saying "Howdy" and talking to every bleary-eyed ballplayer on the team (and, of course, touching up a few of them for a few dollars). Maybe Clarke figured one of his worthless players would stuff a pillow in this idiotic rookie's mouth, but an hour or so later, Rube again appeared, pounding on Clarke's door. Oblivious to Clarke's ever crustier mood, Rube earnestly reported that he'd met everybody just as he'd been told, but he wanted Clarke to know that there was one player he could not awaken. Rube said he had pounded hard on this player's the door for a good fifteen minutes, but the fellow would not stir. He figured he'd better tell Clarke, as something must be wrong. There was nothing wrong. The player was an outfielder named William Ellsworth Hoy. He was a deaf-mute. The team referred to him as "Dummy" Hoy.* (Ballplayers were a sensitive lot back then.)[2]

Honus Wagner never stopped loving to tell the story of Rube Waddell's first night in the big leagues. It was indeed quite an introduction for Waddell, Clarke, and the Colonels. It would not get much better.

NOTES

1. *Louisville Courier*, July 26, 1897, p. 6.
2. Clippings File, Cooperstown; Spink, "Rube Waddell," p. 7.

*Hoy's presence in the National League gave rise to the umpire's signals of "strike," "safe," and "out" that remain in use today.

Chapter 4

A Second Cup of Coffee

"Dummy" Hoy was well rested and ready to play on September 8. The rest of the Louisville team looked a bit bedraggled. They left Washington that morning and boarded a train for Baltimore where they were slated for a series with the very tough Orioles, champions of baseball for the previous three years. The season was all but over for the Colonels. Baltimore, meanwhile, was in the thick of a pennant race with Boston. Fred Clarke figured he owed a certain rookie a little payback for the previous night's escapades. When the Colonels arrived at the ballpark, someone asked Clarke who was pitching. The manager coldly pointed a finger at his night visitor and barked "that man." He was tossing this Rube out to start against the nasty likes of Willie Keeler, Wilbert Robinson, John McGraw, and the rest of the defending champs. He sent Rube out with a rookie catcher, too. His name was Ossee Schreckengost. (One newspaper simply referred to him as "Louisville's catcher with an unpronounceable name.") Neither Rube nor "Schreck," as Rube would come to call him, had any knowledge of the hitters. They had no knowledge of the strengths and weaknesses of their teammates. Despite all this, as one reporter noted, "considering the hard task before him, the showing [Rube] made was an exceptionally good one."[1]

The Orioles jumped on Rube at the start for two runs in the first inning. Rube was jittery and had walked three. Thereafter he settled. The Orioles scratched another run in the second. Two scored in the fourth, during which Rube gave up but one big hit, a double to Hughey Jennings which scored the two runs. It would have been worse, but Schreckengost nailed several runners trying to steal, and he would have gunned down several more but for the throws simply being dropped. After the fourth inning, Rube settled completely and shut the Orioles out with four perfect innings, except for his hitting Jennings with a pitch. Maybe it was payback for the double, but, like Sandy Koufax, Rube Waddell never threw at anyone intentionally.

The Colonels could score but one run all day, so Rube had a loss on his record, but he proved he could overcome jitters and more than hold his own against the very best in the game. "The kind of ball he pitched," noted a Louisville paper, "would win more times than it would lose."[2] Schreckengost would not catch another game for the Colonels. He had gone 0 for 3 at the plate and dropped several pop flies. Clarke immediately dropped him. Schreck ended up playing for Cleveland the next season. He and Rube would meet again, however.

Like any bad year, 1897 wound down slowly and painfully for Clarke and the Colonels. The next day against the Orioles, some bad calls by the umpire so enraged Clarke that he pulled the entire team off the field. He refused to continue the game and accepted a forfeit. It was hot, the team was terrible, but this new kid Waddell seemed oblivious to the demoralization that lay all about him. He was in the big time, and he was going to enjoy it. Clarke would not be amused.

Clarke gave his crazy rookie a few days rest. On September 12, the Colonels were scheduled to be in Indianapolis to play an exhibition game against the "Indians," a team that was part of the Western League, a minor league one cut below the National circuit. Back in the 1890s big-league teams played such in-season exhibitions quite often. Clarke figured it was as good a time as any to send Rube out and give him another look. Besides, some of his antics on the bench were a little weird and irritating. Louisville won 9 to 3, but Rube was touched up for 11 hits. Still, players, fans, and reporters all noted how much speed the kid had, how wide his curves were, and how his long, rangy motion seemed to summon the pitch out of his entire body as well as his big left arm. He was raw, but the stuff was there. One reporter surmised: "It looks like the club has made a good haul in the hayseed."[3]

The Colonels were back home for a doubleheader on September 15 against Pittsburgh. Clarke was away in Chicago, attending the wedding of a friend and enjoying a "needed rest," as the *Courier Journal* poignantly noted.[4] Veteran first baseman Perry Werden managed in his place. The Pirates were not much better than the Colonels, so this was a classic end-of-season match of tailenders where anything could happen. It did.

The Colonels won the first game. In the second game, the Colonels' starting pitcher, William Magee, proved to be off even his mediocre game. He gave up seven runs in three innings, so Werden yanked him and inserted the young Waddell to make his first appearance before the home crowd, such as it was. Werden also sent Rube out to coach first base when the team was up at bat. (Werden did not like Rube on the bench any more than Clarke did.) On the mound Waddell held the Pirates to just one more run, but the game was beyond reach, as Louisville could garner only two runs.

Somehow all the exposure before a big home crowd brought out the theatrical in Rube, the likes of which neither Louisville nor most any other baseball city had ever seen. "It was necessary to be at the park yesterday afternoon," noted the *Courier* "to properly enjoy what transpired there."[5] Rube was an entire three-ring circus. While in his wind-ups, he contorted his body in every odd way imaginable, yet he still got the ball over effectively. He used a hesitation move, one Satchel Paige would later make famous, to throw off the batters' timing. Rube provided an additional feature to his hesitation, as he made certain "noises" at the top of his windup before hurling a strikes, adding a new aura to the term "fireball." Rube particularly enjoyed striking out Patsy Donovan, the Pirate player/manager who had released Rube that spring. Indeed, Rube loudly reminded Donovan of the spring release after he had fanned him and sent him trudging back the dugout. Rube did handsprings and cartwheels from the mound to the bench between innings, and he bantered with everybody — his teammates, the umpires, the Pirates, and the fans. He was non-stop with the jokes and wisecracks. The Pirate players tried their best to psyche Rube (in the 1890s such a tactic was called "guying"*). But nothing worked. Rube was acting strangely, and everything designed to throw him off his game only made him all the more effective and zany. It was a combination no one had ever seen or could possibly fathom. And the fans loved every minute of it.

Rube's work in the coaching box had the fans splitting their sides even more. He broke into comic mimings of the opposing pitcher's windups (with a few more of the hesitations and "noises" he had employed on the mound). His jokes were non-stop. He also began directing the runners by making hand gestures and bellowing out cow and pig noises as though he were driving animals about the farm back in Prospect. Ballparks were intimate enough in those days for such field antics to be easily heard, and big Rube was more than audible. The crowd was in stitches.

Manager Werden, meanwhile, was totally befuddled. He had no idea what to make of it. He tried to remove Rube from the coaching box, but the fans protested so loudly that he had no choice but to leave the boy out there. The newspapers gently headlined "Waddell is Witty" and wrote of "the queer antics of Rube Waddell." Baseball had never seen such a show, but there would be more, much more.[6] Rube was a hit, and of course that evening he carried the show from the ballpark through all the bars in downtown Louisville.

Clarke returned from Chicago and learned of the antics. He was not amused. Meanwhile, the team's play continued to deteriorate. They slipped to 11th place. If St. Louis had not been playing sub–.200 ball, the cellar would have easily belonged to the Colonels. Clarke took his baseball in deadly earnest

---

The term "to guy" came from Britain's celebration of Guy Fawkes Day, when startling someone is common banter.

and he had no patience, either with the notion of comic relief for the team or with the idea that one can at least give the fans a good show when you cannot win. To him this kid was just weird, and that was all there was to it. The stories of Rube's escapades about the bars of Louisville hardly softened matters.

The Louisville team hit bottom when they played the Detroit Tigers. The Tigers were then a minor league team, playing in the Western League with Indianapolis. On September 22, the Tigers beat Louisville in an error-filled game, 14 to 12. Rube came in the next day and beat Detroit 8 to 5, but Clarke was still seething about the loss. Rube, meanwhile, decided to celebrate his victory. Clarke took one look at Rube's condition the next day and was furious. How could someone celebrate after giving up five runs to a bunch of minor leaguers? Whether he was pitching against the Orioles or on a sand-lot, it was all the same to Rube, but it was not all the same to Clarke. He had seen plenty of drinking in baseball, and it had always infuriated him. This crazy rookie was not going to be any sort of exception. Waddell also thought nothing of doing a little playing on the side with an amateur team in Louisville. When he showed up for work with a hurt finger from one such game, Clarke really hit the roof. He fined Waddell $50 for his drinking. With inimitable "Rube logic," Waddell pouted, exclaiming, "The team is supposed to give you money, not take it away."[7] If Rube had a point it was certainly lost on Clarke.

Rube was ready to quit the Colonels. The season was nearly over anyway, and Clarke wanted no part of him. (This would happen again.) Having pitched against the Western League Tigers, Rube thought he could give them a try. Clarke made it easy for him. In November the Colonels traded Rube to Detroit.

NOTES

1. *Louisville Commercial*, September 9, 1897, p. 2.

2. Ibid.

3. *Louisville Courier Journal*, September 12, 1897, p. 6; *Louisville Commercial*, September 13, 1897, p. 2.

4. *Louisville Courier Journal*, September 18, 1897, p. 6

5. Ibid., September 16, 1897, p. 6.

6. *Louisville Courier Journal*, September 16, 1897, p. 6; *Louisville Commercial*, September 16, 1897, p. 2.

7. Honig, *Pitchers*, p. 5.

Chapter 5

Tiger Rube

Detroit agreed to sign Waddell for the spring of 1898. Fred Clarke had no desire to hold on to the loony Butler County boy. More thoughtfully, Clarke believed the young Waddell definitely needed more time in the minors to mature. He did not understand Waddell's nature, and he never would.

Rube reported to the Tigers' spring training camp in Nashville, Tennessee, in late March, 1898. He showed great form. In a couple of practice games against the baseball team of Vanderbilt University, Rube mowed down the college boys with ease. Newspapers reported that Waddell's speed was such that the college boys, same age as Rube, were downright scared. In four games he pitched 13 innings, gave up but two hits, and struck out 16. Several times Rube retired the side on nine pitches. It was like pitching for Volant.[1]

On April 8, the Tigers broke camp and headed north, stopping in various towns along the way to play exhibition games. On April 9 came a moment for a little Rube revenge. That day the Tigers arrived in Louisville to play the Colonels. Rube did not start, and Clarke's club pounded out 15 runs in four innings. Rube entered the game in the fifth and pitched the rest of the way. And from there Louisville garnered but one run, a homer by Honus Wagner. They won, of course, 16 to 10, but no one else could hit the Rube, and Clarke struck out twice. Full of himself, Rube celebrated, and on his next slated outing for the Tigers in Dayton, Ohio, he failed to show up. The following day he pitched and gave up 12 hits. Success could always go to Rube's head, usually with the proper lubrication.[2]

The team arrived back in Detroit in mid April, and the city's fans were agog over this new fireballing lefthander about whom they had been reading so much. Only the outbreak of war with Spain was getting more Detroit press than Waddell. On April 14 the Tigers played a practice game against a local team, the Abbotts. "The young 'giant' 'Rube' Waddell" strode in for the sixth inning. Immediately he struck out three. He struck out four more the rest of the way. Two days later, Rube again entered a game in the sixth. This time he struck out the first two batters on six pitches and gave up but one hit the rest of the way. Detroit won both games. A newspaper reported Rube revealed himself to possess more than enough speed "to loan to the Cubans." Apparently Waddell's blazing speed prompted rumors that he had little or no control. But in the two games in Detroit he did not walk a batter, though he did hit one, and in Louisville he walked only one. The *Free Press* assured Detroit fans: "Somebody may have concluded in the past that Waddell was short on control, though very long on speed. His work here has not given evidence of wildness at all." He is, noted the *News-Tribune* "a wonder, chock full of ginger." They predicted great things for the lad, "if," they carefully noted, "the Pennsylvanian does not fall by the wayside."[3] "If" was a word often heard when folks spoke of the young Rube.

While Rube showed great potential, the Tigers were another story. As usual, Rube found himself on a lousy club. Rube pitched on opening day against Indianapolis. He struck out the side in the first inning, and the fans went wild. But as soon as Indianapolis made any contact with the ball, Rube was in trouble, not because the hits were hard, but because no one on the Tigers could field anything. Rube gave up just three hits in the first seven innings. But a slew of errors yielded six unearned Indianapolis runs. Detroit's second baseman made so many errors that he was fired after just three games. Their third baseman was no better. Indianapolis won the opener 6 to 2.[4]

Detroit proceeded to lose its first four games and quickly occupied the Western League cellar. The *Detroit Evening News* began to headline articles about the Tigers with words like "How Not to Play Ball."[5] Rube was the only bright spot. On April 27 he pitched Detroit to its first victory. The game was against the Columbus Senators, and Rube had the Senators "pretty much in a hypnotic state all through the game." The score was 4 to 1, and the one run came in the ninth, when the game was sewn up and Rube was doing a bit of clowning. The clowning did not stop with the ninth inning, however. It continued for several more days, and on the 29th Rube staggered out to pitch against Indianapolis. After five hits, six walks, a wild pitch, and, of course, three team errors, Rube and the Tigers lost another.[6]

After two more losses to Indianapolis and one to the Milwaukee Brewers, under manager Connie Mack, the Tigers' record stood at 1 and 10. The *Free Press* asked in headline "Can They Win a Game?"[7] Rube sobered himself for a game on May 6, and he defeated Connie Mack's Brewers. It was always simple when Rube's head was not fogged. His pitching could be brilliant, no matter his condition, though he was more consistently superb when sober. But it was his hitting and fielding that came apart when he was on or recovering from a "toot." In the game against Milwaukee, his fielding was nimble and included some slick coverings of first base. At the plate that day Rube also got three of the Tigers' seven hits, including a triple.[8]

With Rube sitting down the next day, Milwaukee walloped Detroit, 19 to 13. (No, the teams hadn't switched to football, though Big Rube would have played if they had.) "It was," as the *News-Tribune* tersely put it, "awful. Detroit," they declared, "showed how baseball is not played." The *Free Press* was a bit more dramatic, headlining: "Murder! Murder!" Two more losses followed to Columbus, during which the Senators scored 24 runs. Rube came back to beat Columbus on May 11; again, his fielding was terrific — seven assists. Detroit was now 3 and 13, with all their victories coming via Rube's big left arm.[9]

Amidst such generally putrid play, the Tigers' morale was anything but good. Manager Frank Graves quit on May 12, and the next day the Tigers actually won a game without Rube pitching. The same day that Graves quit, club owner Frank Van Derbeck decided that the club needed some discipline to accompany the management shakeup. Together, it might clear out the team's cobwebs. He decided to focus some of his disciplinary anger on Rube.

When he wasn't carousing or pitching for the Tigers, Rube sometimes went out and pitched with local teams. Derbeck knew that Rube often went out and played on sandlots with kids. He could not do much about this, but he also found out that Rube had pitched four innings for an organized local club in the town of Delray on May 8. This angered Derbeck as much as it had Fred Clarke. For Rube's indiscretion, Derbeck fined him $25. Rube had a hard enough time understanding why Fred Clarke had fined him $50 for drinking. But how could a ballplayer get fined for playing ball? Rube logic! Rube also argued, with some legitimacy, obviously, that he was not the player who needed shaking up, since he was the one bright point over the Tigers' dismal month of play. After the victory over Columbus, Derbeck put the fine in abeyance, declaring that it "might sometime be remitted." That did not satisfy the Rube. "The fine still hangs like the sword of Damocles over the talkative southpaw's head," wrote the *Evening News*. Rube could not do anything about it, but he sure could pout.[10]

Rube's mood worsened when he pitched well against Milwaukee on May 14 but lost 5 to 4. He walked four, and Tiger errors were again critical. The next day the Tigers won without him. Life just was not fair. Like any man, Rube would encounter many such barriers. Sometimes he would run away, sometimes he would stay and fight. This time he decided to fight the best way he knew how. The first-place Minneapolis Millers had lost only two games that season, and Detroit headed out to Minnesota to play them on May 17. Rube wanted a piece of the Millers, and the Tigers' new manager Ollie Beard gave him the ball. Some players said you had to keep Rube laughing or you didn't have a chance against him. This day Rube went out on the field snarling, and nothing would lighten his mood. He struck out five Millers in the first three innings. In the fourth and fifth he fanned four in a row. Every Miller but two struck out at least once; one whiffed three times. In all, Rube struck out 11, a new Western League record. He walked none and gave up only four hits, two clean singles and two little dribblers. At the plate Rube went 2 for 5, scoring twice. In the field he was flawless. It was Rube's first big game as a pro. The *Evening News* printed a cartoon, depicting the Rube, with huge feet, of course, carrying a newspaper displaying a headline: "Record 11 Strikeouts." He was striding mightily across the ball field, with all the other Tigers merely coming up to his knees.[11]

Rube must have figured he'd shown Derbeck his true value, and that the fine situation would now be settled favorably. So naturally he celebrated, and celebrated. On May 21, Beard shoved Rube out on the field in St. Paul to pitch against the Saints. "George Erratic Waddell," as the *Free Press* referred to him, could not see the plate too well that day. "Waddell Walloped" was the headline, as the Saints "reduced Waddell's chest measurement to about 6 inches"; 13 hits, 12 runs — it was ugly. Noting how well Waddell usually fielded, the *Sunday News Tribune* described Rube standing "like a mummy with the ball under his grimy paw." In the sixth inning, after a single, Rube threw a wild pitch and the runner advanced to third. Rube got the ball back from the catcher and just stood there in a fog while the runner stole home. A reporter declared it "enough to drive the catcher to drink," but the catcher did not need to; Rube had done more than enough for both of them.[12]

Over the next week, the Tigers returned to Detroit. Derbeck scolded Rube for his St. Paul game. That week the Tigers proceeded to lose every game, and Derbeck continued his tough guy act, firing manager Ollie Beard. Meanwhile, Rube was nowhere to be found. He had expected praise for the Minneapolis game, as well as forgiveness for St. Paul. He actually told a reporter that the catcher had lost the St. Paul game for Detroit — that he had dropped several throws to the plate and that the wild pitches were actually passed balls. It was oddly detailed level of analysis from someone who could barely see the plate that day. Amidst his confusions, and those of the team, Rube could not sit still. During the week of losses, Rube appeared at the ballpark only once, and he came dressed in a new suit with a bright red tie. He sat in the grandstand, munched down several bags of peanuts and made loud comments about Derbeck. After that nobody saw or heard from him.[13]

Rube skipped town. Not only had he left Detroit, he'd left the country. He'd crossed the river to Ontario and made his way over to the city of Chatham. They had a ball club, and he signed on with them for a few months. He had a great time with the folks over there, and he pitched some great ball. In his first outing against Dunnville, Rube pitched a no hitter, striking out 17 with nine other batters grounding out to him. In other words, at only one point in the entire game did Rube need any teammate but a catcher and a first baseman to be on the field! The very next day, Rube faced Dunnville again and struck out 20.

In a game in Ridgetown, Ontario, Chatham was leading 2 to 1 in the seventh. Rube was full of confidence, even for him. At the request of a fan, he called every one of his teammates but the catcher off the field. He planned to walk three batters then strike out the side. After walking the first two, Rube had trouble with the third batter, who tried to hit Rube's pitches, no matter how far outside they were sailing. He fouled off two, and the count ran to 3 and 2. On the next pitch the batter connected for a fly to the vacant outfield. The two runners scored, but for some reason the batter, befuddled and chuckling at the whole affair, forgot to run to first. Rube retrieved the ball, touched first, and struck out the next two hitters. Chatham came back to tie the game and went up a run in the ninth. Rube then went out and struck out the side to win. He kept the fielders in position this time.[14]

Rube had a great time in Chatham. He was so popular that the team expanded its schedule from two games a week to four and sometimes five. Rube claimed to be making $150 a week. He also pitched in neighboring towns for $25 a game. Before games he would station a pine board in front of the grandstand and bet anyone $10 that he could no only hit it but split it in just three pitches. He rarely lost the wager.

Harry Anderson, subsequently an important editor with the *Toronto Globe*, covered a Waddell game in Chatham for a local paper, the *Planet*. During the game, Rube's catcher was injured. Chatham had no other receivers, so a call went up to the stands for a volunteer. Anderson had been a star soccer forward in Ontario, so he took the challenge and donned a mask and pads. Rube's first pitch tore through the webbing of his mitt and smacked him in the belly. The next one tore his mitt off and sent it flying. The next one he had to take barehanded. The following morning, Anderson's hands were so sore that he had to delay finishing his article. The *Planet* hit the streets late, and Anderson was in trouble with his boss.[15]

Hanging out in many local establishments, notably the Rankin House, Rube was known regularly to carry a shillelagh. He did it not merely for appearance but for protection, given what often occurs in bars. Rube was afraid of no man, but felt he might need help in case of a five-on-one situation. He gave the shillelagh as a gift to a prominent local barrister, G. Grant McKeough (who subsequently gave it to the Baseball Hall of Fame). The story goes that Rube had gotten into a bad back-alley scuffle. McKeough got him off the hook with the local authorities, and Rube, always out of cash, supposedly gave him the shillelagh in lieu of payment. In regard to the truth of the story, McKeough's son later commented: "'good a guess as any."[16]

Either by choice or on the lam, Rube returned to Pennsylvania in August. It may have been late that summer that he played for Homestead. After Rube's departure, folks in Chatham were left scratching their heads: "De Rube, you know, he's a strange one, but he can shir trow de ball, eh?"

NOTES

1. *Detroit Free Press*, April 1, April 3, April 5, 1898; *Detroit Evening News*, April 3, 1898.

2. *Detroit Free Press*, April 9, April 11, April 12, 1898; *Detroit Sunday News Tribune*, April 10, 1898.

3. *Detroit Free Press*, April 15, 1898.

4. *Detroit Free Press*, April 21, 1898; *Detroit Evening News*, April 21, 1898.

5. *Detroit Evening News*, April 23, 1898.

6. *Detroit Free Press*, April 28, April 30, 1898; *Detroit Evening News*, April 30, 1898.

7. *Detroit Free Press*, May 3, 1898.

8. *Detroit Free Press*, May 7, 1898; *Detroit Evening News*, May 7, 1898.

9. *Detroit Free Press*, May 8, May 12, 1898.

10. Ibid., May 12, May 13, 1898.

11. Ibid., May 18, 1898.

12. *Detroit Free Press*, May 22, 1898; *Detroit Sunday News Tribune*, May 22, 1898.

13. *Detroit Free Press*, May 25, 1898.

14. Ernie Miller, "Stumping Around," *Chatham Daily News*, August 8, 1958; *Spalding Baseball Guide*, 1915.

15. Doug Oliver, "Rube Waddell Pitcher Here," *Mafair Magazine*, August, 1958, p. 48.

16. Ibid. Another writer with links to Chatham, Victor Lauriston, held that Rube may have come to Chatham for a reunion in 1904 and given McKeough, then the town's mayor, the shillelagh at that point; see Clippings File, Cooperstown; Spink, "Rube Waddell," p. 7.

Chapter 6

The Senator from Ohio

After his stint in Canada, Rube returned to Prospect. He may have done some late-summer, early-fall pitching in the area. Some say he did a few more turns with the Homestead Club. But the Pittsburgh papers never covered it, and given Rube's already growing notoriety, they would likely have covered any Waddell appearance.

Back in Louisville, nothing could persuade Fred Clarke to take back Waddell's contract. He'd seen the boy pitch. He never forgot the night in the hotel in Washington, and he heard about the escapades in Detroit. Clarke figured more power to anyone who had the wherewithal to handle "the big slob," as he called him. In 1899, Clarke's friend Tom Loftus, part owner and manager of the Columbus Senators of the Western League, decided he would give the Rube a try. Rube had no other offers and thus became a Columbus Senator.

Loftus was a more easygoing personality than Derbeck, and vastly more relaxed than the Marine-like Clarke. He had as good a baseball mind as they, and he'd seen Rube's fastball when Detroit faced Columbus in '98. He figured Waddell would be worth the effort. Rube, meanwhile, was always one to put the past behind him, so a fresh start in Columbus sounded good. And anyway, it wasn't too far from Pennsylvania. So in April, after a winter fattening up in Prospect, Rube was off to central Ohio.

Rube made the starting rotation with ease. He seemed in good spirits, he liked Loftus, and his fastball was hopping. On April 27 the team boarded a train for the first game of the season. Their destination — Detroit. Rube was "the life of the party" en route to Detroit, and he set about trying to talk Loftus and the other pitchers into letting him start against the Tigers. When he wanted something, Rube could wear someone down like nobody else. So everyone eventually agreed, and Rube got the start.

The Senators were not disappointed. The final score was Columbus 4, Detroit 3. But it was not that close. Rube allowed only one run until the ninth inning. He had Detroit completely throttled. He could "mow down the

Detroit team like so many weeds." He was already celebrating when he strode out to pitch the ninth. Then he gave up a hit, whacked the next two batters with pitches, and balked in two runs. Rube steadied himself and won the game; he had just begun to celebrate a bit soon. Rube did that a lot.[1]

On May 1 the Senators were trailing Indianapolis 10 to 2 after four innings. Loftus brought in Rube, and the big fellow gave up only one more run. The game was lost, but Rube again showed really good stuff. Later that week he shut out Buffalo. On May 9 he went back to Detroit and shut them out, too. On May 14 he shut out Indianapolis until the ninth. Then gave up a meaningless run, with Columbus winning anyway. The Senators were in last place at 5 and 8, but Rube was again proving to be a solid winner on a mediocre team.[2] It looked like another year of Rube pitching well on a loser, but the future had more in store for Rube this year.

On May 20 Rube faced the first place Minneapolis Millers, the team he had thrashed the previous year with Detroit. He continued his attack. Of the first sixteen batters he faced, Rube struck out eight. He was running over the Millers' entire order, but his teammates could not score. In the ninth, Rube walked the first man, who advanced to second on a sacrifice. The next man dribbled a single past second, scoring a runner to win 1 to 0. It was a tough one to lose, but Rube was quickly gaining the reputation as the toughest pitcher in the league.[3]

Unlike previous seasons, Rube did not "celebrate" too much after his victories, he just kept on pitching. After the Minneapolis game, he went across the river and beat the St. Paul team that walloped him so badly in '98. From there he took a single day's rest and went out and beat them again. Rube would often pitch on one or two days' rest that spring and summer with Columbus. Sometimes he pitched two days in a row. He went on an absolute tear through the entire league. When Rube first faced Connie Mack's Milwaukee Brewers, Loftus told Mack that he was going to show him a new lefthander, simply saying, "He's screwy, but he sure can pitch." Rube proved Loftus right on both points. He won the game and, while winning it, ran into the stands several times after a strikeout and had a fan slice off a bit of the sleeve of his undershirt for good luck.[4]

By July 10, after another blanking of Milwaukee, Rube's record stood at 20 and 4! It had only been bad luck that gave him the four losses, for in addition to the 1–0 loss to Minneapolis in May, the other three came by scores of 6–5, 8–7, and 7–6. Rube had simply not had a bad outing all season.

Words like "unfathomable" and "invincible" appeared in the papers. And his demeanor was solid. He was still doing his acting stunts out on the mound — cartwheels, constant jokes — but everyone enjoyed them. Who could argue with that kind of success? Many also commented on his sterling fielding. Waddell is "the best fielding pitcher in the league," opined one reporter. "Bunts in front of the plate just don't go," chortled another. Reporters also marveled at how far Rube could hit the ball (usually with a tiny bat). By June, Waddell's mere "name on the scorecard seems to be a bugaboo to most of the teams of the circuit." Single-handedly, Waddell had pulled the Senators into contention. In May they were in the cellar. On June 19 they were in first place for a day, with Rube having won over half their games. On July 11 they stood in third place, two and a half games out of first.[5]

On June 29 came a particularly satisfying victory. The game was against Detroit. Rube had a perfect game for six innings. In the bottom of the sixth Rube singled and then advanced to second with a runner on third. The next batter lined to the outfield. Rube ran, but the runner on third waited, fearing a catch. When the ball landed safely, he belatedly started for home with the Rube chugging right behind. A good throw from the outfielder nailed the runner from third. But as the Detroit catcher, Rube's former battery mate, hoisted the ball triumphantly to show the umpire that the collision with the runner had not jarred the ball loose, Rube slid in safely under his very nose. The crowd went wild. It made up for the steal of home the previous year in St. Paul. Rube went 4 for 5 that day, scored twice, and beat his old team 14 to 3, striking out eleven.[6] A Pittsburgh newspaper predicted that Waddell "is pitching his last season in the minor leagues. If Louisville does not want him next year, a number of teams will."[7]

NOTES

1. *Ohio State Journal*, April 28, 1899.

2. Ibid., May 2, May 10, and May 15, 1899.

3. Ibid., May 21, 1899.

4. Clippings File, National Baseball Hall of Fame and Museum, Cooperstown, N.Y.

5. *Ohio State Journal*, May 23, May 25, May 28, May 30, June 5, June 9, June 11, June 14–15, June 18, June 20, June 22, June 25, June 27, June 30, July 3, July 5, July 7, July 9–10, 1899.

6. Ibid., June 30, 1899.

7. *Pittsburg Community Gazette*, July 17, 1899.

Chapter 7

The Prodigal

Columbus was winning, and Rube was mowing down the league. But though the quality of baseball in Columbus was excellent, as a business proposition, baseball was a loser in the city. Other than on weekends, the team was losing money at every home game. Late nineteenth-century Columbus was a working man's town, without much of a leisure class who cared to attend ball games. (State government was tiny in those days.) The ball yard on the south side on Parsons Avenue was a full three and a half miles from the downtown. There was but one horse-drawn trackless trolley and no connections to the East Side where much of the city's baseball-loving laboring classes lived. Games began at 3:00 P.M., making it impossible for working people to get to the games on any day but Sunday. League rules, drawn up in cognizance of the need for visiting teams to meet post-game train schedules, would not permit later starts. Even if later starts could have been arranged to secure significantly greater attendance, they would have had to have been so late in the day as to imperil the completion of every game with darkness. (There were no stadium light systems in 1899; Cincinnati would not bring that innovation to major league baseball for another 35 years.)

With permission from Western League President Ban Johnson, Loftus began talking with representatives from other towns, mainly Rock Island, Illinois, and Grand Rapids, Michigan. The team thus felt a bit of turmoil. And the pennant race added to the pressure. One positive change at this point came on July 7 with the signing of a young outfielder out of Wahoo, Nebraska. His name was Sam Crawford. While Crawford would prove a valuable asset, the team's immediate concern was where they were going to play. To make moods even darker, Rube took sick with a fever on July 11. It was a legitimate sickness, not a toot, and he did not pitch for a week. While Rube was sick, his girlfriend — Florence Dunning, a native of Georgia — helped take care of him. She was Rube's first girlfriend, and their relationship grew.

On July 12, while Rube was in bed, Loftus sealed a deal with the town of Grand Rapids. The existing Grand Rapids team of the "Interstate League" would move to Columbus. Loftus secured free use of Grand Rapids' Recreation Park. Several Grand Rapids businessmen guaranteed purchases of $350 of tickets for the first games, tickets they easily sold to fans excited about the better brand of baseball coming their way. The local newspaper pushed sales heavily. The Senators were to arrive on July 20. "Every lover of baseball should buy a ticket ... and help make a complete success of the deal." The only question left was what to call the team. Grand Rapids was not Lansing, so "Senators" had all the congruity of "Jazz" and Utah. Owing to the happiness of bigger-time baseball arriving and to the strong strain of Dutch Presbyterianism in the region, the town decided on "the Prodigals." The Rube had truly arrived.[1]

Loftus and the team went on the road on July 16. Rube made the trip. He had not fully regained his strength, but he certainly could not stay in Columbus. He said good-bye to Florence, though he would see her again. The team arrived in Minnesota. Inexplicably, Loftus sent a weak Rube out to pitch against St. Paul on the 18th. They needed a win. Rube shut out the Saints for three innings. Then his strength gave way, and he faltered, yielding eight runs in the next three innings. Loftus had to relieve Rube for the first time in the season. The next day, with Rube clearly too weak, Loftus had to play Minneapolis. He actually put Sam Crawford in the box, who had not pitched since he was in high school. But Crawford won. The team then ventured to their new home.

The day off in Minneapolis proved restorative for Rube, and there was an open day afterwards when the team traveled to Michigan. The Prodigal Rube then opened the Grand Rapids season against Minneapolis on July 21. Sixteen hundred fans turned out (a weekday game in Columbus usually drew 200). The home team chose to bat second, something Grand Rapids fans had never seen before.

The game was about to start, but everyone on the Grand Rapids bench was looking about. They were to take the field, but where was Rube? No one knew. All of a sudden there arose a commotion out in the grandstand. "Here comes Rube!" someone shouted. Sure enough, it was Rube. He'd been out playing with some kids. He cut through the stands, jumped into the field, and ran towards the bench, disrobing as he went. He did that often. "It all took about three minutes," remembered Sam Crawford. Rube would "run back ... and yell 'All right, let's get 'em.'"[2] Rube was definitely restored to health and back in form that day. He struck out nine, as Grand Rapids won 15 to 3. "They may call Waddell 'Rube,'" wrote the local paper, "but he knows how to pitch something besides hay."[3]

Many years after his Hall of Fame career, Sam Crawford recalled the appeal of Rube among the fans in Grand Rapids as well as among the players of the Western League. "You had to notice him. First because he was such a big kid. Then because of that fastball. And once you started noticing him, you never took your eyes off him."[4] Indeed, the fans could not keep their eyes off Rube. It was not just his pitching ability. Others may have had ability, though maybe not to the same degree, but they never possessed Rube's appeal. Charisma has become an overused word in a more narcissistic era, but Rube had it. And he continued to be an entertainer while out on the field, something baseball fans back then had never seen. Baseball was truly a game to Rube, nothing more. Putting out a fire was serious business. Baseball was just fun. He would turn cartwheels, walk on his hands, chat and joke with the fans, make odd noises. He would still run into the stands occasionally and have someone cut a small good luck piece off his red underwear. He used to pour ice water on his arm *before* a game, claiming that if he didn't he'd throw so hard he'd burn up the catcher's mitt. He was serious about that. You never knew what Rube was going to do next, and neither did Rube. Loftus didn't mind — with the way Rube was pitching, how could he? The opposition would join in the zaniness, too. Some thought they were swept up by the fun and force of personality. Sam Crawford had a different slant on it:

> He was always laughing out there on the mound. ...The other side tried to keep him in good humor, even if he was striking them all out. They figured he was tough enough to hit against when he was happy; get him mad and there was no telling. ... If ... he'd really bear down ... you wouldn't have a chance. Not a chance.[5]

Rube kept laughing and winning. From Grandville, Kentwood, Walker, Cutlerville, Jamestown, Holland, and Wyoming (Michigan), from all over Western Michigan folks turned out by the thousands to see the Prodigals. The team was so-so, though Sam Crawford began to hit like a fiend. (He batted over .400 that summer.) Indianapolis and Minneapolis continued to lead the League. Rube's old buddies in Detroit kept pace with Grand Rapids, vying for third all along. This added an element of intrastate rivalry to the excitement. If the team lost a few, no one worried. A losing streak was impossible, for every third day, sometimes every other day, everyone knew who would pitch. On August 1, the Prodigals were in third place, 45 and 38, a half game ahead of Detroit. Rube's record stood at 25 and 6. His only decisive loss had been against St. Paul, when he was really too weak to be out of bed.

Whatever the pull of the planets and stars was on the Rube is a matter neither baseball people nor anyone else could figure. His incomparable talents were bound up in his zany on-field antics, in his runnings off to fight fires, and in his wanderlust. Rube wandered off to firehouses as a kid, and he would wander off to parts unknown when playing ball. "Where's Rube?" was a question many a player, manager, and fan cried out over the years. In early August, Loftus, the Prodigals, and much of Grand Rapids began to ask this very question, for Rube had vanished.

On August 8, Loftus received a telegram. It was from Rube. He was back in Columbus and needed money, or said he did anyway. "As soon as I receive $10 from you, I'll be able to buy a ticket from Columbus to Grand Rapids.— Eddie" The Prodigals had gone 1 and 5 that week and slipped behind rival Detroit. Loftus wired Waddell the money immediately. He waited for Rube to return, and then he waited some more. Rube may not have needed the money; he always had a knack of knowing the right angle to play as he touched someone up for a "loan." Most likely, he went to Columbus on impulse because he missed Florence. Rube could never resist an impulse. Indeed, even the *thought* of resisting an impulse probably never occurred to him.

Rube finally returned to Grand Rapids on August 12. Loftus worried that something may have happened to him during his romp. Rube said he was fine, but Loftus wanted to be sure and sent him out to pitch in an exhibition game against a local team in Manistee. (A young utility player named Roger Breshnahan played for them.) Rube pitched wonderfully. Loftus and the fans breathed more easily, and first-place Indianapolis was due in the next day.[6]

Twenty-six hundred people came out to Recreation Park to see Rube. Repeated applause greeted him, and the applause grew to loud cheers as the game progressed. Rube struck out eight Indians. In the fourth a routine grounder to second saw the Prodigals' second baseman throw wildly. The ball whizzed by the first baseman, and the fans groaned, but only for a moment. Rube had run over to back up the bag. His big legs "looked like the pistons of a steam engine as he sailed over the ground," wrote one observer. Rube blocked the ball with his leg, recovered, and threw the runner out at second. Truly the Prodigal Rube had returned. In the next inning Rube threw so hard to first he nearly decapitated his first baseman. He lifted the whole team, and Grand Rapids destroyed the league-leading Indians 9 to 1.

On August 16 Grand Rapids was in Buffalo for a double header. Rube pitched the first game, winning 4 to 3. He struck out the side in the ninth, and came off the mound feeling rather full of himself, even for the Rube. He asked Loftus if he could pitch the second game. Who could say "no" to the Rube the way he was going? However, Rube did not win the second game. Indeed, he was shellacked for 18 hits and 12 runs. That night the Prodigals boarded the train, arriving back in Grand Rapids the next morning. They had to go straight to the ballpark, as a game was slated for 1:00 that afternoon.

Bumpus Jones was the scheduled pitcher, but he turned up feverish and could barely stand up. It was actually a touch of malaria! Jones would recover, but he was certainly in no condition to pitch that day. Loftus looked at Rube. Rube shrugged his shoulders, and he promptly went out and hurled a shutout. Three games in 24 hours; he was a wonder. (Afterwards, Loftus actually gave him three days off.)

Whether it was the wear and tear of the season, or of pitching so much the one week in mid–August, Rube actually hit a bad patch. On August 20 he lost a close one in Minneapolis, 4 to 3. He tried to best the Millers on the 22d but gave up six runs in four innings and was relieved for only the second time in the season. After coming out of the game, Rube did not even stay around to watch the finish. The Prodigals lost. But Rube was long gone. He didn't go to Columbus this time. He just went fishing; after all, this was Minnesota. He beat St. Paul on August 25 for his 29th victory. Three days later, though, the Milwaukee Brewers beat him convincingly, 5 to 1.

Rube came back to Grand Rapids, having lost three of four. The team was still a half game up on Detroit, and Rube had over half the team's 57 victories, but he was disconsolate. Rube could never deal with emotional ups and downs too well. There was never any telling what he would do. This time he left again. Instead of relaxing with a fishing pole or going to see his sweetheart, Rube went out and pitched more. On Sunday, September 3, Grand Rapids baseball fans learned that their Rube had become a Harvard man. Rube had gone up to Harvard, Michigan, and pitched for the visiting Northern Kents of Cedar Springs, Michigan. How he got it into his head to do that no one could fathom. Rube won 6 to 2. But that did not mollify the Prodigals' fans. The only good thing the *Herald* could note was "The Harvards deserving credit for making a good showing against 'the great and only Rube.'" Folks in Grand Rapids were not pleased.

Cedar Springs had actually tried to hide the identity of their pitcher. Rube certainly looked like a big Midwestern farm boy, so they listed him on their roster as "Ole Olesun." No one knows how the Rube did trying to talk like a Scandinavian immigrant, but the locals were all agog: "Dat Ole, he can shur trow it, you know, hey?" No one in Grand Rapids was laughing, however. The Prodigals were in third and second place Minneapolis was due in that day.

Rube returned to Grand Rapids on Sunday morning. He had clearly been celebrating his victory over Harvard with his newly forged Scandinavian brethren. Loftus had to pitch him. No one else could beat Minneapolis. Rube's little excursion was already common knowledge in Grand Rapids, particularly "to the fans of a speculative turn of mind." Those who were betting with their minds sat bemused, while those rooting with their hearts groaned. Rube gave up five runs in the first inning. The first two batters bunted. Rube bobbled the first and threw wildly with the second. It was a sad contrast to his sober, sensational fielding a few weeks before. Then came a barrage of hits. The Millers scored two more runs in the third. Cries of "Take him out!" reverberated about the grandstand. Loftus obliged. Grand Rapids lost. Rube went off the field limping, but, noted reporters, "The seat of his lameness was really in the opposite end of his armature." Given the regard many townspeople had for the mentality of some of the local immigrant farmers, many in Grand Rapids wondered if "Ole Oleson" wasn't Rube's real name after all.[7]

Rube redeemed himself a little with a good game on September 7. It was his 30th win of the season. But the "balloon ride" Rube had taken in the previous weeks remained on the minds of folks all over Grand Rapids. There would not be time for reparations. The season was winding down. On September 9, Sam Crawford was gone. His spectacular line-drive hitting won him a contract with the Cincinnati Reds. There he began a 19-year career in the big leagues. Rube would see him again.

Rube was slated to start for Grand Rapids on the 10th, but didn't show. He hadn't gone on another toot. He had simply gone; he didn't even say goodbye to Loftus. He had actually left with Sam Crawford. While Crawford stayed in Cincinnati, Rube met the Louisville Colonels there en route to a game in Baltimore. Someone had persuaded Fred Clarke to give the 30-game winning "big slob" another look.

NOTES

1. *Grand Rapids Herald*, July 18, 1899.

2. Quoted in Lawrence Ritter, *The Glory of Their Times: The Story of the Early Years of Baseball Told by the Men Who Played It.* (New York: William Morrow, 1984), p. 49.

3. *Grand Rapids Herald*, July 21, 1899.

4. Ritter, *The Glory of Their Times*, p. 49.

5. Ibid.

6. *Grand Rapids Herald*, August 8 and August 12, 1899.

7. Ibid., September 3, 1899.

Chapter 8

My New Kentucky Home

"How am I going to handle Rube this time?" thought Fred Clarke. The memories of the Washington hotel and the zaniness of September 1897 had not faded, and Clarke had not mellowed at all. He was in his third year as the Colonels' player/manager, and he was only 26, just four years older than the Rube.

The Colonels were mired in ninth place. The season had once again gone down the drain, and the fans were looking for something to cheer about. They remembered Rube's antics. The Louisville papers were full of excitement about the incredible record Waddell had compiled in Columbus and Grand Rapids. The tales of "Ole Olesun" had apparently escaped them. But they had not escaped Fred Clarke.

Clarke needed to see for himself if Rube had developed any toughness. He knew the kid could throw a ball like few others ever had. The question was a matter of the kid's head. After picking up Rube in Cincinnati, Clarke and the Colonels headed for Baltimore. The Orioles had fallen off a bit since their championship years of 1894–96. But with players like Willie Keeler and John McGraw, they were still strong. Clarke wasted no time. He put Rube out right away to start against the Birds on September 12.

The next day the *Courier Journal* headlined the consensus about Clarke's new pitcher: "Rube Waddell Is a Winner." Through eight innings Rube had given up two runs. The Colonels had scored none, but at the top of the ninth they came through with two. Rube went out in the bottom of the inning to hold them. The first batter tripled. With none out, it looked grim, and the fans were doing everything they could to tighten the screws on the big semi-rookie. Out in left field, Clarke held his position — and his breath. Up stepped Willie Keeler. He popped harmlessly to shortstop. Up stepped John McGraw. He also popped to short, and the runner, having taken too much of a lead, was doubled up. Rube had held them. Clarke actually smiled a bit. In the tenth Louisville tallied a run. Rube again went out, this time to win. The Colonel fielders let him down, though, committing two errors and allowing the Orioles to tie it. Rube did not react, though. He hung in. The eleventh was scoreless. In the twelfth Louisville scored one. In the bottom, Rube and the Colonels were perfect. Clarke had his victory. More importantly, he had his answer as to Rube's toughness.[1]

Rube beat Baltimore again in relief on September 15. Honus Wagner hit well and had two marvelous throwing assists from right field. But Rube made the headlines, making "monkeys of the locals for the balance of the game."[2] From Baltimore, the Colonels took the evening train to Philadelphia. The very next day Rube pitched and won again. Clarke figured hard work would keep the kid out of mischief. Rube went on to beat Washington; then he beat St. Louis.

In an outing against Chicago, Rube was pitted against Clark Griffith, whose season record then stood at 21 and 12. Rube went out and struck out 13, an all-time nine-inning record to that date. Louisville won 6 to 1. Griffith had his 13th loss. From the outset, Rube's confidence knew no bounds. In the second inning, he intentionally walked three batters then proceeded to strike out the next three. He would walk only one other batter all day. Several times he sent the catcher to the press box to find out if he had broken the strikeout record. When he struck out the last man, Rube celebrated by dancing a Highland Fling from the pitcher's mound to the dugout. The Chicago crowd delighted in it all.[3]

After five wins and a save, Rube finally lost his first game on September 29 against St. Louis. But Clarke would not let up, and neither would Rube. Even Clarke had to acknowledge the achievement and accept the sideshows. Tommy Leach played third for Louisville that season, and roomed with the Rube when on the road. (What a treat that must have been.) "If they thought he was nutty later," Leach recalled, "they should have seen him then. He was just an overgrown boy. It was a riot."[4] Clarke's intensive use of Rube brought out the best in the lad's pitching, but it could not suppress his playfulness. Somehow, during time off in Louisville, Rube had gotten hold of a flock of geese. He trained them all to skip rope, save one goose that just would not learn. Unruffled, Rube trained that one to hold the other end of the rope while he twirled it. Rube brought the whole flock out to the ballpark one day for a pre-game exhibition. Clarke could only shake his head. Some people wanted to name the goose at the other end of the rope Rube, too.

From the day he rejoined Louisville in mid–September to the final day of the season on October 16, Rube compiled a record of 7 and 2. Besides the one loss in St. Louis, Rube's only other loss was to Chicago in a game that was called for darkness after just six innings. For that stretch of weeks, when Rube was not pitching, the Colonels' record was 10 and 7.

The final game of the season was a joy for Rube. It was in Pittsburgh.

Rube boasted he would beat the Pittsburghers on their own field. His mother, father, and two of his sisters came down from Prospect, as did a whole slew of friends from Butler, from Evans City, and from lots of saloons in between. They all cheered Eddie as he strode out to meet the Pirates. Rube was actually all business, no clowning. As he was mowing down the Pirates, from somewhere in the stands an egg flew out, and it hit Rube right in the head as he was walking out to mound. Tommy Leach recalled: "You couldn't faze that guy. ... He's the only guy I know who appreciated a thing like that." Rube reacted by telling the outfielders to leave the field. Under the rules, that was not allowed. Nine men had to take the field. So Rube instructed the outfielders to stand right behind the infielders. They did, even Clarke did, and Rube proceeded to strike out the side. "I stood there at third base," Leach remembered, "and watched him throw. I wasn't playing. I was watching! 'How can a man throw that hard?' I used to wonder to myself."[5] The Colonels beat Pittsburgh that afternoon 4 to 1. The season was over. The Brooklyn Dodgers had won the pennant. Louisville had finished ninth. For the year, his Columbus, Grand Rapids, and Louisville games combined, Rube compiled a record of 37 and 12.

NOTES

1. *Louisville Courier-Journal*, September 13, 1899.
2. Ibid., September 16, 1899.
3. Ibid., September 23, 1899.
4. Ritter, *The Glory of Their Time*, p. 35.
5. Ibid.

Chapter 9

Back Home

With the final game in Pittsburgh, the National League season ended for Louisville. Rube was home, and he had big plans. He went up to Prospect and saw family and friends but immediately skedaddled over to Columbus. There, on October 18, George Edward Waddell and Florence Dunning were married. Florence and Rube shared a genuine affection. They also seemed to have something in common in regard to social graces. One of Rube's catchers in Louisville, Malachi Kittredge, recalled sitting near the couple at a hotel dining room. The young couple was served a charlotte russe for dessert. The sweet came with a paper wrapping. Florence ate the whole thing, including the paper. Rube asked his love how she liked it, and Florence responded, "The crust was delicious." By all appearances it was a perfect match.[1]

Mutual friends in Columbus must have taken care of all the arrangements, as the local papers described the occasion as "one of the prettiest weddings of the season." Throughout the household lay lovely arrangements of palms, vines, and potted plants. A family friend played Mendelssohn. Friends came in from Chicago, Buffalo, and Cincinnati. The citizens of Prospect, Pennsylvania, sent along good wishes, proud that "Prospect has a place on the map now on account of Rube's pitching." "Shazaam!" thought Rube. He and Florence moved home to Prospect.[2]

The Waddells spent a quiet winter in Prospect. Rube helped work the family farm. After the harvest was in, he coached and played on the Prospect football team. Rube was a terrific football player, not just in the general sense of his ability, but in the added sense that he could absolutely terrify the opposition. The average player on the Prospect team weighed 135 pounds. Rube's winter weight ran around 235, and he was easily the fastest man on the team. "Edward Waddell makes a mighty rush!" noted a local paper after Prospect, mainly Rube, mauled neighboring Butler. One day a team came in from New Castle. They were much larger. The puny Prospect team stood there waiting for their leader to arrive, feeling more intimidated by the minute. Suddenly all heads turned as Rube arrived. Inexplicably, he was sauntering across the field carrying a full keg of nails on each broad shoulder. Rube gave a big smile as he set the kegs down next to Prospect's bench. New Castle did not ask what the nails were for. They just left the field and forfeited the game.[3]

During the off-season, Honus Wagner came up to Prospect to see Rube one day. Wagner described Rube as "a curious card and a pest, to put it mildly — and yet," he reflected, "it is impossible to help liking the eccentric fellow." Rube was already known for his tendency to touch up people for money. "Get introduced to the Rube," Wagner noted, "and in ten minutes he will make a touch. What's more, he will spring so artistic an excuse that it is 3 to 1 he will get away with it." When Wagner took the train up to Butler he made sure he brought only the return train ticket and no other coin with him. Otherwise, "how could I refuse a gentleman who was offering me the hospitality of his home?" Upon Wagner's arrival, Rube immediately discovered that his guest had forgotten his wallet. Rube thought a minute and went to his father asking for $20. Wagner recalled:

> Mr. Waddell, Senior, looked upon his son with doubtful eye. "See here, George Edward," spoke the old gentleman. "I gave you $10 only last night. Where has that money gone already?"
>
> "Father," answered the Rube most earnestly, "you remember that pair of pants I had out in the barn to do the stable work in? Well I thought I could use those pants for a bank to put my nest egg in. So I put the $10 in the pants. Last night, Father, you, in the kindness of your heart told a tramp he could sleep in the barn. Father, that wicked tramp stole those pants and my nest egg with them."

"The old gentleman, shaking his head," laughed Wagner, "coughed up the $20 — and then Rube had $30." Rube and Wagner had a great day painting up the town of Butler.[4]

Rube would go into Butler regularly. He did some work in the fire department, relieved various bartenders, and did a lot of fishing in the nearby creeks. Though he never made much money in the majors, Rube always played the role of the big timer. He would regularly buy a block of theatre tickets for all his friends. They would all sit up in the balcony. One friend recalled that during intermissions Rube would holler, "Who's the best ballplayer in the world?" The group would holler back his name. Eddie did not mind being called Rube anymore.[5]

When contemplating the upcoming baseball season, Eddie and Florence Waddell figured that when the month of March rolled around, he would head South to wherever the Colonels were going to train. But in the off season, the National League did some reorganizing. The season was shortened from 154 to 140 games. The league changed the balk rule a bit. Now only the runners could advance if the pitcher motioned but did not throw to first base, or if he threw to a base without stepping toward it. And home plate would now have five sides, not four. The big changes, however, concerned the makeup of the league's roster of teams.

The existing twelve-team circuit of the National League appeared to stretch the talent pool a bit too much. In 1899 the bottom two clubs — Washington and Cleveland — had been pitifully poorer than such powers as Boston and Brooklyn. In the previous five years, some overlappings of management and ownership had also evolved. The mere hint of such a possiblity as a fixed game or an insider trade raised the spectre of compromising the league's credibility in the public mind. All the team owners knew this could jeopardize their whole enterprise, and they were not about to risk such a catastrophe.

In an age of corporate mergers, big league baseball consolidated itself. As J. P. Morgan reflected, rationalized combination was always better than cutthroat competition. With the consolidation lowly Washington was dropped from the league. Much of the Cleveland team merged with St. Louis. The once proud Baltimore Orioles disbanded, with many of the players going to Brooklyn. Finally, the Louisville Colonels closed up shop, leaving the town with bat manufacturing as its only major baseball enterprise. Owner Barney Dreyfuss, who had lost $16,000 over five years with the Colonels, bought 50 percent of the Pittsburgh Pirates and brought his best players up the Ohio River with him. For reasons of health, Dreyfuss had wanted to get out of the Kentucky distillery business where he had made his money. He had come to America from Germany at age 16 and learned English and baseball simultaneously. Baseball was his passion, and when the opportunity came simultaneously to quit the liquor business and stay in baseball he seized it.

Among the players Dreyfuss relocated to Pittsburgh were Honus Wagner, Rube Waddell, and Fred Clarke, whom Dreyfuss made the new Pirates player/manager, a post Clarke would keep until 1915. For Honus Wagner the move was a great piece of news. He was from the town of Mansfield in Allegheny County, a town since renamed Carnegie, right next door to Pittsburgh. For Rube it was the same. Up in Butler the *Eagle* proclaimed proudly: "Rube Waddell pitches for Pittsburgh next year!"[6]

The National League's consolidation left some hard feelings in some cities. Baltimore, Cleveland, Washington, and Louisville were now without ball clubs. At this point, Ban Johnson, president of the Western League, got busy. It would take him a year to complete the work, but he began developing a rival league out of some of his Western League clubs and other key cities. He would place teams in Washington, Cleveland, and Baltimore, while keeping the Tigers in his booming Western League city of Detroit. He would go into direct competition with the rival National League, eventually starting teams in Boston, Philadelphia, and Chicago. He did the same in St. Louis, moving the former Milwaukee Brewers there to become the Browns. The new Baltimore club, again named the Orioles, would last two years. Then in 1903, with the new league's existence secured, Johnson took on the older league in the big city of New York. Thus Baltimore moved to New York to become the Highlanders, later renaming themselves the Yankees.

Few would have wagered from that point that this two, 8-team league configuration would remain unchanged for 50 years, but it did. At first, the new league created a frantic series of bidding wars for the best players. These chaotic effects lay down the road for Waddell, for Honus Wagner, and for many others. At the moment, the matter may as well have involved classical music as far as Rube was concerned. As they celebrated Christmas in 1899, the only thing the Waddell family knew was that next season Eddie would be playing before home folks.

With the reshuffling of the league, 1900 pennant predictions were flying about many National League cities. Boston and Philadelphia looked strong from the previous year. Brooklyn was the defending champion, and with their pick of the Oriole remnants, they seemed even better. Inheriting good players from Cleveland, St. Louis fans were hopeful too. Chicago, Cincinnati, and New York seemed the only weak teams in the league, though New York was trumpeting the potential of a young pitcher they were wooing named Christy Mathewson, who would soon graduate from Bucknell College. The Pittsburgh Pirates, with their surviving Colonels, felt very confident. Fred Clarke expressed confidence to Barney Dreyfuss, telling him "the Pirates will fool some of the people who are accusing the locals of being shy on brainy players." What new player on the Pirates could possibly have given rise to such talk?[7]

With a new team and stronger possibilities, manager Fred Clarke began the 1900 season more tough minded and determined than ever. After performing so marvelously for Clarke in Louisville the previous fall, Rube picked up the ball in April and continued right where he'd left off. In an exhibition against Memphis, Clarke penciled Rube in for the middle three innings. But Rube was going so strongly, striking out seven players in a row, that Clarke left him in. The fans approved, and Rube naturally launched into one of his goofy routines, turning cartwheels and walking to the dugout on his hands. He let up in the last innings, lobbing slow ones over and letting the Memphis boys hit a few. Rube pitched three innings against the 1899 Eastern League champions from Rochester, New York. No ball ever even got out of the infield. Rube had earned a spot not merely on the Pirate's starting rotation, he was the #1 starter. The *Pittsburg Post* noted, "Waddell's feats with the sphere are still being discussed with admiration among the local fans." The

Pirates would open on the road, but Clarke slated Rube to start in the home opener at Exhibition Park. All the locals in "daan-taan Picksburg" were excited.[8]

The Pirates opened in St. Louis on April 19. In the box for St. Louis was Denton True Young. His nickname was "Cy," short for "Cyclone," which described the weather conditions batters felt they were experiencing when they faced his fastball. Cy Young was in his ninth full season, at this point. He had won 186 games in his first six seasons, and he was at the peak of his powers as he faced the Pirates. Expecting Rube to start against Young, the *Pittsburg Post* predicted "a royal battle."[9] Sam Leever, whom Rube had bested in Homestead, had also had a good spring, however, and Clarke chose to start him against St. Louis. Young had the Pirates completely hog-tied. He gave up but five hits the whole game. Meanwhile the Cardinals jumped on Leever for three runs in the first. Then Leever took a line drive on the finger and had to leave the game. Clarke sent in Rube. Rube gave up seven hits, but no runs. Meanwhile, the Pirates could not do a thing with Young, so the 3–0 lead held up. It was the first time Waddell locked horns with Mr. Cy Young. It would not be the last.

Rube opened Cincinnati's season on April 23. A Cincinnati reporter was watching Waddell for the first time. "Waddell," he lamented, "at no time gave the local aggregation an opportunity to get within hailing distance of a run." Rube struck out six, the Pirates scored six, two by Rube himself as he went one for three. He's pitched a three-hit shutout, and, as Pittsburghers would grow fond of saying, "he had 'em all the way."

News of Waddell's pitching on the road made the locals even more excited about the home opener on Friday the 26th against the Dodgers. Before the game the Pirates staged a parade. Rube marched alongside a furniture store owner who carried a big umbrella to protect Rube from the sun's rays. On the umbrella, the businessman had printed an advertisement of his shop. The crowd loved it; Clarke did not. Rube explained that when or if he sets up a house, he now had a promise of free merchandise. In addition to the parade, the Pirates' management tried an inducement of a free seat cushion with each paid ticket. Eleven thousand turned out at Exposition Park, becoming the largest crowd ever to see a game in the city. Rube chortled with confidence about the game: "There's nothing to it. It's a pipe." It wasn't. The game was a wild and woolly affair. Errors plagued both sides. Rube could often be unnerved in such situations, and this was no exception. He was hit freely, and Clarke lifted him in the fifth. The Pirates lost, 12 to 11. The rest of the series would not be any better. The Pirates lost Saturday, 19 to 5, and on Sunday 7 to 1, with lots of errors. The Pirates a bad series; Rube had had a bad game. The question was whether either could regroup. (The answer would be: Yes and No.)

Rube's apparent solidity worsened that week as he took "sick." The *Dispatch* described it as "his alleged case of pleurisy." Clarke did not schedule him to start again until May 2. This was to be a rematch with Cy Young, but Rube did not show up. He was busy with his new Irish setter. Rube did come to the park the next day, and the Cardinals jumped all over him, pounding out 11 hits. Rube's catcher that day, Clifford "Tacks" Latimer, aggravated matters, with two passed balls and several dropped third strikes. One reporter advised Fred Clarke not to hang on to such a battery, as "neither has more gray matter than the law allows; to allow them to wander about all by themselves was rather a daring venture by Manager Clarke." Latimer was shortly released.[10]

In his next outing, on May 6, Rube took another "balloon ride," the 1900 term for "coming unglued." He shut down Chicago in the first inning. In the bottom of the first, Fred Clarke was on first base. Always aggressive, Clarke barrelled into Chicago second baseman Clarence "Cupid" Childs to break up a double play. Childs took exception to Clarke's high spikes, and a fistfight broke out. Matters cooled a bit, but Clarke was not a happy man when he trotted out to left field to begin the next inning. Rube then lost his focus. He gave up four straight singles, the Pirates made two errors, and Rube hit a batter. Now Clarke was really fuming. He ran in and yanked Rube. Chicago went on to win, 7–6.[11]

Rube had had such a wonderful April. Once he got back to Pittsburgh he was too full of fun, and had too many personal connections and diversions from which to choose. The cliché about the kid in the candy store only remotely describes what was occurring with Rube that spring in Pittsburgh. Clarke decided to sit Rube down for a spell. Some said Rube should pitch only when the Pirates were on the road. Rumors also began to fly about the city that Waddell was so forlorn about being benched that he had jumped off the 6th Street Bridge. Rube later announced that he was going to hunt down and get even with the originator of the rumor about his attempted suicide.[12]

Before "Tacks" Latimer left the club, he had the misfortune of being assigned as Rube's roommate when the Pirates were on the road. Generally, they got along well, though as his position on the club grew tenuous, Latimer would playfully jump onto Rube's side of the bed in the morning, hold his razor to Rube's throat, and make Rube promise to let Tacks catch him on his next start. Rube responded with equal playfulness. Rube always traveled with a shotgun, and he would sit in the room, assemble and load it, and point it right at Latimer. Latimer got the last laugh on Rube before Clarke released him. Besides his uniform, Rube usually owned just one suit of clothes at a time. He would never clean the suit, he would just wear it a few weeks and then get rid of it. Latimer saw Rube about to throw away a suit. "Heck, I can use it," said Latimer, "so why not give it to me." Waddell agreed. Tacks had the suit cleaned and pressed. A few days later, Rube saw Latimer, looking quite spiffy. Rube liked the cut of Latimer's appearance, and offer to trade his new suit for Tacks' "new" one. Latimer agreed, and Rube got his old suit in exchange for his new one.[13]

Clarke had a good sense of humor about matters like suits. He was not amused, however, at stories of razors and shotguns, and he was even more in earnest when it came to matters on the ball field. He felt no choice but to sit Rube down for all his zaniness. Whether it was Clarke's discipline or just the course of time, Rube's balloon seemed to come back to earth. While Rube was benched, Clarke tried other pitchers, among them a youngster named Jack Chesbro. Chesbro would become a great pitcher, but only after he mastered the newly discovered art of lubricating the fingers with saliva before throwing the ball. (The spitball was never illegal before 1919, but no one developed its use until the early twentieth century.) Chesbro would win 41 games with New York in 1904. With the Pirates he was just beginning to show his greatness. Clarke started him against Philadelphia on May 17, and he gave up four runs in the very first inning. Clarke looked down the bench and thought he would take Rube out of mothballs. As Rube strode out to the mound, the crowd looked nervously at one another. But Rube pitched remarkably well. Philadelphia garnered only three hits in eight innings. They scored no more runs, but the Pirates could counter with only three. The game was lost, but Rube had the crowd back in his corner. Clarke was still neutral.[14]

Rube's balloon reascended on May 22 when he faced the Brooklyn Dodgers and their star pitcher, Joe McGinnity. Rube was perfect for three innings. Then former Oriole Willie Keeler tripled to start the fourth. Fans started to razz Rube, and it worked. With only Keeler on third, Rube turned and threw to first where, of course, no one was covering. Keeler scored. The fans were laughing, and Clarke went ballistic. Rube was out.[15]

Rube righted himself on the 25th. Again it was a relief job. The New York Giants were up 4–3 in the sixth when Rube entered the game. Rube promptly struck out five of the next seven batters. He held the Giants scoreless; unfortunately, the Pirates could tally for none. If anyone would have noticed, Rube had shown exceptional poise in relief. He was, after all, a capable fireman. But such specialties were unknown in the baseball of that era.[16]

As with any player, Rube's penchant for losing focus shot around the league. Opposing coaches let Rube have it with every possible insult. Rube would have to deal with this for the rest of his career. But no one ever really knew whether the razzing had any effect. Rube's rhythms were unique. And there were times when all the razzing in the world made not a dent in him. Such a day was May 27. He beat Cincinnati 7–2 and was all business from start to finish. At the end of May the eccentric Rube stood at 2 and 3, with two effective stints in relief. He had struck out more batters (30) than the rest of the entire Pirate pitching staff combined, but he also led the staff in earned runs (32). Clarke was looking for consistency, and he was not getting it. The Pirates were beginning a long road trip from May 30 to June 25. Clarke hoped his mercurial ace would solidify amidst fewer diversions.[17]

In the first few games of the trip, Rube came through. In New York on May 31 he beat the Giants in a tight one, 7–6, striking out seven and working effectively with men on base. Two days later he relieved Jack Chesbro after "Happy Jack" had allowed five runs in two innings. Rube held the Giants to only one more run, but the Pirates lost. Rube beat Philadelphia on June 5, and when a teammate fell ill he came back on a day's rest to beat the Phillies again. In the second game Rube wobbled in the eighth after a walk, a passed ball, and a wild throw yielded a run. The Phillies coaches rode Rube mercilessly. But Rube held in the ninth. He struck out the last Phil and danced all the way to the dugout.[18]

The day Rube danced off the mound, Fred Clarke took ill. The illness was not due to Rube, it was kidney trouble, though Rube doubtlessly did not help the condition.

Whether it was Clarke's departure, the fatigue from pitching twice in three days, or some deeper cause, Rube's wild throw and ghost dance seemed to touch off another ascension. It was a brief one, for he failed to show up for a start on June 9. Where he went remains a mystery. Rube reappeared in Brooklyn on June 11, and interim manager Dick Cooley used him that day in relief. Rube was gaining steadily wider fame among fans, and the Brooklynites were delighted to see him stride to the mound. They were even happier when the great Rube failed to hold a lead.[19]

Three days later Rube lost in his first appearance in Boston. The *Boston Globe* wrote of "the most talked of pitchers of the day, a pleasing faced chap, tall, lithe, muscular, with a wealth of speed and curves." Boston people felt Rube pitched well; the loss was simply due to their club being superior to the Pirates.[20] The Pirates were indeed playing poor baseball. Given the hopes of April, it was a big disappointment, and Rube was certainly one of the players not living up to expectations. On June 17, Clarke returned to the club. Rube stood at 4 and 5. His 65 strikeouts led the league and matched the total of the rest of the Pirate staff. But he was not winning, and neither was the team. Honus Wagner was hitting .440, but no one else was any good. On June 17, Pittsburgh lost its seventh game in a row. Clarke appeared ready to try out some new pitchers. But his kidneys began troubling him again, and he had to take another week off.[21]

Amidst the losing streak and general turmoil, Rube started against

Chicago, who sent out Clark Griffith. It proved to be quite a duel. After 13 innings, the game was scoreless. Both pitchers went the distance. Rube struck out 12. With two out in the bottom of the fourteenth, Rube walked Chicago's eighth hitter, and Griffith stepped in. On a called hit and run, Griffith lofted a twisting pop that just cleared the shortstop and squirted across the left field foul line. The runner raced home, ending the game. It was a tough one for Rube, and for the Pirates it was another loss, the kind that really stings when a club is on a losing streak.[22]

After such a loss, everyone on the club was down. Rube responded with more zaniness. He bragged to the press that he was going to lead the league in strikeouts. Then he disappeared, this time for ten days. He took the liberty to return to Pittsburgh ahead of the team. Rube figured the road trip was coming to an end, and he had just pitched the marathon in Chicago. Generally, though, it is a good idea for a ball player to ask permission before departing like that. Protocol never was Rube's strong suit. Clarke returned to the club on the 27th. He found Rube gone and had to steady himself lest his health relapse. When Rube wandered back on June 29, Clarke promptly sent him out to face the Phillies. With equal promptness, Rube lost, with the Pirates committing five errors.[23]

Clarke decided it was time to have a "Dutch Uncle" talk with his erratic young pitcher. In regard to the many lost games, Rube certainly had his excuses and explanations and pleas of bad luck. But he had no explanation as to why, at the point he was supposed to be starting a game, he was found under the stadium grandstand playing marbles with some kids. Clarke was hardly sympathetic, and Rube seemed unwilling or unable to heed any words from his manager. Clarke grew even angrier when he learned that Rube had been working some evenings for a local theatre. At Hindman and Kummers' Union Scout Theatre Company, Rube had been acting on stage, leading the company band, and, between acts, selling songbooks to the audience (25 cents a piece). He offered to give one to Clarke. Clarke was not buying; he was not the theatre type.[24]

Clarke really hit the roof when he learned that, in addition to keeping late hours and drinking, Rube had actually been doing some ball playing with a few local businessmen and hurt his finger while catching. Then Rube met some boys after a game — something he often did — playing ball, leapfrog, mumblety-peg, marbles, anything. This time the boys had asked him to show them how to throw a curve ball. They had no baseballs, however. Rather than disappoint, Rube tried to show them using a brick. Hurling heavy bricks, Rube hurt his arm. Clarke was now totally fed up. He gave Rube one more chance on July 5 against the Giants. Rube lost it. He had not won a game since June 7. On July 8, Fred Clarke suspended Waddell indefinitely.[25]

Rube learned of the suspension from the newspapers. He went to Clarke and asked if it was true. Clarke snapped, "It sure is, so get your stuff our of here and never come back." "Fred," Rube responded, "I never had any idea you felt that way. Next time I see you I will shoot you full of holes."[26] Whether or not Rube was serious about shooting Clarke was not important at that moment. The question now was where to go.

NOTES

1. Clippings File, Cooperstown.
2. *Ohio State Journal*, October 22, 1899; *Butler* (Pa.) *Eagle*, September 28, October 19, and November 2, 1899.
3. *Butler Eagle*, November 23 and November 25, 1899; *Philadelphia Public Ledger*, May 9, 1915.
4. Quoted in the *Minneapolis Journal*, June 5, 1912, p. 16.
5. Isaac Allen interviewed by John Dell, *Philadelphia Inquirer*, undated, circa 1962, Clippings File, Cooperstown.
6. *Butler Eagle*, December 14, 1899.
7. Clarke to Dreyfuss, quoted in the *Pittsburg Dispatch*, April 18, 1900.
8. *Pittsburg Dispatch*, April 2 and April 6, 1900; *Pittsburg Post*, April 21, 1900.
9. *Pittsburg Post*, April 16, 1900.
10. *Pittsburg Dispatch*, May 1, May 3–4, 1900.
11. Ibid., May 7, 1900.
12. Ibid., May 17 and May 19, 1900.
13. Told by Fred Clarke, *Sporting News*, March 28, 1951.
14. *Pittsburg Dispatch*, May 18, 1900.
15. Ibid., May 23, 1900.
16. *Pittsburg Post*, May 26, 1900.
17. Ibid., May 28, 1900.
18. *Pittsburg Post*, May 31, June 2, 5, and 7, 1900.
19. Ibid., June 12, 1900.
20. *Boston Globe*, June 15, 1900.
21. *Pittsburg Post*, June 17–19, 1900.
22. Ibid., June 22, 1900.
23. Ibid., June 20 and 30, 1900.
24. Ira Smith, *Baseball's Famous Pitchers* (New York: A. S. Barnes, 1954), p. 45.
25. *Pittsburg Post*, July 8, 1900.
26. Recalled by Fred Clarke, *Sporting News*, March 28, 1951.

Chapter 10

Punxsutawney Rube

Hall of Famer Sam Crawford said that it really never mattered to Rube whether he was pitching in the big leagues or on a sandlot with a bunch of kids. It was all the same: to Rube baseball truly was only a game. Two days after his suspension from the Pirates, Rube joined a local team in Millvale and traveled with them for some games in the town of Punxsutawney, Pennsylvania, the hamlet of groundhog fame.

As expected, Rube beat the Punx, striking out 11, though the score was only 1–0. Rube then switched to the outfield, and this time Punxsutawney beat Millvale 3–1. Rube's home run was Millvale's only tally. Rube so liked the crowds in the groundhog town, that he switched sides that evening. The team went home to Millvale, while the Rube stayed put. He pitched for Punxsutawney against DuBois (pronounced Doo-boys). He homered and reportedly shattered several of DuBois' bats with his curves.[1] After three such contests, the DuBois manager told his Punxsutawney counterpart that either he get rid of Waddell or there would be no more games with DuBois that summer. So Rube stopped pitching. Then in a game against Homestead, with Punxsutawney losing, Rube came on in relief in the seventh. The Ground Hogs tied it, but then Rube gave up a home run in the ninth and lost. The Pittsburgh papers printed the story (and Fred Clarke's kidney condition showed improvement).[2]

It was all such a waste, a great young talent like Rube playing out in the sticks. (At the same time, another young Pennsylvania fireballer, Christy Mathewson, left Bucknell College to begin playing for the New York Giants.) Several minor league teams offered to buy out Waddell's contract. New Castle, Pennsylvania, signed former Pirate Tacks Latimer, and they tried to snare his former batterymate Rube for $35 a game. Clarke did not want Rube, but Pirates owner Barney Dreyfuss would not release him. Likely, Rube would not have worried about any barring legalities if any such offer attracted him. But he was happy in Punxsutawney, and Punxsutawney was happy to have him — at least that was how Rube saw it.

Connie Mack was an old friend of Barney Dreyfuss. He was still managing Milwaukee in the developing American League and was in a pennant fight with Charlie Comiskey's Chicago "White Stockings." Mack certainly remembered Rube and that big fast ball from the previous summer at Columbus and Grand Rapids. In his playing days, Mack had been a catcher. Like most catchers, Mack was not only a good judge of pitchers, he was a good handler of men. He had natural gifts in psychology, without the mumbo-jumbo of the trade, of course. He knew well Rube's proclivities for "balloon rides." He felt he could handle the boy, though, and he was certainly convinced, with all Rube's talent, that it was worth an effort.

On July 12, the *Pittsburg Dispatch* noted that Connie Mack was in the city. The new league's leaders were starting to raid the senior circuit, stealing many of their best players, and folks in Pittsburgh were worried Mack had his eye on Honus Wagner. Mack denied it. He told reporters he had just run over from Cleveland to see a game. He actually came over to talk to Dreyfuss to get permission to negotiate with Waddell. As the *Philadelphia Inquirer* once chortled: "A pretty handy man, that Connie Mack. He ... has the patience to wait, and [he] hustles while he waits."[3]

Dreyfuss gave Mack permission to talk to Waddell about signing on with the Brewers, with the proviso that Dreyfuss could recall the Rube when he wanted. Dreyfuss sighed: "Go ahead. We can't do anything with him — maybe you can." Mack agreed to the proviso. That evening he placed a phone call to the Punxsutawney Hotel where Rube was staying.

"Hello Rube!" chortled Mack, forgetting how Waddell felt about the nickname. "Who the hell are you?" was the response. Mack gathered himself and started again: "Is that you, Eddie?" That was better; Rube could forgive as quickly as he could rile. Mack started in: "Eddie, the folks out in Milwaukee would like mighty well to have you wearing a Milwaukee uniform. You'd like it out there, Eddie, and they'd like you." It was no sale, though. "They like me here," Rube said. "They do everything for me. I can't let them down. There's not enough money in Milwaukee to make me run out on them." They talked a bit more, but the Rube was firm. He wasn't leaving Punxsutawney and his loyal fans.

Rube had four passions: pitching, fishing, fighting fires, and liquor, not necessarily in that order. As he thought about the phone call, Mack reflected on this and concluded he should have gone on more about the major industry of Milwaukee and some of its prominent families like Pabst, Miller, and Schlitz. Rube always enjoyed such sociable company. Mack went home to Milwaukee, but he had not given up. For two weeks he sent Waddell daily telegrams, sweetening the offer bit by bit. Finally Rube wired back. The note simply said: "Come and get me." Connie Mack was on the next train.

Mack arrived in Punxsutawney on the morning of July 25. He met "Eddie," as he would always call him thereafter, at the local hotel and took him to breakfast. They quickly came to terms as Rube downed his breakfast — four eggs, home fried potatoes, two pitchers of coffee, and, this being Western Pennsylvania, several stacks of buckwheat cakes, well buttered with lots of syrup.

Rube was willing to leave with Mack, but the train was not due to depart until 3:00 P.M. Rube suggested they take a walk. After that breakfast, Mack thought Rube had a pretty good idea. "Besides," said Eddie, "I've got a few little odds and ends to square up before I take off." The first place they stopped was a dry goods store, where Rube owed a bill. He asked for the bill and gave it to Mack. It totaled $12.35. Mack obliged. Coming all the way from Milwaukee, he was not about to let one little bill stop him. The morning walk continued, with more stops — cleaners, hardware, sporting goods, men's clothing, a pawn shop, and several saloons of course — all with outstanding IOUs. There were twelve such stops, and Mack particularly remembered paying the Addams Express Company agent the $8 Rube owed for a puppy, shipped COD. Since shipping companies were notoriously tight in those days about their "cash on delivery" policy, Mack always wondered how Rube had been able to wangle leaving them with but an IOU. Rube had no idea what had become of the puppy.

Mack's pocket cash was running low, but his biggest worry was getting Waddell out of Punxsutawney. Mack well knew how small towns wanted to hold on to their ballplayers. He began to figure that if the town was even half as devoted to the big pitcher as his credit line indicated, they were going to protest something fierce. So Mack took Rube back to his hotel room and waited quietly. After such a tiring walk, Rube was hungry and wanted to go out to lunch. Mack persuaded him to stay in the room and had some sandwiches sent up. Rube ate four.

With the train due to depart at 3:00, Mack waited till 2:45 to check Rube out of the hotel. He paid that bill, too. They arrived at the train station with five minutes to spare. Mack wanted to give the town's baseball fans as little time as possible to protest the loss of their Rube. When Mack and Waddell arrived at the station, however, an entire committee of townspeople was anxiously waiting. Mack's heart sank. He knew it would be the easiest thing in the world for someone to come up with a pretext to compel the sheriff to hold Waddell in Punxsutawney. Any irregularity would do; besides, the sheriff was standing right there with the committee. Mack's thoughts began to scroll through all the money he had wasted that morning. Then one member of the committee approached. The spokesman was the head of the local ball club.

"Are you Connie Mack?" he inquired.

"I am," was the reply. Then came the surprise:

"Mr. Mack, my friends and myself have come down here to thank you. You are doing us a favor. Waddell is a great pitcher, but we feel that Punxsutawney will be better off without him."

There were many such times when towns tried to hold on to their star ballplayer, and many more when no one cared if he departed. But this was the only time in the history of baseball that a town turned out to make sure the player *left*.[4] (In 1964 some said the aptly named football star Joe Don Looney departed Norman, Oklahoma, under similar circumstances.)

Just how far the "Kid in the Candy Store" metaphor could extend with Waddell was anyone's guess now, for Rube was off to the Beer Capital of America.

NOTES

1. *Pittsburg Dispatch,* July 14, 19, 21, and 22, 1900.
2. Ibid., July 24–25, 1900.
3. Ibid., July 12, 1900; *Philadelphia Inquirer,* July 9, 1902.
4. Peter Martin, *Pete Martin Calls On,* pp. 45–47; *Pittsburg Dispatch,* July 26, 1900.

Chapter 11

Beer Town

With the constrictions in the National League after the 1899 season, Ban Johnson had seized the opportunity to build a new league in the gaps. The small towns of the old Western League like Grand Rapids were abandoned. But Johnson was too shrewd to take on the Nationals straight away. They were strongest on the East Coast; his ties were in the Midwest. He would build where he and his enterprise could grow safely, then take on the Nationals where the big money lay. In 1900 the new American League was thus a transitional arrangement, bigger cities, bigger money, better players than the old Western League, but still regional. Cleveland was a new team, and no one even had a name for it yet. A new team in Chicago provided the first direct challenge to the senior circuit. Otherwise, Johnson had his old friends in Minneapolis, Buffalo, Detroit, Kansas City, Indianapolis, and Milwaukee. The new league was popular. The big risk in Chicago was paying off. Indeed in July, they were leading the league and outdrawing their crosstown rival. One of the Chicago White Stockings' chief competitors in the American League was Connie Mack's Milwaukee Brewers. Mack upped the ante in the pennant race when he returned from Punxsutawney with Rube Waddell.

Connie Mack arrived back in Milwaukee on July 26. Perhaps he wanted to show off his new player. Perhaps he was exasperated with all the bills he had paid back in Punxsutawney or with something Waddell may have done on the long train ride. Perhaps Rube was eager to get at the business of playing ball with a manager with whom he finally felt comfortable. Whatever the reason, Mack took Rube straight to the ballpark and sent him out to pitch against Buffalo. In the first inning Rube gave up a double and threw two wild pitches, though some thought they were passed balls. Behind him, the Brewers committed two errors, as Buffalo scored two runs. It would be one of the few bad innings Waddell would have for Connie Mack that summer.

The Brewers lost the game on July 26. The Pittsburgh papers chortled at Rube's bad performance. The Milwaukee papers, however, put the blame on the shoddy fielding of the Brewers.[1] Rube did not seem bothered by it one way or the other. He was not too comfortable with his catcher and would have preferred to work with Buffalo's receiver, Ossee Schreckengost, with whom he'd once pitched in Louisville back in '97. Mack had Rube work with the Milwaukee catcher a bit, so the receiver could get a little more comfortable with Waddell's fearsome shoots and curves.

After the game Rube did anything but mope. He set out to find some good fishing spots. He found one, of course, and he loved the fact that he could get there simply by taking the trolley straight north from the ballpark to the end of the line. Fishing was the Rube sidelight that seemed least to affect his pitching. If that was going to be Rube's principal vice in Milwaukee, Connie Mack would buy him all the bait and tackle he wanted.

Rube quickly settled into a habit, pitching well every few days and fishing all other times. He beat his old Detroit mates on August 1 with a five hitter. On the 5th he did the same to Indianapolis, and hit a home run besides. It was the first ball hit clean over the fence in Milwaukee that season. The *Milwaukee Journal* happily noted that Rube was reluctant to leave with the Brewers on a road trip: "Rube Waddell has taken such a fancy to fishing that he wanted to remain over and join the Brewers [later] in Minneapolis. ... Rube has done nothing but fish the past week, getting into the city just in time to pitch his game and return by the first streetcar to the lake."[2]

Whether or not it was due to resentment over the fact that he would rather have been fishing, Rube's first outing in Minneapolis did not go well. He lost it 3–2, and appeared to spend the majority of the game jabbering with fans in the bleachers. Fred Clarke would have fumed at such antics. Connie Mack simply sent Rube out the next day to pitch again. He won. Three days later in Kansas City, Rube combined the jabbering with winning, going a full twelve innings to beat the "Blues," all the while maintaining a non-stop vaudeville show for the bleacherites. Then it was on to Chicago where he did another 12 innings, but the game ended in a tie as darkness fell. At last Rube could go back to Milwaukee, catch the trolley and go fishing. Road trips were certainly a nuisance.[3]

The Brewers returned to Milwaukee on Friday the 17th. They were to be back in Milwaukee barely long enough to change their clothes, something Rube rarely did. The schedule had them playing Chicago at home for a doubleheader Saturday and another doubleheader on Sunday. Then it was right back on the train for three games in Kansas City. Mack slated Rube to pitch the first game on Sunday, so Rube stayed at the lake on Saturday and fished. Chicago was in first place, with Milwaukee close behind, so these were important games, and Mack wanted his ace to be content. Rube's Saturday fishing posed no problem to Mack, as long as he showed up Sunday and did his job. That Sunday, Rube would do his job and then some.

Chicago had won both games on Saturday, so the Sunday twin bill was pivotal, lest the Brewers fall too far behind. Some 10,500 Brewer fans arrived on Sunday to cheer Rube. They got their 50 cents worth. Chicago scored two runs early in the game, and from there Rube bore down as he seldom had before. The Brewers scraped back the two runs and put the game into extra innings. On and on the game went, with Rube shutting down Chicago completely. Finally in the bottom of the 17th inning, the Brewers got a man on via a Chicago error. After an out, John Anderson stepped up. "Honest" John, as he was called by his fellow Norwegian immigrants, stroked a triple to win the game.

After 17 innings of great pitching Rube had earned his fishing. But his blood was up, and he asked Mack if he could pitch the second game! Rube had pitched both ends of a doubleheader before, but this Sunday, in effect, he already had. Mack thought a minute and must have felt that despite Rube's eagerness, the obvious possibility of fatigue needed to be headed off with a little added incentive. So the sly Mack went to Rube and told him not only could he pitch, but if he won he would be excused from the Kansas City trip and could spend the three days fishing in Pewaukee, one of his favorite spots. That was all Rube needed to hear. He promptly went out and shut out the White Stockings 1–0. The team traveled to Kansas City. Rube went fishing.[4]

Rube's stupendous feat headlined sports pages around the country. The National League cities read about it, and back in Pittsburgh Barney Dreyfuss was suddenly interested in big Rube again. Still, he had to convince his icy young manager, Fred Clarke. That would take a little time.

Rube had some more hurling to do for Connie Mack. When the team returned from Kansas City (where they'd lost two of three), Rube joined them for a game with Minneapolis. Rube got a little screwy in this one. He had watched a Miller pitcher be effective with a lot of slow junk pitches. Rube decided that looked easy. "Think of the years I will last at this gait," he excitedly told Connie Mack. Mack was not thrilled at the tactic. He tried to dissuade Rube, but to no avail. Rube seemed to have the better of the argument, for he blanked the "Millers" for eight innings, though timely Brewer fielding was the chief factor. Up 2–0, Rube continued his easy ride. He walked one, the only one of the day, then the Millers found their rhythm with Rube's new "speed." They quickly knocked out two singles. One run scored. Mack knew that more talking with Rube would be useless. But rather than relieve him, as most managers would, he had a different idea. Mack went into the stands, found a Brewer fan, and advised him on a few matters he might care to convey to the Rube. "Rube, you big stiff," the fan began to bellow, "you lost your arm?" Rube stopped. Mack recalled how a haze seemed to lift from him. "I'll show you whether it's gone," he hollered back. Rube promptly struck out the succeeding Minneapolis batters, and Milwaukee won the game.[5]

After two more victories over Detroit, Rube stood at 10 and 2. That was ten victories from July 30 to August 29. The Brewers were off to Indianapolis. Upon arrival, they were met by Charles "Chief" Zimmer, a veteran catcher for the Pirates. The Pirates first contacted Connie Mack after Rube's double win over Chicago. Parodying Rube's response to Mack from Punxsutawney, Mack wired Dreyfuss: "Come and get him." Rube also wired Dreyfuss, "I'll quit baseball before I play for the Pirates again." From there, Mack remembered, "I played fair with Dreyfuss. I didn't encourage Rube. ... I wrote a letter to Barney ... advising him to send someone to Indianapolis who could deal with Rube on his own terms." This is why Dreyfuss sent Zimmer, all with the begrudging approval of Fred Clarke.

Rube's work with Milwaukee obviously proved he was worth another try. Besides, the Pirates had regrouped and were in the thick of the pennant race, contending with Brooklyn, Philadelphia, and Boston. If Rube could come through as he had in Milwaukee, and as he had in Louisville the previous September, Pittsburgh could have its first pennant.

The legality of the situation was clear, Waddell belonged to the Pirates. Mack was a gentleman, far more than most of the baseball men of the day. But while Mack would pose no problem, Dreyfuss and Zimmer knew that legalities would make no impression on a free spirit like the Rube. They could stop him from playing for Milwaukee, but that would have just driven him out of either league back to some place like Punxsutawney or Oconomowoc (a town in Wisconsin, where Rube had become a hero when, on a fishing expedition, he helped put out a fire and saved a crying boy's little red wagon left in the burning building).[6] Zimmer had to persuade Rube to return voluntarily. That was why Dreyfuss sent the amiable Zimmer. Fred Clarke certainly was not capable of any such diplomacy. Besides, Rube always had a soft spot in his heart for catchers.

Rube met Zimmer and immediately warned him about the promise he made to Clarke that he would shoot the manager full of holes the next time he saw him. Zimmer wired this back to Pittsburgh. Clarke relayed that he would take his chances. Barney Dreyfuss told Zimmer to use arguments of tangible value. Mack had gone out of his way to be helpful here. "There's only one way to get Rube to go back with you," he advised Dreyfuss. "You have to take him out, buy him a suit of clothes, some shirts and some ties — even some fishing stuff if he wants it." Zimmer understood and did for Rube, much as Mack had in Punxsutawney. Zimmer and Rube took a walk around downtown Indianapolis and began to buy the boy whatever his eyes set upon. He bought him a new pair of shoes, a shirt, a new "electric blue" suit, several ties, bright red of course, and a suitcase. The suitcase purchase appeared to seal matters, for now Rube wanted to pack it up and put it to use. Just like that, they were off to Pittsburgh. Without Rube, Mack's Brewers wound up finishing second to Chicago.[7]

Noting the contrast between Rube's work in Pittsburgh and Milwaukee, reporters praised Connie Mack. "As a lion tamer, [he] has no equal," noted one.[8] It was clear at that point that Rube could do wonders if given a little latitude. The question was whether Fred Clarke had learned anything.

NOTES

1. *Pittsburg Dispatch*, July 27, 1900; *Milwaukee Journal*, July 27, 1900.

2. *Milwaukee Journal*, August 2, 6, and 7, 1900.

3. Ibid., August 9, 10, 13, and 17, 1900.

4. Ibid., August 20, 1900; Clippings File, Cooperstown.

5. *Milwaukee Journal*, August 24, 1900; Mack's recollections were in the *Philadelphia Inquirer*, April 8, 1900.

6. *Sporting Life*, September 1, 1900.

7. *Sporting News*, March 28, 1951; Spink, "Rube Waddell," *Baseball Register*, 1944, p. 10.

8. *Chicago Journal*, August 30, 1900.

Chapter 12

Back to the Burgh

Chief Zimmer and Rube arrived back in Pittsburgh on September 2. In June, Rube had bragged that he would lead the National League in strikeouts. This was one of many things which had goaded Fred Clarke, who preferred his players focus on the team's achievements. Having been counseled by Zimmer en route from Indianapolis, Rube returned and promised Clarke, "I will help you hold second place." At that point the Pirates were in second, four games behind Brooklyn, with Philadelphia and Boston four more back and Chicago five more. Cincinnati, St. Louis, and New York were the only clubs out of the chase.

Despite the threat of shooting Clarke, when Rube arrived the first thing he said to Clarke was a jovial, "Hello there, Freddie." Clarke decided he would keep an eye on Rube and have him room next door to him. The first morning after Rube had returned to the Pirates, Clarke went over to Rube's room and asked if he had a spare button. Rube looked in his trunk, and Clarke noticed a pistol. Clarke began to worry. As Rube's mind seemed to wander, Clarke reminded him that he was looking for a button and returned to his room. The next thing Clarke saw was Rube, hitching up his pants with one hand and coming through his door with a large Bowie knife in the other. Clarke immediately began yelling. "Lookit here, Rube, you cain't do that!" Rube looked incredulous: "Thought you wanted a button, Fred, I just cut one off my pants for you." Years later Clarke remembered, "He had slashed off a button from his uniform pants, so he was in the same fix I was. That was Rube."[1]

While Clarke knew deep down that Rube was good-hearted, there remained something in the chemistry between them that continually brought out the zaniness in Rube, even when he was pitching, and that was the rub. Rube was a crazy character no matter for whom he played, but he could be handled in such a way that he could be brilliant on the field. Connie Mack proved that. One can easily measure pitching performances, and Rube fell off as he switched from Connie Mack to Fred Clarke. It was not all bad, but it was hardly the ten wins a month clip he'd reeled off in Milwaukee. Rube's spirit just could not find stable turf when playing for Clarke.

Rube's first game was easy. It was an important game against third place Boston, and the Pirates jumped out with nine runs in the second inning. With that sort of a lead it was "a pipe." The game was the second of a doubleheader. Boston had lost the opener, and down nine runs in the second, their aspirations were completely deadened. Rube's speed and curves looked sharp. He gave up only four hits and went on to win, 14 to 1. His only problem was a nosebleed that held up the game for five minutes.[2]

Clarke slated Rube for another game with Boston on September 5, but Rube didn't come to the ball park. He didn't come on the 6th, and he didn't come on the 7th. Perhaps he'd found another fishing hole. Rube returned just as the team boarded a train for Brooklyn. Clarke said nothing. He just started him the very next day against Joe McGinnity and the Dodgers. Chief Zimmer had apparently talked to Clarke and advised silence.

Though there were no words between Clarke and Rube, the tension began to show. In Brooklyn, Rube was steady through four innings, but something was bubbling. In the fifth he came up to bat. The score was tied, and there were runners on base with two out. Rube stood in, and as McGinnity watched, Rube began to flourish his arms and dance about the batter's box. He then grounded out. As he went out to the mound, the Brooklyn players and fans got on him something fierce. Rube responded by hitting the first batter with a pitch. The Brooklynites rose with abuse befitting their name and reputation. Rube stayed in. Zimmer did his best to keep things steady. The game remained tied as darkness fell, and Rube seemed on the verge of something bizarre.[3]

Two days later Rube got a revenge, of sorts, against the Brooklyn congregation. On September 9, Rube was not scheduled to pitch, so he parked himself at one of the bleacher entrances to Brooklyn's Washington Park baseball grounds (Ebbets Field would not open until 1913). Saying not a word, but armed with a very large hatchet, Rube hurled the big weapon at one of the Park's largest fence posts and did so repeatedly for about a half hour before the game, as hundreds of wondering fans nervously entered the ball yard. Perhaps Rube had in mind to do to Brooklyn what two kegs of nails had done to the New Castle football 11 back in Prospect. The effect of Rube's demonstration is incalculable, but for 13 years the hacked post went untreated. It stood in mute evidence of what big Rube had done with a large hatchet back in 1900.[4]

On September 11, Rube pitched, and with a runner on third he insisted on throwing over there and pitching out of a stretch position. There was no handling him. He won the game, but it was still clear that he was still not fully of this world. On the 12th, Rube started against the Phillies. With the score tied in the eighth, Philadelphia had two on. The next batter dribbled a slow one at the mound. Directing the play, Chief Zimmer yelled "First base!" for he saw the runners were going. Rube turned and threw the ball right to third. Runners were safe all around, and the play touched off a seven-run rally, forcing Clarke to go to a reliever. The Pirates actually won the game, but Rube was again starting to get a little too weird for Clarke. The next day the *Pittsburg Dispatch* printed a report that Rube had joined a local circus troupe and was learning the refined sideshow art of masticating live snakes. The paper noted further that against Philadelphia, Rube's curve balls had shown a little extra wiggle.[5]

Something strange was going on, even for Rube. His arm was hurting him. In the fire in Oconomowoc, Wisconsin, where Rube had rescued a boy's little red wagon, Rube had singed his fingers on the wagon's metal. (The wagon was worth about $3.50; the doctor's bills came to ten times that amount). At first his fingers were simply numb and he pitched well. Then as the nerves regenerated he began to feel pain and unconsciously altered his motion to compensate. This threw his arm off, and his head was, at least in some way, connected to his arm. As to the throw to third, contrary to Zimmer's directive, Rube claimed Zimmer had indeed told him to throw there, adding the justification, "And Zimmer is president of the union." (Huh?) Zimmer was the Pittsburgh leader in an effort by National League players to form a labor union. Rube actually had little to do with the union. And what a labor union had to do with a throw to third was anybody's guess. It was Rube's childlike, "Johnny made me do it" non sequitur response to any sort of pressure, a pressure that seemed only to grow when he was in the vicinity of Clarke.[6]

On September 13 there was a fire in downtown Pittsburgh. Naturally, no one expected Rube to show up at the park. He did not disappoint, though he returned from this fire with his fingers intact. The next day, the Pirates were to play an exhibition game against a minor league team from Meriden, Connecticut. Clarke tapped Rube, and the papers noted sardonically, "Waddell will pitch, with the understanding, of course, that there is no circus in town." Rube pitched a fine game. Everywhere the Pirates went, and even sometimes at Exposition Park, Rube was the object of crowd tauntings. He was a show, and the fans wanted the zaniness to come out. It was cruel, but that's the nature of professional sports.

The Pagliacci clown act in which Rube felt trapped could have been relieved by some strong pitching. Success covered most any problem in baseball back then, too. Here Rube was simply the victim of bad luck all through September. He began to pitch well, but bad breaks dogged him at key moments. He beat the lowly Giants on the 18th, but that was nothing to brag about. Against St. Louis he came in to relieve Jack Chesbro in the seventh one day and threw three innings of shutout ball, but despite Rube's work the Pirates could not overcome the Cardinal lead. The fans continued to be more concerned about antics they were anticipating to burst forth.

The fans loved Rube, though. They were warmer-hearted than the Pirate manager. With the team having a good year, the city threw them a morning parade on September 20. The parade snaked through the smoky downtown streets and ended with a triumphant entrance into Exposition Park. Clarke received a large floral horseshoe. Rube got a box of hard-shell crabs. The boy loved to eat.[7]

A big opportunity for Rube to get everyone's attention back strictly on baseball came on September 24. He and Cy Young were to face each other again. Young had another 20-win season going, and everyone remembered their duel back in April. A Rube victory could shove aside a lot of nonsense. In the game, the two battled brilliantly. Going into the ninth, neither had allowed a run. In the bottom of the ninth, St. Louis got a man on. A little pop out to the catcher advanced him to second. The next man, only the 28th to face Waddell in the entire game, hit a lazy pop that fell behind second base. The runner was going all the way. He scored, and just like that, the game was over. Ill-luck was following the Rube for sure.

On September 27 he pitched a masterful seven-hitter against Cincinnati, a game one reporter declared would have been "a winner 9 times out of 10." But Rube lost 4 to 1. Cincinnati supposedly used an illegal player that day. Dreyfuss lodged an official protest with the league, but it was rejected. Rube took another crack at the Reds on the 30th. Cincinnati coach John Peltz rode Rube from the third-base box so mercilessly that the umpire actually threw him out of the game. Peltz's tactics worked, though, for in the bottom of the ninth, with the score knotted, two out, and a man on third, Rube threw a wild one. Zimmer retrieved it and tossed it in time to Rube, who had dashed in to cover the plate. Rube dropped it.[8]

The Pirates were still in second place, but the big push everyone hoped the Rube would give just did not occur. Anxious for an explanation, folks looked at all the weird antics. Rube felt trapped, and Fred Clarke provided no zone of comfort.

NOTES

1. Quoted in *The Sporting News*, March 28, 1951.
2. *Pittsburg Dispatch*, September 4, 1900.

3. Ibid., September 8, 1900.

4. Ibid., September 10, 1900.

5. Ibid., September 12–13, 1900.

6. Ibid.

7. *Pittsburg Post*, September 21, 1900; Dennis DeValeria, *Honus Wagner: A Biography* (New York: H. Holt, 1996), p. 81.

8. *Pittsburg Dispatch*, September 19, 23, 25, 28, and October 1, 1900.

Chapter 13

That Poor Pig

Some sort of comic relief was necessary to break the cycle of bad fortune that was plaguing Rube that September. Early the next month came an opportunity. On October 5 the Pirates had an off day, and the management scheduled a "Field Day" at Exposition Park. The players were to contest in a series of skill events before the crowd and close the day with an intra squad game.

To make sure the entire day was taken and seen as pure fun and games, the players were told to come dressed in any sort of costume they wanted. They arrived in all kinds of get-ups. There were tramps, schoolmasters, farmers, policemen, and one maiden with golden hair who "played havoc with many susceptible hearts in the crowd." Honus Wagner came in authentic Dutch clothes. (His family had a houseful of them, of course.) Encouraged by the racial climate of the day, one Pirate came as "a hobbled Chinaman," while another decked himself out as "a Hebrew"; no one ever learned what *landsman* Dreyfuss thought of that. Two pitchers, Jack Chesbro and Jesse Tannehill, came as "a darkey couple." Chief Zimmer naturally showed up as an Indian. Shortstop Fred "Bones" Ely, whose slick fielding was keeping Honus Wagner playing right field all season, came dressed as a ballerina, complete with tutu, and spent the day batting, running, and throwing "like a girl."

Could anyone imagine a more perfect stage for the one and only Rube? Oh yes, the Rube did come through in the clutch. He was, of course, the final player introduced to the crowd. With the headiness of the Spanish-American War victory a not-too-distant memory, Rube hit the perfect note, donning a complete Uncle Sam outfit: full beard, top hat, the whole nine yards. The crowd roared with approval as Uncle Sam trotted out. Rube was in his element, and everyone loved it. Even Clarke seemed happy with it all. He had come as a cowboy, by the way, with *loaded* pistols to keep order as he umpired the intra-squad game.

It was apparently quite a sight, seeing the players performing the various field events in their getups. One event was a timed run in which the participant circled the bases as fast as possible. Off went Uncle Sam, with beard and hat, running the bases, and he did it in 16 seconds. Another event was a 300 foot accuracy throw. Rube missed the mark by just six feet, four inches. In a distance throwing contest, the Dutchman Wagner bested Uncle Sam, though each winged the ball over 129 yards.

The highlight of the day was to have been a greased pig contest. Clarke had purchased a huge specimen for the event. Various Pirates gathered around the animal as the day's festivities were to commence. Some of them had no farm experience and were a little leery about what they were going to do with this great, and, by all appearances, not too friendly swine standing imposingly before them. Rube pushed through the crowd. He had handled many a pig up in Butler County and thought he would do the city boys a favor with a few good pig-handling tips. "Whether a pig's greased or not," counseled ole' Rube, "you cain't pick one up by its body anyway. What you have to do is go for its hind legs like this…" Rube proceeded to grab the great beast by the hind legs and fling all 300-plus pounds of the porker over his great right shoulder. The trouble was Rube flung it with such force, that he broke both the pig's back legs. Now the monster couldn't run or even walk.

One of the coaches was hurriedly dispatched to a local butcher to secure some sort of moving swine, a slab of bacon, or anything to improvise for the occasion. He came back with a poor specimen that, even healthy, could move about as well as the one Rube had crippled. But they went ahead, greased it up, and, with great fanfare, opened the pen gates expecting it to run with the players in hot pursuit. The gate opened and the poor thing didn't move a muscle, assuming it ever had any in the first place. Honus Wagner pounced on it, and the contest was over in less than five seconds. (Wagner could only pinch hit the next day.)[1] A few weeks later, after Rube had gone home to Prospect, all the boys hit him up for stories. They didn't want to hear about baseball, though. Everyone just wanted "a detailed account of the death of that poor pig."[2]

NOTES

1. *Pittsburg Post*, October 6, 1900.
2. *Butler Eagle*, October 18, 1900.

Chapter 14

World Series

After the Field Day, the Pirates had another week to play out the season. Pittsburgh still held second place, and there remained a mathematical possibility of overtaking Brooklyn for first. Rube did his best, shutting out St. Louis on October 8, 8–0, allowing only two hits through eight innings. On October 12 Rube finished out the season with a drubbing of Chicago. He walked out to the mound and struck out three of the first four batters. In the fourth the leadoff man tripled, and there he remained as Rube struck out the next two on six pitches. The next man popped to short. In the eighth Rube struck out the side. He gave up only five hits all day and struck out 12. It was the best strikeout performance that season in the National League.

The regular season was over. Rube had done all he had promised. The Pirates had held onto second place. And, despite missing all of July and August in Punxsutawney and Milwaukee, Rube *still* ended up leading the league in strikeouts with 130; his ERA was 2.37. His strikeout total fell just shy of that of the rest of the Pirate pitching staff.

Though there was now a new rival league, the National League had yet to recognize it, and they tersely sniffed at its inferiority. There would be no meeting of the AL and NL winners — Chicago and Brooklyn. There would be post-season play, however. Most every year, the National League had scheduled a series between the first and second place clubs. It was called the Temple Cup Championship. So in 1900 Pittsburgh squared off against Brooklyn in a best of five series. It would be Rube's only foray into official post-season play.

In game one, Rube was pitted against Dodgers ace Joe McGinnity. Rube was perfect for three innings, so was McGinnity. Then the walls caved in. Rube gave up thirteen hits the rest of the way. Brooklyn won 5–2. Rube did his best to the end. Indeed, in the eighth inning, when McGinnity batted and grounded to the mound, Rube fielded it and raced after McGinnity. McGinnity slid into first, but Rube tagged him just before he got there, being careful to knee the Dodger ace in the head as he fell over him. McGinnity was out for a few minutes. Still wobbly, he went out to pitch. That was when the Pirates got their two runs. Otherwise McGinnity had been unhittable, and he steadied himself and finished the inning.

Brooklyn won the second game. Pittsburgh took the third. The Pirates fell behind 6–1 in the fourth, and Clarke put Rube in. The Dodgers' third base coach Fred Sheckard immediately began razzing the Rube. What Brooklyn-ese he precisely spoke no one knows, but whatever it was, Rube took strong exception. He had had enough of the "guying" from opposing coaches all season, and there was no reason to hold back now. Rube pointed a finger at Sheckard (his index finger), yelled something, then made a rush for the coaches' box. No one was laughing at these antics, least of all Sheckard. Fortunately for Sheckard, umpire Tim Hurst spent his off seasons as a boxing referee. Hurst got between Rube and Sheckard just in time. A sufficient number of Pirates raced out and pacified Rube. Sheckard was ejected, and he made no objection. The game wound down. Brooklyn had their championship. Rube went home to Prospect.[1]

NOTES

1. *Pittsburg Post* and *Pittsburg Dispatch*, October 10–17, 1900.

Chapter 15

Get Him the Hell Off My Ball Team

As the 1901 season approached and the players reported for spring training, Ban Johnson and the American League took off the gloves. Johnson had prepared well, and he was ready to go into direct competition with the senior circuit. The Chicago White Stockings had more than held their own against their cross-town rivals. Johnson kept the Tigers in Detroit, and he maintained the team in Cleveland which had yet to decide on a name. (The city's NL franchise of the 1890s had been called the Spiders, and that remained in common usage.) The smaller towns of more regional appeal in the old Western League — Buffalo, Kansas City, Minneapolis, Milwaukee, and Indianapolis — were abandoned. (They would reestablish clubs, and join with Toledo and Columbus to reform the American Association.) Johnson set up teams in two of the cities the NL had abandoned — Baltimore and Washington. And he placed three more teams in direct competition with the National League, setting up shop in St. Louis, Boston, and Philadelphia. Connie Mack moved from Milwaukee to Philadelphia to manage the new Athletics.

The baseball wars heated up even more when the owners of these new teams began raiding National League rosters, offering fat salary increases to lure players away. Many jumped. St. Louis manager–third baseman John McGraw returned to the city of Baltimore to manage the new Orioles. Joe McGinnity left Brooklyn to join him. Cy Young left St. Louis for the Boston Pilgrims. Future Hall of Famer Jimmy Collins shifted from NL Boston to AL Boston. Connie Mack tried a similar intra-city grab, signing the superb hitting second baseman Napoleon Lajoie from the cross town rival Phillies. (The elder Philadelphia club threatened legal proceedings. With Johnson's urging, Mack avoided intra-state venue problems for the league and sent Lajoie to Cleveland.) Many lesser players followed the money and switched. Clark Griffith, manager of the Chicago White Stockings, tried everything to land Honus Wagner, but Wagner remained loyal to his hometown Pirates.*

The name Waddell certainly occurred to some of the American Leaguers. Rube was not yet 25, but he was already quite the item. An Ohio team that spring was singing the praises of one of its new young pitchers. "He will prove to be a second Rube Waddell" was their claim. No pitcher in baseball had ever become such a benchmark so quickly as did the Rube (though a champion two-year-old race horse that year was named "Honus Wagner"). The Pittsburgh papers postulated that, despite his fame, or rather because it, Rube would be secure. "Everyone knows Waddell is a good pitcher, but everyone in baseball is also aware that he is hard to handle."[1] The American League owners had agreed with one another as to who could court which player. Rube was "given" to Boston. The Pilgrims knew all about Waddell. Nonetheless, they were "hard after Rube," according to Barney Dreyfuss. The Pilgrims offered Rube nearly double his salary. Rube was firm, though: "Not on your life," he proclaimed. "I'll pitch for Pittsburg or for no one. I don't like that town of Boston anyhow. I'll stick to Pittsburg — or go to Homestead." Boston would indeed prove to be a bad luck town for Rube, his "hoo doo" town, as he called it. After Cy Young signed with Boston, Dreyfuss actually sent Chief Zimmer out East to induce him to jump back to the NL and play for Pittsburgh. Whether in Pittsburgh or Boston, Cy Young and Rube Waddell would have made quite a staff. But it was not to be. Young remained in Boston, and Rube would stay put. Connie Mack went quietly behind the backs of his Boston brethren and wrote Rube that if he went to Boston and did not like it, he could pitch for Philadelphia and earn $2000 more than either his Boston or his Pittsburgh figure.[2]

Mack later reflected that Rube was never concerned with money; he had the mind of a child. A child will always focus on the positives, and Rube was doing just that amidst all the baseball raiding that spring. Things were good in Pittsburgh, and Pittsburgh was where he was going to stay. He was not going to think about any previous problems, let alone matters like labor unions or salary offers from competitors, and he likely believed, albeit naively, that others like Dreyfuss and Clarke felt the same way. To Rube this wasn't business, it was baseball.

Aside from third baseman Jimmy Williams, who signed with Baltimore, the Pirates were less affected by the AL raiders than other teams in the National

*Wagner hoped that his show of loyalty would, in addition to his regularly leading the league in hitting, stolen bases, and virtually every other offensive and defensive category, prompt owner Barney Dreyfuss to grant him a raise. Dreyfuss would not raise his $5000 salary for several years, however, and Wagner had to threaten to quit baseball altogether and open a garage in Carnegie before Dreyfuss budged. He eventually made $10,000, the first major leaguer to crack that level.

League. Having nearly won the pennant in 1900, Clarke and the Pirates were then quite optimistic about the new season. They all went off to Hot Springs, Arkansas, for pre-season training. Rube was the life of the party on the train, singing songs all the way down. Connie Mack once pleaded with Rube to give up his life of "wine, women and song." Rube responded by asking if it was all right if he just gave up singing. On that long train trip down to Arkansas that spring, many a Pittsburgh Pirate wished he had, as the Rube could always be depended on to sing very badly and very loudly.[3]

Clarke put the team through daily regimens of running, calisthenics, and baseball. The first day out, the team ran a three-mile loop. Rube got lost. He made the most of it, though. He had brought a gun with him, so he got in some hunting and arrived back proudly displaying several ducks. Clarke shook his head. There was a method to Rube's madness here, however. The previous day it had been raining, and everyone stayed inside except Rube. He went out looking for the ball field. During his search he got lost then, too, so bringing the gun along for the next day's run seemed a good idea. Rube logic![4]

The Pirates were celebrities in Hot Springs. Honus Wagner was a hit among the boys in the local pool halls (and apparently he was quite the hustler). Wagner, pitcher Sam Leever, and the Rube put on a trap shooting demonstration, at which all were skilled marksmen. Rube was the toast of the town, naturally. Out of the blue, folks sent him baskets of Easter eggs. When the team went to Hot Springs' new movie house, the band struck up "When Reuben Comes to Town." Rube immediately took the podium and conducted. Thankfully, he did not break into song.[5]

Clarke and the Pirates were a rough and tumble lot. Modern managers would have heart attacks at some of the "training" Clarke employed, given how it imperiled his star players. On April 5, for example, Clarke oversaw an intra-squad game — of football — with no pads, no helmets, just a ball and a bunch of very large men. And this was no mere game of "two-hand touch." Honus Wagner took a mean elbow in the face and spent much of the afternoon repairing his bleeding countenance in a cold stream. Rube took the game seriously, though he brought no kegs of nails this time. Midway in the game Rube was going after a loose ball and, in the rugby-style rules of the day, attempted to kick it. But just as he gave a mighty swing with his leg an opponent grabbed the ball. Rube thus did a "Charlie Brown," kicking nothing but air. His momentum swung him completely around. He landed on his head and "made a large noise like an Indian." The rest of the team thought he was faking, and the game went merrily on. The doctor said Honus Wagner had a fractured nose and Waddell a sprained ligament in his right hip. Both turned out for practice the next day anyway. Rube was a little stiff and sore, so two days after the football game he was excused from practice. He went out to the gate, sold tickets, and greeted fans. Baseball, springtime, and the Rube; it was an irrepressible combination.[6]

The Pirates left Arkansas and journeyed to Cincinnati for the season opener. Unfortunately it rained. Clarke was never willing to sit still, if only for the mischief Rube would doubtlessly create. He secured use of the practice facilities at a nearby army base, Fort Thomas. The servicemen all turned out, mainly to see the Rube. A number of them were recent veterans of the war with Spain, and Rube ended up receiving a host of souvenirs from Cuba and the Philippines. It is impossible to estimate the quantity of barroom braggadocio for which these "medals" served as evidence for the next months. A troupe of actors was also staying at the same Cincinnati hotel as the Pirates. Rube was a hit among them, too. This gave him some new ideas.[7]

The Pirates finally opened their season against Cincinnati on April 22. They won. Clarke showed the extreme heights of his humor when he told the press that if rain stops Pittsburgh from playing any more games, he would bet the Pirates either tie or win the pennant race. Rube was in earshot of this statement and, in deadly earnest, waded into the meeting insisting Clarke accept his wager of $200 on the point. Rube logic? It took Chief Zimmer and Sam Leever two hours to convince Rube of the error in his higher mathematics.[8]

Rube's first start came the next day against St. Louis. He was great for six innings. In the seventh, however, "the balloon could easily be seen going skyward." The Cardinals scored five runs, two of which came via a wild throw from Rube as he was fielding a bunt. Rube could be troubled when dealing with pressures, and he was feeling them since one of the new National League rules demanded rosters be trimmed to sixteen players by May 1. The Pirates were over the limit. Rube pitched in a practice game the next day against a local college. The following day the Pirates sounded an old refrain: where is Rube?

Rube had gone home to Prospect, with a few refreshment stops on the way. His father brought him back to Exposition Park on May 2. John Waddell, Sr., had once met with Pirate management and asked them to be patient with his son, feeling screwiness ran in the family and admitting to being a bit off himself. Barney Dreyfuss had smiled at it all, but no one could mollify Clarke with such a tidbit of insight.

Clarke immediately tossed Rube out to the mound to face the Chicago Orphans, as they were then called (sometimes they were called the Remnants. "Cubs" came in 1905.) With his father in the stands, Rube showed nothing — no speed, no snap on his curves, no control. In the first inning he gave up three hits, a wild pitch, and four walks. Rarely before had Rube walked four in a game. On this afternoon, Chicago had batted all nine players before Clarke relieved Rube with just one out in the first.

The day after the loss to Chicago, Rube received a letter from a local furniture dealer: "If you lose your position with the Pittsburgh club owing to the game you pitched against Chicago on Wednesday, we will give you $50 a week to drive one of our delivery wagons." Rube was certainly big enough to handle the task of furniture moving, and, annualized, the weekly salary topped the paltry $1200 Dreyfuss was paying him.

Maybe Rube should have taken the offer from the furniture company, for that night Clarke stormed into Dreyfuss' office. "Sell him; release him, drop him off the Monongahela Bridge," Clarke fumed. "Do anything you like, so long as you get him the hell off my ball team!" When Rube heard he had been sold, he ran into Dreyfuss' office and demanded half of the selling price. "You can't have it all," Rube argued. (Rube logic!) Dreyfuss went him one better, however. "You can have it all," Dreyfuss calmly replied. "It's right here on my desk." And there it all was — a cigar. Rube had been sold for a stogie. On May 3, the Chicago team left Pittsburgh, and Rube was on the train with them. He was now an Orphan.[9]

NOTES

1. *Pittsburg Dispatch*, March 18, April 24, 1901.
2. Ibid., March 18, 26, 30, and April 8–9, 1901.
3. Ibid., April 1, 1901.
4. Ibid., April 2–3, 1901.
5. Ibid., March 30, April 2, 4, and 8, 1901.
6. Ibid., April 6–7, 1901.
7. Ibid., April 20, 1901.
8. Ibid., April 23, 1901.
9. Ibid., May 2–4, 1901; *Pittsburg Enquirer*, January 14, 1915.

Chapter 16

Life in the Big City

Rube's manager in Chicago was none other than Tom Loftus, the man who had managed him in Columbus and Grand Rapids. Loftus certainly knew what Rube was capable of, both on and off the field. Meanwhile, Chicago had a terrible team in 1901. Across town, the White Stockings of the new American League occupied first place and were outdrawing the Orphans by a wide margin. One of Loftus' major problems was that he had no left-handed pitchers on his roster. Given these circumstances and with the memory of Rube's performance in 1899, Dreyfuss' offer to toss Rube on the next train out of Pittsburgh for the price of a cigar was hardly one Loftus could refuse.

In the seasons with the Pirates, Rube had compiled a record of 1 and 10 at home while going 10 and 1 on the road. Chicago was a long way from Butler County, Pennsylvania, so Loftus figured Rube would have fewer "home distractions." The trouble was that Rube could "make himself at home" most anywhere he went. Indeed, as Loftus was leaving Pittsburgh, Dreyfuss' assistant, Harry Pulliam, offered him a bet. Pulliam wagered that within 12 hours after reaching Chicago, Rube would know more people in the city than Loftus knew himself. Loftus declined.[1]

The Orphans reached Chicago on May 4, and the Pirates were right with them, as the schedule had them playing the Orphans in Chicago that afternoon. The papers in both cities had covered the trade and the events surrounding it. Both team president Jim Hart and manager Loftus wanted to waste no time capitalizing on the new fan interest. Rube was a meal ticket.

"Rube Starts Out Gunning" was the headline in the next day's *Chicago Tribune*. The *Trib* meant it literally. Rube did not pitch in the first game against Pittsburgh. Rather, he sat conspicuously in the grandstand, with a big smirk on his face, proudly brandishing a loaded Smith and Wesson revolver he had just purchased. Rube had promised he would "get even" with several of his former teammates. Some of the Pirates were a trifle alarmed when they saw the big guy up in the stands, fully "loaded." Still, they beat the last-place

Orphans that day. The next day, though, they would face Rube and his big fast ball.[2]

All the pre-game hype worked. Some 14,000 fans came to West Side Park on May 5 to watch Rube's debut in a Chicago uniform. It was the largest crowd of the year. Hart and Loftus milked it for all it was worth. Rube began warming up by throwing balls into a board next to the dugout. The slams of his fast balls echoed around the stands like rifle shots. Young Frank Chance was to catch Rube that day, and when he went out to warm up with his new battery mate, he facetiously bid fond farewells to several friends in the stands, as though he was off to meet his doom. Rube pitched his heart out that afternoon. Unfortunately, his teammates committed four errors, which led to three Pittsburgh runs. The Pirates were up 4–0 going into the bottom of the ninth. Rube stepped up with two on and knocked a triple to right. Only Honus Wagner's good throw kept him from scoring. The crowd had been cheering Rube's every strike all afternoon. With his triple they went absolutely mad. Here was Paul Bunyan in a baseball uniform. Singlehandedly, Rube was trying to beat the first-place Pirates for the cellar-dwelling Orphans with both arm and bat. Rube should have tested Honus Wagner's great arm, for that inning he could go no further than third base. Chicago just could not hit. They lost 4–2, but their fans now had a new hero.[3]

There is a story about Fred Clarke's first day opposing Rube and Chicago. Clarke had apparently been trying to needle Rube in the early parts of the game, to no avail. Between innings he supposedly spoke to Rube, inviting him to his ranch in Kansas after the season to hunt and to train a new dog. "What kind of dog," perked Rube. "Just a pup, and you can have him if he takes a fancy to you," offered Clarke. Rube confidently chortled: "They all do. He's as good as mine." The next inning Pittsburgh allegedly scored five runs off Waddell, whose mind was on something besides baseball. (The story is not true, but it's part of the lore that grew about the Rube.)[4]

The Chicago newspapermen loved Rube. He was the greatest, never-ending sports story that ever hit town. Rube lavished praise on Loftus, and he minimized the dissension on the Pirates and how Clarke "harps at his men instead of jollying them." Loftus was extravagant too, predicting Rube would "not lose more than one game for us the balance of the season."[5]

The Pirates would play two more games with Chicago that week. Rube begged Loftus for another crack at them, but Loftus preferred to wait, lest another loss to the tough Pirates burst the bubble. Lowly St. Louis was due in next, and Loftus figured they would be a better team against whom Rube could begin building some winning momentum. By the time the Cardinals arrived in Chicago, the Orphans were certainly in need of a win. The Pirates had gone on to sweep the series.

Rube came through splendidly. He mowed the Cardinals down for four innings, and the fans cheered loudly. A particular fan named Frank Childs, known for his booming voice and biting wit in regard to any Orphan miscue, was suddenly a Rube cheerleader. In the top of the fifth it looked like disaster had struck. With two out, batter Art Nichols grounded to first. Rube ran over to cover the bag, and Nichols knocked him down hard. Nichols was clearly out at first. His knock-down of Rube appeared to be a deliberate attempt to derail the big guy. The fans booed Nichols, of course, but their boos turned to cheers as Rube popped up from the collision and turned several of his patented back somersaults as he returned to the mound. Not only did Rube finish the inning, in the bottom of the fifth he stepped up with two on and blasted a 2 and 0 pitch out of the park for a three-run homer. It was one thing for a hero to win unblemished. But here was the hero of a cellar dweller, jumping up from a knock-down, answering back with utter defiance, and swinging on 2 and 0 when he could have waited for a walk. The bravado was breathtaking.

Rube finished the game in style. With two out in the ninth, the fans booed an Orphan error, fearing Rube would again be robbed of a well-earned victory. Rube just smiled and struck out the last man. A crowd of young boys cheering "Rube! Rube!" greeted Waddell as he left the park. He had gotten over his earlier discomfort with the nickname. Three days later, he beat the Cardinals again. This win pulled the Orphans out of last place, and Rube was the toast of State Street.[6]

NOTES

1. *Chicago Daily News*, May 6, 1901.

2. *Chicago Tribune*, May 4, 1901.

3. *Pittsburg Dispatch,* May 6, 1901; *Chicago Record Herald,* May 6, 1901; *Chicago Tribune,* May 5, 1901.

4. Christy Mathewson, *Pitching in a Pinch* (Lincoln: University of Nebraska Press, [1912] 1994), p. 134.

5. *Chicago Daily News*, May 4 and 6, 1901.

6. *Chicago Daily News,* May 10, 1901; *Chicago Record Herald,* May 11, 1901; *Chicago Tribune*, May 11 and 13, 1901.

Chapter 17

The Theater Type

It was a good thing that Tom Loftus had not taken up Harry Pulliam's wager about how many friendships Rube would establish on his first day in Chicago. Rube quickly became quite a fixture in the city's night life. At the turn of the century, Louisville, Detroit, Milwaukee, and Pittsburgh could not hold much of a candle to the night life of the city with the big shoulders. Comparisons with Columbus, Grand Rapids, Butler, and Punxsutawney need not be drawn. Rube had never had such a life and was whooping it up all over Chicago. He sure could make friends easily.

When Rube worked at Pittsburgh's Union and Scout Theater and when he met the Cincinnati theater people the previous April, he had gotten a taste for the kind of folks with whom he had a whole lot in common — people who had a passion for standing up in front of others and entertaining them. Rube discovered the theaters of downtown Chicago and began to frequent them, apparently becoming a hit with many of the actors. Soon Rube was welcome backstage at many houses.

One night Rube visited one of his haunts, where *The James Boys in Missouri* was playing. The play was a typical late nineteenth-century melodrama — men torn between the hard shoot-'em-up life of the frontier and their pangs of love for their good, noble women. As the play progressed Rube was backstage fidgeting with the props. He came upon an arsenal of weapons, all loaded with blanks, ready to use for the gunfire scenes. The play was shifting to its most tender moment — when the hero revealed to a weeping heroine his deep, abiding love for her. At the key moment they were to kiss, Rube knocked over the weapons and some 40 cartridges discharged. Fortunately, the hero was a quick-witted actor, and he saved the moment with an ad-lib. "My God," he shouted, caressing his stunned heroine, "the sheriff is approaching. He is shooting at my sentinels!" The actor rushed from the stage. With the play disjointedly continuing, the actor guessed who was back among the props. He quickly rounded up the three burliest stage hands he could find. They collared the big Rube and ran with him out the back door. As they all tumbled into the alley, the perky actor and his henchmen jumped up and ran back inside, bolting the door securely. Rube was left to nurse his bruises and find another theater.

On another evening about town Rube was watching an animal act. He was taken with a lion on stage and decided to wander up and play with the big cat. He fooled with the great beast until it playfully clawed at his arm, his right arm, fortunately. Loftus and Hart were prepared to fine Rube for his stupid recklessness. But the ever-resourceful Rube spun a tale of being held up by a highwayman, claiming he resisted the brute until he was stabbed. He was not fined.[1]

NOTES

1. "Reminiscences of Rube Waddell," *Baseball Magazine*, XII, January, 1914, pp. 43–45.

Chapter 18

Last Place

The Orphans were off to the East Coast after Rube had twice blanked the Cardinals. The lowly New York Giants were first on their schedule. The New York fans knew well the success their Brooklyn counterparts had had "guying" the Rube to throw off his rhythm. The coaches around the league were still on him, but Rube seemed to be a lot happier and less vulnerable to taunts now that he was playing for Loftus. One advantage the Brooklyn bleacherites had enjoyed was the fact that their team was so good that their opponents would already feel pressure; taunting just salted matters a bit. The Giants were another case. They were the team the Orphans had surpassed as Rube lifted Chicago out of the cellar.

Rube stepped out on the Polo Grounds to face the Giants on May 17. The New York fans immediately tried to goad him, but he just smiled and thrashed their boys. For the first few innings, Rube continually yelled at batters, "When I get through with you there won't be a run to your credit." For seven full innings he was true to his word. Meanwhile, the Orphans hit and fielded well behind him. With the score 11–0, the Giants rallied for three runs in the eighth. During the rally the bleachers erupted, hoping the floodgates would open on the Rube. Rube quickly settled, though, allowing no more runs, and in the ninth he actually turned to the particularly loud right field crowd, bowed politely, walked over to their end of the field, and made a brief speech, insisting that he had meant what he had said, but that circumstances beyond his control prevented him from carrying out his shutout plans fully. Rube meant every word of it, and he ended up winning over a lot of the New York bleacher bums, not just with his pitching but with his sheer audacity. Boxer Jim Corbett was in the stands that day, and that evening he met Rube in a New York establishment. They became fast friends, Corbett commenting that he admired Rube's work greatly. Rube told Corbett he felt the same.[1]

When last-place teams square off, the tendency toward poor play often snowballs. No aspect of the game is immune, including umpiring. Nerves fray, and occasionally everything comes unglued. This occurred during that week's

Orphans-Giants series. Plate umpire Billy Nash had made some terrible calls against Rube and the Orphans. This was one thing that helped Rube endear himself with the New Yorkers. The Giants enjoyed the largesse of Nash's incompetence, but it did nothing to make them more accepting of bad calls when they came their way. Quite the contrary, their respect for Nash went lower and lower. They were primed to kick with a vengeance if any calamity befell them, as of course one would.

Later in the series, when Rube and the Orphans were up at bat, Chicago attempted a double steal of second and home. Nash called the runner safe at home. New York catcher Jack Warner was sure he'd tagged the runner. The fans were up in arms, and Warner immediately turned around, kicked Nash in the shins, and jumped on his feet with his spikes. Nash called for the police. But the 50 or so of New York's finest at the Polo Grounds that day were all Giants fans. Other than laughing at the sight of it all, they made no move. Warner was ejected. The game went on with the crowd frothing at the mouth.

In the next inning Nash called one of the Orphans out with just two strikes on him. Though on the winning end of the call, New York's pitcher Luther Taylor, a deaf-mute (his nickname was "Dummy"), walked to the plate and made several exaggerated hand gestures at Nash. Taylor's gestures appeared to resonate with the crowd, and when Nash then ejected Taylor the fans were ready to rumble. At game's end the bleachers emptied onto the field, but Nash, who knew better than to rely on the police, left the field quickly and escaped harm.

Jack Warner received no discipline or fine for his actions. Indeed, Giants president Andrew Freedman actually demanded that National League president N. E. Young discipline Nash. Freedman knew that the National League needed New York. The Polo Grounds was the National League's only big park. Freedman's receipts were three times that of Cincinnati's, for example. If League finances grew tight, everyone in the circuit knew only New York could finance a bailout. League finances were especially tight at this point. The American League's player raiding had forced salaries upward, and the AL was beating the senior circuit in attendance, outdrawing the NL in the four cities where each had a team — Chicago, St. Louis, Boston, and Philadelphia.

Chicago president Jim Hart criticized Freedman for his position and called upon Young not to cave in to the New York arrogance. His was a lonely voice. Brooklyn Dodgers owner Charlie Ebbets demurred. He solemnly spoke of how the Nash matter was "not our quarrel" and how we in Brooklyn "like to be on good terms with our neighbors." With that, a sardonic chorus of "Soitenly" erupted from Flatbush.

Young caved into Freedman's pressure. While recuperating in the hospital, Nash learned that he had been suspended for two weeks and that the umpires' schedule had suddenly been rearranged with Nash never to umpire in the Polo Grounds for the remainder of the season.[2] (In subsequent decades, players receive such "stiff" fines as a five-game suspension, with pay, for spitting in an umpire's face. Such "progress" took 95 years.)

Rube's zaniness was first cousin to the frontier-type violence that lay at the edge of many ball games. Ballplayers were great athletes, but many were not much different than common thugs. It would be many years before the game would rise in both popularity and gentility to give it a thicker veneer of civility. For now it was wild and woolly, and Ty Cobb had not yet arrived on the scene. Cobb's contribution involved making the game more scientific, but hardly more civil. Before then the nature of the game and its fans lay somewhere between a Rube belly laugh and a Warner fistfight. And when last-place teams like the Giants and Orphans got together, there was not much quality of play to mediate the extremes.

Later that season St. Louis fans stormed an umpire. The St. Louis manager threw himself on top of the ump to save him from serious injury. Both the manager and the umpire were hurt anyway. In July, Jack Warner was at it again, throwing a ball point-blank into the stomach of an umpire in Cincinnati. There were no arrests or fines for any of these acts.[3]

Jack Warner had been brought up short only once for his antics. This had occurred in Louisville, two years before, and only because the umpire literally took matters into his own hands. Warner went after umpire Tim Hurst, the boxing referee. He tried to hit Hurst, and hurled a slew of obscenities his way. Hurst was made of sterner stuff. He immediately threw Warner out of the game. Warner went up to the grandstand and continued his verbal assaults. Having stuffed his coat pockets with baseballs, Hurst walked to the side rail and began hurling the balls at Warner. Fundamentally a coward, Warner fled with baseballs crashing around him. When Hurst ran out of baseballs he turned to Honus Wagner, who was kneeling, quietly bemused in the on-deck circle, and lamented "I'd give $40 for an arm like yours." Wagner acknowledged with a quiet nod.

Subsequent generations like to think they have eclipsed such incivility, but the bemusement we get from such stories speaks a bit to the contrary. Ballplayers were then on the same page as boxers, in the newspapers and otherwise. Though we may be loath to admit it, the difference between that era and later ones may simply be a civility enforced by well-paid layers of bureaucracies. The reckless humor of a Rube is a joy that has now been blocked out of the game.

Rube and the Orphans mucked about the National League cellar that spring and summer. Rube continued to strike out hitters more rapidly than the rest of the Orphan staff. The rules had changed and strikeouts became more common. League officials were interested in shortening the games. That way they could start games later in the weekday afternoons, draw bigger crowds, and not worry about nightfall hanging over every game. It was in 1901 that a foul ball was denoted as a strike before a two-strikes count. Before then it counted for nothing. This did speed up play, and strikeouts went up markedly. Simultaneously, being hit by a pitch gave a batter first base; formerly he merely got one ball.

Strikeout king Rube naturally liked the new rule, and he was ready to defend it against any purist who felt otherwise. One evening after a game in Philadelphia, Chicago happened to be staying in a hotel where a group of senior Presbyterian ministers was holding a meeting. In the hotel lobby, Rube plopped himself down next to one elderly gentleman of the cloth and inquired as to the purpose of their assembly. The gentle pastor informed the big fellow that they were considering a proposal to "change the creed." Hearing that, Rube animated. "I don't care how much you change it," he exclaimed, "but don't cut out that foul strike rule. It's a great thing for the pitchers." "Yes, my son," said the bemused reverend. Umpires may miss calls, but perhaps Rube had missed his calling. Other ministers gathered around, and they had a jovial evening with the one and only.[4]

NOTES

1. *Chicago Record Herald*, May 17, 1901; *Chicago Daily News*, May 17, 1901.
2. *Chicago Daily News*, May 18, June 12, 13, 1901.
3. *Chicago Tribune*, July 9, 1901.
4. Ibid., May 20, 1901.

Chapter 19

The Great Mathewson

The Orphans continued to lose and remained mired in the cellar with the other lowlifes like the Giants. New York's season, however, began to pick up largely on account of the team's new pitching ace, Christy Mathewson, then in his first full year. By the end of May, the Giants had begun a climb up the league ladder. Meanwhile, even though he had been with the team less than a month, Rube accounted for a third of Chicago's victories, and he was batting .347. Across town the other Chicago team was in first place, and the Orphans' attendance out at West Side park was terrible. Everyone went to the "Sox" games. Indeed, when schedules happened to put both Chicago teams in Boston one week and the Orphans found themselves with a day off, *they* went to the AL grounds to root for the White Stockings.[1]

In Chicago the Orphans cut the admission price to 25 cents. It seemed, though, the only way folks would turn out for the Orphans was if the White Stockings were on the road and Rube was pitching. Otherwise, as one newspaper said, "the Orphans [were] in a comedy role." In one game they committed ten errors. The *Chicago Tribune* compared them unfavorably with the team from "the Blue Island Grammar School." Rube was the one redeeming feature, the "one pitcher on the staff who seems able to bag a contest." With the new foul/strike rule, games were shorter. Reporters saw redemption there, too. And there was entertainment. Bleacher jockey Frank Childs became a fixture at West Side Park. After the inevitable Orphan error, he could be counted on to stand up and holler, "Well, well, well" and proceed with a litany of witticisms and insults. The fans began to look forward to Childs' performances as part of their quarter's worth.[2] That was life in the cellar, a little baseball, a lot of comedy.

Rumors resurfaced that Rube was going to jump to the American League, but he emphatically denied them. Rube was having too good a time in Chicago. With all the losing, both Jim Hart and Tom Loftus grew testy. Rube was doing his usual absence routine—fishing and drinking. Hart grew impatient and decided on some action, no matter the risks. On June 14, Rube showed up at the park with a battered right hand. Hart immediately concluded that Waddell had gotten into some sort of bar fight and slapped him with a $50 fine. Rube came forth with the "honest truth." He admitted that, indeed, he had been in a saloon, but, he pleaded, "I was only drinking pop, when I heard this guy say that Jim Hart was a _____!" Rube looked Hart straight in the eye and proclaimed, "Now I wouldn't let anybody call you nothing like that, so I hit him and hurt my hand!" Hart actually bought Rube's tale and lifted the fine.[3]

In addition to Rube's blarney, Hart may have had second thoughts about the fine because he needed his ace in an upcoming series with the Giants. When the Orphans traveled to New York in May, Pirate club secretary Harry Pulliam made a special trip there in hopes of seeing Rube Waddell square off against Christy Mathewson. The clubs' rotations did not bring them together that series, but they did meet in June. That afternoon, 12,000 showed up in Chicago, and the fans came expecting to see not comedy but first-class baseball. Mathewson had graduated from Bucknell College the previous spring and joined the Giants that summer. It was highly unusual in those days for a college graduate to play major league baseball. Mathewson was the hope of many, not only to turn the consistently bad Giants into winners, but to bring greater respectability to the game. He did not disappoint. In 1901 he reeled off a string of victories and conducted himself always as "the Christian gentleman" that he truly was.

This fine Bucknell gentleman came to Chicago to face the Rube. Outlining the matchup, the papers noted that Rube *had* attended night school. Here the media was being both unfair to Volant College, which was no mere night school, as well as generous to the Rube, since he had never attended a class. Everyone was waiting in a bit of awe for the big matchup. Even Rube was circumspect: "I expect to go in tomorrow's game and do my very best to win," he humbly intoned, "but I am not egotist enough to claim a victory until the game is won. Mathewson is a hard man to beat." Mathewson's presence brought polite tones out of everybody. (Though he could have avoided World War I service at age 37, Mathewson enlisted in 1917. In the trenches he suffered poison gas inhalation. The effects eventually killed him in early October, 1925. For the remainder of that season and through the World Series that year, all baseball players wore black armbands, so great was the game's respect for "the Christian gentleman.")

Rube and Mathewson were two of baseball's, indeed all of American sport's, first matinee idols. Together they embodied much of post-frontier America's notions of manhood and heroes. Mathewson represented all the good, conscious thoughts about respectability that comes from Christian charity. Rube appealed to that part of the imagination in men that resents limits and somehow clings to the notion that, left unconstrained, he can achieve more. These were two pathways in the imaginations of Americans who were nostalgic about a frontier that was gone and yet optimistic about the nation's burgeoning new day on the horizon. Both were images which resonated deeply with the fans of America's game. The images were part of what made baseball's popularity grow so enormously in these years. Mathewson was never quite (though almost) the choirboy people saw him to be, but Rube was every bit the rogue, and his young death, while tragic too, was not quite so noble.

In the initial contest with Mathewson, Rube came through. Hurt right hand and all, he bested his gentleman rival. Each walked four, a high number in either case. Mathewson struck out eight. Rube fanned ten, including three whiffs of Mathewson. The key to the Orphans' victory was psychological. Rube so discouraged the Giants with his curves and shoots that they appeared to sulk. Meanwhile, Chicago grew confident. They played errorless ball and hit Mathewson for nine runs. Final score: Chicago 9, New York 2.[4]

New York went on to win the rest of the games in the Chicago series, as the Orphans' miseries continued. Losses mounted, in the standings and in the team balance sheets. Rather than hoisting the team, the great Rube began to be pulled down to the team's level and flounder with them. On June 20 he was up 5–3 on Boston with two out in the ninth. Then came two walks, including one of the pitcher, a wild pitch, and two Orphans errors, as Boston rallied for three runs to win. Against Brooklyn on July 24, Orphan runners found themselves picked off first or second base five different times. Rube was one of the picks, and it occurred with two out and the bases loaded. With several players injured, Rube was pressed into playing some first base (Loftus hoped this would also tame some of his habits; it didn't). On one key play Rube forgot to cover the bag. On June 29 he had a rematch with Christy Mathewson in New York. Unlike the first game, this one was a farce. Rube gave up nine runs in four innings as the Giants destroyed Chicago 14–1.[5] No one that day would have wagered it, but this forgettable game turned out to be the last time these two great young pitchers would ever face each other.

NOTES

1. *Chicago Tribune*, June 18–19, 1901.

2. Ibid., June 3, 7, 1901; *Chicago Record Herald*, June 3, 1901.

3. "Reminiscences of Rube Waddell," *Baseball Magazine*, XII, January, 1914, pp. 43–45.

4. *Chicago Tribune*, June 16, 1901; *Chicago Record Herald*, June 16, 1901.

5. *Chicago Tribune*, June 21, 25, 30, 1901.

Chapter 20

A Big Toad

In early July a little gallows humor in Brooklyn lent Rube and the last place Orphans a touch of relief. It was the Fourth of July. The fans were eager to celebrate the national holiday and to return the favor of big Rube's hatchet hurling of the previous summer. The Dodgers management had intentionally left the hacked fencepost unrepaired after Rube's dandy work on it. About 7000 Brooklynites came out on the 4th. In the middle of the game, with Rube on the mound, they began shooting off revolvers, cannon crackers, and other artillery. "Take that you big country Rube!" was their message. Rube was anything but befuddled. He smiled that big grin of his and pitched Chicago to a victory.[1]

But, the next day, the Orphans' slide continued. By July 7, they were not only in last place, they were seven and a half games behind the seventh-place club. The *Chicago Tribune* sarcastically called for readers to go easy on the Orphans. "*Nil Mortus Nisi Bonum*," they headlined ("Do not defame the dead").[2]

Jim Hart was beside himself with frustration. He cut several players. He even banned Frank "Well, Well, Well" Childs from the ballpark. Rube protested. Hart claimed Childs used offensive language during a Giants game. Naturally, all Chicago fandom understood how unaccustomed New York ballplayers were to offensive language, particularly their sensitive catcher Jack Warner. In June, Hart's first baseman, Irish-born John Joseph "Dirty" Doyle, had jumped into the Polo Grounds stands and slugged an abusive fan. As a way of getting back at the Giants management for the Jack Warner incident, Hart had refused to discipline Doyle. Yet here in July he was tossing a paying customer merely for his language. It was absurd, and it hardly helped the team's miseries.

Through early July, Rube's losses began mounting almost as quickly as Hart's and so did his absenteeism. Willing to try anything, Hart and Loftus demanded the team buckle down. They began requiring regular morning practices, even on game days. Getting up in the morning was not Rube's strong suit. He missed every morning practice for a week, and on July 14 Loftus suspended him.[3]

Rube was upbeat: "I got a little bad, but Tom's a good fellow, and I expect to be reinstated all right."[4] Meanwhile, several offers came to Rube, one from a minor league team in Ogden, Utah, another from Connie Mack. Hearing Rube had received "several telegrams," Loftus quipped, "What were they, from your wife, Rube?" (Rube and Florence's bliss was indeed fading.)[5]

Though he covered himself nicely with the rhetorical flourish, Loftus knew that he could lose Rube, and he certainly did not want that. Rube was reinstated, and he immediately went out and beat the Giants, 7–4. His performance was actually stronger than the score indicated. The Giants scored their four runs in an error-filled third inning. Other than that, Rube was unhittable, striking out eight. He also hit a triple. Three days later he beat the Giants just as convincingly. Two days afterward, Rube entered in relief against St. Louis. Down 6–0, Rube shut the Cardinals out from there. The Orphans rallied but fell short with only five runs.[6]

While Rube's effectiveness was heating up in St. Louis, the weather was getting even hotter, and it put the skids to Rube's little renaissance. Even by the standards of St. Louis in late July, the weather was miserable. One day the official temperature reached 113 degrees; who knows what it measured on the ball field. In the hotel no one could sleep, with night temperatures hovering in the 90s. Rube pitched in the heat on July 24 and lost 2–1. He gave up two key walks, and failed to back up third base on a play in which the Cardinals scored the winning run. Pitcher Jack Taylor criticized Rube after the game. In all the heat, Rube was in no mood to hear it from a teammate who had never even pitched .500 ball. He took the opportunity to express his opinion of Taylor's workmanship on the mound, adding a few words about the workmanship of Taylor's face, to boot. Taylor responded "with all the enthusiasm of an Irishman who finds his neighbor beating *his* little boy." (The pair got in another fight on the train back from St. Louis, too.[7])

Upon the club's return to Chicago, Rube commented on how tired he was of the whole mess. "I never was on a tail-end club before," he sighed, "and that's made me sick of the business." Taylor actually made threats, stating he would pitch one more game, but unless Waddell was fired, that would be the limit. Rube suddenly took one of his leaves, probably for the cooler Wisconsin fishing country. The team headed for Cincinnati without him. There Taylor actually won two games.[8]

Loftus let the fighting blow over as just one of those things brought on by the heat. Rube showed up on August 1. Gratuitously, Loftus fined him a mere $10 for missing practice. Rube actually claimed Loftus' arithmetic was unfair here (this coming from the math whiz who wanted to bet Fred Clarke that a 1–0 record could not theoretically stand up as a pennant winner). Though another pitcher (not Taylor) was warming up, Loftus started Rube. There were 7000 school boys in the stands that afternoon, one of Hart's promotions. Rube had been out in the stands with the boys before the game. When Rube walked out to pitch, they let out "a howl of delight." Rube won, fanning nine. It was corny but true, the idolatry of schoolboys washed out the team's conflicts. Rube was back, and Jack Taylor said not another word about it.[9]

Again the euphoria would be short-lived for Rube and the Orphans. This time it was not the weather. On August 4 came a hint of trouble in the offing. The score was tied 3–3 as Rube saw a fly ball land between two inept outfielders for a triple. Moments later he stood on the mound, gazing at the ball for a moment, and the runner nearly stole home. He ended up losing 4–3, anyway. After a win in Cincinnati, it was on to Pittsburgh. There was the trouble. Awaiting Rube in Pittsburgh was not only the Pirate ball club but the Allegheny County Sheriff. Rube owed some board bills to his Pittsburgh rooming house, and the creditor had become totally exasperated trying to collect from the elusive Rube. The sheriff collared him. Loftus paid the bill. It was all of $21. After all this ruckus, Rube went out to face his old team. It was a weekday, yet the game still drew 7000. Rube showed great delight when he fanned Fred Clarke. Otherwise the day was forgettable. Rube gave up 11 hits; the Orphans committed five errors. Chicago lost again.[10]

Rube breathed a sigh of relief, getting out of Pittsburgh and pitched a strong six-hitter to beat St. Louis on the 17th. He had the Cardinals completely throttled and hit a homer, too. Four days later he pitched a marvelous three-hitter against Cincinnati, perhaps his best outing of the season. Then he went fishing again. On the 26th Rube returned. Whether it was true or motivated by the anticipation of another fine, Rube came to the park with an affidavit, signed by a railroad conductor, attesting that the train which bore him back from his fishing trip had wrecked. Like a first-grade teacher, Loftus accepted little Eddie's excuse. Rube went out and beat the Cardinals 5 to 3. After the game he asked Hart for a loan of $13.50. He said he had an Irish setter due on delivery any day.[11] Hart paid it.

Another Rube win over Cincinnati on the 28th gave him four victories in a row. Chicago was now in a virtual tie for sixth, along with lowly Cincinnati and the reslumping Giants. It wasn't much, but after being so far down anything looked good.[12]

Then, all of a sudden, Rube was nowhere to be found. For the first few days, folks figured it was just another fishing trip. But after ten days Loftus, Hart, and the news boys figured something more was afoot. On September 8 the Orphans learned that Rube had joined a ball team in Gray's Lake,

Wisconsin. Rube said his new team's contract allowed him six days a week for fishing. The Gray's Lake manager certainly knew the right inducement. On September 6, Rube started against Libertyville, Illinois. He won 32–0, and no, he had not changed to football. Asked why he had switched to such a league of ball, Rube said he was tired of morning practices. He confided to one reporter that "he would rather play piano on the streets of Chicago." After all, Rube noted, "the piano can be made to play as you want it to." With syntax straddling the garbled and the surreal, Rube opined, "It is greater to be a big toad in a small puddle and fish."[13]

For the next month, Rube's whereabouts were a mystery. He pitched no more for Gray's Lake. The Chicago papers could not pinpoint him, neither could nearby Milwaukee's. On September 22 he was to reappear in Chicago to pitch for the local White Rocks against the Corncrackers. The White Rocks manager had paid Rube $5 in advance. (He did not know the Rube, obviously.) Three thousand fans came to Hand's Park for the event. No Rube, no $5. Rube did resurface in Kenosha, Wisconsin, on October 6, pitching for Burlington, Illinois. He struck out 17. Kenosha's catcher, Peter Breen, touched Rube for three hits, though, and Burlington barely won 6–5.[14]

Rube had won 13 and lost 16 for the Orphans that long, crazy summer. No other Orphan did as well. Rube failed to lead the league in strikeouts, something that would not occur again until 1908. In October of 1901, however, it looked like Rube had retired from baseball. But that month a couple of Chicago players tracked Rube down. They asked him to go with them on a barnstorming baseball tour of the West Coast. Rube had never been out West before.

NOTES

1. *Chicago Tribune*, July 5, 1901.
2. Ibid., July 7, 11, 1901.
3. Ibid., July 10, 15, 22, 1901.
4. Ibid., July 16, 1901.
5. *Chicago Record Herald*, July 16, 1901.
6. *Chicago Tribune*, July 18, 21, 23, 1901.
7. Ibid., July 27, 1901; *Chicago Record Herald*, July 26, 1901.
8. *Chicago Record Herald*, July 25, 1901; *Chicago Tribune*, July 28, 31, 1901.
9. *Chicago Record Herald*, August 2, 1901; *Chicago Tribune*, August 2, 1901.
10. *Chicago Daily News*, August 9, 1901; *Chicago Tribune*, August 11, 12, 1901; *Pittsburg Post*, August 11, 1901.
11. *Chicago Tribune*, August 18, 22, 26, 1901.
12. Ibid., August 29, 1901.
13. Ibid., September 8, 1901; Clippings File, Cooperstown.
14. *Chicago Tribune*, September 23, October 7, 1901.

Chapter 21

Loo-Loo Land

Rube and friends had a great time barnstorming about the West Coast. Somewhere between the long Chicago summer and the trip west, Florence decided to leave Rube and their home in Prospect. She headed back for Columbus. The locals in Butler County were understanding of Florence, which was meaningful given divorce's rarity and the stigma attached to it in those days. "It's no surprise to Butlerites to learn that the lady had secured a legal separation.... Rube isn't the kind of a fellow to hanker after the comforts of his own fireside.... If the girl had used the same degree of sense at the start that she did in applying for the divorce she would have less cause to regret a foolish act."[1] There would be more women in Rube's life, but Florence was the only one Rube would mention on his death bed. But the marriage had ended, so Rube had little reason to go back to Pennsylvania, not for a while anyway. After the barnstorming tour, he decided to remain in the West.

The West Coast was quite a separate culture from the East and Midwest, and the difference was reflected in the game of baseball. Until 1958, the western-most major league baseball city was St. Louis. On the West Coast, fans read in their papers and magazines of the major leaguers, but the games and players may as well have been in Japan, especially in the days before radio. The major cities of the West had their own teams and their own leagues. The play was not at the same level as the AL and NL, but comparisons were irrelevant, as they could only be abstract. The Western leagues simply put the best teams together they could, and their fans were loyal.

When teams of Eastern players came West, baseball lovers were certainly curious to see them. This was the only way to experience their play beyond the mere words in the papers. As he did everywhere else, when the Rube came to the Western cities, he was an immediate hit. The exhibitions involved American League players against National Leaguers. Rube pitched for the Nationals and was unhittable. He struck out 27 in two consecutive games.

The Los Angeles team owner James Morley saw the games and signed Rube to play for him permanently. His salary set a league record—$275 a month. Rube was an instant celebrity. Rube had actually signed with Oakland and San Francisco as well as with Los Angeles. They all ordered him to report. Rube could have been in legal hot water for this, but no one pressed matters. Rube told the three club owners to shake the dice for him. L.A. won, and Rube reported there.[2]

Los Angeles was not a large a city in 1902. Its population was under 20,000 (New York's was four million). There was no movie industry. It was a middling town even by Western standards. The San Francisco Bay area was far more populated. When he came to Los Angeles, big Rube just bowled the little place over. Back in Chicago people predicted that in tiny L.A. Rube would wear out his welcome, run out of people whom he could touch up for loans, and come back.

The nature of league scheduling in California certainly suited the Rube. There would be five games a week, all occurring between Thursday and Sunday, with a doubleheader on Sunday. This gave Rube plenty of time for fishing and imbibing the local culture. (Still, Rube would have his usual share of absences going to fires, to fishing holes, and to parts unknown.) There were but four teams in the league — the Sacramento Mosquitos, usually known as the "Skeeters"; the San Francisco Has Beens (no kidding); the Oakland Mud Hens; and the Los Angeles Looloos. Rube was definitely the star Looloo.

After witnessing the exhibition and barnstorming games, the sports people in the West declared Rube "the best that ever pitched in Los Angeles." On April 5, a crowd came out to Chutes Park with great anticipation to watch Rube and the Looloos open the season against Oakland. Oakland was the top team of the California four, and they showed it. Rube also showed that he had begun celebrating the night before the game. He yielded 11 hits and struck out only one, as Oakland won easily.[3]

Rather than being disgraced by the performance, Rube found himself ever more the darling of the crowd. When he did not pitch, Rube played outfield or, occasionally, first base. The next day, when Rube trotted out to right field in the first inning, 8000 fans cheered, "anxious to lift Rube back to the top of Chutes [Park] Tree, off which he had fallen kerplunk the day before." Rube's personality was such that it inspired fans who wanted a reason to forgive him. Sure enough, Rube made several good catches, and in the bottom of the ninth he knocked in the winning run to beat the Mud Hens 3–2.[4]

The next day the *Los Angeles Daily Times* printed a Looloos promotion item: "Next Thursday and Friday will be Ladies day, and every lady going to Thursday's game will receive a full-length picture of Rube Waddell who will pitch that day." Amidst higher-pitched and more intense cheers, the Rube won one for the ladies, fanning seven Mud Hens, giving up just four hits, each one meeting with cries and groans.[5]

Whether in victory or defeat, Rube could do no wrong. On April 11, the Looloos lost, but Rube, playing right field, went 2 for 4 and hit a homer. This was the first home run hit in Chutes Park that season, and it won the Rube a suit of clothes. The Looloos lost again the next day. The score was 7–6 in 11 innings, and the deciding run came on a Looloo error, committed by the very right fielder who had replaced Rube in the eighth. ("It would-n't've happened if...," fans mused.) Rube had been given a rest because he was to pitch the next day, and when he did he redeemed Looloo virtue with a victory. He struck out eight in the process.

With a defeat of Sacramento on April 18, the Looloos took over first place. Rube pitched the next day. He lost in a ten-inning heartbreaker. In the seventh inning two men were on base with Rube batting. He hit a screamer. Alas, the Skeeters' shortstop made a great play and saved the game. The drama of it made up for the loss.[6]

Rube continued to tear up the West with his bat, his big left arm, and his off-field antics. One afternoon before a game he got together with heavy-weight boxing champion Jim Jeffries, and not just over a beer. They got in the ring. It was quite an event for the folks in L.A. No damage was done in the exhibition, but Jeffries thought Rube had all the tools of a fine boxer. After hitting Jeffries, Rube went out and hit the ball. On Saturday the 26th he went 2 for 3. On Sunday he pitched a shutout with nine strikeouts in the first game of a doubleheader. Rather than resting, he played first base in the second game and went 1 for 3, as he had in game one. On May 1 he faced San Francisco, gave up only three hits, and struck out ten. In the ninth inning he was up 3–0 when his fielders committed two errors, allowing two runs to score. With the lead now imperiled, Rube calmly waved to the crowd, reassuring them that the big sheriff had the situation in hand. He struck out two and ambled slowly off the field, tipping back his cap, just as the sun was setting behind him.[7]

The Oakland Mud Hens were in town on May 8. They remained the Looloos' chief rival for league supremacy. Rube was pitching, and the game was a tight one. Then everyone's attention suddenly shifted away from base-ball. In the fifth inning a fire broke out. The fire was not down the street and Rube was not prompted to run off the mound. Rather, it broke out right in Chutes Park. A large mattress had been hoisted in front of the grandstand behind home plate to serve as a backstop. Some grease had been applied to lift it along the grandstand wall, and the grease had either prompted a spon-taneous combustion under the mattress' weight or had been ignited by a care-lessly tossed cigarette. The fans scattered in panic, as did most of the ballplayers. Chutes Park was a wooden structure, and everyone feared a com-plete catastrophe. Like the legendary Big John, Rube stepped in. He ran over and tore the burning mattress from its moorings and plopped it on the field, where it burned harmlessly. The imperiled Chutes Park was saved with no damage but a little singed grass. Rube then continued the game, beating Oakland 9–6. If the aggressive Promethean spirit could not stop Rube, how could a mere flock of Mud Hens? The Looloos beat rival Oakland again the next day. As everyone talked of Rube's heroics, he hit a key double in a rally that put the Looloos in the lead to stay.[8]

While Mother Nature could not conquer Rube with fire, in a game against lowly Sacramento she would try again. In Chutes Park the batters faced due west. On May 17 a big Santa Ana wind blew through, blessing batters with gale winds that turned pop-ups into home runs. Sacramento would thus steal a victory off Rube, 10 to 8, but Rube was still the day's hero. In the seventh he caught a liner in the hand and dislocated his thumb. Refusing to leave the game, Rube had the trainer jam the thumb back in place and he finished the contest, bent in thumb, but unbroken in spirit.[9]

Years later a former major league second baseman named Lennie Randle was playing in a fledgling pro baseball league in Italy. (He had been blackballed from the majors after beating up Texas Rangers manager Frank Luchesi after Luchesi, in a fit of nepotism, had cut Randle in favor of the son of former Dodgers star Maury Wills. "Bump" Wills was not as good as Randle, and, despite the hype over his lineage, he never amounted to much.) In Italy Randle was a hit, and he commented on the particular nature of the Italian passion for baseball. There, he said, victories were not quite so much the point as they were in America. Rather it was the graceful long ball, safe or out, and the sparkling play that fans wanted to see, for that was *bello*. There was something of that in the appeal of the Rube. Whether in Los Angeles or anywhere else, Rube was more than just *bello*. In victory, in defeat, he was *bellissimo*.

Rube always pitched well on special days — Ladies Day in L.A., Kids Day in Chicago. Friday, May 23, was a very special day, and Rube won handily. His new "lady love" was in the grandstand. She was there again on Sunday for a doubleheader, with Rube going 5 for 8 on the day, with two homers. He was now batting third in the lineup, even when pitching.

Back on the mound the next Thursday, Rube excited the crowd with the "switch" play on an attempted double steal against San Francisco. With runners on first and third, the play involves the runner at first breaking for second, drawing the catcher's throw, allowing the other runner to dash home. Anticipating this, the "switch" involves the catcher throwing hard, not to second but to the pitcher, who then easily cuts down the lead runner. Rube and the Looloos worked this to perfection. The catcher is usually the brains behind the play, but Rube sure got the credit from the crowd.

The game with San Francisco had more excitement in store for the fans. Tied 5-5, the game went into extra innings. At the top of the eleventh, San Francisco scored a go-ahead run. In the bottom of the inning, with two out and a runner on third, guess who stepped up to the plate? Cheers erupted everywhere. A reporter described the noise as "a regular Mont Pelee bombardment." Rube nearly fell down swinging for strike one. This Casey-like drama stirred the crowd even more. Ever theatrical in instincts, Rube took his time regathering himself and stepping back into the box. The pitcher was equal to the drama and slowly hitched up his pants, took the sign, and went into his windup. The crowd leaned forward, Rube swung, and crack!— he popped a dinky fly to short. It was not quite "Casey at the Bat," but Rube was a fable even in defeat.[10]

Amidst Rube's L.A. Looloo-land dramatics, back East the American League pennant race was heating. Connie Mack had a solid team which he felt could contend with first-place Chicago. In early June, Mack's A's were behind Chicago in a virtual tie for second with St. Louis and Boston. Luck was definitely on Ban Johnson's side. The four best teams in his adolescent league were those in direct competition with National League cities. The other four AL cities — Cleveland, Detroit, Washington, and Baltimore — had weaker teams, but their fans had nowhere else to go.

Ill fortune had befallen Connie Mack that spring. Before the 1901 season, Mack had succeeded in luring second baseman Napoleon Lajoie and pitchers Bill "Strawberry" Bernhard and Chick Fraser over from the crosstown rival Phillies. Lajoie had responded with quite a season for Mack, leading the new league in virtually everything — hits, doubles, runs, RBI, home runs, and batting (.422). Bernhard had won 17 games; Fraser 22. In 1901, the Phils' angry owner, John Rogers, sought an injunction to prevent Lajoie and the others from playing again for the A's. He lost in a lower court, but in 1902, two days before the new season was to begin, the Pennsylvania Supreme Court handed down a decision barring Lajoie from playing for any Pennsylvania team but the Phillies.

After this State Supreme Court decision, Chick Fraser went back to the Phils, as did Bill "Frosty" Duggleby, another Philly pitcher Mack had just signed. The A's manager recognized there was nothing he could do to hold onto Lajoie. League president Ban Johnson agreed, but he had one final card he wanted to play. With Ban Johnson's blessing, Mack sent Lajoie and Bernhard to Cleveland, along with Elmer Flick, a future Hall of Fame outfielder Mack had also just signed over from the Phillies. This wily move kept the talent in the American League and bypassed the intra-state court issue.

The legal clouds lifted, but Mack now had some huge holes in his lineup. Ban Johnson would be of no help here. Mack signed Danny "Kid" Murphy to replace Lajoie at second and Socks Seybold to play outfield. Murphy would prove a great talent, though he was no Lajoie. Seybold would hit 16 home runs in 1902, a major league record no one would break before Babe Ruth. Still, after losing Fraser, Duggleby, and Bernhard, Mack had no pitching staff aside from one promising right-hander named Eddie Plank, though another youngster, Bert Husting, carried the load nicely in the early part of the season. To make matters worse, Mack, thinking he had signed the young Christy Mathewson away from the hapless New York Giants, found Matty subsequently deciding to remain with the senior league. Many a Philadelphia fan came to wonder just how spectacular a team the A's could have had in the early 1900s if the fates had only turned a little differently. Mack could have ended up with Lajoie, Flick, Mathewson, Plank, and Waddell all playing together. Connie Mack was not the sort to sit and dream, however. He simply had to beef up his pitching staff. Otherwise, he knew he would never hold on against the likes of the White Stockings. In June, before a game in Detroit, Mack was handing in his lineup card to umpire Jack Sheridan and he sighed: "I wish I had a pitcher who could go nine innings." Sheridan replied: "Why don't you get Waddell back? He's pitching for Los Angeles." Mack's mind turned two summers back to Milwaukee and that big fastball. With Rube out in Los Angeles, it was Punxsutawney all over again.[11]

Rube really liked Connie Mack. A personality such as Rube's needed to feel comfort and could not easily find it. On Mack's team, Rube had been most content. Mack knew the sacrifices necessary to keep Rube productive, but he was convinced they were worth the effort. Desperately in need of pitchers, Mack cabled Rube. Rube cabled back, asking for $100 and transportation. Mack sent a railway ticket and the money, and Rube agreed to come east. After a winning series against Oakland, Rube headed for the train. Looloo teammates and management got wind of Rube's action and they headed there, too. This was *not* Punxsutawney. The team pleaded with Rube not to leave, and the Rube literally broke down in tears. Whether it was the team's pleadings, management's legal threats, or pangs about his new lady love, Rube stayed. He cried to his manager, "I never did want to leave you; you have been so good to me." He even gave Looloo manager James Morley his unused train ticket as proof of his sorrow and sincerity.[12]

When the A's were in Chicago, a man arrived at the Victoria Hotel to see Connie Mack. The man had been at the L.A. train station and relayed to Mack what had occurred. Undaunted, Mack wrote again, and Rube, with his usual emotional attention span, wrote back agreeing again to join Mack, this time with the same words he had written in 1900: "Come and get me." Mack also sought out Ban Johnson in Chicago, who took Mack to an office of the Pinkerton Detective Agency.

On June 14 the Looloos headed north for a couple of weeks play in Sacramento and San Francisco. Mack figured it would be easier to get Rube out of California if he could nab him somewhere besides Los Angeles. He also knew that the Rube could be too easily dissuaded from making such a jump. The folks in Punxsutawney could have cajoled the big kid into staying even with Mack at his side so Connie Mack hired a couple of Pinkerton detectives and sent them to San Francisco with orders to advance the big left-hander $200 and bring him back. (Mack did not specify "bring him back alive," but the Pinkertons understood, if only because of the $200.)

On June 19, Rube lost a tough one to San Francisco. He struck out ten, hit a home run in the ninth to tie it, but lost it in the tenth on a passed ball by the catcher. The Pinkertons met him at the hotel. Maybe it was the loss of the game, but Rube went along. He quietly packed his cases and tipped a young boy at the hotel to carry the bags over to the train station. Saying good-bye to no one, Rube boarded the Sante-Fe Limited that evening.[13] He was back in the big leagues.

Nothing with Rube could ever go smoothly, of course. En route, he began to harbor doubts. In Kansas City, Rube met a prizefighter, William Rothwell, known as Young Corbett. Corbett had just defeated Terry McGovern for the featherweight championship. Rube was starstruck and followed Corbett around like a puppy. The Pinkertons feared Rube was about to wander off. They wired Mack of the troubles afoot. Mack was in St. Louis at this point, and he promptly boarded the next train to Kansas City. Rube wanted to show off to Corbett, and Mack feared he would thus get drawn into pitching for a team in Kansas City. There were two teams in K.C., and either would have eagerly snapped up such a player as Rube Waddell. Mack arrived and met Rube. Rube wanted to go out to the ballpark. Mack agreed to go with him, fearing that Rube would start pitching and never leave. "I don't know how I did it," recalled Mack, "but I talked Rube out of pitching that day and got him on the train … before anyone else could grab him." Mack personally accompanied the big lad back east.[14]

NOTES

1. *Butler Times*, May 1902, Clippings File, Cooperstown.
2. Spink, "Rube Waddell," p. 11.
3. *Los Angeles Daily Times*, April 6, 1902.
4. Ibid., April 7, 1902.
5. Ibid., April 7, 11, 1902.
6. Ibid., April 12–14, 18–20, 1902.
7. Ibid., April 27–May 2, 1902.

8. Ibid., May 9, 1902.
9. Ibid., May 10, 18, 1902.
10. Ibid., May 30, 1902.
11. Spink, "Rube Waddell," p. 11.
12. Clippings File, Cooperstown.
13. *Los Angeles Daily Times*, June 20, 1902.
14. Clippings File, Cooperstown; Spink, "Rube Waddell," p. 11.

Chapter 22

The Planets Shrink in Fear

With Rube in hand, Connie Mack arrived back in the east on the morning of June 26. The train pulled into Baltimore, where the A's were to play the Orioles. Mack and Rube headed straight for Union Park. Rube had forgotten all about L.A. and wanted to pitch that very day with no rest. Mack was never one to say "no" to the Rube, so he sent him out, just as he had when he arrived in Milwaukee from Punxsutawney. Rube pitched his only bad game with Milwaukee when he started straight from the train with no rest. Mack may have forgotten that.

The Orioles' manager was John McGraw. In the previous season he had jumped leagues from St. Louis. McGraw had seen Waddell back in the Louisville days, and he knew how good Rube could be, as well as what he could do about it. McGraw decided to bench-jockey Rube all he could that day, and John J. was one of the best at such tactics. Whether it was McGraw's mouth, the lack of sleep, the newness of it all, or a catcher with whom he was uncomfortable, Rube's debut with the A's was a dud. He lost to the lowly Orioles 7–3.[1]

Rube's loss to Baltimore brought a little chortling out of some Philadelphia papers. But Mack never fretted. He told Rube to settle in and get some rest. The team was heading back to Philadelphia, where Rube could get a fresh start.

Mack also switched catchers for Rube. Mike "Doc" Powers (he held a degree in dentistry) was a fine catcher, but he had trouble with Rube's curves, something readily apparent in the game with Baltimore. Rube was indeed tough to catch (on the field, too). Mack decided to pair Rube with a catcher named Ossee Schreckengost. Back in Louisville in '97 the two had played one game together but had quickly parted. Mack had just picked up Schreckengost from Cleveland. Everyone called him Schreck. The newspapers did not want to spell out his whole name and seldom did; most players and fans could not pronounce it anyway. Indeed Schreck got his other nickname — "Rocking Horse" — during a game in Cleveland when a pitcher, directing traffic on a pop-up, yelled "Take it Schra...; take it Shu...; aw ____, take it Rocking Horse!" The name stuck.

Mack was an old catcher himself, and he loved to watch Schreck at work. Mack later said that Schreck's glove work was the best he ever saw behind the plate, including that of such later stars as Mickey Cochrane.[2] While there were no formally selected all-star teams in those days, many newspapers independently named such squads, and Schreck was a regular choice here. Like most catchers, Schreck was tough as nails. He wore a mask only reluctantly. Sometimes he wore a chest protector, but he disdained those new things called shin guards. He could also be seen on the bench, yanking wads of padding out of his mitt. It was not merely that his hand could take the pounding; Schreck had

Connie Mack, manager of the Philadelphia A's from 1901 to 1950, seen here at an early point in his career. Though Mr. Mack would gain a reputation in his later years for sleeping on the bench and for general forgetfulness, in his prime, as this photo implies, he was a most intense field boss as well as a great handler of ballplayers. Of Rube Waddell, he once commented that after 67 years in the big leagues as a player and manager, he'd seen every wild and crazy ballplayer that ever took the field. With a rueful smile, he noted that not one of them could hold a candle to the Rube. (National Baseball Hall of Fame Library, Cooperstown, N.Y.)

more in mind than mere machismo. Though fans certainly loved the sight of a Rube fastball making loose padding fly out of Schreck's glove, Schreck wanted a mitt that was flexible. Paul Richards is sometimes given credit for developing a big flexible catcher's mitt when he managed the Baltimore Orioles in the late 1950s and wanted to help catcher Gus Triandos handle the fluttering knuckleballs of Hoyt Wilhelm. Schreck invented the "hinged" catcher's mitt before such a thing had a name. He did not have a factory make one for him. He just took a regular mitt, undid the stitching, and pulled out stuffing in the appropriate spots to make the mitt flex as he wanted. With such a mitt he could use his glove like an infielder, and he did so expertly. He caught with one hand, and while the thinner padding may have occasionally pained his glove hand, he could sure keep his good throwing hand in a much safer spot. Schreck could handle Rube's pitches with ease, though sometimes he would be a little behind Rube's curve.

Rube and Schreck became instant buddies. As jazz cornetist Bix Biederbecke had his J. C. "Tram" Trumbauer and Charlie Parker had Dizzy Gillespie, Rube had Schreck. They were roommates, drinking buddies, hunting and fishing pals, general partners in crime. Connie Mack said Schreck was the fizz powder in the pinwheel that was Waddell.[3] When Rube and Schreck were together, one knew to expect anything except tranquillity.

On July 1, Mack slated Rube for his Philadelphia debut. The "Main Line" crowd may not have been interested in the "coming out" of this sort of rogue, but the rest of Philadelphia sure was. Besides, it was the Orioles who were in town, and Rube was itching for a rematch. A few baseball aficionados, scouring for some hint of weakness in Waddell's *on*-field legacy, have pointed out that the Rube never threw a no-hitter or a perfect game. Not quite true. Rube 'n Schreck did have a perfect game of sorts, and it was on July 1, 1902. In the second inning an Oriole player dribbled a grounder past third for a single. As the runner bluffed a steal on the next pitch, Schreck immediately picked him off first without even coming out of his crouch. The Orioles' only other hit came in the fifth. Desperate to get something going, McGraw immediately sent the runner off to steal second. Schreck gunned him down. Otherwise, Rube never walked a batter and struck out 13 Orioles, to boot. He struck out the side in the third, sixth, and ninth innings. It was the same three players each time — Billy Gilbert, Harry Howell, and John Cronin. In the sixth, he fanned the hapless three on nine pitches. Like any pitcher who throws a perfect game, Rube faced but 27 men that day. He also drove in a run. It was as perfect and fearsome a game as one could imagine. At the top of the ninth, Rube stood on the mound and waved to the crowd. "It's all over, go on home," he yelled and promptly struck out the final three batters. The crowd did not go home, however. They rushed out and carried Rube off the field on their shoulders.[4]

Baseball people spoke in awe of Rube's July 1, 1902, blanking of Baltimore. Connie Mack said folks were still talking about it 20 years later. The papers who had sniffed at Rube's anti-climactic opener in June were all aflutter. A mediocre poet on the staff of the *Philadelphia Inquirer* even penned a short verse:[5]

A Reuben to the diamond came, the rooters rooted free.
You've all heard rooters just like them before.
He spat upon one horny hand and wiped it tenderly.
You've often seen them wipe it there before.

["Mediocre" may be too generous a description of this poet.]

Up to the bat the Orioles rose, his face was filled with glee.
There're various brands of glee you've seen before.
"Strike one," the umpire cried, "strike two"—
the umpire said "strike three."
But you've seldom seen those kind of strikes before.
For when Reuben twirls the sphere,
The Planets shrink in fear.
And the sinuous sea serpent
Its sorrow tries to drown.
Then the cyclone hides its head,
And the birds go right to bed
For there's doings on the diamond when Reuben comes to town.

The A's were in second place when Rube joined Mack and the A's—five and a half games behind first-place Chicago. On the back of their new horse, the A's and the city of Philadelphia would enjoy a wild ride to the top.

NOTES

1. *Philadelphia Inquirer*, June 27, 1902.
2. Quoted in Spink, "Rube Waddell," p. 12.
3. Harry Grayson, "Eccentric Waddell Prepared to Fish," April 30, 1945, Clippings File, Cooperstown.
4. Clippings File, Cooperstown; *Philadelphia Inquirer*, July 2, 1902.
5. *Philadelphia Inquirer*, July 2, 1902.

Chapter 23

Goodbye, John McGraw

Since John McGraw had tried to ride the Rube so mercilessly in his two outings against the Orioles, Rube found his flawless shutout of the Orioles on July 1 especially sweet. He was not through with his revenge, however, and the results would prove unexpectedly far-reaching.

Connie Mack always knew that his young Rube had to be kept busy, not to eliminate but at least to minimize the "balloon rides." After the blanking of Baltimore, Mack told Rube he would need him the following afternoon to help coach. Rube took this in earnest, and the next afternoon he showed up in fine fettle and took his place in the first base coach's box. Whatever pent-up energies Rube harbored from not celebrating the night before came out sideways that afternoon along the first base line at Columbia Park. The game was a great pitcher's duel. Eddie Plank faced Joe McGinnity, whom McGraw had induced to jump to Baltimore from Brooklyn. Both pitchers were future Hall of Famers. But the Rube was the real star of the game. As in Louisville, coach Rube began to do some bizarre things. He turned hand-springs and cartwheels in the box as well as to and from the dugout, quite amazing feats of athleticism for someone so tall and broad shouldered. He made loud farm animal noises, and barked out commands to runners like a cattle drover. His banter and jokes were ceaseless. And he taunted the dour McGinnity with comedic imitations of his windup, complete with his hesitation noises. He was definitely full of beans.

McGraw had tried to derail Rube many times. With all his antics, it was now Rube who would get to McGraw. "Mugsy" McGraw had a fearsome temper, but he usually used it to his advantage. He rarely lost control, he just seemed to, often to the intimidation of opponents and umpires. This day Rube got completely under his skin. Irritated to distraction, McGraw began to take his frustrations out on the umpire, kicking at minor matters. Rube, Mack, and the Philadelphia crowd loved every minute of Rube's show and McGraw's reactions.

McGinnity actually bested Plank in the game 2–1, but the result was a sidebar in view of other outcomes. After several rows with the umpires during the game, McGraw was ejected. The umpires reported both McGraw's behavior and his actual words to American League president Ban Johnson. (Johnson and McGraw absolutely hated one another.) In regard to his choice of language, McGraw held, "I indulged in a little pleasant sarcasm, but umpire [Thomas H.] Connolly became obstreperous and ordered me to the clubhouse." Needless to say, Johnson was not convinced of McGraw's innocence, and he suspended Mugsy.[1]

Such an explosion between McGraw and Johnson was inevitable. Each was a man who needed total command, and neither was the sort who could ever take orders from anyone. McGraw would not bow to Johnson's authority. He demanded reinstatement. Johnson refused. McGraw left. He left the Orioles, and he left the American League. On July 10, the last-place New York Giants hired McGraw as their manager. McGraw took McGinnity and several other good players with him — John Cronin, Dennis McGann, and Roger Breshnahan. At this point, Joe Kelly and Cy Seymour also jumped the Orioles for Cincinnati. Baltimore was decimated. They were suddenly the weakest team in the AL and would finish dead last. Their attendance fell off, and Ban Johnson had to secure money from the other clubs to keep the Orioles afloat. Ultimately, Johnson capitalized on this state of affairs, shifting the Baltimore franchise to the big city, taking on the NL directly, plunking a new AL team — the New York Highlanders as they would be known (later the Yankees) — right in McGraw's back yard.[2]

Johnson predicted failure for McGraw. "I wouldn't be surprised," Johnson snorted, "if the National League would be glad to get rid of him in a little while."[3] Of course, McGraw would go on to great fame as the Giants manager. He would lead them to many championships and remain at their helm for 30 years. In July, 1902, however, he appeared to be running away, and every fan in the American League was loving every minute of it. While the fuel was already mixed when McGraw and Johnson found themselves in the same league, Rube's antics of July 2 struck the match. The thought of it all certainly made Rube, Mack, and the rest of the A's chuckle heartily.

As he left the league for New York, McGraw held forth to the press about what a bush-league operation the American League was. He had some particularly choice words to say about the Philadelphia Athletics. "The Philadelphia club," he opined, "is not making any money. It has a big white elephant on its hands.... [The owner, Ben Shibe,] cannot see a penny coming in at the gate. No money was made last year, and no money will be made this year."[4] As the Athletics drove for the pennant in the summer of 1902, attendance surpassed that of all other teams in both leagues. Profits soared. At Columbia Park, and in papers like the *Inquirer*, the "White Elephant" became a favorite image. With a smug grin, the entire Philadelphia community came to adopt the symbol of the white elephant, confronting McGraw's enmity by rallying behind it. White elephants were posted all over town. Mack had white elephant emblems sewn on all team sweaters and jackets. It took decades for the symbol to fade as an A's trademark, and in the 1960s, after the team had moved to Kansas City and subsequently to Oakland, owner Charles O. Finley readopted the old white elephant as the A's symbol. It all began with the anger of Mugsy McGraw.

McGraw would meet Connie Mack and the A's many times in the future. He would get his revenge. But the fates never allowed him again to meet Waddell on a ball field in a real game situation with anything at stake.

NOTES

1. *Philadelphia Inquirer*, July 3, 1902.
2. *Reach's Baseball Guide*, 1903.
3. *Philadelphia Inquirer*, July 10, 1902.
4. Ibid., July 14, 1902.

Chapter 24

A Blaze to Glory

Rube's victory over Baltimore on July 1 set him on a blaze through the American League that was like no other half-season any pitcher would ever have. When it was over, Rube and the A's were the champions.

Rube was zany, but Mack figured out how to keep an eye on him. Boxer Young Corbett and his trainer Frank Newcomb followed Rube to the east from Kansas City when they read of his success. Rube badly wanted Mack to hire Newcomb to be the team's trainer. Rube liked boxers and wanted to be groomed like one; he had a sense for conditioning, but none of the discipline. Mack hired Newcomb, but not as a trainer. He made him Rube's shadow, with strict orders to report to Mack on Rube's whereabouts at all times. Rube soon grew tired of Newcomb following him everywhere he went. When he complained, Mack told Rube that if he didn't like it, Newcomb would have to be fired. Rube had no heart to fire anyone, so Newcomb stayed, and Mack thus kept a good watch on his star pitcher all season.[1]

On July 4 the Athletics hosted Washington in a doubleheader. Double-headers in that era were all-day affairs. The first game would begin at 10:00 A.M., the second at 3:00 P.M. Between games the fans cavorted, ate the new-fangled sandwiches called "hot dogs," strolled about the field, and generally had a gay old time. With this double bill being on July 4, the between-games fiesta had the added gaiety of firecrackers. July 4 was always a big holiday all over the country, of course, but nowhere was it taken with such earnestness as it was in Philadelphia. To do other than whoop it up with total abandon was downright unpatriotic. This is why Mack had Rube start the *second* game. There was no use giving the boy an excuse to join in the party any sooner than he had to.

Amidst all the hoopla, Rube took the mound that afternoon. The 14,000-plus excited fans hoped for another stellar performance from their new Rube. They didn't get one. Rube gave up five runs in the first inning. Now the grandstand was filled with a strange mixture of holiday mirth, fear, disappointment, and hope.

Though Rube was not his best, the A's battled back, overtaking the Senators and winning 12 to 9.[2] This victory was actually almost as important as the July 1 perfecto. The Baltimore shutout on that day proved to everyone that Rube could pitch like no other. His coaching on the next day proved he could behave like no other, as did subsequent reports of his nightly carryings on. But the win on July 4 showed the team and the Philadelphia fans that Rube was not a complete head case. He could come back when down. He could work effectively with men on base. He would not be bothered by distractions as extreme as fireworks popping during his windup. While the A's already knew Rube could win *for* them, now they knew Rube could win *with* them.

There are pitchers who have all the stuff, but who never seem to be able to ignite the team behind them. Having snuffed out that possibility of July 4, Rube and the A's illustrated their newfound mutual admiration on July 8. On the road in Boston, the A's were up 9 to 6. In the fifth, Mack brought in Rube. He shut the Pilgrims down for two innings, while in their half of the sixth the A's came up with 12 runs. They ended up winning 22–9.

With the juices flowing, Mack sent Rube out to start against Boston the very next day. Rube's opponent was a Bill Dineen. Dineen was great pitcher in the midst of a streak in which he would win 20 games four times in five years. This year he would win 21. The game was a wonderful duel. It was knotted 2–2 after nine innings. On and on they went into extra innings. Rube would not give an inch and neither would Dineen. Rube set a new baseball record, striking out 16 batters that day, and after striking out the last man in the 14th he cartwheeled all the way to the dugout. Naturally, the fans loved it, and it answered any Pilgrims' prayers that the young lad was tiring. In the top of the 17th, the A's rallied for two runs, the second run being a Rube RBI. In the bottom of the inning Rube blanked Boston. He and the A's were ablaze.[3]

Boston and Philadelphia had another series the very next week in Philadelphia. This series set a rematch of Rube and Dineen. Before the game Boston's big first baseman George LaChance, with the prior approval of manager Jimmy Collins, decided to play around with Rube, joshing him about fishing and hunting. Never one to back away from any sort of gaming, Rube gladly took the challenge. They gnawed at each other verbally, and this escalated to a few gentle pushes and shoves. Finally they decided to wrestle. Mack knew better than to be too much of a killjoy when it came to Rube's antics, so Rube and LaChance went ahead with the match, all this taking place as game time approached with thousands of fans entering the ballpark and watching. It was all in good spirits, there would be no kicking or fists, just good ole wrasslin'. For a half hour these two big oafs pushed and shoved at each other. Rube would get the better of it — in more ways than one. With the crowd now roaring its approval, Rube pinned LaChance's ears to the ground. After the long match, LaChance sat down, completely exhausted. He told manager Jimmy Collins that he would have to put someone else on first base that day. If LaChance was too tired to play first base, how was the Rube going to pitch? Rube went out, full of beans, and tossed a complete game, the A's winning 3–2. The next day the *Philadelphia Inquirer* printed a cartoon, depicting Rube handing a beaten LaChance a fan. This was more than just winning; it was fun.[4]

Rube beat Chicago on July 15, besting his old rival Clark Griffith. Griffith thought he had Rube's number, for Chicago scored one in the first and two in the second. But again it was Rube *and* the A's that Griffith was facing. Rube shut out the White Stockings from there, while the A's came back with nine. Three days later Rube faced the Sox once more, and again he was a trifle wobbly, giving up six runs. He was also wobbly in the legs. (Mack knew what was going on in the evenings.) Rube singled in the fifth, for example, but when Danny Murphy singled after him, Rube was thrown out at second by the outfielder. The A's came through for him, though. This time it was Schreck. He doubled home the seventh run in the bottom of the ninth. Rube joined the crowd that carried his roommate off on their shoulders. The A's were rolling; they were now only five games out of first.[5]

Eddie Plank started against Cleveland on July 21. Larry Lajoie and company scored ten runs through seven innings; so did the A's. Rube came in to complete the game. He shut down Cleveland completely, and the A's again came through with a run in the ninth. That night Rube went out and refereed a boxing match, celebrating afterward with the winning fighter. The next day Cleveland was again piling up the score. In the fourth inning Mack called for Rube. He gave up two singles that inning, but from the fifth through the ninth he put down 15 batters in a row, while the A's rolled ahead. With two out in the ninth, and two strikes on centerfielder Harry "Deerfoot" Bay, Rube paused. He took off his cap and waved good-bye to the crowd, telling them it's all over, you can go home. Then he turned and struck out Bay with the next pitch. On and off the field, Rube had a style unlike any who had ever played the game.[6]

By July 25 Chicago had 42 wins and 31 losses; Philadelphia stood at 41 and 32. Boston and St. Louis were still in the thick of it, but it was the Athletics that had made the biggest move of the month, a month in which Rube Waddell had gone 9 and 0. Pennant fever in Philadelphia was everywhere. On Saturday, July 26, St. Louis was in town, and Rube was slated to pitch. The grandstand at Columbia Park held a little over 15,000. By 9:30 in the morning all those seats were filled. Around the outfield and along the very baselines more fans poured in. Out on Columbia Avenue and Oxford Street people could be seen standing on buggies, automobiles, and rooftops. Many had climbed telephone polls. Philadelphia had never seen anything like it. Downtown in front of the *Inquirer* office a crowd gathered as newspapermen, getting word of the game's progress by telephone, would relay information via megaphones out to the people on the street. This was Rube's kind of day.

As the game progressed, the crowd was in agony, as inning after inning St. Louis put runners in scoring position, but each time Rube reached back and kept the Browns from scoring. Rube and the A's were up 3–0 going into the ninth. With one out the Browns got a man on. The next batter hit a fly to the outfield. Normally it would have been an easy out, but the crowds that had built up around the outfield grass had inched in and made the catch impossible. The umpire awarded the batter a double, thus granting a run. Instead of the game being over, the tying run was stepping up to bat. He worked Rube to 3 and 0, with the crowd dying a little on each pitch. The same thing was happening downtown among the crowd in front of the *Inquirer* office. This was pre-radio "radio," unbearably exciting. Rube took charge, responding with three straight blasts into Schreck's mitt for a strikeout. When the next batter grounded feebly, it was all over.[7]

Philadelphia was now a complete A's town. The Phillies were an afterthought. The same thing was occurring in Chicago, St. Louis, and Boston. One week up in Boston, the NL Beaneaters and the AL Pilgrims both played at home. The Pilgrims drew 5046 on July 23; the Beaneaters 600. The next day the difference was 4000 to 400; the day after, 5000 to 300. The A's were doing much the same to the Phils. One of the keys here involved the intensity of pennant races. While the AL race was a hotly contested four-team affair, the NL championship was a foregone conclusion. Fred Clarke, Honus Wagner, and the Pirates had put together an unbeatable team. As of August 6 they had an 18-game lead on second place Brooklyn, a wider gap than the AL-leading White Stockings had on last place Baltimore.[8]

After the draining victory over the Browns, and knowing what Rube had likely done Saturday night, Mack felt Rube should rest a few days. There was no game Sunday (never on Sunday in Philadelphia!). Mack also had Eddie Plank and other pitchers who were now showing some spark, like Bert Husting and a young kid out of Holy Cross College named Andy Coakley. By Tuesday Rube was itching to get back out there, but Mack thought it was still too soon, given the work Rube had done that month. But Mack relented. It turned out to be Rube's only loss of the month, the first time he and Schreck came out on the short end. During the game St. Louis second baseman Dick Padden said one too many things to Rube. Rube rushed right at Padden. The rest of the A's got between them in a hurry, and the storm passed.

Rube persuaded Mack to send him out after just another day's rest. He wanted another piece of the Browns. This time the results were inconclusive. A bit of bad luck hurt Rube that day. In the third inning a Brown batter popped to short center. The field was damp, and Rube's centerfielder, Dave Fultz, slipped. The ball glanced off his body and scooted across the first base line into the clubhouse area. The umpire made no call, and as the A's searched for the ball, the runner scampered home for a rather strange home run. That run was significant, as the score was knotted 4–4 after nine innings. One more inning was played before darkness fell. The final two outings of the month may have indicated Rube was a bit frayed. Still, all in all, 10 and 1 seemed a reasonably good month.[9] Mack was certainly satisfied. The A's were still in second place, dead even with Chicago in losses, four down in wins. On August 1, the A's boarded a train for Chicago.

Rube lost to Chicago 3 to 1 on August 3. So strong a following had Rube attracted the previous year with the Orphans that the highly partisan Chicago fans cheered him as the game began. Early in the game, a wild throw from the outfield yielded one Chicago run. In another play, with one on, Rube fielded a bunt. His throw to first hit the batter. The ball caromed into foul territory and another run scored. Rube pitched strongly the rest of the way, and when it was over the Chicago fans gave him another cheer. Chicago went on to win two of three from Philadelphia. Their lead thus widened, and both St. Louis and Boston inched past Philadelphia.

Rube's next start came against Cleveland. Again he hurled a strong game, striking out 12. But he lost 5–4. Cleveland's fifth run was a terrible one for the A's to stomach. With a runner on and two out, the batter popped in front of the mound. Third baseman Lave Cross, first baseman Harry Davis, Rube, and Schreck all converged on it. The four did a classic "you take it" as the ball landed between them and the runner scampered home. It looked like the city's pennant celebrations had been premature.[10]

To add to the A's sudden malaise, Rube played hooky. Connie Mack had promised Rube that if he beat Cleveland he could go with his mother, who had come to the game, to visit his sister in Michigan. The team's next stop was in Detroit, and Rube could rejoin the team in a few days. Rube lost in Cleveland but went away with his mother anyway. No one heard from him for five days.[11]

If this had been the Pirates, Fred Clarke would likely have suspended Rube. When Rube drifted into Detroit in the early afternoon of August 11, Mack said nothing but, "It's your turn to pitch." Rube did. The A's offense had been sputtering since the beginning of the Chicago series. Rube showed his teammates he could wait for them to ignite. If they could not score any runs, he would gladly see to it the Tigers didn't either. After 12 innings of tense 0–0 baseball, Rube lost patience, however. He stepped up to bat with a runner on first and stroked a triple. Now he had a lead and went out and blanked Detroit in the bottom of the inning.

Detroit and Philadelphia did not play on the 12th. Instead both traveled back to Philadelphia. Rube got home that night and went to a club to catch some prizefights. On the 13th Mack asked Rube if he could pitch again, Rube said "sure" with a wonder in his eye as to why there could be any reason he couldn't. He shut out the Tigers again and this time the A's bats came to life, as they scored eight.

Mack knew the team would come out of its slump; he just needed something to hide behind while he got through it. He hid behind the Rube. Mack's tactic worked, for on the 14th, the A's swept a doubleheader from Detroit. On the 15th they won two more. Rube worked *all four games*! That marked six games in a row. In the bottom of the ninth in the last game, Rube tried to send his outfielders off, forgetting this was not allowed. So Rube had them squat down directly behind the infielders as he struck out the last man.

On the day of the first Detroit doubleheader, the Phillies were also in town. It was a Thursday afternoon. The A's attendance was 5,918; the Phils drew 218. After the second doubleheader, the A's learned that both Chicago and St. Louis had lost. Rube had pitched in six straight wins in four days. Philadelphia was now in first place with Chicago due in the next day.[12]

With the enormous fan interest, Athletics' president Ben Shibe found his "white elephant" was now so successful that he had to come up with imaginary measures to accommodate all those people who wanted to fork over their money. He increased the precious seating capacity of Columbia Park. He narrowed the bench seats and charged for the overflow standing areas. By the time Saturday's Chicago game was ready to begin, 18,765 tickets had been sold. (Shibe began to think he might need to build a new park.) The 18,000+ was not just a team record; it was a league record, and Shibe could have likely sold many more tickets given the great numbers of people out on the cars, rooftops, and telephone poles. There even was a crowd downtown in front of the *Inquirer* office.

The game with Chicago was tense and scoreless through four innings. In the top of the fifth, Rube rushed in to cover a bunt. He slipped while picking up the ball and threw it over first into the bleachers, allowing the runner to scamper to second. The next batter also bunted successfully, leaving runners at the corners. The runner on first immediately tried to steal second on Schreck. Schreck threw in time, though on a bounce, and shortstop Monte Cross misplayed it. The runner on third scored, and Chicago had the lead. Schreck came back to bench steaming. He said nothing, but knocked in runners his next two times at bat. Schreck's RBI were enough to hold the lead into the ninth. With the crowd roaring, Rube struck out the first two men

he faced. The third batter bounced one between first and second. First baseman Harry Davis snared it. He threw to Rube, who ran over to cover the
bag. The umpire immediately signaled "out," and thousands of joyous fans
streamed onto the field. To the Sox it looked like Rube had bobbled the throw,
and amidst all the post-game confusion they tried to protest. The umpire
looked at the crowd and threw up in his hands in futility. His call stood.
Chicago was mad as hell. Rube had a victory. Their lead over the Sox widened,
and all Philadelphia celebrated.[13]

After a Sunday off, the A's beat Chicago again and the Browns lost, too.
Now the A's were a game and a half ahead of the pack. Mack gave Chicago
another crack at Rube on Tuesday. They made the most of it, winning 5–2.
For Rube it was his first real loss, one where the game was not in doubt, since
his first outing off the train against Baltimore back in June. It had been almost
two months.[14]

Mack may have thought Rube and the rest of the team needed a rest
after the pressure of the Chicago games, but that was out of the question. For
as the Sox were boarding the train at Broad Street station to leave Philadelphia, the St. Louis Browns were arriving for three games. It would be an A's
sweep. After the first two victories, a third-game loss would have yielded a
jump of only one game in the standings, but feeling a bit confident, Mack
started non-ace Fred Mitchell. Mitchell gave up three runs in the first inning.
The crowd began to stir, and the players were getting fidgety. Mack yanked
Mitchell during the first inning, and brought in Rube. Other than an unearned
run later in the game, Rube completely baffled the Browns the rest of the way.
In the bottom of the third Schreck hit a home run. Then Rube stepped up
and hit another one. Everyone knew who was in charge that day. The rest of
the A's bats then came to life and they won going away, 12 to 4. Philadelphia
went crazy.

Cleveland came in the next day, and 21,000 came to the park to watch
the A's win another one, 12 to 1. Rube celebrated hard during the Cleveland
series, and he missed a start. But Philadelphia went on to sweep Cleveland
anyway. The A's had won 16 of their previous 17 games and were now in front
by three. Rube had at least timed his "toot" precipitously, for there a big road
trip lay ahead. Mack hoped Rube had gotten the celebrating out of his system; he would hope that a lot.[15]

Amidst the hoopla in Philadelphia, the Brooklyn Dodgers tried to induce
Rube to jump leagues. They offered him $500 a month for the rest of 1902
and 1903, plus a $1000 cash bonus and off-season use of a seaside house for
hunting and fishing. "You know Connie Mack is a skin[flint]," urged the
Dodger representative. Did Rube consider the offer? As Connie Mack once
reflected, "Rube had the mind of a child." Can one imagine a ten-year-old

boy, his favorite team in the thick of a pennant race, being induced to give
up rooting and turn his attention to another team in another league? So much
for Brooklyn.[16]

After the sweep of Cleveland, the A's were off "around the western circuit"—Chicago, St. Louis, Detroit, and Cleveland. The road trip was critical. If the A's could hold their lead while on the road, the pennant would be
virtually assured because most of their remaining games were at home. In
Chicago, the Sox were still mad about the August 16 call on Rube's alleged
bobble at first base. They prepared themselves, as well as their field. A doubleheader was scheduled on the 28th. Chicago won the first game. Rube
started the second game. Manager Clark Griffith had decided that Rube
needed to be pressured, though not with words; that was not working anymore. Instead, Griffith had his players bunt incessantly. In addition to the
fielding pressure by itself, Griffith had his grounds keeper heavily dampen the
area around the third base line. With Rube being so big, Griffith hoped he
would rush in on the bunts and slip. It worked a couple of times. Mack was
not happy about it. But Rube slogged through it. Rube also came up with
two remedies for the situation. First, he struck out seven (you can't bunt when
you can't get your bat on the ball); second, he went two for four at the plate.
With the score tied 4–4 in the eighth, Rube singled in the lead run, and he
made it hold up the rest of the way.[17]

The next day bad news came for the A's, and especially for Rube. The
Pittsburgh Pirates were still way out front in the National League. Knowing
a pennant was assured, reporters pressured Barney Dreyfuss as to whether he
would be willing to accept the challenge of a series with the winner of the
new American League. Such a prospect was certainly enticing to Rube. He
had faced Clarke and the Pirates before, but only with the lowly Chicago
Orphans behind him. Now he had a team. He badly wanted to go home and
face his old mates.

With all the bad words and inter-league player raiding over the past two
years, the suggested playoff was no cinch. At this point, Dreyfuss was particularly angry. He had not lost many players in 1900-1, but more recently
several of his players, notably Jack Chesbro, had signed with American League
clubs. Other key players were leaving too, though *not* Honus Wagner. Dreyfuss was angry. Like other NL leaders, he clung to the faint hope that the new
league would fail, as had other rivals in the 1880s and 1890s. A playoff series
would only give the upstarts more credibility. Thinking they may even expand
into other cities, like Pittsburgh, Dreyfuss reflected on what AL competition
had done to Chicago, St. Louis, Philadelphia, and Boston. Yes, the Pittsburgh
Pirates would make money on the proposed championship series, but so would
the new kids, who needed cash more desperately than he. There would be no

championship series in 1902. A retired umpire named Joe Cantillon would propose a few exhibition games between the Pirates and a team of American League all-stars. Dreyfuss agreed to this, but it was hardly the same.[18]

Mack would not let his team dwell on the prospect of no playoff against the NL champion. Too much lay ahead just to secure the AL pennant. After saving the A's from a doubleheader sweep by Chicago on August 28, Rube performed the same feat on the 30th. The A's lost game one. In game two, Rube struck out only four, but he went 2 for 4 at the plate, and here he added a few twists. He imitated his opponent's windup while standing in the batter's box, arrogantly accepting a called strike as a meaningless price for his display. In the eighth inning, the score was again tied. Rube stepped into the box with a man on. He broke into no comical imitations this time. He belted a triple and shut the Sox out from there. In late July and early August, Rube suffered three close losses and a tie. The breaks were going against him. But baseball teaches that breaks even out as long as one's effectiveness does not ebb. Rube had effectiveness to burn (and how he would burn it!), and now the breaks were falling his way. Clark Griffith was not happy about it. Rube ended the second win in Chicago with a strikeout and an exhibition of handstands. He didn't just win; he rubbed it in.[19]

While Clark Griffith had tried to dampen down the baselines on Rube and the A's, the St. Louis Browns were ready with their own tricks. Manager Jimmy McAleer planted a man out by the centerfield scoreboard with a pair of binoculars to try to pick up the A's signals. Into the series, the wily Connie Mack caught on. He went to the umpire. The ump spoke to McAleer, who naturally denied everything. Other Browns had come out during the rhubarb to support McAleer and pressure the umpire. Mack would not back down, but the denial was holding up. Then one of McAleer's outfielders, the good but not terribly bright Jesse Burkett, blurted out, "Well, we had it for four games anyway." (Oops!) McAleer was tossed, and the A's won the game.[20]

St. Louis would take two in the series from the A's. With that, second-place Boston pulled to within one game. It looked like the A's train may be derailing. The symbolism of that became all too real as the team left St. Louis for Detroit. Rube told a reporter he was sleeping and having a dream that he was pitching to Jesse Burkett. In the dream, recalled Rube, "I sent a swift, straight one across the plate; Jess swung and pow — the train wrecked." The dream was not real, but the train *had* wrecked. Pitcher Howard "Highball" (and not for the location of his pitches) Wilson was lying in bed when the wreck occurred. He shrugged when someone told him what had happened and said: "Well I can't help it. The train isn't mine," and he went back to sleep. The rest of the A's disembarked, however. There were no injuries and the trains were righted, with fireman Rube helping get the job done.

With the train wreck, Rube and the A's arrived in Detroit seven hours late with no sleep, save for Highball Wilson. Their league lead had dwindled to one game, and they had to play the Tigers in two hours. Rube went out, with no sleep, no meal, and won it for them 5–1. Going without sleep was nothing new to Rube.[21]

Mack insisted Rube rest a few after the Detroit game. Giving Rube time off was no guarantee he was going to rest, however, particularly because Rube still had lots of friends in Detroit. One evening that week, Mack was in the hotel lobby. Rube suddenly walked in with a policeman. The officer explained to Mack that Rube had created a disturbance, that he had... Mack politely interrupted the constable, as it never took much to convince him that Rube had done something wrong. Mack asked the officer what would happen as a result of the misdemeanors. (Mack's sizable assumption was that the problems did not involve felonies; fortunately, that was the case here.) The officer said that Rube would be arrested and would have to pay a fine but nothing more. Mack asked if the fine could be paid right then and there. The officer agreed and told Mack that $10 would cover it. Mack immediately gave the officer the $10 and sent Rube to his room. An hour later Mack decided to take a stroll before going to bed. Down the street, he passed a saloon and glanced in the window. There was Rube and the "officer" drinking up the $10.[22]

On September 4, Rube's playfulness continued on the ballfield. He shut out the Tigers for the first six innings. On the mound he was full of fun and games. He even feigned an argument with Schreck, claiming there were three outs when Shreck signaled there were two. The next man singled. Mack sensed that Rube had lost his stuff, and because the A's had a big lead, Mack relieved Rube for the first time in the season. The A's went on to win, 13 to 4.[23]

Cleveland was the next stop, and Mack was a little worried that pulling Rube may have upset him. He still wanted to rest his ace, though, so he sent him out as a pinch hitter in the ninth inning. It was not a pressure moment. The game was already lost (10–7), and the crowd loved it anyway. Rube popped to second.[24]

Now "rested," Rube won a lucky one in Cleveland on September 6. He was out pitched by future Hall of Famer Addie Joss. Rube gave up seven hits to Joss's four. Joss fanned four while Rube struck out only two. The A's defense was superb all day, however, shutting down several Cleveland rallies with good plays. They won it for Rube, 3–2. Two days later, Rube's luck would continue in another start against Cleveland. He got cocky with the bottom of Cleveland's order, throwing a lot of slow junk. They made him pay for it, and several times Rube faced the top of the Cleveland order with men on base. Rube dug the deepest such hole for himself in the seventh, when he faced Larry Lajoie with the bases loaded. Fortunately, Lajoie popped, and Rube had another victory.[25] As Yogi Berra might have said, Rube could sure skate thin ice and get himself into hot water.

If the road trip had lasted any longer, Rube may have found himself testing the fates once too often. But the Cleveland series ended the western trip, and the A's came home still atop the league, two up on St. Louis. Thousands of fans, complete with a marching band, greeted the team at the Broad Street Station. The lowly Orioles were coming to town. Everyone felt confident.

With a doubleheader slated with Baltimore, Mack thought he could give weak Fred Mitchell another start, but after four runs in two innings, he had to yank him. Rube came in to put out the fire. He gave up only three more hits, and went 2 for 4 at the plate. The A's came back with nine runs to win. In the second game, the Orioles were again ahead. This time it was 3 to 2 in the seventh. In came Rube. He immediately gave up a double and a single, yielding another run. Everyone on the bench began to glance Mack's way. But Mack stayed with the Rube, and it worked. Rube gave up just one more hit and struck out three the rest of the way. The A's scored three in the bottom of the seventh, giving Rube his second victory of the day. The next morning the *Inquirer's* cartoonist depicted Rube wearing a crown of laurel leaves.[26]

The A's went on to sweep Baltimore. They were now four up on St. Louis and Boston, and the Pilgrims were due in the next day. Boston trotted out Cy Young for the opener, so Mack asked Rube if he could go again. Rube was eager for another joust with Young. Neither pitcher really got the better of it; Young struck out seven, Rube fanned eight. But Young allowed four runs; Rube let in five. It was no disgrace. The Philadelphia crowd gave Young a big cheer in the top of the ninth and Rube an even bigger one in the bottom.[27]

Rube had pitched in Philadelphia's last three outings, and nearly won all three. His "capacity for work," noted the *Inquirer*, "is only equaled by his willingness." Mack rested Rube until Monday the 15th. Boston was still in town, with the series winding up with a doubleheader. Rube and Cy Young hooked up again in game two. This time Rube took it going away. He struck out ten to Young's two as the A's won easily, 9–2. Over 16,000 people came to Columbia Park that Monday afternoon. Down on Broad Street, the other Philadelphia team had played the other Boston club before 956. Amidst the pennant fever, the Phillies had become the idols of dozens.

The A's were now five up on Boston and four up on St. Louis. Washington was due in, so the A's winning continued. The following week, Boston had one more crack at home against the A's. The series gave Rube and Cy Young a rubber match. Rube took it 6–4. Then he came back two days later to win another one. That second win in Boston marked Rube's 24th victory since July 1. Between August 22 and September 22, Rube had pitched 14 games. When he struck out his eighth Pilgrim on the 22d, Rube's season total stood at 210. That led the league, despite the rest of the pitchers having a three-month head start. It had been quite a blaze. He even batted .286.

By September 20, though, other clubs still had a mathematical chance to win the pennant, and Philadelphia's leaders were already planning a championship parade for the 29th. (Such hubris would haunt the city, but it would take a full 62 years to materialize fully.) Rube was given a gold watch by some adoring fans. Within days, Rube lost the watch. With tears in his eyes, Rube asked Mack what could be done. Mack put an ad in the papers, offering a $20 reward. Magically, the watch was soon found by a saloon keeper. Rube and Mack went down to the establishment. Rube retrieved his watch, and Mack paid the reward. Rube returned to the saloon, as he now had a $20 credit with one of his favorite barkeeps.[28]

Rube "lost" his watch several more times, and Mack paid the reward each time. But Connie Mack's mother had not raised a fool. Mack had made up his mind that the way to handle Rube was to go along with whatever tall story he told. Rube once appeared at a team hotel dazed and bloody, and told Mack he had been watching Willie Hoppe play pool. With the performances he extracted from the eccentric one, particularly compared with what Fred Clarke's management had yielded, who could question Mack's methods? With the low salary he was paying Waddell, furthermore, and with the huge crowds Rube was turning out for Mack and Ben Shibe, $20 here and there was a pittance, indeed, a pathetically low bonus. The joke was on anyone but Connie Mack.

On September 24, after winning four in a row from Baltimore, Philadelphia won the pennant. The parade was well planned and proved quite an affair. Some 350 clubs and organizations sent bands and other marchers. The delirium so washed over all local laws and customs that even the Philadelphia Giants baseball club was allowed to march. (They were a "colored outfit.") Some eyebrows were raised at this, but Rube sure didn't mind. He sometimes played with them. Indeed, the Giants' top pitcher, a savvy artist named George Foster who had taught Christy Mathewson to throw the "fade away," beat Rube one day. From then on Foster was known as "Rube." Others would take the name too, hoping some of the magic would transfer.

With the pennant, the season was over. There would be no series with the Pirates. Since Pittsburgh had declined the challenge of a playoff, the A's could legitimately claim to be the champions of baseball. From there, the team could only play some exhibition games. The players always needed a little more cash, so they eagerly went off for several weeks. But it was all rather anti-climactic. Covering the A's playing teams the likes of Camden, Reading, and Wilmington, the *Inquirer* bluntly advised, "cut it out!"[29]

Rube should have heeded the *Inquirer*. The day after the victory parade, he pitched in an exhibition against Wilmington. During the game, he took a line drive on the wrist. He continued to play exhibitions, but largely in the outfield. If there had been a World Series, Rube could not have pitched. Such ill luck would return a few years later.

Rube had also signed to play professional football that fall with a new team, also named the Philadelphia Athletics and managed by Connie Mack.[30] Rube traveled and caroused with the team that fall, but he never played a game. Some said he was a bit afraid of playing with folks his own size and bigger. Even if it was true, Rube did not really need to play; he had done enough playing without a helmet anyway.

NOTES

1. Spink, "Rube Waddell," p. 12.
2. *Philadelphia Inquirer*, July 5, 1902.
3. Ibid., July 9–10, 1902.
4. Ibid., July 13, 1902.
5. Ibid., July 16, 19, 1902.
6. Ibid., July 22–23, 1902; *Philadelphia Record*, July 23, 1902.
7. *Philadelphia Inquirer*, July 27, 1902.
8. Ibid., July 26, August 6, 1902; *Philadelphia Public Ledger*, July 26, 1902.
9. *Philadelphia Inquirer*, July 30, August 1, 1902; *Philadelphia Record*, August 1, 1902; *Philadelphia Public Ledger*, August 1, 1902.
10. *Philadelphia Inquirer*, August 7, 1902.
11. Ibid.; *Philadelphia Record; Philadelphia Public Ledger*, August 8–13, 1902.
12. *Philadelphia Inquirer*, August 13–16, 1902.
13. Ibid; *Philadelphia Record; Philadelphia Public Ledger*, August 17, 1902.
14. *Philadelphia Inquirer*, August 18–20, 1902.
15. Ibid., August 23–27, 1902.
16. Ibid., August 27, 1902.
17. Ibid., August 29, 1902.
18. Ibid., August 30, September 6, 1902.
19. Ibid., August 31, 1902.
20. Ibid., September 1, 1902.
21. Ibid.; *Philadelphia Record, Philadelphia Public Ledger*, September 2, 1902.
22. Martin, *Peter Martin Calls On...*, p. 51; Clippings File, Cooperstown
23. *Philadelphia Inquirer*, September 5, 1902.
24. Ibid., September 6, 1902.
25. Ibid., September 7–9, 1902.
26. Ibid., September 11, 1902.
27. Ibid., September 12-13, 1902.

28. Ibid., Sept. 20–23, 1902; Martin, *Peter Martin Calls On...*, p. 52.
29. *Philadelphia Inquirer*, October 11, 1902.
30. Ibid., October 3, 1902.

Chapter 25

If He Does That Again, I'll...

Rube and the A's were on top of the world after the 1902 pennant. Success in the prime of youth can breed a sense of invulnerability, and Rube would certainly show that — not that he had never done so before. His wrist healed fully. He played a few more post-season exhibitions and went back to Prospect for some of the winter. As spring training approached, Rube decided to get an early start. Connie Mack planned to take the team to Jacksonville, Florida, for much of the month of March. Rube told him he would meet him there. In early February, Rube and Schreck headed off for Florida. They ventured down to Winter Park amidst the lakes north of Orlando. In 1903 central Florida was a fairly primitive, undeveloped area with a few farms and fruit groves, and lots of swamps. Rube and Schreck discovered an ostrich farm. Farmer boy Rube had never seen such an animal and was fascinated with how big and fast it was. The farmer had a young son, and Rube watched as the boy rode the ostriches bareback. Naturally, Rube thought he would try it. It must have been quite a sight, with the six foot, 225 pounder attempting to clamber on and ride the animal. In any case, the ranch owner was not pleased when he saw what Rube was doing. The ostriches never said how they felt about it, but Rube and Schreck were summarily tossed off the ranch.

Undaunted, Rube and Schreck next took up alligator hunting. The two were out in a canoe scanning the swamp water. Rube thought he saw something just off the right side of the canoe and decided he would reach for it. He found something, all right: it was an alligator, and it took quite a nip at Rube's hand. It was his right hand, fortunately. Rube and Schreck headed for Jacksonville with Rube's big right hand all bandaged up. Mack was delighted to see them, of course, though the sight of Rube's paw gave him a jolt.[1]

Mack and the rest of the team arrived in Jacksonville ready to start work. Mack knew that ballplayers did not always keep themselves in the best of shape in the winter months. He wanted them to come along slowly, lest injuries crop up and hamper their play in the early season. Rube was no exception to the rule, and, because of the alligator bite, Mack felt even more strongly about the need to go easy. Unfortunately, this left Rube with more time on his hands.

While at the ostrich farm in Winter Park, Rube and Schreck saw the farmer had quite a collection of alligators. He raised them and sold them for their hides, and hired someone, usually referred to as a "greaser," to keep an eye on them. Like many so employed, this "greaser" also trained the alligators so he could periodically take his act on the road to circus sideshows. There he would wrestle the beasts and pass the hat to the customers for extra cash.

Rube, as sketched by a Philadelphia newspaperman in 1903. The intensity of the eyes reveals a different person than the childish buffoon many have cast him to have been. His drinking and carrying on would wear him down, but until the alcohol caught up with him he was a marvel, at least on the ballfield (*Philadelphia Inquirer*).

Rube saw what the greaser did with the gators and apparently thought he should try his hand at it, too. Determining how much alligator wrestling Rube actually did down in Winter Park is much like learning from a drunken angler the real length of the fish he caught. Apparently Rube did actually climb into the pens and do some sparring with the gators. After Rube got through talking to the folks down in Winter Park, they were all humming of his many heroic deeds. Subsequently, Rube's gator bragging knew no bounds among the A's in Jacksonville. Schreck said nothing one way or the other.

The same alligator tamer happened to come north to ply his trade among the tourists in Jacksonville, and he hit town the same time the A's were training. Rube went to the sideshow. After all the bragging he had done, he could not pass up an encore without losing face. Rube showed up, and, after the "greaser" completed his act and was passing the hat among the crowd, Rube climbed in and put on his own show. The "greaser" didn't give a hoot if one of the gators bit off Rube's left arm, but he certainly didn't want this idiot to hurt one of the beasts he had trained to fear him. Wanting no one meddling with his livelihood, the greaser sought out Connie Mack. Mack received him and jovially asked, in view of his trade, if he knew "Rube Waddell the famous alligator handler." With that the greaser growled: "What; do I know that stiff of a 'gator eater? Why I got that Rube beaten fifty different ways." The greaser calmed down, but he left Mack a note telling him to keep his pitcher away from his alligators, and threatening, "If he

Ossee Schreckengost (everyone called him "Schreck," though his nickname was "Rocking Horse"). Schreck was Rube's batterymate, roommate, hunting and fishing buddy, and general partner in crime. Connie Mack, himself a former catcher, said that Schreck was the finest defensive receiver he ever saw (and that included Mickey Cochrane). Schreck got along fine with Rube but could not stand the big oaf's habit of eating animal crackers in bed. In 1903 Rube had to sign a contract promising to cut out the habit. (*Philadelphia Inquirer*).

does that again I'll slit his throat."[2] Rube heeded Mack's subsequent advice.

Rube's right hand was slow in healing, so Mack had him do a little jogging and calisthenics. But pitching was out for a while, lest working with his bad hand subtly throw off his motion and hurt his pitching arm. Idle hands may be the devil's workshop, but when the hands were Waddell's, the devil needn't trouble himself. Not far from the A's training camp in Phoenix Park, Rube found a bunch of small pigs. Every day Rube would run over and chase one down, and play with it just like a small child would pet a puppy. Schreck told reporters that Rube was trying to learn "Hog Latin." Rube brought one of the pigs into the camp and kept it as the team's spring training mascot. He named him "Dick."[3]

By March 9, Rube's hand had pretty much healed. Itching to pitch, Rube broke out of Mack's restriction when he learned that Shibe had arranged for the A's to play the Phillies in a city championship series in the week before opening day in April. Rube announced that he wanted to pitch every game. Then he ran out to pitch and began humming fastballs into Schreck. The loud pops attracted a crowd of youngsters. Rube sure looked good, but Mack made him call it off. He still wanted Rube to go easy.

Still with time on his hands, Rube found a racetrack. This one didn't run horses, it ran those new beasts called motorcycles. A race promoter named Jack Prince knew a crowd pleaser when he saw one. He invited the A's to see a race. Naturally, this brought out more people. Rube could not resist the situation, and he climbed on one of the machines. He had no idea what he was doing, but he came out unharmed. He assisted some of the riders with their starts. He made such a hit that the riders made him a track official. The crowd was so taken with the big hurler they clamored for a pre-race speech from him. Rube obliged, and "the large crowd rent the air with cheer upon cheer." Alas, a text of the vital speech did not survive the occasion. Amidst the roar of the engines it is doubtful that many heard it anyway, which was probably for the best.

On March 14, Mack finally let Rube out of his cage. He started an exhibition game against a local team. Rube began lobbing in pitches from all sorts of odd angles and positions. Every once in a while he would burn one home to Schreck and make everyone jump. The small crowd was delighted by the antics. The A's won 20–0, and Rube said he would pitch the next day and guarantee no hits, no runs.[4]

The prediction brought out a good crowd the next day as the A's faced the Jacksonville Cummers. Rube did not quite fulfill his promise; he gave up two hits. The A's won this one 12–0. Rube struck out 14, and would have struck out more had he not goofed around with slow ones in the last innings. In the third inning Rube instructed Schreck to sit on the ground, not in a crouch, just park himself on the dirt. Schreck obliged and held up his mitt, as Rube struck out the next man on three pitches. Rube fielded flawlessly, nailing several runners with throws behind his back. In the ninth, after a couple of innings of slow ones, Rube picked up the pace again. He struck out two. Then he intentionally walked three. With the bases full, Rube ordered all the fielders off the diamond. With just Schreck on the field with him, Rube struck out the last man on three pitches. The crowd chanted "RUBE! RUBE!" and he cartwheeled all the way to the bench. Many gathered around the hero of the day. Several wanted to feel his muscles, with Rube happy to oblige. A few days later Rube did the same stunt, calling in the fielders at the top of the ninth inning. He struck out the side on nine pitches.[5]

The day against the Cummers had gone all too perfectly. In the locker room, Schreck asked Rube to throw him his shoes. Still in a pitching mode, Rube hurled the shoes at Schreck, smacking him in the forehead and opening a nice little gash. Schreck was OK. He got hit in the head in a practice game a week later. He fell like a log, but "Doc" Powers revived him with a little ice. "It will not injure him," Powers assured reporters, "you can't kill him unless you hit him hard." If Schreck could handle Rube, what were a few knocks in the head?[6]

After retiring the side with no fielders behind him, Rube disappeared from camp. No one knew where he'd gone. After a few days the team's curiosity began to grow. By now the possibilities were limitless. Was he back with the alligators, was he fishing, drinking, riding ostriches or motorcycles (or all of the above)? Mack sent various folks out to scout the saloons and other establishments, but no one turned up a clue. There was a rumor that Rube was heartsick over a lost love and had tried to commit suicide by jumping off a bridge. The tale had it that he survived by landing in shallow water which covered four feet of soft mud. It was all untrue, but it certainly made good copy, and papers printed cartoons of a chagrined Rube standing in deep mud with onlookers splitting their sides with laughter.

The A's finally gave up looking for Rube. They figured they'd see him when they'd see him. One night, resigned to the situation, the A's finished dinner at their hotel and turned out on Bay Street. A local minstrel show was doing a promotion with a band parading up the avenue. Standing in front of the hotel as the band approached, all the A's began to grin and shake their heads. Guess who was leading the band? In full scarlet uniform, complete with a furry, three-foot shako hat and baton, was Rube. The boy was good at drum majoring, too. He could do stunts with the baton and throw it high in the air and catch it without missing a beat. Connie Mack, fearing his presence might dampen the occasion, didn't want Rube to catch sight of him, so he crouched down next to a mailbox as the band approached. Rube marched by. Without missing a step, he ducked down for a second and said, "Hey there, Mack," and kept right on going. Mack later commented that he would never forget that look of "ineffable bliss on Rube's face." Some of the A's followed the band to the theater to attend their concert. Rube banged away loudly on the bass drum.[7]

Three days later Mack decided he had had enough. He put Rube on an early train out of Jacksonville. The team would stay to practice, but Rube was to work out in the Eagles' gymnasium in Philadelphia. Boarding the train, Rube looked at the reporters and thanked everyone. "You guys in Jacksonville are just too sociable," he complained. "I have been to all kinds of towns and cities, but this one skins them all."[8] Connie Mack would bring the A's back to Jacksonville for spring training many more times in his long career, but as long as Rube was on the club Mack would never go near the place again.

NOTES

1. *Philadelphia Inquirer*, March 2, 1903.
2. Ibid., March 3, 1903.
3. Ibid., March 3, 11, 1903.
4. Ibid., March 15, 1903.
5. *Philadelphia Record*, March 16, 1903; *Philadelphia Inquirer*, March 16, 23, 1903.
6. *Philadelphia Inquirer*, March 16, 26, 1903.
7. Ibid., March 26, 1903; Pete Martin, *Peter Martin Calls On...* (New York: Simon and Schuster [1936] 1963), p. 51.
8. Article by Bill Foley, Clipping File, Cooperstown.

Chapter 26

Animal Crackers

Before the 1903 season began Mack sat Rube down to go over some contractual matters. Rube signed the standard player contract but with an added provision especially for Rube that Mack insisted he accept. The provision stemmed from discussions with Ossee Schreckengost a few days earlier. Schreck easily came to terms with Mack, but he made one little request — that Rube be forbidden from eating "animal crackers" in bed. In those days, roommates shared a bed when the team traveled. It was standard practice throughout baseball. Schreck was the only man who could live with Rube. But the one thing that got under his skin, literally, was Rube's munching animal crackers in bed. "The big bum has got to where he eats these little animal crackers every night. I didn't mind the flat crackers so much," Schreck complained. "But for a whole week last year I woke up with elephants' tusks and cowhorns stickin' 'tween my ribs."[1]

The mere thought of having to assign another player to room with Waddell made Mack instantly agree to Schreck's odd little codicil. Rube made no fuss about it. He liked Schreck and didn't want to rile him. Not another word was said about the animal crackers, and Rube never ate animal crackers in bed again.

A few days after the cracker deal, Rube did exact a little revenge, not on Schreck but on Mack. The team was still in Florida, and late one night Rube knocked on Mack's door. Mack answered "I am in bed, but come in if you'd like." Rube did, and proceeded to speak some inanity to Mack as he ate a sandwich. While eating, Rube made sure he dropped an appropriate amount of crumbs and other sandwich contents in Mack's bed. The sandwich didn't contain animal crackers, just raw onion and limburger cheese.

Mack had one other item he needed to discuss with Rube that spring. He thought one "Dutch Uncle" talk with the Rube about drinking couldn't hurt. He brought Rube into his room and sat him down. He took out a glass and dropped three live worms into it. Then he poured in three fingers of whiskey. He asked Rube to watch closely, which Rube did dutifully. The worms quickly died, of course, and Mack asked Rube if he understood what he was trying to tell him. Rube smiled and thanked his manager, concluding: "You're just trying to relieve my mind. It's sure good to know that a drinking man ain't never gonna have to worry about worms in his stomach." Rube logic! Mack nodded with resignation and sighed: "That will be all, Eddie."[2]

Time and again, Rube logic would get the best of Connie Mack — and provide humorists and baseball historians with anecdotes for years to come. Bennett Cerf told about the time that Rube, during an A's road trip in Detroit, trashed some hotel property after a night of drinking. The next day, the ever-honorable Connie Mack conferred with the hotel office and determined the cost of repairing Rube's handiwork. An amount was agreed upon, and Mack made the proper restitution. Later that week, after the A's had arrived back in Philadelphia, Mack called Rube into his office. "Edward," intoned Mack, "I'm going to have to fine you $100." "What for?" demanded Rube, who was hardly able to remember much of anything from the road trip. "It's for that disgraceful hotel escapade in Detroit," answered Mack. Rube drew himself back, and with his best Clarence Darrow voice solemnly swore on his own behalf: "Mack, there ain't no Hotel Escapade in Detroit!"[3]

NOTES

1. Quoted in John J. McGraw, *My Thirty Years in Baseball* (New York: Boni and Liveright, 1923), p. 25; see also Jack Newcomb, *The Fireballers: Baseball's Fastest Pitchers* (New York: G. P. Putnam's Sons, 1964), p. 35.

2. Quoted in Milt Shapiro, *Laughs from the Dugout* (New York: Julian Messner, 1966), pp. 73–4.

3. Quoted in Bennett Cerf, *The Laughs on Me; 2000 Stories, Anecdotes, and Amiable Observations* (Garden City, N.Y.: Doubleday, 1959), pp. 90–91.

Chapter 27

A Rocky Start

After such a month of "training" as Rube had taken in March, how would he and the A's fare when the season began? When the A's returned to Philadelphia, all baseball talk about the city centered around two things: the upcoming exhibition series with the Phillies and the fact that few reporters and baseball people were predicting great success for the A's in 1903. Some people had the A's finishing as low as sixth place. Boston was the favorite. Cleveland, St. Louis, and Chicago all appeared strong. Some even had high hopes for the New York Highlanders.

The A's opened in Philadelphia against a couple of college teams — Brown and Villanova. They were supposed to open the series with the Phillies on Saturday April 4. Unfortunately, it rained. Some of the players complained that they should share in some of the receipts from the games with the Phils and threatened to boycott. At first, Ben Shibe and Connie Mack balked, but they worked out a deal and a strike was avoided. The next day was lovely, but it was Sunday, and no such games were allowed in the city. (They did play in St. Louis on Sunday, and the Cardinals upset the favored Browns. McGraw, meanwhile, would not let the Giants play the Highlanders).[1]

The A's-Phillies series finally began on Monday. "The Great and Only Rube Waddell will be in the box, one of the pitching wonders of the decade," announced the *Inquirer*. Wham! The sound of Rube's fastball could be heard all over Columbia Park as he warmed up. He went out and struck out the side in the first inning. The crowd roared its approval. The A's seemed to be picking right up where they had left things in September. "Seemed" was the right word. Rube was fine. Indeed he pitched nine innings of no-hit ball, striking out ten. The only man to reach first base did so in the second inning, as Rube made an error fielding a scratch grounder. Rube had wanted another strikeout, so after he had picked up the ball, he threw to first baseman Harry Davis as hard as he could. Though the throw was a trifle wild, Davis could have caught it, but he misplayed it. Thereafter, Rube pitched perfect ball through the ninth.

Unfortunately, while Rube hurled to perfection, the A's bats were absolutely dead. The Phillies' starter, A's castoff Fred Mitchell, gave up just four hits and no runs. In the bottom of the ninth, the A's had runners on first and third with one out, but they could not bring the run in.

Rube took the mound for the tenth inning with the sense that he should now be holding something in his big left hand besides a baseball. Others would appear to have taken leave of their senses, too. Rube walked the first batter, his old Pittsburgh mate, Doc Zimmer. The next man grounded to the mound. Rube picked it up and took so much time throwing to second that Zimmer was safe. The next batter popped to first. The umpire ruled it an infield fly. For some reason Zimmer raced to third anyway, so Harry Davis caught the ball and ran to second, but the umpire refused to call Zimmer out. He later admitted to the newspapers he was wrong, but in the game the call stood. Rube returned to the mound shaking his head and hit the next man to load the bases. A sacrifice fly followed, scoring one run. The next batter garnered the Phils' only hit of the day, scoring the second run. The A's went quietly in their half of the tenth. So the Phils won 2–0, despite Rube's near-perfect nine-inning performance. All of Philadelphia was scratching its head. One pattern was set, even though Mack did not yet know it: the 1903 A's could not hit.[2]

The series shifted to the Phillies Park at Broad St. and Huntingdon Avenue. Eddie Plank started for the A's. He couldn't hold the Phils, and Mack sent in a rookie, a full-blooded Chippewa named Edward Bender. In Florida the team had quickly come to call him "the Big Chief." This was soon shortened to "Chief," and it stuck. Both Plank and Bender would go on to Hall of Fame careers, but on this day neither could do well. The Phils won again. Mack came back for game three with Howard "Highball" Wilson. Wilson had highballs both the night before and during this game, as the Phils shellacked him for six runs. Bender relieved him and pitched well, prompting war whoops from the A's faithful. The Chief's strong showing didn't matter because the A's again could do little at the plate. The AL champions were down to the lowly Phils three games to none. The Browns had lost to the Cardinals, and in another pre-season exhibition the Brooklyn Dodgers beat the Washington Senators. Dreyfuss was wishing he had played Philadelphia in October, after all. All National League purists were chortling.[3]

Rube bailed the A's out in game four, winning 7 to 1. The only run for the Phils came on a wild throw — Rube's. He had tried to pick a man off first and threw it into right field. When the series with the Phils was first agreed upon by the two managements, some members of the A's had protested, because the extra games were not part of their contracts. With the team playing so poorly, some Philadelphians were beginning to speculate that they were deliberately blowing games in protest.[4] The Phils won again on the 12th to take the series four games to one. The A's had played so badly, and the stories of Rube's high jinks in Florida had spread so widely, that a Cleveland newspaper asked: "What did they go to Florida for, to catch alligators?"[5]

The A's woes continued on April 20, opening day in Boston, Rube's "hoodoo" town. Rube started and lost 9–4. Boston Manager Jimmy Collins devised a strategy to use against Waddell — bunt on him incessantly, make him field his position, and tire him out. Rube always pitched better than he fielded, particularly if his previous evening's training had been indiscreet. Back in Grand Rapids he often fielded brilliantly, but alcohol was already eroding a few skills, particularly those that were not as deeply instinctive as pitching. The night before the Boston game, Rube had been out partying, and his fielding showed it. The A's won the next day, however, and came back to Philadelphia for their home opener, again with the Pilgrims. After the Phillies series and the loss in Boston, a certain darkness pervaded the ceremony as the 1902 pennant was officially hoisted at Columbia Park. Rube lifted the gloom. He struck out ten that day, and the A's won 6–1.[6]

The April patterns would continue. On Saturday the 25th, Rube again faced Boston. He struck out 11 but lost 4–0. The A's just could not hit. Rube felt like an Orphan again. Matters seemed to turn around at the end of the month. On April 28, Rube beat New York and the A's scored seven runs for him. The next day the A's scored 12 runs in another rout of Boston. The hitting seemed better, but while the A's were pounding Boston, another problem cropped up. Rube was nowhere to be found. No one had any idea where he had gone. There were a lot of saloons in Philadelphia, and in the off season Rube had developed a circle of regular establishments as far away as Reading.[7]

Rube finally surfaced on May 6, only it was not at the ballpark. He was down at the police station. Around noon that day Rube had been on Market Street. An express wagon whizzed past him and nearly knocked him over. Rube took offense and ran after the team of horses. He grabbed the lead one by the bridle and led it to the side of the road. The two "teamsters" in the wagon jumped down, and they were not a happy pair. Words turned quickly into fists. Then a policeman arrived. He could not restore peace, so he hauled all three down to the station. Explanations were heard in front of a magistrate, and the judge decided to let all three go. The next day one Philadelphia newspaper noted a little byline on the front page: "Even a policeman can't preserve order in alcohol." Two days later Connie Mack announced to the press that Rube had been suffering from a bad cold but would soon be back.[8]

Rube did come back on May 8 and beat Washington 5–3. He gave up the runs in the first three innings. Thereafter he was unhittable, striking out nine. On May 12 he won a lucky one in Chicago. The game went 11 innings, and Chicago had men in scoring position in every inning after the fifth. But Rube worked out of every jam, striking out 13. After the game Rube walked into the Chicago dressing room and scrawled on the blackboard:

> The only Rube Waddell struck out 13 White Sox today.
> This is a record.
> The other record was 12 strikeouts against the White Sox.
> Rube Waddell also held that record.
> Rube Waddell and Connie Mack travel together.

After the game, Rube went off fishing — without Connie Mack.[9]

Mack did not see Rube for three days. The boy wandered back on May 14, and Mack told him it was his turn to pitch. Mack did not see what Rube had brought with him. Somewhere in his wanderings Rube had purchased a four-foot toy elephant, bright red with white letters. Perhaps Rube felt it was close enough to the White Elephant symbol of 1902, and that it would stir his teammates. In any case, they were not stirred. They just looked at one another nervously. Wherever Rube's mind was that day, it certainly was not on the White Sox. The Sox hit him hard in the first, though no runs scored. In the second, Rube walked the first man. The next batter bunted, and Rube just stood there as the ball rolled by him. The next batter bunted, too. Rube fielded this one and threw the ball into the stands. Three runs scored. In the top of the third it was Rube's turn to bat, and he took the little red elephant up to the plate with him, carefully setting it down right next to the batter's box. A strange kind of silence fell over the ballpark. Rube struck out, and at that point Mack decided it was prudent to put in a reliever.[10]

Some say people can profit from sitting by a calm pond, both literally and metaphorically. The placid lake can be so still that we can see ourselves, and in the calm of such a day the waters of our soul can also grow so still that we can gain a true reflection of our spirits. Writers like Ralph Waldo Emerson and Henry David Thoreau may have believed in such transcendental notions. Rube's sojourns to the lakes either proved them wrong or proved the world to be so cracked that it could not appreciate the higher purposes that were at work in Rube's soul out at the Chicago ballpark on May 14. We'll never know for sure, but Connie Mack was not taking any chances. He put Rube right back on the mound the next day in St. Louis. Jesse Burkett homered with a man on in the first, but Mack was patient. He left Rube in, and Rube went on to give up no more runs while striking out 13. The A's came back with four runs. In the ninth inning Rube ended the game by striking out the side and doing an Indian war dance. The next week Rube pitched two strong wins against Cleveland. "Cleveland Wants No More Waddell" was the headline in one Cleveland paper. At the end of the month against the New York Highlanders, Rube won his fourth straight. He again struck out the side in the ninth inning, this time concluding by dancing a jig. In those four games, Rube struck out 39 batters. On June 1 he blanked Washington, facing only 28 men the whole contest, one shy of a perfect game.[11]

One never knew what crazy stunt Rube would do next. Mack hoped that when Rube was rolling on a hot streak, as he clearly was in late May, nothing would upset his rhythm. Everybody held their breath in early June. Then Rube did something really bizarre. He didn't wrestle alligators. He didn't run off with a minstrel band. He didn't chase a fire engine or even go off on a bender. This new act would prove more self-destructive than any of those. Rube went off and got married.

Sometime in early 1903 Rube had met a woman. Some said they met as a result of her writing him a fan letter. Others said not only had they met by mail, but that they never actually met face to face until Rube presented her with an engagement ring. Rube and a woman were seen buggy-riding around Philadelphia at various times that spring, but whether it was Rube and his newly intended cannot be determined. Right after the Washington game, Rube left Philadelphia for Lynn, Massachusetts. There, he and the former May Wynne Skinner were wed. Rube gave his bride "a magnificent diamond broach." They had a brief reception at the home of the bride's parents. Then they went right back to Philadelphia, with Rube returning to the ball club. The wedding and ceremony had the leisure of a Waddell fastball. The marriage would have the steadiness of a Rube bender.[12]

NOTES

1. *Philadelphia Inquirer, Philadelphia Record,* April 3–6, 1903.
2. *Philadelphia Inquirer,* April 7, 1903.
3. Ibid., April 10–11, 1903.
4. Ibid., April 12, 1903.
5. *Cleveland Leader,* April 20, 1903.
6. *Philadelphia Inquirer,* April 21–22, 1903.
7. Ibid., April 26, 29–30, 1903.
8. *Philadelphia Record,* May 7–8, 1903.
9. *Philadelphia Inquirer,* May 9, 12, 1903; *Chicago Post,* May 17, 1903.
10. *Philadelphia Inquirer,* May 14, 1903.
11. Ibid., May 16, 24, 27, 31, June 2, 1903.
12. Clippings File, Cooperstown; *Philadelphia Record,* June 3, 1903; *Boston Globe,* June 3, 1903.

Chapter 28

Summer of Chaos

When Rube rejoined the A's, his teammates gave him good wishes, but, of course, their attention was on the pennant race. As of June 3, the AL lead was a virtual four-way tie between Boston, St. Louis, Philadelphia, and Cleveland. Each day saw one team climb up, only to drop down a day or two later. No one seemed to be able to break out. Mack looked for something that could ignite the A's and get them in the thick of it. In the previous year, Rube had been just that sort of spark. Mack hoped his newly wedded ace could find some stability and perform again as he had the previous summer. The question was what marriage would do to Rube. Everyone in Philadelphia naturally hoped he would find some constancy. Few were optimistic, however. One writer speculated: "Whether his [Rube's] usefulness as a pitcher will be impaired for the balance of the season remains to be seen. As a rule most bridegrooms play poor ball — during the honeymoon at least."[1]

Rube pitched one inning of relief on June 4, as Detroit beat the A's. The next day he started against the Tigers' ace "Wild Bill" Donovan. Donovan outpitched his rival: fewer walks, fewer hits, more strikeouts, but the A's edged him 4–3. As Rube floated through that victory, it seemed to buoy his sense of invincibility. In his next outing he faced the rival White Sox. He pitched a masterful four-hitter, winning 7–1. In the fourth inning Rube stood in the batter's box and decided to call the balls and strikes himself. The pitcher quickly took advantage and hummed in two strikes. Then he tried to be as playful as Rube and lobbed one over. Rube put the bat on his shoulder and drove the ball deeply to left. He circled the bases and clearly had a home run as he rounded third. Then five feet from the plate he stopped running, fell to his knees, and loudly prayed that the catcher would drop the throw. He was tagged out, and the crowd went berserk. The A's won, however, and they were now in first place.[2]

Rube took his seven-game winning streak back home and on June 12 faced Cleveland and Addie Joss. The *Inquirer* called it "a game future old timers will talk about for years ... the most sensational game of ball ever played in this city." Joss came out with smoke. He pitched a perfect game for five innings. Rube struck out five in the first two innings; he fanned 14 altogether. Each team scored a run in the sixth. That would be all the scoring for a long time. Rube threw perfect ball the rest of the way, and the game went 14 innings. Ollie Pickering homered in the 14th to win it, and fans streamed onto the field to carry him off. The *Inquirer* proposed laurels and a monument to Waddell. Fans had the sense that the previous summer's miracle was about to reoccur. A record crowd of 24,227 came to the park the next day. Chief Bender won the game with a five-hitter.[3]

Rube won again, beating St. Louis 9–3 on the 16th. That made nine in a row for him. He celebrated by winning an ice cream–eating contest. (Rube could down a half gallon of the richest confection without blinking.) He felt invincible. He had not lost in over a month, not since the day of the Red Elephant. Bender won the next day. The A's were now a game and a half up on Boston and were off on a key trip around the western circuit.

Waddell and the A's were in synchronization. They rose together. When Waddell was the best in the game, the A's were a good team. When Waddell fell to the mere status of "good," the A's lost. The positives of late May/early June would reverse themselves on the road trip, as Rube wandered off on several inexplicable sojourns.

Rube's first road outing came in Chicago on June 19. He gave up five runs, and the A's garnered only five hits. Chicago beat Eddie Plank the next day 11–1. The team slinked off to St. Louis. That summer the "Mound City" had been beset by flood problems. And when the A's arrived there, Rube went off for two days, not to repair levees but to try his luck fishing in some of the flooded areas. That endeared him to the St. Louis crowd even less than it did his teammates. The crowd cheered as the Browns beat Waddell 4–3 on June 24.[4]

Without any train wrecks, the A's traveled to Detroit. There, Wild Bill Donovan got one back from Rube, 2–1. Three days later Cleveland bested Rube 4–3. Rube had lost three in a row, each by a single run. The A's headed home. Having begun the trip a game and a half up on Boston, they were now three behind. On the way back to Philadelphia, the team stopped in Harrisburg to play an exhibition game against a local club. They lost that one, too, 4–0. They reached Philadelphia on July 3, with the *Inquirer* running a cartoon depicting Connie Mack pulling a red wagon full of A's. All were sitting glumly. Rube, of course, was only half on the wagon, leaning most of the way out with a fishing line in a puddle of water.[5]

The fans were hoping the home stand would revive things for the A's. A crowd of 20,679 came to Columbia Park to celebrate July 4 and to watch Rube again face Wild Bill Donovan. It wasn't even close. Rube gave up five runs through four innings. The crowd began to yell "take him out!" Rube tightened down from there, allowing no more runs, and at one point striking out six in a row. But the A's bats were dead, as Donovan breezed to an easy shutout. After nine wins in a row, Rube had lost five.[6]

With his team on the skids, Mack turned to Rube after only a day's rest. Rube had come through this way before. He went out and won the game, all right, but the way he won it was not the best thing for team spirit. He took a 6–5 lead into the ninth. With one out, Rube walked two. The next batter popped to Schreck. Then Rube walked a third batter to fill the bases. Many felt he did it deliberately. "Hey Rube," many were thinking, "this isn't some exhibition game in Jacksonville." The next man hit a screaming liner to left. "Topsy" Hartsel was there to catch it. The A's came off the field with a win, but felt like they had been driven home by a drunk who had just missed killing them and upon arrival at the door slurred at them: "See, I told you I could handle it." Morale did anything but rise, and the next day Detroit won 8–7, with Philadelphia committing seven errors.[7]

No one on the A's needed any more evidence of the team's precarious position, nor of the way Rube's behavior contributed to it. Then the fates hit them with a symbolic blow: the death of the Washington Senators' star player, Ed Delahanty. Delahanty was one of the best hitters in baseball. His lifetime batting average was over .340. Philadelphia had a special affection for him, as he played most of his career with the Phillies, twice batting over .400 for them. He had jumped leagues for better money with Washington.

Delahanty had had a drinking problem and a vile temper. On July 5 he fought with Senators manager Tom Loftus when the team was playing in Detroit. He left the team and hopped a train across Ontario toward Buffalo. While on the train Delahanty downed several glasses of whiskey and began running about the Pullman sleeper, threatening people with his razor. The conductor had to eject him from the train at the next stop, in Bridgeburg, Ontario, situated right at the American border on the Niagara River. Perhaps the conductor should have waited until he could put Delahanty in police custody, but the danger Delahanty posed to passengers was too extreme. Drunk, disoriented, likely depressed, Delahanty endeavored to traverse the railroad bridge and cross the Niagara River to the American side. The bridge attendant attempted to stop him, as foot crossings were illegal, but Delahanty uttered several unrepeatable words to the bridge man and pushed him aside. The attendant was trying to contact authorities when he heard a splash. The drawbridge was open. Delahanty had fallen into the river. At the time no one on the train or on the bridge knew the drunkard's identity. The suitcase Delahanty had left on the train would reveal it.[8] The Delahanty family suspected foul play, and rumors flew about the baseball world. But Ed Delahanty had died drunk. Few could candy coat that sad fact, and the implications for Rube and the A's were obvious.

After his rather untidy victory over Detroit, and amidst the unfolding news about Delahanty, Rube disappeared once more. Rumors flew about Philadelphia that Rube had returned to California. But on July 10 Rube reappeared in the seventh inning as the A's were losing to Cleveland. Mack immediately sent him out to coach. The players on both sides were wearing black armbands in honor of Delahanty. Rube had not been aware of the commemoration, so he trotted out to the coaching box without a band. This looked even more untidy. It was ignorant, but not irreverent, though it was taken for the latter, and given Rube's well-known tendencies, it hardly looked good. To top off the day, Cleveland won the game.[9]

Mack sent Rube out the next day. This time the heavens conspired to maintain the A's slide. It was a rainy day. Play was halted several times, but the umpires would not cancel the game. Groundskeepers spread sawdust everywhere, but couldn't keep pace with the rate at which the turf was turning to mud. Players slipped all over the place, and Rube did his share. Cleveland proved the better set of mud horses. Nothing, it seemed, could get the A's rolling again.[10]

Looking for some point of optimism, the *Inquirer* noted on July 13 that on the same day in 1902 the A's were in fourth place, seven back of Chicago. Now they were in second place, five back of Boston. Rube came back on the 14th with "one of his good days," as the *Inquirer* put it with a note of nostalgia. He shut out the White Sox 2–0 with 14 strikeouts. Still, the A's hitting was weak. The next day, however, Chief Bender and Eddie Plank took a doubleheader from Chicago as Boston lost. Now the margin behind Boston was just three games. Rube came back on the 17th and beat St. Louis, striking out 12.[11]

It looked like the veil was lifting from Rube and the A's, but an event occurred during the St. Louis game which clouded matters, particularly for Rube. In the second inning Rube had faltered a bit. He walked three and gave up his only run of the day. Even though it was a home crowd, some of the spectators on the first base side were giving Rube the devil of a time. St. Louis players were even relaying to them suggestions of particular things to say.

The intensity of the language grew after Rube's pitching proved effective and it had become clear that the A's would win. A major reason for the fan abuse was that, with the A's still seemingly mired in a slump, gamblers had gone short and taken bets on the Browns. Many fans naturally resented such people, and the mix in the crowded stands wiped away all civility. With blessings from league president Ban Johnson, Ben Shibe was determined to get rid of the bettors from Columbia Park. Corruption from betting had nearly killed professional baseball in 1877, when scandals revealed fixed games. No one wanted such destruction again. Shibe sent some plainclothesmen over to pinpoint the ringleaders. Mack had first baseman Harry Davis coach first base so he could steadily monitor the situation, too.

With two out in the seventh, Rube was fully in command of the game and decided to answer some of the taunts. He struck out the last man and walked over to the first base side of the stands. Davis had tipped him off as to who was the prime culprit. The fellow was easy to spot: he was wearing conspicuously loud clothes and a big gold diamond ring. Rube yelled a few things, hoping the answer would verify Davis's determination. It did. Rube shouted at him, "I've got you!" and, with his father and wife in the stands, he vaulted the railing, climbed up the rows, and seized the gambler, a well-known ticket scalper named Maurice Blau. Rube landed one good right to Blau's nose and ripped some of his fancy clothes. Then the crowd separated them. "There was murder in the eye of the famous pitcher," rhapsodized one newspaperman. Another said, "Rube shook the gambler like a terrier would a rodent."

Schreck, Harry Davis, and others induced Rube to return to the field. Play was halted for a few minutes as first-year umpire James Hassett met with Connic Mack and Ban Johnson, who was in attendance that day. Play resumed, and, as is so often the case when a good play in the field ends an inning, Rube was first up in the bottom of the seventh. There were a few hisses from the crowd, but they were drowned by the cheers, particularly from the ladies. Men waved their hats, and Rube stroked the first pitch for a double. He later scored. Meanwhile, two plainclothesmen and the A's big grounds-keeper had hauled Blau away. It seemed the evil gambling spirit had now been driven from Columbia Park. Baseball could be fun again, and the A's put the game away.

While the A's "hoodoo" appeared broken by Rube's action, the law still had to do its turn. The next morning, the A's attorney, Lewis Hutt, went before a Philadelphia magistrate. He brought two witnesses who declared that Blau's provocations were extreme, justifying Waddell's actions. Blau sent an attorney who argued, of course, that culpability lay with Waddell. Neither went to jail. Blau and Rube each had to post $500 bond. That was easy for Blau. George Schaeffer, a friend of Connie Mack, posted Rube's.

The matter looked like a win for Rube and the A's, but Ban Johnson still had something to say. He was certainly concerned about gambling but he also wanted to curb vigilantism. He sent Mack a telegram: "I was present and saw the entire occurrence. While Waddell was given great provocation, he must be punished for his action, and perhaps it will be a lesson to clubs to give better protection to their players. I insist that rowdyism must be cut out of

American League baseball, and if that cannot be accomplished one way we must try other methods. Waddell's sentence is suspension for five days." Mack didn't like it, but he had no choice but to go along with Johnson's ruling.[12]

The A's slump appeared to be over, but now the league had suspended Rube for what most saw as heroic, decisive action. Meanwhile, outfielder Danny Hoffman was threatening to quit the team and jump to Los Angeles. Left fielder Topsy Hartsel was hurt. Chief Bender was playing left field when he wasn't pitching. Rumors about a new round of National League player raiding were starting up again, with Harry Davis and Rube mentioned frequently. (Davis led the A's in hitting that season.) Even if all the rumors were false, A's fans wondered how the team would do without Rube. Even more, they wondered how big Rube would react to the suspension.

Without Rube, the A's lost the next day to St. Louis. But then they rebounded to sweep a doubleheader from the Browns and then defeat lowly Washington. The team was to go to Washington, and Rube was supposed to join them, but as they gathered at the Broad Street station, the old question came up: "Where's Rube?" He missed the train. More than likely, Rube had spent the suspension in bars. Mack sent telegrams all over Philadelphia, as well as to Reading and Prospect, to try to locate him. Rube resurfaced on July 23; Mack sent him out against the Senators. He started with four perfect innings, and everyone breathed a sigh of relief. Rube and the A's won easily, but this was against the worst team in the league.[13]

Chief Bender lost to Washington the next day. Two days later the Senators beat Rube 2–1. After the loss came a Sunday off. (Washington never played on a Sunday; no team in the East did, not even New York.) The A's had more games to play with Washington. Rube went to Mack and said he wanted to pitch the very next one to avenge the Saturday defeat. Mack gave him the ball, and Rube tossed a shutout. The next day the *Inquirer* was effusive in Shakespearean praise: "Time cannot wither nor custom stale the infinite variety of Rube Waddell" (after *Antony and Cleopatra*). But no one considered Cleopatra's ultimate fate. For the moment, all seemed well; no slump was resurfacing. There was the lingering, season-long pattern of the A's just not hitting. Rube was pitching well, but Boston was still five games ahead.[14]

After Plank beat Washington on Tuesday, there were two more games in the series. Wednesday's game ended in a tie as darkness fell, so they played a doubleheader on Thursday. Rube won the first one. After it was over, with Plank still not fully rested, with Bender still needed in the outfield, and with the other pitchers undependable, Mack went to Rube and asked how he felt about pitching the second game. Forty-five years later, Mack still remembered the Rubenesque response: "I don't know, let me go warm up and see how I feel." Rube had just pitched nine innings in late July, in the heat of Washington, D.C., no less. How warm did he have to be? Rube went out and won another one. Mack did relieve him in the seventh.[15] Rube had pitched five games in seven days. In another Paul Bunyan act, he had single-handedly picked up the team. After the doubleheader against Washington, the A's trailed Boston by two and a half games.

The New York Highlanders were the next club to come to Philadelphia. Ban Johnson had induced Clark Griffith to leave Chicago to manage and play for the Highlanders. He wanted his new AL team in the big city to do well, draw crowds, and compete with the rival NL Giants, particularly since they were managed by his nemesis John McGraw. Griffith had come through for Johnson, and by late July the Highlanders were a solid team, markedly better than the Baltimore Orioles of the year before. On July 31, Griffith pitched New York to a 3–1 victory over the A's and Chief Bender. Meanwhile, Boston defeated Washington. The next day was critical, and the game pitted Rube against his old Pittsburgh teammate Jack Chesbro. It was a tight game with some odd aspects. Rube fanned 13 Highlanders, and he gave up just four hits, all to one player, shortstop Norman "Kid" Eberfeld. But Eberfeld's hits came on the back of some key walks, and gave the Highlanders three runs. "If I would have walked him four times," Rube reflected, "I would have pitched a no hitter." The A's had two runs going into the ninth. With two out, Schreck touched Chesbro for a triple. Rube was due up next. Could he come through? The Philadelphia fans would never know, because Mack chose to pinch hit with Doc Powers. He flied harmlessly to right field. Boston lost, too. The next day Eddie Plank took one from New York, while Boston took another one from the Senators. Boston's margin over the A's was still two and a half games.[16]

On August 5 the Boston Pilgrims arrived in Philadelphia for a three-game series. The two teams were then to head for Boston and play three more. Everyone knew these six games could determine the outcome of the AL race. Pilgrim manager Jimmy Collins selected Bill Dineen to pitch game one. Mack picked Waddell. Dineen gave up but three hits, Rube gave up four. Dineen struck out seven, Waddell 11. Boston's Patsy Daugherty, their leading hitter that year, had been on an absolute tear, going 17 for 24 in his last six games. Rube held him 0 for 4. The difference in the game was defense. The A's made two key errors. Rube made a mental error in the seventh. After a one-out double, he threw to third on a bunt when Schreck directed him to first. The runner was safe, and then he later scored on a sacrifice fly. The two errors also were costly, and Boston tallied three. The A's again just could not hit, and they were shut out.

Chief Bender came through the next day with a 4–3 win over Cy Young. On Friday the 7th Boston came back and trounced Eddie Plank 11–3.[17] This was certainly not what A's fans had hoped for, but other things began to occupy their attention. After his loss on Wednesday, Rube disappeared again.

After the Friday loss, the team went to the train station to head for Boston. Rube had not been seen since Wednesday, and he did not show up at the station. Mack was exasperated and told reporters that he cared little whether Rube turned up again. That was some statement, coming from the reserved Connie Mack.[18]

On Saturday, as the A's were opening the do or die series in Boston, Rube resurfaced. He was pitching for a team in Camden, New Jersey. Reportedly, he had signed some sort of contract with them and had hurled a one-hitter against Norristown, Pennsylvania, striking out ten. All of Philadelphia yelled a loud "So what!" Still, Rube's troubles the next night soon made everyone forget that bit of silliness in Camden.[19]

On Saturday nights Rube worked in a bar in Camden. He often ventured over there. The owner of the Camden bar had been capitalizing on Rube's drawing power. He had also been letting Rube sleep upstairs. Rube's appearances behind the bar made business boom. While he was tending bar Saturday night, Rube found himself hauled off to jail.

Several things had occurred. Rube was not arrested for failing to show up for work with the A's. That was not the issue. Mrs. May Wynne Skinner Waddell was simply fed up. She had been threatened with being turned out of her boarding house because Rube was far in arrears with his bills there. It was said that the main source of food Mrs. Waddell received from Rube were unfinished bags of peanuts Rube pilfered at the ballpark. Mrs. Waddell had appealed to Connie Mack and Ben Shibe for help. They had been discreet about saying anything to the press about the matter, but they had lent her the services of the team's attorney, Lewis Hutt.

Hutt had Mrs. Waddell go directly to the Camden saloon keeper to see if she could reason with him. He turned her away, telling her Rube was welcome to stay at the saloon as long as he wished. Rube happened to be there at that moment, and Mrs. Waddell asked her husband to come home. He refused.

Hutt then planned to appear in license court to seek a revocation of the saloon keeper's permit and to bring suit against Rube for non-support of his wife. Meanwhile, probably at the inducement of the A's management, George Schaeffer, the man who had posted Rube's bond in the Blau affair, vacated the bond. With that, Rube ended up spending Saturday night in Camden's City Prison.

Rube was later asked about the non-support issue by a reporter. Rube held forth that he was home every night. The reporter then queried a series of "what about's" — when the team is on the road, when you're refereeing boxing matches at various Philadelphia athletic clubs, when you're tending bar over in Camden. Each time Rube nodded in acknowledgment. The reporter finally asked, "But you're home most Sunday nights?" "Oh absolutely!" Rube confidently replied, adding, "except for a couple of hours when I play pool."[20]

While in prison, Rube must have first held the romantic notion that all the boys down at the bar would learn of his plight, chip in the necessary cash, and go down and triumphantly bail him out. After a few hours it finally dawned on him that nobody was coming. Then depression started to hit. Mrs. Waddell told reporters: "It's the first time he has had a chance to do a little pondering, for when a baseball hero is in the midst of a howling mob of admirers, he's got no time to think." The police detective took the opportunity to rub it in: "Rube, you're a fool," he admonished, "and the sooner you know it the better it will be for you. The fellows who pat you on the back call you a fool and a pinhead out of your hearing." In the presence of his wife and several detectives, Rube broke down and cried like a baby. He promised to reform.[21]

Newspapers were full of hope after Rube's release. The *Philadelphia Record* wrote:

> Waddell is easily led astray and his peculiar actions in deserting the club at such a critical time as this is thought to have been the result of temptations hung out by false friends, rather than a deliberate determination to disregard the terms of his contract with the A's. The question now is: How long will Waddell continue to be good? He needs a guardian in every town of the AL circuit, for he has hosts of blood-suckers who call themselves friends in every city.[22]

Connie Mack dearly hoped that Waddell had learned something from this emotional bruising. Like the *Record*, he believed Rube was basically goodhearted, but completely immature. When Rube was released from prison early Sunday morning, Mack wired him a note of forgiveness at the police station. Mack was obviously prepared to make this gesture, so long as Rube showed some proper contrition. The whole effort was a gamble to get Waddell in line. Whether the impact would be long lasting or not, Rube was immediately on the 8:05 A.M. train for Boston.

After winning but one of three in the series in Philadelphia, the A's had lost the Saturday and Monday games in Boston. Mack started Rube on Tuesday. He lost. He gave up two runs in the first, one in the second, and two more after that. The A's offense could generate only one meaningless run in the eighth. Boston had thus won five of six in their week against the A's. Philadelphia had fallen to six and a half games out. The New York Highlanders were only three games behind the A's. Fighting now to stay in second place, the team embarked on a western road trip. If Rube needed more time to "heal" at home, he was not going to get it.

Chief Bender won the first game of the trip in Chicago. Rube started the second game on August 14. He shut out Chicago for five innings, striking out the side in the fourth. In the sixth inning Chicago tried some new tactics. Since they obviously could not hit Rube, they tried just to make contact with the ball, bunting, slapping at it, hoping something could come of it. Left fielder "Ducky" Holmes bunted down to third. Rube left it to third baseman Lave Cross, who was unable to field it in time. Rube struck out the next batter, but Holmes stole second. The next batter bounced one over the shortstop, leaving runners at the corners. Right fielder Danny Green grounded to first. Rube neglected to cover the bag, and a run scored. This flustered Rube, and the gates broke open. A single scored two runs. A double scored another. With a runner on second, Rube threw a wild pitch into the stands, moving the runner to third. When the next batter singled to right, the runner walked in with the fifth Sox run of the inning. Mack yanked Waddell. Meanwhile, Boston beat Detroit.[23]

Two days later Rube's sad state continued in the second game of a doubleheader in St. Louis. The Browns had beaten Chief Bender in game one, so a victory from Rube in game two was important. Certain events surrounding the game heightened its importance. Rube had been engaged by a St. Louis theater manager, William Garen, to perform in a vaudeville show after the '03 season (another side activity which irritated some of his teammates). On Friday, seeking to advertise his theater, Garen had publicly offered a wager of $1000 versus $800 that Waddell would beat the Browns that Sunday afternoon. A young St. Louis pitcher named Willie Sudhoff learned of the wager and grew angry. He asked manager Jimmy McAleer for the start. McAleer obliged. Sudhoff promised $200 of his own money and asked his teammates for the remainder to cover Garen's wager. (With that, Garen grew a trifle unnerved and cut his wager by half.) All this would be illegal in subsequent decades, but in 1903 it was an open, accepted part of the game.

Over the weekend, the Sudhoff/Waddell contest thus built up with great intensity. It took on a David and Goliath aura. The A's drew first blood with an unearned run in the top of the first. In the bottom of the second inning, with one on, one out, Browns second baseman Bill Friel hit one past first. It twisted and spun toward the stands and rolled under the pavilion steps. It was only a short single, but with the added time it took to get the ball from under the steps, both runners took an extra base. Baseball of more recent vintage would have had ground rules for such eventualities. In those days, fielders just had to play through it. The next batter popped a short one to right. Danny Hoffman caught it, but, in his haste to cut down the tagging runner, he threw over Schreck's head into the stands. Two runs scored. From there, the Browns could do absolutely nothing with Rube, but the A's continued their hitless ways. 2–1 held as the final score. St. Louis won the game and the bet.[24]

Eddie Plank beat the Browns on Monday. On Tuesday Rube wanted revenge. He got it. Not only did he win, he struck out 12 and went 2 for 4 at the plate. When the last batter popped to short, Rube dropped to his knees, gazed skyward and intoned a loud monologue, lamenting he had been robbed of the final strikeout. Such efforts at comedy were wearing thin, however. By this point in the season they were doing little but irritate the rest of the team.[25]

Detroit was the next stop. (It was always the same loop: Chicago, St. Louis, Detroit, Cleveland, with each of the four eastern clubs following one another.) On Wednesday rain canceled the game, so a doubleheader was slated for Friday. Bender and Plank lost both ends of the twin bill that day. Now third-place Cleveland was only a half game behind Philadelphia. Mack was out of fresh pitchers, save one. He asked Rube to handle both games, hoping a Herculean feat would lift both Rube and the whole team.

In the first game, Rube hooked up with Wild Bill Donovan in another great duel. The A's put one across for Rube, and that was all he needed, as he blanked the Tigers with six strikeouts and held them to three hits. In the second game, Detroit scored one run in the third. The A's offense produced nothing. In the eighth, with runners on first and third, the A's hit a line drive which struck the shortstop in the knee. The carom went straight to the second baseman, who touched second and threw in time to first. It was a ridiculous fielder's choice, but it tallied a run. With two outs, Danny Hoffman and Schreck singled, and then up stepped Rube. With the best opportunity before him, Rube hit a one-and-one delivery to right. His old teammate Sam Crawford made a great shoestring catch. The A's had four hits that inning, but only one run to show for it. The breaks were just not with them.

Rube went out to pitch in the eighth, his 17th inning of the day. After Lave Cross muffed a grounder at third, Detroit called a hit and run. The batter grounded one at Danny Murphy, who, seeing the runner break, had moved to his right to cover the bag. The ball rolled into right field, and the runner tried to leg it all the way home. The throw was there, and Schreck made the tag. But Schreck looked up and saw the umpire signaling safe. He exploded, and the whole A's team ran out of the dugout. There was no reversal from the umpire, of course. The A's went quietly in the ninth, and Rube's second game was lost.[26]

The next day, Bender lost in Cleveland. The A's were now in third behind Cleveland. With Sunday off, the A's played an exhibition game in Zanesville, Ohio. They lost that one too, 14–5. Thoroughly disheartened, the A's went back to Cleveland to face Addie Joss on Monday. Joss hurled a one-hitter to down Eddie Plank 3–0. Meanwhile, the team was chanting an old refrain: "Where's Rube?" He was supposed to start in Cleveland on Tuesday. He had taken the train with the team from Detroit, but Mack had not seen him since. Rube did not appear for his start. Mack finally saw him at 5:00 A.M. the next morning. Mack declined to ask Rube for one of his lame excuses, he just released him. Rube begged for another chance; Mack refused. "Released" meant permanently dropped from the team, hence free to sign with anyone else. The papers clarified the wording the following day; Rube had been "suspended for the season."[27]

Rube went back to Camden to tend bar and pitch for a local club. He threw a one-hitter against the Dale Athletic Association. Connie Mack and Ben Shibe came to see the game. They claimed they were there to scout prospects, but everyone knew they were there to talk to Rube. Rube struck out 17, did some clowning, and dropped a pop-up in the process. Mack did not need to see any such work, but he wanted to secure Rube for 1904.[28]

Mack did not want to admit that he needed Rube. He still had a team to run for the rest of the season. One Philadelphia newspaper proclaimed, "Baseball loses nothing by Waddell's suspension."[29] The A's did little better without Rube. But the disgust with Rube's antics prompted a kind of denial throughout the Philadelphia baseball world. Rube was responsible for the team's play. Without him they would prove it. The proof, however, focused on a persnickety joy at finishing in second place. Team morale was better, but without an effective Rube there could be no run at league-leading Boston. Mack knew all that. He also knew that a major reason the A's failed to repeat as champions was the drop-off in hitting. In 1902, five of his players batted over .300. This year only Harry Davis did. The team batting average fell from .287 to .264, and the decline did not fully reflect the failure to push runners across at key times. But the patient Connie Mack wisely went along with the popular enthusiasm for the diminished goal of runner-up. He hoped the resentment at Rube would give way to renewed optimism the following spring. The A's did finish second, a half game up on Cleveland, but a full 14 games behind Boston. Boston would subsequently best Pittsburgh in the newly established World Series.

The year 1903 was an eventful one for Rube. He wrestled alligators, chased pigs, rode ostriches, and reportedly attempted suicide. He led a marching minstrel band, acted on stage, tended bar, posed as a department store mannequin, and raced motorcycles. He got married, fought a couple of teamsters on Market Street, brought toys up to the batter's box, and climbed into the stands and slugged an obnoxious fan. Three times he was criminally charged, twice for assault and once for spousal non-support. Numerous times he disappeared from his team, and twice he was suspended from baseball. Throughout all this, his month-shortened season record was 22 wins and 16 losses; his ERA was 2.44. Despite all his time off he led the league in complete games (34), and his strikeout total of 302 was then the best in the history of the game. No one else in the league even topped 200 (Detroit's Bill Donovan was second with 187). Future Hall of Famers Addie Joss and Cy Young *combined* for 302 strikeouts that year, and each was at the top of his game. Besides the A's, the best team strikeout total that year was Boston's 579. Rube thus totaled better than half that of any other team. Not only was 302 an all-time record, other than Rube's half-year total of 210 in '02, no one in the league had *ever* topped 200.

With such a mind-boggling strikeout figure, Rube presented quite a case. Here was a crazy man whose ability was so utterly compelling that folks had to take a chance with him. The fact that a pitcher who puts up such numbers is dropped from a team is testimony to his bizarre character, to be sure. But it is also testimony to the sense of just how much greater people felt the man could have been. As Connie Mack later reflected: "That Waddell, if only he had ever grown up, my my my my goodness me!"

NOTES

1. Francis Richter, *Sporting Life*, June 4, 1903.
2. *Philadelphia Inquirer*, June 5, 10, 1903.
3. Ibid., June 13–14, 1903.
4. Ibid., June 20, 25, 1903.
5. Ibid., June 28–July 4, 1903.
6. Ibid., July 5, 1903.
7. Ibid., July 7–8, 1903.
8. Ibid., July 6–9, 1903; see also Mike Sowell, *July 2, 1903: The Mysterious Death of Hall-of-Famer Big Ed Delahanty* (New York: Macmillan, 1992).
9. *Philadelphia Inquirer*, July 11, 1903.
10. Ibid., July 12, 1903.
11. Ibid., July 15–18, 1903.
12. *Philadelphia Record*, July 18–19, 1903; *Philadelphia Inquirer*, July 18–19, 1903; *New York World*, July 18, 1903.
13. *Philadelphia Inquirer*, July 20–23, 1903.
14. Ibid., July 24–28, 1903.
15. Ibid., July 28–30; Clippings File, Cooperstown.
16. *Philadelphia Inquirer*, August 1–4, 1903.
17. Ibid., August 6–8, 1903.
18. *Philadelphia Record*, August 8, 1903.
19. Ibid.
20. Clippings File, Cooperstown.

21. *Philadelphia Press,* August 10, 1903; *Philadelphia Record,* August 8–10, 1903; *Philadelphia Inquirer,* August 8–10, 1903.

22. *Philadelphia Record,* August 10, 1903.

23. *Philadelphia Inquirer,* August 14–15, 1903.

24. Ibid., August 17, 1903.

25. Ibid., August 18–19, 1903.

26. Ibid., August 21–22, 1903.

27. Ibid., August 23–26, 1903.

28. *Philadelphia Record,* August 30, 1903.

29. *Philadelphia Press,* August 27, 1903.

Chapter 29

Unhand That Woman!

Back in May of 1903, the enterprising St. Louis theater manager, William Garen, had signed Rube, at $40 a week, to perform at his theater after the season ended. When Rube signed on, many speculated as to what parts the Rube could play. The *Philadelphia Inquirer* speculated about him standing in the mists next to a grave, holding a ball, and soliloquizing: "Alas poor baseball..." Garen chose a lower level of drama and featured Rube in an 1890s melodrama entitled *The Stain of Guilt*. Between acts Rube also appeared in an especially programmed tableau entitled "Reuben Striking Them Out."

The Stain of Guilt was an eminently forgettable play, typical of the stilted Victorian emotions of the theater of the era. The plot concerned a woman torn between a good and bad suitor. Contrary to the dictates of typecasting, Rube did not take the role of the bad one. He played the heroine's simple, but kindly brother.

In one of the climactic scenes of the play, the bad suitor has the noble girl in a compromising situation when, in the "Ta-Daa" nick of time, Rube enters. Often he did so wearing his baseball uniform. Audience cheers inevitably greeted him when he stepped on stage. In this thrilling scene, Rube was to stride forward and loudly exclaim: "Unhand that woman, you cur!" Then he was to deliver a hard punch to the villain and save his noble sister.

The play met with great box office success. Serious drama critics made little comment. The play ran into trouble, however, because Rube could not master the art of the theater punch. Likely he was the only man in the theater taking the drama with any seriousness. Rube found some time in the summer when the A's were in St. Louis to rehearse with his stage colleagues. At the first rehearsal, Rube threw such a powerful left hook that the actor playing the villain was knocked over the footlights and into the orchestra pit. This happened several times in actual performances. The director and the other actors coached Rube, and the "villains" kept pleading with him, "Just touch me and I'll fall." Rube responded to this coaching about as well as he did to Connie Mack's.

The play's director, Joe Finnigan, tried to eliminate the punch, using a little wrestling instead, but the result was the same, as actors found themselves tossed into the orchestra like so many sacks of potatoes. Wrapping Rube in a chivalrous robe and sword was another idea, but that made the villains even more nervous. They were spared a punch only once, when Rube stepped out in full baseball uniform and a boy in the gallery shouted "Throw it here, Rube!" Rube instantly went into his windup. The crowd roared, and the evening's play came to a screeching halt. Some nights, of course, Rube failed to appear and was found tending bar somewhere down the street. Even so, the troupe took the play on the road to Chicago and New York, and they packed the houses wherever they went.

In the cinema version of Neil Simon's play *The Odd Couple*, a scene takes place in which the New York Mets pull off a triple play, a play which sports reporter Oscar Madison misses because of a needless phone call from Felix Ungar. Whether true or not, the story goes that during the filming the director asked Pittsburgh Pirates great Roberto Clemente to hit the ball to third that would start the 5–4–3 double play. Given Clemente's incredibly accurate batting skills, this was going to be a simple matter to film. But baseball instincts reportedly took over, and every time Clemente stepped up, he knocked the ball into the seats. The director finally had to turn to Bill Mazerowski (who hit only one good home run in his life). Maz reportedly grounded it right to the third baseman on the first take.

Like Clemente, Waddell's instincts kept taking over in *The Stain of Guilt*. While Roberto may have been wasting film and baseballs, Waddell was knocking out some of the actors. Rube's *theatre verité* was so fearsome, that the troup began to run low on actors. Men could not or would not take the part of the villain, and the production had to close prematurely.[1]

After the play closed, Rube stayed in St. Louis, tending bar at a local, and now ever more popular establishment. He was content for the winter months. His wife remained thrilled at the continued neglect.

NOTES

1. *Philadelphia Record*, August 14, 1903; *Philadelphia Inquirer*, May 20, 1903, October 2, 1903; Pete Martin, *Peter Martin Calls On...*, p. 50; Ed Burkholder, *Baseball Immortals* (Boston: Christopher Publishing House, 1955), p. 37; Clippings File, Cooperstown.

Chapter 30

Coon Hunts and
Straight Baseball

As Connie Mack anticipated, by the time spring training rolled around in 1904, the Philadelphia sports fans were ready for a new season and seemed prepared to accept Rube back into the fold. Commenting on the physical conditions of the various players at the outset of spring training, the *Inquirer* jauntily noted, "The Rube will not have the slightest trouble in working off his surplus *avoirdupois*." Had Rube turned his life around? Again, the *Inquirer* was careful to note positively that as Rube and the A's gathered at Broad Street Station to head off to train, "Mrs. Waddell was there to see him off."[1]

Remembering the zaniness of Jacksonville, 1903, Mack sought a different site for the A's training, one with few distractions. Maybe the name of the town resonated in regard to his desires for the team, but Mack took the A's to Spartanburg, South Carolina. Spartanburg was indeed a plain, tiny town in a rural setting. There was one school in the region, tiny Wofford College. There was little to do but play baseball. The locals' diversions were fishing, hunting, and "coon hunts." As Mack recalled from the Milwaukee days, if Rube's muse turned him only to fishing he would play great ball.

In Spartanburg, the A's played ball. Otherwise they went native. Rube and Chief Bender did a lot of horseback riding, at which both were very good. Naturally, Rube made his mark on the locals but did generally healthy things. The *Inquirer* noted that Rube "has become a great favorite with the residents down here, and but for the fact that he has to go through some training motions, he could spend all his time in fishing and gaming." He always went out late in the afternoon after practice and returned at sundown with ducks, quail, and fish. The team ate well that month.[2]

Rube and his fishing buddy Schreck did not go in for the coon hunts, however. It wasn't that Rube and Schreck were averse to the idea of hunting raccoons. A coon hunt had nothing to do with raccoons, anyway. It went this way: Lave Cross and a few other of the more "urbane" A's bought Roman candles and shot them off in the direction of the left field fence. Then began the "coon hunt," as the Republican *Inquirer* described to the smirking delight of a lot of Philadelphia's Main Line readers: "The boys made a charge on the colored men and pickaninnies who were basking in the sun on the bleachers. The [Roman candle] balls fell short, but the result was as though they had landed. The colored people showed more activity than you would have thought them capable of.... Taking it all together, the charge was a brilliant success."[3] Rube and Schreck were not part of the coon hunting crowd. They spent some time lounging out in the sun with the bleacher folks. The *Inquirer* photographed Schreck in shockingly friendly pose with one of the local "coloreds." The stern post–Victorian moral code of the rising Philadelphia middle class involved a strict drawing of the color line in all matters social. It also demanded non-abuse or outright abstinence from alcohol, and an outwardly chivalrous treatment of women. Rube and Schreck violated all the rules.

In 1904 the middle-class sports world, in Philadelphia and elsewhere, was experiencing the rise of black boxer Jack Johnson. Former champions like John L. Sullivan and then-champion Jim Jeffries were notorious for their hatred of blacks, in America or anywhere else. Sullivan refused to fight several great black fighters of his day, and several were considered to be his equal, especially the Australian champion, Peter Jackson. While champion, Jeffries refused to fight Jack Johnson. He did fight him eventually, but only after Jeffries had retired and Johnson had taken the crown from one of his successors, Tommy Burns. Both Sullivan and Jeffries would have fallen in popularity had they shown any less virulence in their racism. Boxers embodied the atavisms which middle-class men believed they otherwise controlled. Savage forms of racism lurked just beneath the smooth veneer of middle-class propriety. Neither boxers nor overt racism were terribly welcome in polite company, yet both were nurtured behind the masks. Baseball players were evolving away from the status of nasty boxers, but they were not yet too far removed. And in a few years, Ty Cobb would greatly slow this evolution. Part of Rube's unsettling impact on the sports world was that he lay outside all the mores of the day, including those which subsequent generations righteously damn. A lesser player of his nature would have been sent packing. But Rube's incredible athleticism forced a contending with his incongruous ways.

In rural South Carolina, Rube clashed with no veneer of bourgeois sensibility, for little existed. He endeared himself to the locals with his skills with a gun and a fishing rod. He also gave them one especially joyous afternoon on the ball field. In an exhibition against the baseball team of Wofford College, after Eddie Plank and Chief Bender pitched the first six innings, the crowd rose in delight as Rube came in for the final three. The A's had scored two runs, and on an error they had allowed one to the Woffords. Rube held them through the seventh and eighth. In the ninth Rube walked the first batter named Harry Bradham. The walk may have been deliberate. As Rube struck out the next two batters, Bradham stole second and third. With the tying run on third and two out, Rube motioned his players off the field, leaving only Schreck to keep him company. Then he motioned the crowd onto the field. They gathered around the baselines. Had the next batter connected sharply with one of Rube's shoots, someone could have been seriously hurt. But Rube wasn't worried. He knew he had the batter at his mercy, and this was a crowd that had adopted him. He wasn't going to let anyone be hurt. The first pitch came — strike one! The intimate crowd let out a roar. The next pitch had the same result and an even bigger roar. With two strikes, Bradham figured his teammate had as little chance of hitting Rube as anyone in the park. So when Schreck tossed the ball back to Rube, whose left-handed stance left him facing a little toward first base, Bradham raced for home. If Rube did not instantly see what was going on, the crowd certainly tipped him off. Rube winged it back to Schreck. Bradham was out, and the Spartanburg crowd went home with broad smiles on their faces. Like Jacksonville, Spartanburg was yet another city where for years thereafter parents described to their children what the great Rube Waddell did when he visited their town.[4]

Mack and the A's left Spartanburg with everyone in good shape, ready for the season. They stopped off in Richmond, Virginia, where they played a team from Montreal. Afterwards, Rube took the team to the theater. Rube was able to use his actor's card to secure his teammates the best seats. Rube was still a "corker," but the team and the press were confident that he, and thus the team, were ready for a season of serious baseball. "Last season," noted the *Inquirer*, "Rube was not always himself. His theater venture did much to distract his attention.... This year Rube is going out to break all his previous records. There will be no sideline diversions for him this year, just plain, straight everyday baseball. And when the Rube is hooked up that way, he is practically invincible."[5]

Rube would give Philadelphia a season of straight, everyday baseball. Only one pitcher in the league (Cy Young) would win more games. Rube would set a strikeout mark that would not be broken until the major league season was lengthened. But the season would be a "dud" for the A's. Weak hitting would continue to plague them.

NOTES

1. *Philadelphia Inquirer*, March 13, 15, 1904.

2. Ibid., March 25, 1904.
3. Ibid., March 18, 1904.
4. Ibid., March 25, 1904.
5. Ibid., April 4, 1904.

Chapter 31

The Cy Young Series

One of the highlights of the 1904 season involved the duels between Rube Waddell and Cy Young. They squared off four times that year. Of the four duels, only one was even a trifle lackluster. The rest were truly memorable. The first occurred early in the season, on April 24. Both teams had high hopes. The A's expected to contend for the pennant as they had in 1902. Boston, of course, was the defending champion. At the outset of the first April game, Rube started blazing. He had a perfect game going for five innings. Meanwhile, the A's had put two runs over in the first inning. Thereafter, Young completely handcuffed them. After the first, the scoreboard man hung up nothing but 0's and the fans heard only the loud pops of Young and Rube fastballs as they hit their catchers' gloves.[1] Round one went to the Rube, 2–0.

The next time Rube and Cy Young squared off was on May 5. Both teams' expectations for a strong season were proving true, and they were in the thick of the early-season scramble for the lead. Three days before, Rube had pitched a one-hitter against Boston. The Pilgrims' one hit had been but a limp, slow roller in the fourth inning, which Rube actually could have fielded, with the runner legging it out for Boston's only single. The only walks Rube yielded came in the ninth inning, when he got a little cocky and the outcome of the game was certain. In the wake of the one-hitter, Rube was feeling utterly full of himself, even by Rube standards. Just before the May 5 game, he strutted haughtily in front of the Boston dugout, bragging about what he was going to do to them. "I'm going to give you the same thing I gave … the other day." George LaChance was on the bench, but he refused to come out and wrestle. Cy Young heard every word, however, and he got his own dander up a bit. Old Cy didn't need to do any wrestling; he would let his pitching speak for itself. "I'd been watching him," Young recalled. "He was a damned fine pitcher, but he ran his mouth quite a bit. I figured he was calling me out and I had better do something about it."

Rube went out and pitched well, though Boston touched him for three runs. Meanwhile, Young gave up no walks, he hit no batters, the Pilgrims made no

Rube on the practice field in 1904. The original caption of this photograph states: "The Erratic Twirler of the Philadelphia Athletics who is, without doubt, The Champion Strike-out Pitcher of the Country." Rube was indeed the most feared pitcher in baseball. In an era when hitters swung not for the fences but only to make contact, homeruns and strikeouts were more rare. Yet in 1904 Rube would strike out 349, a mark that would stand for 60 years, even as home run swings made strikeouts increasingly commonplace and the season lengthened. Rube's total of 349 was more than half the number compiled by any other team in the league that year; the next best individual total was 180 by Cy Young (National Baseball Hall of Fame Library, Cooperstown, N.Y.).

errors, and the A's got no hits. It was the first perfect game in the history of modern baseball. Young modestly recalled, "I had good speed and stuff." There had been two perfect games back in 1880, when pitchers threw from just 45 feet away and could "run up" their deliveries like cricket bowlers. But no modern pitcher had ever reached the perfection Cy Young achieved that day against Rube. None could ever surpass it. Fittingly, Rube was the 27th man to face Young in the ninth inning. With a 2–0 count Rube flied harmlessly to right field. As he rounded first and trotted off, Rube doffed his cap to Cy. In Young's next outing, against Detroit, he pitched a no-hitter for seven innings, and went on to throw a 15-inning shutout, finally winning 1–0. That made 16 no-hit innings and 24 scoreless innings in two games. Cy Young was a "damned fine pitcher" too.[2]

Through June, Rube was still his cocky self, blazing away with a record setting season strikeout pace. He tried to pitch three days in a row against Chicago but lost two of the three. Then he ran off a string of victories in mid–June, which were the A's only victories in the middle of that month. After he beat Detroit on June 16, Rube wanted to face the Tigers the very next day. Mack refused, and started Bender instead. The Chief lost. Rube was strong, but the A's were not. Boston, meanwhile, had raced to the league lead, with Cleveland, New York, Chicago, and Philadelphia bunched tightly from second to fifth.[3]

Philadelphia ventured up to Boston on June 23, hoping to pull out of their doldrums and gain some ground on the Pilgrims. Cy Young was waiting for them, and the Pilgrims were waiting for Rube. They pounded Rube for six runs in two innings. Mack relieved him. Young actually gave up six runs himself, but Boston won by a run. The A's won the next two. Rube and Bender then beat Washington a couple of games. Despite the loss to Young, things were looking up, and Boston was due in for a series in Philadelphia.[4]

The first game with Boston brought Rube and Cy Young together for the fourth time in ten weeks. The day was rainy, and several times fielders slipped while making plays. Rube and the A's were up 3–2 in the eighth. Rube slipped while fielding a grounder. His throw sailed into the outfield, and the runner ran the circuit, tying the score. In the ninth his old wrestling buddy LaChance singled. After a bunt sacrificed him to second, catcher Lou Criger hit one to right. LaChance legged it home. Danny Hoffman's throw appeared to be in time, but the umpire rule safe. Schreck kicked, but the call stood. Young held the A's in the bottom of the inning to win his third from the Rube.[5] They would meet again.

It was simply not in the cards for the A's to make a sustained run at the Pilgrims that year. There would be a few spurts, but the hitting just wasn't there. Aside from first baseman Harry Davis, none of the A's batted above

.300, or even above .290, and Davis was hurt much of the summer. Monte Cross batted an anemic .189, and Schreck slumped to an abysmal .186. In addition to Boston, other teams were quite tough that year. The race came down to Boston and the feisty New York Highlanders, led by Clark Griffith and spitball wizard Jack Chesbro, who expectorated his way to a phenomenal 41 victories that year, a modern-era record. Boston would finish the season a mere game and a half up on the Highlanders. Wherever the A's went, people came out to see the blazing Rube. Otherwise, the team was largely a middle of the pack ball club that year, finishing 12 back in fifth place.

One game against Detroit was clearly a Rube day. He shut out the Tigers 5–0. At the plate Rube went 3 for 4. In his first at bat he hit a hard liner to center that flew directly to the outfielder. Otherwise, everything fell Rube's way. In the fifth inning, with Schreck on second base, Rube strode up to the plate. Knowing he was clearly on a streak, Rube defiantly motioned at the fielders to move back, way back. At the first pitch, Rube took a mighty cut. He barely nicked the ball, and it popped almost straight up. The pitcher and the catcher both ran for it. They collided, as the ball dropped a mere two feet in front of home plate. As they lay there in confusion, Schreck scored, as would Rube later that inning. Rube had things going for him all right, but the A's sure didn't.[6] When Rube was going off on his toots, as he did so often in 1903, the A's were in contention, and everyone lamented how a steady Rube could have made the difference. Now Rube was steady, for him anyway, and the A's were mediocre.

The only low point in the season for Rube came in a game against St. Louis on August 2. A second baseman for the Browns named Harry Gleason stepped in. With Gleason batting in a crouched stance, Rube figured he could smoke one by the kid. But Rube's pitch curved into Gleason, and Gleason reacted by trying to duck. The ball caught him behind his left ear. Gleason instantly collapsed, and both sides rushed to the plate. Rube insisted on helping carry Gleason off the field. Ice was immediately applied. But as blood started coming out of Gleason's ear, Rube was completely unnerved. He finished the game, striking out only four, one of the few low marks for a full game Rube would record that year. His heart just wasn't in it that day, nor was anyone else's. Gleason eventually recovered, though the next season with the Browns would be his last in the majors. Two years later Danny Hoffman was beaned. Everyone rushed out but stood helpless. Rube rushed off the bench and carried Hoffman out to the street, flagged down a vehicle, took him to the hospital, and sat there with him all night, applying ice to his head. Danny also recovered, and played until 1911. Though he lived only another 11 years after he retired, for the rest of his 42-year life, Hoffman said he owed what longevity he had to Rube.[7]

Rube continued to win. The A's made a modest run at the league leaders in mid–August. At one point New York, Chicago, Boston, and Philadelphia were only two and a half games apart. At that point in the season, the A's returned to Philadelphia after a 10 and 2 road trip. Two thousand people had turned out at the railway station to greet them. At the end of the month, some patrons invited Rube and several others to a big celebration in the woods near Reading. Many thought "Uh-oh, there goes Rube." But Rube was back the very next day to beat Chicago, striking out five of the first six he faced.[8] Rube continued to come through. The team's weak hitting just could not sustain anything.

On September 15 the A's were seven games out of first place. Rube was pitching against Washington. In the second inning Rube chased a runner caught between first and second base. The runner tried to duck under the tag. Rube got him, but he tripped and tumbled onto his right shoulder. He had to leave the game. The diagnosis was a slight separation, and for the first time in his life Rube had his arm in a sling. "Out for a few days" was the team's prediction. "A few" turned out to be "12," during which time the A's went 3 and 8, ending what flickering chances they had to climb into the race. With little to do, Rube hoisted a few and managed a bowling alley. He came back on September 29 and pitched against the Browns with his right arm and shoulder still swathed. He looked odd, but only three Browns reached first base that day.[9]

The season would likely not have turned out too differently had Rube not gotten hurt. Boston edged out New York for the pennant. Arrogantly, John McGraw refused to let his NL champion Giants play Boston after the season, so Boston claimed the sport's championship by default. Since then, there has only been one other missed World Series.

That winter everyone wondered what would have happened if the Pilgrims and the Giants had squared off. Then and since, baseball people have wondered even more just how many strikeouts Rube could have added to his 349 total had he had the four or five more starts from which the injury kept him. So often with the Rube come the words "what if."

Regardless of the missed starts in September, Rube's 349 strikeouts in 1904 was phenomenal. As in the previous season, his total bettered half that of any other team in the league. New York's Jack Chesbro was a distant second, 110 behind the Rube, and Chesbro pitched 72 more innings.

The '04 season, coupled with the previous year, despite all the zany antics and suspensions, left Rube with another mark few pitchers would match — two straight years striking out more than 300 batters. Few pitchers ever struck out 300, the equivalent of a batter hitting 50 home runs in a season. Fewer yet have done this twice, and no one until Sandy Koufax would do it two years in a row. Rube can be called the Babe Ruth of strikeout artists, and Koufax the Mark McGwire. (Koufax, like McGwire, broke the record in a longer season, but he passed Waddell's mark within the number of games Waddell had in 1904.)

Rube's 349 strikeouts not only stood for decade upon decade, few even approached it. Walter Johnson's best was 313. Christy Mathewson never topped 267. Lefty Grove, Carl Hubbell, and Dizzy Dean never approached it. The great Bob Feller made a run at it in 1946, now in an era in which swinging for home runs was normal and the number of strikeouts in the game had risen. Feller actually thought he had broken Waddell's record. He was having an outstanding year, and with the pennant out of reach, Cleveland manager Lou Boudreau began giving his ace lots of extra starts and some relief stints in August and September so he could go after Rube's mark. So arrogantly conscious was Feller of the record that he actually chastised hitters he felt were deliberately trying to save themselves from being fanned. Feller finished the season with 348. At that time, the official record had Waddell at 343, but in the off-season, baseball statisticians ran over the box scores carefully and corrected Rube's figure to 349. After 40 years, the Rube still stood at the top of the mound, and until the season was lengthened no one would topple him.[10]

NOTES

1. *Philadelphia Inquirer*, April 24, 1901.

2. Ibid., May 6, 11, 1904; see also Donald Honig, *The Greatest Pitchers of All Time* (New York: Crown, 1988), p. 45.

3. *Philadelphia Inquirer*, June 5–18, 1904.

4. Ibid., June 22–24, 1904.

5. Ibid., June 30, 1904.

6. Ibid., July 28, 1904.

7. Ibid., August 3, 1904; Pete Martin, *Peter Martin Calls On...*, p. 52; Howard Liss, *Baseball's Zaniest Stars* (New York: Random House, 1971), p. 48.

8. *Philadelphia Inquirer*, August 27–30, 1904.

9. Ibid., September 16–29, 1904.

10. *The Sporting News*, October 9, 1946.

Chapter 32

Mardi Gras

Connie Mack and John Shibe may have thought Rube had reformed in 1904. On the other hand, maybe they just weren't thinking, given the site they chose for the A's 1905 spring training — New Orleans. They did bring trainer Frank Newhouse along, however, and his principal duty was to look after Rube.[1] He did not do a very good job.

Rube reported to the train station on time. He was a trim 212 pounds, "never in better shape," he proclaimed. He was rarin' to go, and for more reasons than he let on. He had spent much of the winter in Lynn, Massachusetts. He stayed in great shape working as a woodchopper in Lynnfield Woods. He made himself something of a hero in Lynn with one of his fireman escapades. During a local blaze, Rube rushed into a house. The house had an oil stove. If it exploded the whole house would have been lost. Rube grabbed the stove, and it was hot. He heaved the whole thing out the window, and it landed harmlessly in a snowbank. That the stove did not badly burn his hands or explode as he manhandled it was a complete miracle. Rube's other doings that winter in Lynn were neither heroic nor miraculous.[2]

While in Lynn, Rube tried to save something of his marriage. That didn't work out too well. He lived with his wife after moving there in October, but by December he had moved out and was living with his in-laws in the town of Peabody. That did not work out well, either. Rube was making money chopping wood, but he spent it all at the local bars. Rube's father-in-law, Edward Ross, grew irritated with his presence. In early February, Rube decided to move out. On the evening of February 8, he arrived at the house, drunk and with an expressman and a wagon. Obviously knowing Rube was leaving, Mr. Ross inquired as to what Rube was going to do about his "board bill." Rube never liked to hear about debts, and, drunk as he was, he found this inquiry especially irksome. He flew into an absolute rage. He grabbed a flatiron off the stove and pummeled Ross in the head and stomach. Mrs. Ross tried to intervene with a broom, but Rube dropped her with a chair. This raised the ire of Mrs. Ross's big Newfoundland dog, who attacked Rube, tore his trousers, and took a bite out of his big left arm. Waddell was able to punch the dog, grab his trunk, and, while bleeding freely, head down the road with the rather dazed expressman. Mr. Ross secured help from neighbors. His wife was not injured, but he had lost six teeth, his eyes were blackened, and had lacerations on his face and contusions to the stomach and limbs.[3]

Rube said a not-too-fond farewell to Massachusetts, got out of town fast, and headed for New Orleans. Such bizarre bouts often brought out the best in Rube's athleticism. The 1905 season would bear this out. For now, though, it was Mardi Gras time.

The thought of Rube Waddell going South to train during Mardi Gras is mind boggling. On the way down, Rube and the boys had a gay old time on the train. The railway people did not plan for the realities of traveling with a team of hungry athletes or with the Rube. Halfway to New Orleans the food ran out. When the train stopped at King's Mountain, Tennessee, the ravenous A's ran into the little train station and ate everything in sight. Rube reportedly collared an entire marble cake.[4]

Rube did nothing that outraged New Orleans folks during Mardi Gras. Quite the contrary, he fit right in. "The famous and unique 'Rube' Waddell," as the New Orleans Picayune described him, met the Mardi Gras "Rex," David Hennen Morris. Rube was made a member of the New Orleans "Eagles" Club. One night he joined with a group of masked paraders known as the Jefferson City Buzzards and went out along Canal and St. Charles streets dancing and greeting the many folks gathered on the route. Rube was having one hell of a time. When he pitched against a local team — the New Orleans Pelicans — 2500 left the Mardi Gras festivities to see the Rube perform. "Of massive build, with genial sort of face," wrote the Picayune, "his manner wins the spectator at once. When he makes a wild pitch or gives the batter the best of the argument, he whistles and grins a grin that can be seen from the business office of the park to the clubhouse."[5]

After five days in New Orleans, Connie Mack moved the team up to Shreveport. (It did take a few days to plan and make the move, an indication of how quickly Mack realized his error.) The first night in Shreveport, Rube went out on the town. The team countered, concocting a conspiracy with the local sheriff. Rube woke up the next morning to the sight of the sheriff, who told him his actions of the night before were such that he was to be placed on a chain gang that very instant. He put the irons on Rube. Rube let out a yell, and the sheriff let him scream a while before informing him that the whole thing was a prank.[6] For the rest of the time in Shreveport, Rube went fishing. Mack was happier, and the team got down to the business of training. Rube still did his share of on-field clowning for the locals. There was just no stopping his becoming a celebrity wherever he went.

The A's finished in Shreveport and went on a tour of some Southern cities. As always, fans turned out to see the Rube. In Birmingham, Alabama, Rube pitched a game and then went out on the town. Late that night he was beaten up by a couple of thieves, but he still pitched the next day in Atlanta.[7]

The A's arrived back in Philadelphia on April 1. They played eight exhibition games against the Phillies, splitting them evenly. Rube won one of them on a four-hitter.[8] After a mediocre 1904 and with basically the same team, everyone wondered whether the 1905 season could bring anything special. It would, but it would be bittersweet.

NOTES

1. Recollections of Andy Coakley, *New York World-Telegram and Sun*, March 5, 1955.

2. Jack Newcomb, *Fireballers* (New York: Putnam, 1964).

3. *Boston Globe*, February 9, 1905, p. 1; *Boston Journal*, February 9, 1905, p. 1.

4. *Philadelphia Inquirer*, March 2, 1905.

5. *New Orleans Picayune*, March 5–7, 1905; *New Orleans Times Democrat*, March 6, 1905.

6. Coakley, *New York World Telegram*, March 5, 1955.

7. *Philadelphia Inquirer*, March 20–24, 28, 1905.

8. Ibid., April 1, 7, 11, 1905.

Chapter 33

When the Breaks
Fall Your Way

Whether it was partying at Mardi Gras, being beaten up in Birmingham, not resting afterwards, or pitching too hard in cool weather against the Phillies, Rube began the 1905 season with a sore arm. Mack was loath to start him. The A's would have to commence the season with their ace a trifle lame. Speculation about the new season grew fearful.

The A's first games were on the road, in Boston. Mack sent Chief Bender to open against the Pilgrims, who came out wearing their flashy new red socks. The fans took a shine to the new apparel. The Chief squared off against Cy Young. Rube squirmed a bit, but Mack wanted him to rest. The Chief came through and the A's won. The next day Mack started young Andy Coakley. Coakley had pitched only 11 games in the previous two years with the A's, but Mack still believed he had some promise and wanted him on the staff another year. Coakley gave up five runs in the first three innings that day. Rube was growing so fidgety that Mack relented and relieved Coakley with Waddell. Rube hurled a shutout the rest of the way. The A's came back with four runs in the eighth inning. In the ninth, with two out, they tallied two more. In the last of the ninth Rube shut down Boston for a win. It was a good omen for Rube, and an even better one for the A's. Rube seemed healthy, and the A's showed they could get hits when they needed them.[1]

The A's spent the first week of the season on the road and won every game. By April 20, they were the only undefeated team in the league. John McGraw's Giants were off to a similar start in the NL. When the Giants lost on April 20, Philadelphia celebrated, for not only were the A's now the only unblemished team, it was the Phillies who had knocked McGraw and his ugly New Yorkers off the pedestal.[2]

The A's opened at home on the 21st against Boston. Mack went with Andy Coakley. As earlier in the month, Boston touched up Coakley, this time for four runs. Mack lifted him for a pinch hitter, and in came Rube. Again,

Rube shut out the Pilgrims, and the A's rallied for five runs in the eighth. Rube topped it off by striking out the side in the bottom of the ninth. He had struck out two in the bottom of the eighth, and the papers groused that bad umpiring had robbed him of the third strikeout that inning.[3] That was all that A's fans could find to complain about. It was quite a season's start.

Boston came back with two wins. The April euphoria faded, and the A's fans settled in for the grind of a long baseball season. While such a process is as old as the game, the settling-in process brought a strong tinge of anger to Philadelphians in 1905. The same day the A's lost their second game to Boston, the Giants had been in town to play the Phillies. Like fans all over the country, Philadelphians were unhappy with McGraw's refusal to play Boston for the championship in October. Fans taunted the Giants wherever they went, and Philadelphia fans still remembered McGraw's "white elephant" knock of 1902.

On April 24, as the Giants were leaving the Phillies' Broad Street grounds and heading back to their hotel up Dauphin Street, jeering crowds greeted them along the way. Amidst this, a boy tossed a handful of dirt at the Giants' open bus. He hit catcher Roger Breshnahan right in the face. The big Irish-born catcher was not about to take that. He jumped off the carriage, chased the boy down, and slapped him hard across the face. A crowd quickly gathered. Breshnahan would have been in real peril if the police had chosen to delay their intervention. (Were this New York and the roles reversed, there would likely have been a delay, shown by the "protection" New York's finest gave umpire Bill Nash in 1901 when Jack Warner kicked him.) But the Philadelphia police gave Breshnahan safety. They ducked into a grocery store and called for a covered police wagon. As the police escorted Breshnahan away, fruits and vegetables pelted the wagon. Breshnahan got out unscathed. When Rube had climbed into the stands and hit a known gambler, he was suspended for five days. Breshnahan had slapped a mere boy and received no fine or suspension. All Philadelphia held a grudge against McGraw and the Giants for the rest of the season and then some.[4]

The A's losses to Boston did not precipitate a slump. Their high-flying ways continued throughout April. Particularly important was the fact that they were winning the close ones, often coming up with the right hit late in the game to pull it out. Winners always seem able to do that.

Mack continued to use Rube as a reliever and as a "closer," though there was no such term in those days. Without realizing it, Mack may have worked a little magic in the way the eccentric Rube could best be combined with the rest of the team. With Rube out of the rotation, the A's had to jell as a team somewhat independent of him. Simultaneously, the breaks went their way. They would win, with Rube sometimes coming in from the sidelines. This was similar to 1902, the last time they won a pennant. That year, Rube joined a team with its rhythms already set. This is what Mack inadvertently did in 1905, holding the slightly sore-armed Rube out of the lineup for the first month. In previous seasons, when Rube was fully on the team from the outset, his eccentric ways seemed to prevent the team's most fruitful jelling. Though there were certainly many factors, the A's disappointing showings in 1903 and 1904, as well as the rally the A's made in September of 1903 when Mack had dropped Rube, show that the eccentric one had too strong a personality when placed at the center of a team. Sam Crawford had said "you just could not keep your eyes off him." Tommy Leach was also mesmerized: "I wasn't playing. I was watching."[5] The inexplicable ways team formations occur make a convincing analysis difficult here, but Mack may have happened upon a good prescription. The patterns of 1902 and 1905 are striking, and the results of each year were phenomenal.

With the team in a groove, Mack sent Rube out for his first start on May 4. Several times previously, the *Inquirer* had listed Rube as the day's starter, but Mack had used someone else. Rube was not absent, Mack was just holding him back. The start came against the Washington Senators. Washington was the surprise of the early season, and was contending for the league lead. On May 13, 1904, Washington's record had been 1 and 15. A year later it was 12 and 10. Mack wanted to derail them. He sent out Rube, and the Rube made the most of his chance, tossing one of his patented shutouts, giving up two meaningless hits and no walks. The A's won easily. Eddie Plank faced Washington on May 5. After eight innings, Washington was up 1–0. In the ninth, the A's rallied for two and won. The A's pattern of coming through in the late innings was holding, now with Rube back in full swing. Two days later came even better news. The A's again scored the winning run in the ninth inning, and this time they did it with Rube on the mound.[6] This sure seemed like 1902.

While in Washington, Rube was his old self in other ways, too. Early one morning, a fire broke out in a livery stable near the A's hotel. Mack and some of the A's rushed over. "When we got there," Mack recalled, "who should we see coming out of the second-story window, with a fireman's hat on his head and dragging the nozzle of a hose, but Waddell."[7]

Later in May, Rube pitched against Cleveland. He was winning, but in the fourth he appeared to be heading for one of his balloon rides. Inexplicably, he walked off the mound and sat on the grass. The rest of the team immediately gathered around. They were not going to let Rube take them out of their winning zone. Doc Powers grabbed Rube by the foot and yanked off one of his size 13's. Monte Cross and George Davis kicked him a couple of times. Meanwhile, the Cleveland crowd was jeering, but the team's cohesion was too strong for the noise to make any impact. Rube suddenly began to smile, and he got up and won the game 6–1. The A's were together.[8]

By late May, Washington began to fade from the picture. The A's were left with their expected rivals — Chicago, New York, Cleveland, and of course Boston. After the team gave him a swift kick in Cleveland, Rube set the league ablaze through May and into June. By the time Rube beat Chicago on June 6, his record stood at 11 and 0, and the A's were in the thick of a pennant race.

NOTES

1. *Philadelphia Inquirer*, April 15–16, 1905.
2. Ibid., April 17–20, 1905.
3. Ibid., April 22, 1905; *Philadelphia Record*, April 22, 1905.
4. *Philadelphia Inquirer*, April 25, 1905.
5. Ritter, *The Glory of Their Times*, pp. 35, 51.
6. *Philadelphia Inquirer*, May 2–6, 1905.
7. Clippings File, Cooperstown.
8. *Philadelphia Inquirer*, May 22, 1905.

Chapter 34

Cy Young Again

It took bad breaks and some tenacious play from the Chicago White Sox for Rube finally to lose a game. He started against Chicago on June 9 and breezed easily into the fifth inning. In the fifth with a man on first, Rube ran for a slow roller down the first base line. He slipped on the wet turf. He recovered in time to get the runner at first, but he tried for the lead man. He rifled the throw in time, but he hit the sliding runner in the shoulder. The ball caromed into left field. The runner raced home. Topsy Hartsel tried to throw the man out from left, but he threw wildly and both runners scored.

Rube went back to the mound absolutely red-faced. Sam Crawford once said that opponents tried to keep Rube happy, because if you got him mad they would have no chance. Chicago learned this the hard way for the next few innings. Rube had an expression that people only saw on him when he was fighting a fire. He gave up just two hits and struck out ten over the next six innings. Even Schreck was shaking his head at how hard Rube was throwing. While Chicago was powerless, the A's were having their own troubles with the White Sox's young pitcher, Guy "Doc" White. They scored two in the fifth, but that was it. As the game dragged on, Rube was pushed to the limit. He walked one in the 12th, his only walk of the day. The next man legged out a roller to shortstop. With two on, the next batter connected for a line drive that struck Rube squarely in the stomach. He recovered in time to throw the man out at first. Mack called time. Rube told him he was fine. With runners on second and third, Rube got up and struck out the next man, and the crowd went bezerk. The game dragged into the 14th. Chicago opened with an infield hit to third. The batter went to second on a grounder and scored on a single. The A's opened the 14th with a double, but they were hitless from there. It was a tough loss, Rube's first of the season, and one that showed an eerie sign of a return of the A's old hitless ways.[1]

Rube's next start was another masterpiece of pitching. His opponent was Detroit's Wild Bill Donovan. Donovan pitched equally well. A's fans gave Rube a gift of a safety razor set that afternoon as he stepped up for his first

Cy Young, the winningest pitcher in baseball history. Though nine years Rube's senior, the two hooked up in some memorable duels. (National Baseball Hall of Fame Library, Cooperstown, N.Y.)

BOSTON

	ab.	r.	bh.	tb.	sh.	sb.	po.	a.	e.
Dougherty, lf	4	0	1	1	0	0	0	0	0
Collins, 3b	4	0	2	2	0	1	0	2	1
Stahl, cf	4	0	2	2	0	0	2	0	2
Freeman, rf	4	0	0	0	0	0	2	1	0
Parent, ss	4	0	1	1	0	0	3	1	2
La Chance, 1b	4	0	0	0	0	0	7	1	0
Ferris, 2b	3	0	0	0	0	0	3	3	0
Criger, c	3	0	0	0	0	0	7	1	1
Young, p	3	0	0	0	0	0	0	2	0
Totals	33	0	6	6	0	1	24	11	6

ATHLETICS

	ab.	r.	bh.	tb.	sh.	sb.	po.	a.	e.
Hartsel, lf	3	0	1	1	1	0	2	0	0
Pickering, cf	4	1	0	0	0	0	2	0	0
Davis, 1b	4	0	2	3	0	0	13	0	0
L. Cross, 3b	3	1	2	2	1	1	1	3	1
Seybold, rf	2	0	0	0	0	1	2	0	0
Murphy, 2b	3	0	0	0	0	0	2	5	0
M. Cross, ss	3	0	0	0	0	0	1	5	0
Schreckengost, c	3	0	0	0	0	0	4	0	0
Waddell, p	3	0	1	1	0	0	0	2	0
Totals	28	2	6	7	2	2	27	15	1

Boston —

Runs	0	0	0	0	0	0	0	0	0	-	0
Base hits	2	1	2	0	1	0	0	0	0	-	6

Athletics —

Runs	2	0	0	0	0	0	0	0	x	-	2
Base hits	2	0	0	1	2	1	0	0	x	-	6

Two-base hit — Davis. Left on bases — Boston, 6; Athletics, 5. Struck out — by Waddell, 3; by Young, 5. Double plays — Ferris and Parent; M. Cross, Murphy and Davis. First base on error — Boston 1; Athletics, 3. First base on balls — off Young, 1. Missed grounders and fumbles Collins, Stahl (2), Parent (2), L. Cross. Wild throw — Criger. Umpires — Carpenter and Connolly. Time —1.25.

The box score of a match between Rube Waddell and Cy Young in 1903. Young yielded two runs in the first inning; from that point neither hurler gave up a thing.

BOSTON

	ab.	r.	bh.	tb.	sh.	sb.	po.	a.	e.
Selbach, rf	7	1	1	1	0	0	3	0	0
Parent, ss	6	0	2	4	2	1	3	10	1
Burkett, lf	9	1	3	4	0	0	2	0	1
Stahl, cf	9	0	2	3	0	0	2	0	0
Unglaub, 1b	9	0	2	3	0	0	31	1	0
Collins, 3b	8	0	2	2	0	0	3	4	2
Ferris, 2b	9	0	0	0	0	0	4	12	1
Criger, c	8	0	3	3	0	0	12	2	0
Young, p	8	0	0	0	0	0	0	4	0
Totals	73	2	15	20	2	1	60	33	5

ATHLETICS

	ab.	r.	bh.	tb.	sh.	sb.	po.	a.	e.
Lord, lf	9	0	1	1	0	0	5	0	1
Hoffman, cf	9	1	1	1	0	0	6	0	0
Davis, 1b	9	1	3	6	0	0	21	1	0
L. Cross, 3b	8	0	2	3	0	0	4	6	0
Seybold, rf	8	0	1	1	0	0	5	1	0
Murphy, 2b	8	1	0	0	0	0	4	5	1
Knight, ss	7	0	2	2	0	0	3	4	1
Schreck, c	8	1	3	5	0	0	11	1	0
Waddell, p	8	0	0	0	0	0	0	5	1
M. Cross, ss	0	0	0	0	0	0	1	0	0
Totals	74	4	13	19	0	0	60	23	4

Boston
2 0 0 0 0 0 0 0 0 0 0 0 0 0 0 0 0 0 0 0 - 2
Philadelphia
0 0 0 0 0 2 0 0 0 0 0 0 0 0 0 0 0 0 0 2 - 4

Two-base hits — Burkett, Stahl, L. Cross, Schreck, 2; Unglaub. Three-base hit — Parent. Home run — Davis. Double Plays — Davis and Knight. Parent, Ferris and Unglaub; Seybold and Knight; Collins, Unglaub and Criger. First base on balls — off Waddell, 4. Hit by pitched ball — by Young, 1. Struck out — by Young, 9; by Waddell, 11. Passed ball — Schreck. Umpires — McCarthy and Kelly. Time 3.31. Attendance — 12,666.

The most memorable Young-Waddell duel came, fittingly, on July 4, 1905. The game went 20 innings; both went the distance. Rube gave up two runs in the first, then pitched 19 consecutive scoreless innings. The game quickly became the stuff of legend, and Rube made the most of it. He traded the game ball at a Philadelphia bar for free drinks. By the end of the month a dozen or so other Philadelphia establishments and at least a dozen more around the American League were also displaying "the ball." No one could play the angles for free drinks like the Rube.

at-bat, perhaps symbolic with the close loss he had the previous outing. (Such little gift giving often happened in those days.) Rube and Donovan each gave up only four hits. One of Detroit's was a home run by Rube's old teammate, Sam Crawford. The home run proved enough for the Tigers to win. When the St. Louis Browns shut out the A's the next day, concerns about the A's hitting deepened. No one was worried about Rube, however. His pitching was as tough as ever. He had simply lost a couple of close ones. The A's work at the plate was another matter, and with the loss to St. Louis the team had slipped to third place.

Rube came back with only a day's rest, and he seemed to lift the entire team. He gave up one run to the Browns, and the A's came to life with ten. With two out in the ninth, Schreck defiantly sat squarely on his haunches as Rube struck out the last batter on three pitches. The A's had won without Rube. They had won with him. Now they seemed able to profit from his leadership.

Cleveland was leading the league in mid June, and the Naps (their new team name, from their popular player/manager Napoleon Lajoie) ventured into Philadelphia on June 19. Rube went out and proved invincible through five innings. In the sixth, however, he made a mental lapse. After giving up two hits, Rube bluffed twice on a throw to second. Then he bluffed a throw to hold the runner at first — then as now a balk. With the runners moving up, the man on third scored on an infield grounder. It turned out to be the winning run. The A's then fell five back of Cleveland.[2]

In his next outing against Washington on June 28, Rube seemed to unravel. He was up 3–0 through seven innings, and had struck out eight. In the eighth it all changed. After three singles, a double, a walk, and an error, Washington led 6–3. It was Rube's first bad outing of the season, one in which *he* lost the game. The next day the New York Highlanders pounded Chief Bender 13–4. The promise of the early season team play and of Rube's May-June brilliance all seemed to be fading.

Eddie Plank started the following afternoon in New York. He had a 7–4 lead into the ninth. Then New York began with two sharp singles. Mack stirred. Rube was standing off to the side of the dugout next to the grandstand, chewing tobacco, lifting 200-pound weights, and chatting with the crowd. Mack told him to go in. Two strikeouts later, Willie Keeler stepped up, the tying run. Keeler had hit .432 in 1897. He was no longer that great, but he was still dangerous. But Rube got him to dribble a little one which Schreck easily tossed to first. Rube had saved it, and Mack started him the following afternoon. Rube gave up two runs in the second, but that was it. The A's could only tie it, but Rube did not let up. The A's pushed one across in the 11th. Rube handled it from there. There had indeed been a hint of a team slump, and Rube had expunged it.[3]

No early twentieth-century ball player enjoyed playing to the crowd quite like Rube. Special days brought out the best in him. On July 4 in Boston it was Rube's turn in the rotation. He seemed to be a bit dizzy with the stadium festivities and gave up two runs in the first inning. It was a ho-hum beginning, but then he settled completely. His opponent that day happened to be none other than Mr. Cy Young. He was fully settled, too. Young's first mistake came in the sixth inning. With a man on, Young yielded a home run to the A's big first baseman, Harry Davis. With the score tied, the game went on, and on. Both teams hinted at rallies, but they were snuffed out. Three and one half hours later, the game had rolled into the 20th inning. The scoreboard man had run out of 0's to hang up. No one needed to see them anyway.

At the top of the 20th, Danny Murphy hit one to third. Third baseman Jimmy Collins bobbled it, and Murph was safe. Young beaned the next batter. With two on, Schreck attempted a bunt sacrifice. He popped it over Young's head. Second baseman Hobe Ferris fumbled it, leaving the bases loaded. Up stepped Rube. He hit a hard bouncer right at shortstop Fred Parent. As Parent attempted to throw home he lost control of the ball for a second. He recovered but could only toss it to third. With one run in, Danny Hoffman singled Schreck in from second.

Rube took the mound for the last of the 20th. With one out, Rube gave up a double, and the crowd stirred. Jimmy Collins, whose error had started the A's rally that inning, stepped up looking for redemption. But he could only pop a Rube fastball to shortstop. Hobe Ferris was Boston's last hope. He flew to left.

It was still light after this exhausting game, and a doubleheader had been slated. Mack started Andy Coakley. Coakley struggled, giving up 12 hits, though only two runs. In the ninth, with one out, Boston hit two quick singles. Mack had seen enough, and he sat Coakley down. He put in Rube! Rube put on his shoes and walked out to the mound. He took no warm-ups and promptly struck out the first man. Journeyman infielder Robert Unglaub then stepped up. Rube blazed three fastballs by the helpless Unglaub. The A's had the sweep and drew to within a game and a half of first place. After 21 innings (the last 20 of which were scoreless), a win, and a save in the same day, the Rube legend reached new heights.

The *Inquirer* called the July 4 Young/Waddell duel "the greatest game in the history of the league." Young himself called it "the greatest performance either of us has ever shown."[4] Rube did not argue the point, he capitalized on it. He returned to Philadelphia in triumph and strode into one of his favorite establishments. He had the game ball in his pocket and negotiated a deal with the saloon manager. Rube got a credit of several dollars worth of drinks, and the barkeeper got to display the ball in the front window. It was such a good deal that by the end of the month there were about 20 saloons in Philadelphia and several dozen in other American League cities each displaying the ball.[5] Rube had himself quite a ball.

NOTES

1. *Philadelphia Inquirer*, June 9, 1905.
2. Ibid., June 14–16, 20, 1905.
3. Ibid., June 28–July 1, 1905.
4. Clippings File, Cooperstown.
5. *Philadelphia Inquirer*, July 5, 1905.

Chapter 35

Pennant Drive

Three days after their legendary July 4 performance, Rube and Cy Young squared off once again. As before, Rube gave up a run in the first, then nothing but 0's filled the scoreboard. Young yielded nothing. In the top of the eighth, Boston shortstop Fred Parent bounced a hard one at the mound. It struck Rube on the top of his hand between the thumb and index finger — his *left* hand. Mack came out, and Rube insisted that he could still pitch. Mack left him in, but after the next batter singled on the first pitch, Mack put in Chief Bender. The A's tallied for a run in the bottom of the eighth to tie it. Bender held the Pilgrims scoreless. In the bottom of the tenth, Young walked two, the first walks he'd yielded in 30 innings. Danny Hoffman singled home the winning run. A's fans were again jubilant, but everyone was concerned about Rube's pitching hand.[1]

The next day there was a near riot at Columbia Park, not because of any event on the ball field, but because too many people turned out to see the game. The small grandstand filled hours before game time. Ben Shibe allowed thousands more to purchase entry and squeeze in wherever they could. They ringed the entire field, around the outfield, and along the baselines 12 deep. Foul balls shot into the crowd like mini-cannon balls. The seated crowd could not see much of the game and began tossing bottles and cushions. One foul ball shot into the crowd and five hats flew up in the air all in a row. Anything but concerned about the safety of the people blocking their view, the grandstand simply laughed uproariously at the sight. Outside the park 5000–6000 ticketless people milled. Amidst this the A's and the Pilgrims split a double header. The crowd behavior halted the game several times. Mounted police were finally called in to maintain sufficient order for play to continue. Pennant fever had gripped Columbia Park, and the Park could not take the heat. Ever more, Shibe knew he needed to build a bigger playground.[2]

Still concerned about Rube's hand, Mack told Rube to take a few days off and be ready for an upcoming series in Cleveland. Rube headed off for St. Mary's, a town out in Elk County, Pennsylvania, where his parents had moved in 1903. St. Mary's was over 200 miles northwest of Philadelphia, only an hour or so from Punxsutawney. Mack hoped he would not have to venture out to the hills of Western Pennsylvania to retrieve Rube again. He did not need to pick up any more IOUs. Rube did go native for a few days. He fished, of course. The locals asked him to play ball with them. Rube obliged. Whenever he came to St. Mary's in the off season Rube usually performed in a local theater, his performance highlight being the splitting of a two-inch plank with a baseball. When asked to play this time, Rube begged off pitching because of his hand. He played first base. As it turned out, Rube saw little action at first, for the score of the game was 36–23.[3]

Rube did not return directly to Philadelphia. He promised Mack he would meet the team in Cleveland. Mack made the trip a trifle fitfully, but Rube actually kept his word. Contrary to every image conjured up by Mack and the A's as to how Rube was spending his time, Rube arrived at the Cleveland park with his mother.[4]

Larry Lajoie had been injured for several weeks, and Cleveland's hold on the league lead had been slipping. Chicago and Philadelphia were set to knock them off. On July 12, Mack gave Rube his first try, bad hand and all. It was too early. Rube lost it 9–3. He could not get the ball down. And when he threw low, the pitches were fat. Rube tried Cleveland again on the 16th. He looked better, but he gave up four runs in the sixth, two of them unearned, and Cleveland won 4–3. Cleveland now stood two games up on the A's, and a mere half game up on Chicago. Boston had faded ten games back and were battling the surprisingly tough Detroit Tigers for fourth.

Rube's maturity was such that the frustrations of an injury were not easy to bear. He would try to play when he needed more rest, and of course he could never discipline his off-field antics. The presence of his mother was likely even more unsettling to him when matters did not go perfectly. In his next outing against St. Louis, Rube relieved his pent-up energies. He was usually composed, often humorous on the mound. This day he raged, yelling at his teammates, and at the umpires. Mack did not bench him. That would have been the worst thing to do. (Fred Clarke would likely have sat him down.) As long as the game was secure, it was better to let the kid get it out of his system. The A's won 7–3.

In a key series with the White Sox, Rube won one and lost one. His strikeouts were good, but his control was a little shaky, causing him to spot the ball, not a good thing to do with a strong team like Chicago. His injury and the time off had disrupted him from the unhittable streak he had been on at the outset of the season. The question was whether he could regain form. Given his character, that was a big question.

The cohesion of the A's held amidst Rube's July struggles. Plank, Bender, and young Coakley all pitched well, and the hitting was there at key times. After terrible years at the plate in 1904, Monte Cross batted .270 and Schreck batted .272. Other than Rube's one loss in Chicago, the A's swept that series. Cleveland had faded; Chicago appeared the only rival. On August 1, the A's returned to Philadelphia. Mack tried Rube once more. As often, Rube was not focused at the outset. He gave up three runs in the first, with four walks and a hit batter. The fans were yelling "Take him out!" Mack paid no heed. With the bases loaded and one out, Rube struck out two. From there he gave up but two more hits, one walk, and no runs. The A's came back to win it. Rube now looked fine, and with the victory the A's were back in first place.[5]

Rube and the A's then went on a tear. By August 15 the A's lead had widened to three games. In one spread of nine days at the end of August, Rube appeared five times. Three times he started and threw shutouts. Twice he appeared in relief and allowed no runs there, either. He saved a game for Andy Coakley, shutting out the Senators for an inning on September 3. The next day he started against Boston and blanked them for eight innings. That made 44 consecutive innings of scoreless baseball. No one had ever done that before. It was a record that would stand until Walter Johnson broke it in 1913. (Johnson's record would stand until Don Drysdale broke it in 1968.) But in 1905 the recovered Rube stood atop the league. So did the A's.

NOTES

1. *Philadelphia Inquirer*, July 7, 1905.
2. *Philadelphia Record*, July 8, 1905; *Philadelphia Public Ledger*, July 8, 1905; *Philadelphia Inquirer*, July 8, 1905.
3. Clippings File, Cooperstown.
4. *Philadelphia Inquirer*, July 12, 1905.
5. Ibid., July 13, 17, 19, 26, 29, August 2, 1905.

Chapter 36

A Fatal Straw Hat

Rube's streak of 44 scoreless innings ended in Boston in the ninth inning on September 4, 1905. (Rube always said Boston was his unlucky town, remembering especially, of course, that Boston was where his wife came from.) The run also tied the game. It came when a runner, on base thanks to an error, reached third and scored on a wild pitch. Some said it was a passed ball. Schreck retrieved the ball and appeared to have time to throw to Rube covering the plate. But he elected not to. Afterwards, Rube and Schreck had a talk, "with varying shades of chagrin and disgust." But Rube went back out and finished the inning. Boston scored no more runs, and Rube held them scoreless through the 12th. Meanwhile, the A's got runners in scoring position in each of the next four innings but could not score. Boston won it in the 13th. One reporter described Rube's luck that game as that "of a starving man in a shower of consommé with only a fork in his hand."[1] It was indicative of how tough an opponent Rube was in 1905 that it took such extreme ill fortune to beat him. Ill fortune was not through with the Rube that month.

Rube shrugged off the loss. The A's won the next two in Boston. Andy Coakley pitched the second game, and he asked Mack for time off after the game to visit his family in Providence. Mack granted it and told him to meet the team at the station in Providence on Friday, where they were to change trains en route to New York. Rube started on Friday and did not pitch well. Mack pinch hit for him in the second inning, and the A's came back to win it. Now they were four and a half games up on Chicago.[2]

After the game on Friday, the A's left Boston. They disembarked at Providence, and while they were waiting for the New York train, Coakley appeared on the platform as planned, his gear in his shoulder bag. Coakley was a careful dresser, and this day he appeared his usual dapper self, complete with a straw hat, neatly adorned with a red ribbon. There was an unwritten rule among ballplayers that straw hats were never to be worn after Labor Day. After all, the summer was over. It was a manly ritual in the late nineteenth and early twentieth centuries. One bought a new straw hat on Decoration Day and discarded it on Labor Day, usually after punching a hole through it. After Labor Day, baseball players would make a slapstick comedy routine out of the ritual, breaking every straw hat they could find. Rube, of course, was one of the leaders in this rite for the A's, and when Coakley appeared on the platform, Rube saw the straw hat and was eager to pounce.

Within seconds of Coakley's arrival on the platform, Rube rushed at him. Coakley had removed his straw hat and placed it under his coat. Rube had seen the hat, however. All Coakley saw was this huge maniac charging at him. He swung around to avoid Rube, and as he swung, the spikes stored in his shoulder bag whacked Rube right in the chin. Dazed, Rube thought Coakley had thrown a punch. Now his fun-loving spirit gave way to anger. As he let out a roar, other players, recognizing the misunderstanding, jumped at Rube to contain him. Rube tossed the first few players over his shoulder like bags of apples. Quickly more piled on, though, and they all tumbled over a stack of suitcases.

The players were able to calm Rube down after a few minutes. Rube could get angry, but he would never stay angry. He still wanted to break Coakley's hat. But they all got on the train and eventually put the silly matter aside. Rube sat glumly by the window the whole trip. Teammates cajoled him. The Pullman porter suggested Rube shake hands, kiss, and make up with Coakley. Rube agreed to shake hands but said he'd be damned if he would kiss him. The matter was forgotten.[3]

When Rube fell at the Providence platform, he had landed on his left shoulder. Rube felt a bit sore from this, and traveling on a train next to an open window was not a good thing to do, but he was not conscious of any problem. Two days later, however, Rube ran to Connie Mack almost in tears. "I was shaving, and I felt this click in my shoulder," he shouted. Mack took out his old catcher's mitt and calmly said, "Let's go see." Rube could barely throw the ball. Something was seriously wrong with his pitching shoulder.

On September 11, the papers reported that Rube would be out for at least a week. With the A's in first place, everyone in baseball was primed for the upcoming series between the AL and NL champions. The inter-league player raiding wars had ended, as the leaders of both leagues agreed to respect one another's contracts. (No anti-trust entered here, and this would render players powerless with respect to the owners. Ultimately, Justice Oliver Wendell Holmes would rule in 1922 that baseball was exempt from anti-trust strictures, on the dubious basis that the game was not a matter of interstate commerce.) In New York and Philadelphia, particularly, folks were not concerned about anti-trust and the long-term financial welfare of the players. In 1905 the peace between the two leagues had only one implication: the World Series was definitely going to be played that autumn, and looked like it was going to be the A's versus the Giants.

John McGraw's New York Giants had a big lead in the National League. The guarantee of a world championship series excited many baseball people. The A's and the Giants appeared a good match, particularly in the pitching department. Joe McGinnity vs. Eddie Plank was one duel people looked forward to. But most exciting was the prospect of Christy Mathewson facing Rube Waddell. They had faced one another back in 1901, but only when each was playing for a tail-ender and before each had reached his full potential. Now they were on pennant winners and at the absolute top of their games. When Rube got hurt, rumors began to fly about the whole matter of the shoulder injury being a hoax and that gamblers were involved to keep Rube out of the World Series.[4]

Mack was obviously concerned about the loss of Rube and what it could mean for the upcoming series with the Giants. But that matter lay far on his horizon. The A's still had a pennant to win. Chicago was only four games back the day Rube hurt his shoulder. From September 12 to 21, the A's went 6 and 5, and Chicago pulled to within two games.[5]

By September 26 the A's lead had dwindled to half a game. They had just lost to Detroit. The Tigers had risen to third place, ahead of St. Louis, Boston, and Cleveland. The Tigers had an 18-year-old rookie named Ty Cobb, who joined the team in mid season. He batted only .240 in the 41 games he played, but he was quite a presence. His keen fighting spirit seemed to lift the rest of the team. He was also a great outfielder, with the best speed in the league, speed he employed with great abandon on the base paths.

On September 27, Mack and the A's again faced the Tigers. A's pitcher Weldon Henley, one of the starters who tried to fill Rube's place in the rotation, was down 8–7 in the eighth after giving up two singles and two doubles. Mack tried a call to the Rube. Rube was greeted by great cheers from the Philadelphia fans. But "it was evident to the most superficial observer," wrote the *Inquirer*, "that he wasn't right." Rube delivered three straight balls outside and high. The hitter knocked the next pitch hard. Fortunately it flew straight to the center fielder to end the inning. Mack replaced Rube with Bender for the ninth. Though the A's lost, Chicago did, too. But now, while still concerned about the pennant, Mack was even more worried about Rube. Chicago was due in the next day for a series that would likely decide the race.[6]

Eddie Plank and Chief Bender came through with key victories over Chicago the next two days. Each day the stands were packed, the field was ringed with standing-room entrants, and over 10,000 more were turned away. The tightening of the race with Rube's injury certainly boosted gate receipts. The three-game series with Chicago drew 64,899. It could have been larger with a bigger stadium. Even in tiny Columbia Park, the A's drew over a half a million in 1905, a new city and league record.

Eddie Plank tried to come back for the third game with Chicago and pitch on a day's rest. He lost, but with the first two victories the A's now had a bit of a cushion. Mack also reported that Rube was coming around. Rube tried to go out and practice the next afternoon. Unfortunately he "windmilled" his arms to warm up. Again he felt a snap in his shoulder and had to stop. All these points were known to the press. Despite this, and despite the poor showing on the 27th, rumors continued of a sinister conspiracy to keep Rube out of the World Series. Some New Yorkers were also chiding that Rube was simply afraid to face the great Christy Mathewson.[7]

In early October, Philadelphia swept three games from St. Louis, while Chicago went 2 and 1 against Washington. Each had six more games to play. Bender had won in St. Louis. In the next series against Washington, the Chief picked up for the Rube. He won the first game against the Senators. In the second, Andy Coakley started, but was down 3–0 after two innings. Mack put the Chief back in. He held on as the A's came back to win 9–7 with the Chief going 2 for 3 at the plate with two key RBI. The following day Chicago lost to St. Louis, and Philadelphia had their pennant.[8]

Now that he had won the pennant, Mack let others do the celebrating. He had a series with John McGraw to prepare, and he had to see what, if anything, could be done with Rube. Mack tried Rube in relief against Washington on October 6. He walked three runners in the third inning. Then he seemed to find a bit of rhythm, only giving up one hit from the third to the eighth. He did walk two and slipped while fielding a bunt, however. Then in the eighth he gave up four straight singles, a wild pitch, and a wild throw, yielding three more runs. This gave the game to the Senators, and no one needed to be told how such pitching would have fared against McGraw's Giants. Rube wanted another chance the next day, so Mack gave it to him. He pitched one inning and gave up two runs. It was evident to all that Rube was still not right.[9]

No baseball series had ever received the hype which preceded the 1905 A's-Giants matchup. The inter-city rivalry was long and deep, and based on some real political and economic matters and not just the game of baseball. New Yorkers were already notorious for their arrogance. McGraw, as well as team president John Brush, typified this perfectly, as had Roger Breshnahan's little incident in May when he slapped a young Philadelphia boy in the face. Writer George Bernard Shaw once described John McGraw as the most typically American man he had ever met. Philadelphians preferred to believe that their gentility remained the finer light in the firmament of the American character, but a light which boorish New York materialism had garishly outshone.

Philadelphia was the largest city in the nation in its early decades, and many in the Quaker City felt that New York's rise had marked nothing but a cultural devolution. All of John McGraw's obnoxious comments about the American League, about the A's "white elephant," and his personal feud with Ban Johnson underscored the image and were part of the resentment and rivalry between the two cities.

Rube's bum shoulder did not diminish the pre-series hype, but it sure caused Mack and the A's to worry. If there were professional gamblers at work on the Rube, Mack was certainly earning an award for acting, as was Rube with his poor performances on September 27 and on October 6–7. (The quality of Rube's stage work the previous fall certainly spoke against the notion that the shoulder injury was a fake.) All over Philadelphia, meanwhile, New Yorkers were descending with big rolls of cash. The loudmouthed New Yorkers gave A's fans odds of 10–9 and 9–8. On Wall Street, where open baseball betting was still acceptable, the line was 5–4 in favor of the Giants. The bettors would have calculated differently with a healthy Rube.

Mack knew he had to give Rube more rest, and he still had Plank, Bender, and Coakley. Meanwhile, McGraw had Iron Man Joe McGinnity and Mathewson, "the Christian Gentleman." The series opened in Philadelphia on October 9. Rube was there hamming it up with reporters, but this did not dispel rumors that he was being kept from the game by gamblers plying him with liquor and women. Before the game started, A's captain Lave Cross greeted McGraw at the home plate ceremony with the umpires and presented John J. with a gift of a toy white elephant. McGraw accepted it gracefully. He waved to the crowd and placed the elephant on his head as he walked back to the dugout. Such fun and games were unimportant to him.

Mathewson squared off versus Plank that day. The Giants touched Plank for ten hits and three runs. The A's, meanwhile, could do absolutely nothing with Mathewson. There was only one man in the American League who threw with such speed and who could curve it so many ways, and the A's never had to face him. Mathewson gave up only four hits and threw a masterful shutout.[10]

Chief Bender faced Joe McGinnity in game two. The Chief returned Mathewson's favor, pitching his own 3–0 shutout. Rube was at the game, despite more rumors of professional gamblers, whiskey, and women. Game three was to have been the very next day, and McGraw wanted to start Mathewson. Fortunately for McGraw, it rained, and Mathewson got another day's rest. The speculation about the series being fixed included the idea that the rain-out had been engineered, too.[11]

Game three came the next day, Thursday, October 12. It was still raining a bit, and the air was cold. McGraw started a rested Christy Mathewson.

Mack went with Andy Coakley. As Coakley took the field at the game's outset, several fans stood up conspicuously wearing straw hats with bright red
ribbons. The Philadelphia fans took care of them promptly. The A's hit Mathewson fairly well that day, far better than they had in game one. But the Giant
fielders were equal to the task, and the A's went 4 for 30. Only one man
reached second base. The A's committed four key errors in the field. Coakley pitched well, but the errors were disheartening. The Giants won it easily
9–0.[12]

The A's were thus down two games to one as the series shifted to New
York's Polo Grounds. Mack had to have a victory. He warmed up Rube before
the game. McGraw's eyes nearly popped out of his head when he saw Rube
walk out and start to throw along the sideline, but he quickly calmed down.
Rube's warm-ups were terrible. He had little speed and no control. One of
his pitches actually sailed into the stands and conked a fan in the head. Mack
had to go with Eddie Plank.

Plank pitched a masterful game in New York. Two Philadelphia errors
in the fourth inning gave the Giants a run. That proved all that Giant starter
Joe McGinnity would need. In addition to the errors in the field, the A's ran
the bases poorly. In the eighth inning Topsy Hartsel walked. He was the fastest
man on the team. Mack signaled a steal. The batter, Bris Lord, stood and
watched a fat pitch go by. He looked up and there was Hartsel still standing
on first. Lord flied the next pitch to center. The next batter, Harry Davis,
connected with a Texas leaguer down the left field line. The Giant third baseman Arthur Devlin made a great play, catching the ball over his shoulder as
it veered away from him. With the catch, Devlin crashed into the grandstand
but held onto the ball. All the while Hartsel remained like a statue, standing
on first base. Lave Cross singled McGinnity's next pitch to right. *Now* Hartsel scampered to third. Had he gone to second on either occasion before, he
would have scored. He died on third. McGinnity had his 1–0 shutout, and
the Giants were up three games to one.[13]

"Cheer up," wrote the *Inquirer*, "two years ago Boston was down 3–1 to
Pittsburgh." That was indeed the case, but Boston had not had to face Christy
Mathewson. Mack sent out Bender. The Chief was less effective than he had
been in game two. He gave up three walks, two of which led to scores. He
walked two in the fifth, and the Giants pushed a run over with a bunt and a
sacrifice fly. In the ninth, Bender walked Mathewson. Roger Breshnahan doubled him to third and he scored on an infield grounder. On the mound, Mathewson was again very tough. The A's garnered six hits. Only one man reached
second base. That was Doc Powers, who led off the fifth inning with a double. But Powers made a running error when the next batter, Bender, grounded
to short and Powers found himself caught between the bases. Mathewson

pitched his 27th consecutive inning of shutout baseball, and the Giants were the champions. McGraw had his revenge.[14]

If there was any kind of fix on the '05 World Series, Rube was not the one involved. Judging by their errors on the base paths and in the field, the A's had many candidates. Their hitting was also weak. The team went 25 for 155, an average of .196, against a season average of .255. (The Chicago White Sox would hit better in the infamous 1919 series.) The A's silence at bat can be ascribed to the masterful pitching of Mathewson and McGinnity. Mack was never one to make many excuses. He did point out that the team had had to claw for the pennant to the very last week of the season and was not well rested going into the series.[15] But he did not say — he did not *have* to say — what was on everyone's mind: what would have happened if Rube had been there to face Mathewson? "Would have" "might have" — these words kept appearing in connection with Rube Waddell.

Poor Andy Coakley! He played but one more year with the A's, then played a few seasons with the Reds, the Cubs, and the Highlanders. From 1914 to 1951 he was the head baseball coach at Columbia University, where he coached Lou Gehrig. After retiring from Columbia, he enjoyed success as a midtown Manhattan insurance broker. He had a good life, in baseball and beyond, but he could never get away from the "straw hat." Fred Merkle, whose failure to touch second base in a key game with Chicago contributed to the Giants losing the 1908 pennant, spent the rest of his life having to suffer almost daily questions from fans about his "boner." When Ralph Branca gave up a home run to Bobby Thomson to give the Giants the 1951 pennant, he never heard the end of it. It was not quite the fate of Mrs. O'Leary and her cow after the great Chicago fire, but wherever Andy Coakley went for over 50 years, he never stopped having to answer questions about "the straw hat that kept Rube Waddell out of the 1905 World Series."[16]

Just as McGraw never blamed Merkle, Mack held no grudge against Coakley. It was not his fault. Rube did not have to attack him on the platform. It was purely accidental that Coakley's spikes caught Rube on the chin. Still, Rube seemed to attract accidents.

Rube suffered much bad luck in life, but never did it come at so critical a time as it did that day in Providence. Rube had compiled an amazing year on the mound. He was undefeated and unhittable from April to June. He lost a few in June and July after injuring his thumb and forefinger from a line drive, and despite such pains, most of the losses in June and July were close ones that could have gone either way. Once Rube's hand recovered by late July he was again unhittable, reeling off a string of 44 consecutive shutout innings in August and early September. Then came the straw hat incident. The prospect of what a healthy Rube could have done to McGraw's Giants ate at many A's fans. Rube's notorious lifestyle led their anguish to cling to the rumors of Rube's injury being a product of sinister arrangements with gamblers, rumors which echoed for years.

Rube's great 1905 season was reflected in the statistics he compiled. He led in strikeouts of course, though his total that year fell to a mere 287, still greater than anyone else had ever achieved. Plank and Cy Young tied for second that year at 210. Rube also led the league in appearances (46), wins (26), ERA (1.48), and saves (4). Since 1902, the A's fans had wondered what Rube could do for them if he spent a year playing serious baseball. He certainly showed them. But after the season was over, the only thing any baseball fan in Philadelphia wondered about was what the A's *and* Rube could have done to the Giants were it not for a silly straw hat.

NOTES

1. *Philadelphia Inquirer*, September 5, 1905.

2. Ibid., September 6-8, 1905.

3. Letter from Andy Coakley to J. G. Taylor Spink, February 11, 1943, quoted in Spink, "Rube Waddell," p. 16.

4. See, for example, Harold Seymour, *Baseball: The Golden Age* (New York: Oxford University Press, 1971), p. 15.

5. *Philadelphia Inquirer*, September 9–21, 1905.

6. Ibid., September 28, 1905.

7. Ibid., September 29–October 1, 1905.

8. Ibid., October 2–7, 1905.

9. Ibid., October 8–9, 1905.

10. Ibid., October 10, 1905.

11. Ibid., October 11–12, 1905.

12. Ibid., October 12–13, 1905.

13. Ibid., October 14, 1905.

14. Ibid., October 15, 1905.

15. *Philadelphia Record*, October 26, 1905.

16. See, for example, A. H. Tarvin, "How a Straw Hat Kept Waddell Out of a World Series," *Louisville Courier Journal*, October 15, 1943, reprinted in *Baseball Digest*, vol. 2, #9, November 1943, pp. 1–2.

Chapter 37

Usual Spring High Jinks

Philadelphia A's fans looked forward to 1906 with great optimism. They lost the World Series to the Giants, and there was no way to candy coat that one. But the pennant-winning team had not changed much. Mack had sold 40-year-old third baseman Lave Cross to Washington. Other than that, everyone was back, including Rube.

Rube had spent the off-season with his family back in St. Mary's, mostly hunting and fishing. (He wasn't about to go back to Massachusetts.) He was so popular with the folks in Elk County that there was talk of hiring an agent to promote Rube on a campaign for lieutenant governor. No word came forth as to the reactions of Pennsylvania's Prohibitionists.[1]

Rube arrived in Philadelphia on March 1 to join the team at the train station and head off for another spring training. A crowd gathered to see them off, and Rube was the center of attention, of course. As happened to the A's once en route from St. Louis to Detroit, their train derailed on the trip south. And again Rube took charge of the rescue operation. The engine had to be abandoned, and the cars hitched to a mail train out of Atlanta. There may have been symbolism there, but at spring training time everyone is an optimist.

The team began to train in Montgomery, Alabama. Connie Mack was not going to set Rube loose in Mardi Gras again. Rube appeared to be in reasonable shape, though a trifle overweight. He had done some barnstorming in late October and threw well then, adding to the rumors that he could have pitched during the World Series. By March his shoulder was fine, so the only thing with which Mack had to concern himself was getting Rube's weight down. He did cut Rube's salary, citing his carelessness about training and the high jinks which led to the shoulder injury. The cut was severe, too: from $2400 to $1200. Rube accepted it. Issues like salary were beyond his ken anyway. Whatever he had he spent, and whatever more he needed, he secured by touching up people for loans. Some rumored that Mack was trying to help Rube here, as May Wynne was beginning divorce proceedings. Rube could now more legitimately plead poverty in regard to any charges of non-support. Mack later denied this.[2]

One disciplinary trick Mack employed with Rube was to commission him "Captain of the Balls" during practices. This meant that every player had to report to Rube in order to get a baseball at the beginning of the day. Given the drinks that Rube had pilfered with baseballs after his July 4 duel with Cy Young, Rube fancied the job at first. He had not reckoned, though Mack had, that his officership would require him to retrieve all the balls fouled over the fence. Indeed, Rube began to grow suspicious of some of his teammates' whose bat swings appeared weaker at times and seemed to hit a few too many awry. Mack wanted to get Rube's weight down, and making him chase a few dozen extra foul balls every day was just the way to do it.[3]

As always, Rube endeared himself with the locals. One day, on the way to practice, Rube passed by a corner where a few folks had gathered. It seemed a heavy wagon was stuck in the trolley tracks. No one could move it, and it was tying up the whole trolley line. Rube stepped out, pulled the wagon out of the tracks, and was the hero of the hour. Later, in a game against a group of local Alabamians, Rube stabbed a line drive with his bare hand. The drive was headed straight for the head of the umpire (in games with one official, the umpire usually posted himself behind the pitcher). Folks said Rube saved the man's life.[4]

On another evening, a fire broke out on Decatur St. Rube heard the sirens, ran to the scene, donned a helmet, and grabbed a hose. The locals were impressed, though the fire was not deemed terribly important since, as a reporter of genuine Alabama stock noted, the "property belonged to ... a Negro; the loss is insignificant."[5]

Even though Montgomery was not New Orleans, Rube, Schreck, and company did seek out their share of high jinks. The second day of practice, it began to rain. Mack canceled the day's activities, leaving the players to their own devices. Rube had spied an indoor roller rink near the hotel, and he corralled a group to go over and try their luck with a sport which was, for most of the party, something brand new. It must have been quite a sight, these big athletes rolling around largely out of control. Rube and Schreck frequently sailed into the adjacent chairs. Rube had never before experienced the effects of centrifugal force so sharply, not while sober anyway. Schreck once whizzed by the chair section, through the rink's doors, seemingly out of control. Beyond the doors lay a tall flight of stairs, going *down*, and everyone thought Schreck could be in trouble. Fearing the worst, many of the A's began to turn toward the door. But an instant later, boom! The doors flew open and in skated Schreck, head up, in complete control, with a large cigar in his mouth, jauntily pointing northwest. He'd gotten the hang of it.[6]

Rube found himself in a bit of trouble while in Montgomery, naturally enough. This time, though, he was not the criminal but the victim. While imbibing in the local night-life, Rube found himself wandering about some poorly lit streets. On Bell St. he was knocked in the head and relieved of $40. Friends found him with a gash on his head, and he was treated. Was it a legitimate story? Connie Mack was dubious. The Alabama police concluded the attack was the work of "Negro highwaymen." The locals were embarrassed that their newly beloved Rube had been so roughed up, but their humiliation was not too severe, as the local paper noted: "It remained for Montgomery, little old Montgomery, to be the place where the mighty Rube has pocketed the loser's share in any financial transaction."[7] In an age with little media, it was remarkable how a man's personality and reputation could so deeply penetrate so many corners of the nation's culture.

After breaking camp, the A's toured a few Southern cities. They played the New Orleans Pelicans again, but Mack would not let Rube stay there long. Rube showed off a new weapon in his pitching arsenal. When he threw his "slow one," a change-up or a knuckler, he would trumpet a loud horse laugh, which one of his actor friends taught him. The laugh strained a batter's concentration, and of course the crowds loved it.[8]

Mack divided the team into two groups. Each toured different cities. Rube and Schreck were split up this trip. Whether Rube seized the moment and started eating animal crackers in bed again is not known. But the absence of Schreck did affect his play one day in Memphis. Rube tried one of his favorite exhibition game ploys — clearing the field of all but the catcher in the final inning. Doc Powers was catching, and he had more trouble with Rube's curves than did Schreck. Rube fanned the first two with no problem. He struck out the third man, too, but Powers dropped the third strike. The batter took first. The next two batters bore down and simply tried to make contact with the ball. They were successful. Rube had to run himself ragged, chasing down popups. With the bases loaded, Rube looked to the bench for help. Harry Davis was acting as manager, and he would do nothing for Rube. Davis and everyone else just sat there, laughed, and yelled: "You get out of this yourself, Rube! We're just going to sit here." Rube struck out the last man. He came off the field a winner, but he was more than a little chagrined and winded. Of course, Connie Mack wanted him to do more running that spring.[9]

NOTES

1. Clippings File, Cooperstown.
2. *Philadelphia Inquirer*, March 1, 1906; Clippings File, Cooperstown.

3. *Philadelphia Inquirer*, March 4, 1906.
4. Ibid., March 10, 17, 1906.
5. *Montgomery Advertiser*, March 20, 1906.
6. *Philadelphia Inquirer*, March 2, 1906.
7. *Montgomery Advertiser*, April 13, 1906.
8. *Philadelphia Inquirer*, March 20, 1906.
9. Ibid., March 24, 1906; Clippings File, Cooperstown.

Chapter 38

Bum Thumb

The A's returned to Philadelphia at the beginning of April and played their annual pre-season series with the Phillies. Plank won; Bender won; Coakley lost; and Rube won. "Hey, Rube, you are all right," declared the *Inquirer*. Rube's arm did look good, though his control seemed a little off, as he struck out 11 but walked six. Bender opened the season in Washington on April 14 and defeated the Senators. Rube did the same the next day. Both looked very tough, and fans rejoiced. If there was any rivalry between the pitchers, no one detected it. The next week, Bender won the home opener. Rube's first home appearance came in relief the next day. He entered the game with a three-run lead. He lost the lead in the seventh inning, then lost the game in the tenth. This was not the sort of game the A's lost in 1905.[1]

Rube bounced back from the loss with two great games. On April 20, he whipped New York, going 3 for 3 at the plate. On the 24th he had another contest with Cy Young in Boston and threw a 5–0 shutout.[2]

Rube did a little too much celebrating after his victory over Young. He faced Boston again on the 27th. He totally dominated them for five innings, giving up just one hit. Then with two outs in the sixth, he walked three and gave up three singles. With two on he fielded a grounder, turned and threw it into the right field corner. Rube still had his great stuff, but when he drank his consistency fell off, and his hitting and fielding suffered. No ballplayer has ever pitched so well that he could not be handicapped by his own poor fielding, and Rube was no exception here, though at times he came close.

Few were noticing any inconsistency in Rube at that point. His mediocrity was most anyone else's excellence. As of May 3 the A's were 9 and 5 and in first place. Rube's record stood at 3 and 2. The trouble was after April 27 he was nowhere to be found.[3]

Rube showed up on May 4. Chief Bender started that day against New York. Normally the Chief was a most phlegmatic man, at least outwardly. He was not a drinker and he did not take part in the team's shenanigans, much less any of Rube's. Whether it was Rube's sudden reappearance or some other factor, something lit up beneath the Chief's stoicism that day. In the fifth inning against the "Yankees," as a few folks were just starting to call the New York club, Bender thought he had picked a man off first. The umpire signaled safe, and the Chief became furious. He threw his glove down, and kicked and yelled at the umpire non-stop. He was ejected, something that had never happened to him before. The New Yorkers began yelling "Rube!" Mack obliged them and sent out the woozy one with two on. There was still no such thing as a warm-up in those days. After a walk and a single, Mack yanked Rube in favor of Eddie Plank.[4]

Rube and Mack had a lucky break in that the team left New York the next day for the upstate town of Troy to play an exhibition. Mack used Rube there for a couple of innings. This gave the crowd what it wanted, and it gave Rube what he needed — some work where there was no pressure. The safety valve worked, as Rube shut out Boston the very next day. He struck out three, walked none, and appeared to grow stronger as the game progressed. The team appeared to have been sparked by this, too, as they swept the next three games from Boston.

In his next outing against Chicago, Rube showed that his rhythm was back as he threw another shutout. Typical of Rube, he felt so good that day he got cocky. In the fifth inning he gave up two hits with nobody out, the only time that day Chicago garnered two hits in a single inning. Rube responded by striking out two in a row and then intentionally walking the next batter to load the bases. He struck out the next man on three pitches and cartwheeled off the field. Schreck crashed a big homer over the 29th Street fence and clear out of the lot to win the game. "Never get too low or too high?" Not Rube, who should not have felt too good about beating up on Chicago. They were mired in seventh place and were a very weak-hitting team. No one expected them to go anywhere that season.[5]

The A's continued to win. By May 17 they were 17 and 7, four games up on second-place Cleveland. Third-place Detroit came to town. Rube had been out the previous night, drinking and chasing a fire engine. Connie Mack usually had a scout on Rube's tail and thus knew what Rube had been up to. Rube walked into Columbia Park after his all-nighter and Mack immediately told him, "You pitch today." The first man Rube faced was Ty Cobb. Cobb was in his first full season with the Tigers. He drag bunted Rube's first offering down third base and beat the throw. Cobb would make a career of terrifying the opposition and throwing them completely off their game. But he would have absolutely no effect on Rube that day. Cobb died on first, and for the rest of the game Rube threw a no-hitter. It was almost as perfect a day as his first outing with Schreck against Baltimore in 1902. Plank and Coakley won the next two, giving the A's 11 straight wins. In 1905 the A's had to fight their way to the top, and did not get there until August. This year it looked to the fans like it was going to be a breeze.[6]

Cleveland needed 13 innings to snap the A's streak the next day. Rube had started and had a 1–0 lead into the ninth. He had struck out 13, and every man on the team at least once. In the ninth, Rube walked the first man. The next batter singled the runner to third, and he scored on a sacrifice fly. With the score tied, Mack pinch-hit for Rube in the bottom of the ninth. The A's did not score that inning. Mack sent Bender in for the extra innings, and the Naps hit a home run in the 13th to win it. The loss seemed to take a little starch out of the A's. The next day they committed four errors and lost 8–5.

The A's little streak of bad luck magnified off the field. After he had pitched the Cleveland game, Rube hired a carriage, took his dog out, and went for a drive. At the corner of Ridge Avenue and 22d Street, Rube entered the intersection as a delivery wagon cut in front of him. Rube turned his horse, but when the collision appeared inevitable, Rube leaped out. As he jumped, he caught his thumb in the whip socket—his *left* thumb. He had some lacerations on his hand. Worse, X-rays showed that he had fractured the thumb. First reports said Rube would be out for six weeks. (He lost his dog in the accident, too.[7])

Rube came to the game the next day to the great cheers of the crowd. He sat in the press section, nursing his thumb and smoking a big cigar. The A's won that day, and went on to win three of their next four. So Rube's injury initially met with mirth. Then the A's went on the road, and without Rube they lost six of seven. They fell out of first place and were now bunched with Cleveland and New York.

On June 5, Mack thought he would give Rube and his thumb a try. Rube had been asking for a start for several days, even though the injury was just two weeks old. The game was against the hitless White Sox, so Mack figured it could be a good time for a test. As with the shoulder injury of the previous September, Rube was trying to come back prematurely. The bum thumb did not affect his speed, but his control was off. He walked seven in the first three innings. In the third, he let up on his speed to gain control, and the batters teed off on him, scoring five runs. Rube had simply come back too soon. The reality that Rube was going to be gone a good deal longer cast even more of a pall on the slumping A's. Chicago swept the series. The A's fell to third place, and fourth-place Detroit was breathing down their necks.

Rube responded to his poor showing in Chicago by going off on a bender. The A's won three in St. Louis with Rube sleeping it off in a bar somewhere. In one of these saloons, Rube met Frank Gotch, a professional wrestler. Rube wanted to try his hand with Gotch. Gotch was a champion, far better than George LaChance. He didn't want to wrestle Rube, but the big dolt would not take heed of "no." So the floor was cleared and they went at it. Rube futilely tried a few grabs and holds. Gotch easily held off Rube's attacks and let the big oaf tire himself out. Then he picked up the Rube and body slammed him. Rube had a sore back and was laid up for several days. The A's left St. Louis and went to Detroit and Cleveland, where they lost three of five. They held on to third, as neither New York nor Cleveland could put on much of a spurt. Meanwhile, Detroit crowded into contention. Even lowly Chicago was showing some spunk, though few took them seriously.[8]

Plank beat Cleveland on June 18, and Mack gave Rube another look the next day. Rube faced Addie Joss again, and they hooked up for another great duel. Joss outpitched Waddell, giving up five hits to Rube's seven, one walk to Rube's three; he struck out seven while Rube fanned five, and Rube threw one wild pitch. But the A's got lucky when Rube scored on a bad-hop single in the fifth. The batter later scored when he kicked the ball out of the catcher's mitt while being tagged. The two runs would be all Rube needed.

With the two wins, and with New York losing to Detroit, the A's had regained the league lead. The next day Cleveland bounced back, and Detroit again beat New York. Now two and a half games separated the first four teams. This was nothing like the four-game lead the A's had enjoyed in mid–May, but they had their Rube back — at least they thought they did. Three days later Chicago swept a series in Detroit and found themselves two and a half games out of third place. Chicago? A club with a team batting average of .230? Folks around the league knew this couldn't last.

Rube's thumb was bothering him after the Cleveland game. He had probably reinjured it, but in the heat and with the adrenaline of the game, he couldn't be sure. Mack used him in relief for a few innings against Boston, and he was effective. He gave Rube a start against lowly Washington on June 28. Again, the problem was control. Rube walked six, and when he let up on the speed to gain more control, the Senators' bats were waiting. He lost 4–2, with the A's stranding eight runners in scoring position. This was 1904-level hitting with an injured Rube, not a good combination.[9]

Rube wanted to try again against Washington and pleaded with Mack for another chance. Mack sent him out on June 30. It was a mistake. The Senators came up with five runs on seven hits. The A's made two key errors, but that was not central. Rube was just not pitching well, and no one could discipline him to rest and let his thumb recuperate. In subsequent eras of larger rosters and farm systems, a player in Rube's situation could be sat down, rested fully, and given a few weeks in the minors to test his recovery. The teams had no such systems in 1906. Minor leagues carried their own contracts. The major league teams carried 15 players. If Mack wanted to pick up another player, he would have had to release Rube and risk someone else signing him, which Rube would have accepted if only because he always needed money. With no self-discipline, and being uncontrollably headstrong, Rube kept trying to pitch. Meanwhile, his drinking was not helping one bit. Indeed, as he failed to perform on the mound, his drinking grew worse.[10]

After the last game of the Washington series, the Senators were preparing to depart. Many had already boarded their bus, when the vehicle suddenly began to rock and bounce. There was no earthquake, it was just Rube, already a few beers into the post-game, eager to create a little havoc. Such incidents were still funny to many fans, but bit by bit people were starting to sense how it was all starting to fray. For the key was that Rube seemed ever less able to generate the havoc he used to create for the opposition *on* the field. As the balance shifted, the humor of it all began to fade.

As of July 1, the AL race was a complete thicket. Chicago was six games back in fifth place. A's fans felt the excitement, but the feeling came with a certain anguish. With a healthy Rube, the A's were hot in May, so the tension of a tight pennant race was not what they had imagined for the summer months. New York had a one-game lead on the A's when they arrived in Philadelphia for a doubleheader on July 2. The first game encapsulated the whole season. Plank started and was strong, taking a 4 to 1 lead into the ninth inning. New York suddenly rallied for three runs in the ninth to tie the game. But the A's came back to win it. The A's fans were certainly rooting for the win that inning, but they seemed to be doing so with a tinge of "Why are we being put through this?"

Andy Coakley started game two, and the contest was again a tight one. New York's Al Orth would win 27 that year, and he was pitching well that day. The "Yankees" were up 2–1 in the eighth. Mack pinch-hit for Coakley in the bottom of the inning. The move came to naught, and the Yanks kept their lead. In the ninth Mack sent in Bender. The Chief did not have good stuff that day. After two singles, a walk, and a double it was suddenly 5 to 1.

Psychologists can paste various fancy terms on what happened from there. But after five hours of highly tense baseball with first place in the balance (against a team from detested New York), the tension was now over and everyone was disappointed. Fans began to leave rather than wait for the meaningless bottom of the ninth to be played out. The logistics of little Columbia Park were such that the exit stairs brought fans toward the field, not away from it. With the desire not to let the reality of the loss invade their spirits too greatly, the departing fans may have somehow resented the intrusion of being compelled to get closer to a game they wanted to put behind them. The resulting ambivalence led many to hesitate and stand near the field at the exits.

As the edge of the field grew crowded, Harry Davis stepped up and

grounded harmlessly to second. Now more people started to leave. Socks Seybold then grounded to short, and the departures turned into an exodus. Up
stepped Danny Murphy; first pitch — strike one. That was it; the crowd
around the left field exit broke onto the ballfield, and everyone else then did
the same from other points in the park. There was no violence, just a mass
milling, a mass display of narcissism worthy of fans some 90 years later, save
for the non-violence. The umpire called time and notified Connie Mack of
the need to restore order. There is a spell, an illusion that any game like baseball casts. It shatters when fans intrude into the viewing space. Once the space
is shattered, the authority of the illusion — like Connie Mack's — is gone.
There can only be the authority of the everyday law, and even that would be
resisted in such situations. Mack and the A's could do nothing to restore
order, and they saw no point in calling for the police. If the A's could not
win, the fans, still expecting victories, seemed to be saying that the loss would
have to be consigned some other place, like in their own laps. The game thus
had to be forfeited, with the official score in such situations being logged at
9–0.[11]

Baseball owners and managers had seldom seen such spontaneous dis-
plays. They did not ponder the psychological dynamics at work in the mass
behavior. They just thought even more deeply now about the need for a bigger stadium with better logistics for crowd control. Modernity with its
promises of financial glory and possibilities of spiritual deracination, had
invaded the Philadelphia sports world. Rube was one of the leading players
who straddled the old and new worlds. He brought the closeness of small town
ways to the masses of fans, so much so that the means of display buckled under
the numbers. People like Rube and Christy Mathewson could stretch themselves only so far. Beyond that was the need for corporate control and protection. The development of the appropriate new means lay ahead. For now
the tension was palpable, and the question was how Mack, the A's, and Rube
would handle it.

NOTES

1. *Philadelphia Inquirer*, April 1–19, 1906.
2. Ibid., April 21, 25, 1906.
3. Ibid., April 25, 28, May 3, 1906.
4. Ibid., May 4, 1906.
5. Ibid., May 4, 6–10, 12, 1906.
6. Ibid., May 17–19, 1906; Clippings File, Cooperstown.
7. *Philadelphia Record*, May 23, 1906; *Philadelphia Inquirer*, May 22–23, 1906.

8. *Philadelphia Inquirer,* June 6–16, 1906.
9. Ibid., June 19–23, 29, 1906.
10. Ibid., July 1, 1906.
11. Ibid., July 3, 1906.

Chapter 39

Hitless Wonders

While the A's split a doubleheader with New York on July 2, Cleveland won one and the White Sox won two. This bunched the 1906 AL race even more tightly. Just two and a half games now separated the first five clubs. When it rained on July 3, New York and Philadelphia had to schedule a double-header for July 4.

Mack tapped Rube and Chief Bender to take on the Yankees. Rube faced his old Pittsburgh buddy, Jack Chesbro. Chesbro had won 41 games in 1904. He had fallen to a mere 21 the next year, but he could still be murderous with his spitball. The rain of the previous day had not fully let up, and the field was a mess. For five innings there was no score. The New Yorkers had gotten a hit off Rube every inning, but they had not been able to push a run across. Yankees manager Clark Griffith was trying the same tricks he had used against Rube in Chicago: bunt on him and hope he slips on the turf and loses concentration. The Yanks got some runners on base, but Rube never lost his focus and pitched out of every jam. New York stranded 11 men that day. Rube and the A's won, but it was not the kind of victory about which they could feel too proud. It was certainly not the sort of thing that begins a winning streak.

In the second game, the luck of the day reversed, as Bender pitched a masterful game but lost 2–1. The previous year's July 4 saw Rube triumph over Cy Young in 20 innings under a clear Boston sun and then come back in relief and win another. This July 4 was a weird misty day that ended in a meaningless split. It was quite a come-down. Elsewhere, Chicago won.[1]

A sweep over Washington provided some reprieve from the pressure. New York kept pace, however, and Cleveland was due in right after Washington. Rube started the Cleveland series on July 7. He blanked the Naps for six innings. In the seventh Cleveland tallied a run when Rube misplayed a bunt. He steadied from there, however, and in the bottom of the seventh he helped himself offensively, bunting successfully on a squeeze play, not only scoring a runner but beating the throw to first as well. After nine innings, the score was tied 1–1. In the tenth it looked bad. Nap Lajoie had popped in back of second base. The A's shortstop, second baseman, and center fielder all converged on the ball. They looked at one another for a second, and the ball dropped. Lajoie subsequently scored. But in the bottom of the tenth two A's were on and Schreck knocked them in for the win. The crowd of 22,000 went wild. The A's won, Rube seemed healthy. New York had also lost, so Philadelphia was in first place again.

As quickly as the A's had taken first, they gave it back. They rested on Sunday, of course, then Cleveland beat them on Monday and took over first. The next day it rained. With the extra day's rest, Mack turned to the Rube again on Wednesday. Rube came through. His thumb was still a bit sore, and his strikeout numbers were lower than in May. But he seemed sharp enough, and the A's were coming through with the timely hits.

Detroit was the next visitor. Plank lost the first game, and New York again took first. On Saturday, Mack turned again to Rube. He was using him almost as incessantly as he had in 1902. He had little choice, as Bender was ill and no one else was effective. In the pre-game warm-ups, Rube was playing pepper with Schreck. Playfully, Schreck rifled one back at Rube and hit him right on his bad thumb. It swelled, but Rube insisted on pitching. He shut out the Tigers in the first two innings. In the third he gave up a walk, two singles, and a double as Detroit scored four. In the bottom of the inning Detroit pitcher George Mullin returned the favor, allowing the A's to score five. In the rally, Mack lifted Rube for a pinch hitter. Andy Coakley finished the game, and the 5–4 lead held up. The A's won, but once more Rube was hurting. If the A's had won the 1905 pennant by a nose, it looked as though they could lose this flag by a thumb.[2]

After Sunday off, the A's beat Detroit on Monday while Chicago beat New York. This put the A's in first again. They held first place this time, as New York and the A's matched records for a week. On July 25 Rube tried to pitch against Detroit. He lasted only two innings. In the second he walked three in a row. He began to yell at the umpire and was ejected. His thumb was hurting even more.[3]

With neither New York nor Cleveland able to put together much of streak, the A's maintained their tenuous lead. Detroit was lagging, too, as Ty Cobb was injured and out of the lineup for several weeks in late July and early August. Chicago was the only team that seemed healthy. But they seemed to have a hitting problem. It was a strange pennant race. Who would break out was anybody's guess.

Rube rejoined the A's on August 5. The team was still two up on New York. Chicago and Cleveland were each seven back. That day Philadelphia was to start a series in Chicago. The White Sox won the first two games. Rube pitched the first game. Spitball artist Ed Walsh was Rube's opponent, and he had a great day. Not one of the A's reached second base. Rube pitched nearly as well, but the White Sox got all their hits at key times. Plank pitched well the next day, but Chicago won it 1–0. On Thursday, August 9, the A's touched Chicago pitchers for nine hits. Chicago garnered just two hits, yet they won. The papers were starting to call the White Sox "the hitless wonders." Connie Mack was certainly wondering. He had just lost five in a row, despite good pitching. New York was now only a half game out, and Chicago had climbed fully into the race, a mere two and a half games behind.[4]

Rube's sensational pitching of earlier years had inspired fanfares and poetry. Now his travails were prompting different types of verse:

Waddell's Roundelay

In fishing it is my delight
To take a bottle on the trip,
And though I never get a bite
I frequently can take a nip.[5]

When the team began to slide, such verses did not touch the hearts of the A's and their fans, they just got on their nerves.

After losing five heartbreakers in Chicago, the A's limped off to St. Louis. They lost there 1–0; New York also lost in Chicago. New York thus gained no ground on Philadelphia, while Chicago gained on both. Mack felt snakebit, and Rube's thumb was still sore. On Saturday the 11th, Coakley started against the Browns. He had the lead 4–2 into the fifth. Then he blew up. Nine men came to bat for St. Louis that inning, three runs scored. Mack lifted Coakley for a now-healthy Chief Bender, who held the Browns from there, but the A's hitters did nothing. Meanwhile, Chicago beat New York again, leaving the league completely bunched:

	W	L
Philadelphia	59	41
New York	57	40
Chicago	60	43

On Sunday, August 12, Philadelphia was in St. Louis; New York was in Chicago. The rest of the league was in the God-fearing East where there were no Sunday games, so the entire AL schedule was devoted to the question of who would lead. Mack hoped Chief Bender could end the A's slump, since he had closed well for Coakley on Saturday. The Chief could not do it this day, however. The Browns jumped on him right off, scoring four runs in the first inning. Rube was there, but only to coach first, and he didn't have much to do. Chicago blanked New York, and the Hitless Wonders were in first place for the first time in the season.[6] Baseball fans in Chicago were going absolutely mad. Not only were the White Sox leading the AL, but their NL team, now called the Cubs, was way out in front of McGraw's Giants and had the pennant sewn up.

Rube went to the theater in St. Louis after the Sunday loss. There he proclaimed that he would either win the game the next day or quit baseball. Alcohol is great stimulant for rank prognostications, though less useful for the healing of a thumb fracture. Mack was desperate. Danny Murphy was hurt. Bender and reserve pitcher Jack Coombs were ill. Plank was hurt, as were outfielders Bris Lord and Socks Seybold. Mack gave the Rube a chance the next day to make good on his promise, and Rube came through. He scattered six hits en route to an 8–0 shutout. With the theater hype, the St. Louis fans were all over Rube, but he paid no heed. He turned no cartwheels, made no animal noises. He was all business. His blazer was not quite there, as he struck out only three, but he had snapped the losing streak.

Mack had little in reserve, and he must have figured he had best "ride the horse" as long as it would run. So he tried to revive 1902 once more, starting Rube in the second game of the scheduled doubleheader. Rube wanted to do it, of course, and, as Yogi Berra would have put it, this proved to be the wrong mistake. Rube shut out the Browns 1-2-3 in the first. Then it all went south. After five hits and three errors in the second, four runs crossed the plate. Mack pulled Rube, and the Browns never looked back. Chicago and New York played to a 0–0 tie as darkness fell. All of Rube's efforts thus came to naught. The day was one of complete non-movement atop the league. The sense of futility was no less demoralizing than the losing streak.

Darkness left the next A's-Browns game tied, as Chicago shut out hapless Boston and New York beat Cobbless Detroit. The A's went home and hosted Cleveland. Rube lost the first game with one bad inning in which Cleveland scored all four of their runs. The A's scored only once. Bender won the second game. The next day they split again. Chicago won on both days.

In the first three weeks of August, Chicago went 17 and 1. The A's had fallen 4 behind. Given the A's sicknesses and injuries, it was not that bad. There were still six weeks left in the season, and everyone believed Chicago's incredible luck could not last. But the demoralization factor is strong in cases where the baseball gods seem to smile and frown on different teams. It affects players and fans. In a game against St. Louis on August 22, Jack Coombs was up 5–1 in the ninth. He gave up two runs, and the fans started to boo. Mack inserted Rube, and even here the cheers and boos were evenly split. Rube's drinking and general carrying on were better known than ever, and they had ceased to be funny amidst the pressures of the pennant race. Rube's first pitch

Rube at mid-career with the Philadelphia A's, caught here, likely, after a long night out, as the facial expression and leaning-tower posture indicate. A certain melancholia is clearly beginning to take over from the intensity he previously displayed. (National Baseball Hall of Fame Library, Cooperstown, N.Y.)

was a strike, and the noise that rang out had that unmistakable smirk of a mock cheer. The Philadelphia crowd had soured — on the A's and on the Rube. The A's were playing mediocre ball. Excuses like illness, injuries, and Chicago's luck would not suffice. Rube retired the side for a win, but the tenor of the whole season had changed. The A's were in second place with six weeks to go, but the hearts of the team and their fans seemed to have grown faint. The next day against Detroit, Rube relieved Coakley and took the game into extra innings. Sam Crawford touched him for a double with two on in the tenth. Detroit won, and the crowd really let Rube have a piece of their mind.

A little hope flickered on Saturday the 25th. With only a day's rest, Rube started another against Detroit. He pitched superbly for six innings. The *Inquirer* noted he "gave a suggestion of his old time form." The 1905 season seemed so far in the past now, such nostalgia could already resonate among Philadelphia fans. Rube faltered in the seventh, but the A's tied it in the ninth. Mack relieved Rube for a pinch hitter that inning. The A's won it in the 12th, *and* the White Sox lost a doubleheader to the Washington Senators. With the Sunday day off, the A's could rest. They were four back, and Chicago was due in for a big series starting on Monday.[7]

Few expected a game on Monday. It rained all morning, but the clouds broke at 3:00, and Mack turned his card into the umpire, who yelled "Play ball!" Jack Coombs held Chicago down for three innings. In the fourth he erred in judgment. With one on he fielded a bunt. He had plenty of time to cut down the lead runner, but he chose to go to first. The next batter singled in the run. Meanwhile, big Ed Walsh's spitball proved unhittable. He had a no-hitter for five innings. The A's garnered one hit in the sixth, but the runner went no farther than first base. As the sixth inning ended, the skies opened again, and right there the game ended, 1–0. Elsewhere, New York beat St. Louis, pushing the A's deeper into third place.

More rain on Tuesday prompted a doubleheader on Wednesday. In game one, Chicago came right back with Ed Walsh. Mack started Jimmy Dygert, a young pitcher out of Utica, New York in his first full year in the majors. Dygert was effective, but the Hitless Wonders lived up to their name, scoring three runs in the first two innings on no hits. Mack pinch-hit for Dygert and put Rube on the mound. Rube was fine through the fifth inning. The A's got to Walsh and took the lead in the fifth. The heavens returned the favor to Chicago with a downpour at the end of the inning, making the A's the winner. It was a little revenge — very little.[8]

Chicago continued to win, and Rube and the A's continued to sputter. It was New York that stayed close to Chicago through September, not the A's. In a typical game for the A's in that long September, Rube was pitching against New York with the score tied 1–1 in the ninth. He had allowed a run in the first and been perfect ever since. The first batter singled. Willie Keeler was then safe on an error. A sacrifice put the runners on second and third. The next batter grounded to Jack Knight at third. As Knight ran to field it, he collided with Keeler. Keeler got up, rounded third, and scored, with the batter ending up on second. The A's protested interference. The umpire would not relent. First baseman Harry Davis kicked so fiercely that he was tossed, but Davis kept yelling, so the umpire forfeited the game to New York.[9]

It was during that trip in New York that Rube had a kick that was stronger than Harry Davis'. As he walked on the streets of New York, Rube was sideswiped by an automobile. The motorist did not stop, and Rube took off after him. Rube hopped on the running board and began yelling at the driver like a maniac. Rube didn't want to have the man arrested, he just wanted $15 to replace his clothes. The driver ultimately complied.[10] That was Rube, the same kid who jumped in the stream after a fish that was getting away from him. Folks enjoyed the story, but it seemed a sadly poignant metaphor for Rube and the faltering efforts of the A's. Chicago and New York were bolting past them. Protests were yielding but small change.

New York was in the midst of what proved to be a 15-game winning streak. They seesawed with Chicago for the lead through the month, and left everyone else behind. The A's simply played out the string. Rube had another rematch with Cy Young and beat him 4–0. The *Inquirer* referred to the game as a match between "those old war horses." Rube was only 29, but he seemed an old 29, and he was not about to heed any voices telling him to change his ways, even when he pitched a charity game for a tuberculosis hospital in Connecticut. Rube felt no foreboding.[11]

By September 23, the Philadelphia newspapers were not even giving much coverage to the A's games. They reported the scores, but added maybe a half dozen lines of description. All eyes were on the Sox and the Yankees. Mack was playing a lot of rookies. One good one was a shortstop named Eddie Collins. Collins was still a student at Columbia University and did not want to lose his collegiate eligibility, so at this point he played under the name "Eddie Sullivan." In a practice one day, Rube had so discouraged Collins that the rookie contemplated quitting. Rube loved to pitch extra hard in practice to the rookies. In ten minutes against Rube, Collins had not even hit a foul ball. "Half the time," Collins recalled, "I never saw the ball." Connie Mack tried to be encouraging, telling Collins no one could hit Rube when he was in form like that. Rube also saw that he had been too hard on the youngster, so he took Collins aside and gave him a few pointers. Collins decided to give it another try.[12] He would play 22 more seasons, hit .300 19 times, and make the Hall of Fame ahead of Rube.

In addition to toying with rookies, Rube had some fun with the press.

One cub reporter rushed back to his office with a great scoop from Rube. He told his sports editor that he had the inside "skinny" on the A's—Connie Mack and Doc Powers play poker together. Lave and Monte Cross have drinking problems. Schreck never touches liquor, and Rube has lasted so long in baseball because of no drinking and clean living. The cub was convinced he had a bombshell. His editor chuckled, informing the gullible lad that Mack never gambles, smokes or drinks, that the Cross brothers live a similarly clean life, and that Rube and Schreck were anything but models of saintly living. The editor knew the source of the cub's misinformation.[13]

The White Sox won the American League pennant that year. They did it with what remains the lowest team batting average (.230) ever to win a pennant in either league. To the surprise of all but their most faithful, they went on to beat the heavily favored Cubs in the World Series, though they did it with some surprisingly strong hitting.

The A's finished a disappointing fourth, 12 games behind Chicago. All the valid excuses were there. Players were hurt. Breaks did not go their way. Attention focused in no small measure on the Rube. Everyone accepted that his left thumb was a problem from late May all through rest of the season. But with the shoulder in '05 and now the thumb, people could not but wonder if this was a problem, not of fakery, but one related to high, undisciplined living. On both occasions, alcohol clearly slowed Rube's recovery. Connie Mack believed that Rube lacked the maturity to handle the soreness in his arm that came with age and with the shoulder injury of 1905. He reacted, said Connie Mack, by drinking more and growing morose.[14] The high jinks that led to the shoulder injury and the aggravation of the thumb problem were certainly connected to his boozing, as were many other shenanigans. It just wasn't funny anymore.

It was one thing when Rube was acting nutty yet was still setting strikeout records with the A's winning. But now the results were starting to dim. Rube *did* lead the league in strikeouts in 1906, but his total was 196, fewer than he had posted from July through September in 1902. Rube's mediocrity may have been many others' excellence, but his failure to live up to anything close to his own potential was beginning to irritate a lot of fans and teammates. He went out barnstorming in October, and it was all great fun to the folks in places like Wilkes-Barre and Scranton. But when the exhibitions were over, the A's fans still wanted winners, as they had had in the past. Nothing else would do, and the Rube's zany antics did anything but compensate. The joke had been told once too often.

NOTES

1. *Philadelphia Inquirer*, July 5, 1906.
2. Ibid., July 6–8, 9–11, 12–13, 1906.
3. Ibid., July 26, 1906.
4. Ibid., August 6–10, 1906.
5. Anonymous poem, 1906, Clippings File, Cooperstown.
6. *Philadelphia Inquirer*, August 11–12, 1906.
7. Ibid., August 13, 14, 16–17, 23, 26, 1906.
8. Ibid., August 26, 29, 1906.
9. Ibid., September 4, 1906.
10. Told by Connie Mack in Spink, "Rube Waddell," p. 18.
11. *Philadelphia Inquirer*, September 15–17, 1906.
12. Connie Mack's recollections in Pete Martin, *Peter Martin Calls On...*, p. 53; and in Spink, "Rube Waddell," p. 18.
13. C. T. Rankin, "Anecdotes of 'Rube' Waddell," April, 1912, Clippings File, Cooperstown.
14. Clippings File, Cooperstown.

Chapter 40

Mule Fritters

Connie Mack once shrewdly observed that from management's financial standpoint, the best thing a team could do was to contend for the pennant, then lose. That way the fan turnout would be maximized, yet before the next season the players would not be able to bargain effectively for raises since management could trump them with, "Well you didn't win it." Mack was indeed a tough bargainer. All the baseball leaders of the early twentieth century were notoriously tight with a dollar. Mack had a far greater reputation for kindness than did such counterparts as Charlie Comiskey, John McGraw, Clark Griffith, or Barney Dreyfuss, but he was no less parsimonious. None of the A's got a raise after 1906. Rube had to promise further to stay in shape, lest his salary be cut. Given his drinking, the demand was hardly unreasonable.

Rube stayed in shape during the off-season. There were some rumors that he had signed on to tend bar in Detroit, but there was nothing to them.[1] Rube had learned to roller skate the previous spring in Alabama, and, like a child with a new toy, he kept on with it during the winter. It seemed silly but it did help keep him in shape. When Rube arrived at the train station in March of 1907, he looked "hard as nails" to all the reporters gathered to see them off. His weight was down to 210, which was a good playing weight, and spring training had not even begun.[2]

Connie Mack chose to take spring training in Marlin, Texas, that year. As the team traveled south, the *Inquirer* reporter noted that all boded well for the team: "There was no train wreck to send Rube to the rescue, nor a holdup in which the same Rube could star." The spring hope was that maturity would reign, but even when this appeared to be working, the lingering fear among Philadelphia baseball people was that they were sitting on a Reuben volcano.[3]

Marlin was a tiny town, about 100 miles south of Dallas, surrounded by woods. It was like Spartanburg. There was little to do but hunt, and Rube made the most of it. Ben Shibe's club secretary, Sam Erwin, made a promise that he would eat all the game brought in by any of the players. Rube promptly went out and shot a mule. He dragged it into the practice grounds. Erwin immediately reneged on his promise.

One reason Mack chose to take the team to Marlin was that McGraw and the Giants were training in Texas, too. He and McGraw had arranged to play some exhibition games. They would bring a little of the excitement of the '05 series to the South and make a tidy profit for one another in the process. That was the plan, anyway.

After the A's had practiced a few days in Marlin, they went up to Dallas for a few exhibition games against local clubs. Rube pitched a game on Sunday, March 10. Six thousand Dallas folks turned out to see him. It was the largest crowd ever to see a baseball game in the history of the city.

The A's were in and out of Dallas a few more days, and the business prospects of the exhibitions looked fine. But suddenly Rube was gone. Mack had no idea where to look for him. Three days later, the Dallas fire department was conducting drills for the rookies. Standing in front of the hotel, Mack saw one hook and ladder truck whiz by, and there was Rube in the driver's seat in full uniform — metal hat, rubber boots, red flannel shirt, the works. Rube did not look up as he had when leading the band in Jacksonville. This was serious business, and he was intent on making the grade. John McGraw and his team were also in Dallas at that point. He and some of his players were lounging in front of the hotel and they saw the same thing. "Imagine our surprise," recalled McGraw, "to see Rube Waddell on the driver's seat in full regalia." McGraw's boys all yelled out to Rube, but he didn't even give them a glance. As McGraw noted, Rube "was intent on his job." McGraw had never seen Rube look so serious.[4]

Mack retrieved the erstwhile fireman, but Rube continued to wear his red shirt under his uniform just in case. It was just as though he was back in Butler (and it was the only time he wore any underwear). Three days later Rube was gone again. This time he'd somehow met up with a group of cowboys who were headed for a cattlemen's convention over in Fort Worth. He spent a couple of days there refereeing boxing exhibitions and hoisting a few with the boys.[5]

Mack collared Rube and got him out of town. The A's had exhibitions to play with the Giants. These were slated for New Orleans. Before one of the games, Rube was throwing, looking very strong. "We knew," McGraw remembered, "the chances were that he would beat us." So McGraw gathered a few of his players around him and instructed them to follow his lead. They began taunting Rube on how weakly he was throwing. The clubs were warming up at the back of the outfield, and Rube responded to McGraw by picking up a ball and hurling it on a line, straight to home plate. "You call that

a throw!" chided McGraw. "Why my grandmother could…" McGraw succeeded in getting Waddell's dander up. Rube proceeded to whip several shots
straight to the plate, so much so that he was spent after the first few innings.
Fortunately, Mack had not planned to use him for the full game anyway.[6]

The games were popular with the New Orleans fans. McGraw's quixotic
ways got the better of him, though, and to the financial detriment of all
involved. In one game, McGraw ran out in the first inning to protest what
he saw as an umpire's failure to call a balk. Eddie Plank was the pitcher in
question. The umpire would not reverse himself. McGraw continued to argue.
He was tossed but refused to leave the field. The umpire ultimately forfeited
the game to Philadelphia. Few managers have been ejected from exhibition
games. But perhaps only John McGraw could get himself thrown out of and
have to forfeit a game in which he stood to make money from the receipts.
For after a one-inning forfeit, the fans demanded refunds and got them.

McGraw damaged the rest of the series, too. Former Pirate catcher Doc
Zimmer was now retired and had moved to New Orleans. Mack knew Zimmer and knew he had aspirations to be an umpire. So he engaged Zimmer
for the Giant series. After getting tossed, McGraw seemed to turn a trifle
paranoid. There were seven games slated, but McGraw withdrew after the
fourth. The A's had won all four. McGraw told the press that Zimmer and
Mack had been colluding. Mack, McGraw claimed, had a financial interest
in the New Orleans Pelicans baseball club. Zimmer, he pontificated, wanted
to umpire in the Southern League, in which the Pelicans play. Thus, he concluded, Zimmer had been making calls in favor of the A's to curry favor with
Mack, who would use his influence with the other Southern League owners
to get Zimmer into the league's umpiring corps.[7] This outburst made
McGraw's "White Elephant" claims of 1902 appear downright phlegmatic. If
Bernard Shaw thought McGraw to be the most quintessentially American
man, Shaw must have felt Americans possessed quite a persecution complex.

Rube enjoyed McGraw's antics. Not to be outdone, Rube and Schreck,
staying at the St. Charles Hotel, were having dinner and found a steak not
to their liking. They sent it back, and it returned even tougher. (Perhaps Sam
Erwin was sneaking some mule meat their way.) Schreck got hold of a hammer and some nails, and they loudly pounded the piece of leather into the
wall. Schreck always knew what to do with a catcher's mitt that was too stiff.
The hotel manager threw them both out.

The triumph over the Giants, odd as it was, made the A's fans feel good.
They had gotten the better of McGraw; Rube was in fine fettle, to boot. He
was suffering from an upset stomach, but his thumb was fine. Baseball fans
in Philadelphia were hoping that 1907 would prove to be a repeat of the good
seasons, not of the last one.

NOTES

1. Newspaper note, October 6, 1906, Clippings File, Cooperstown.
2. *Philadelphia Inquirer*, March 2, 1907.
3. Ibid., March 5, 1907.
4. John McGraw, *My 30 Years in Baseball*, p. 28; Pete Martin, *Peter Martin Calls On...*, p. 49.
5. *Philadelphia Inquirer*, March 21, 1907.
6. McGraw, *My 30 Years*, p. 28.
7. *Philadelphia Inquirer*, March 29, 1907.

Turkish Bath

Rube and the A's seemed ready to start another season. The victory over the Giants was too strange to cause too much celebrating, though Rube did anyway, of course. In an exhibition out in Lancaster, Pennsylvania, Rube continued to be playful. He struck out one batter using a lemon instead of a baseball. In the annual "Quaker City" series with the Phillies he gave up an unearned run in the first inning of game one. From there he pitched a shutout but lost the game 1–0. It was a bad sign, but Rube was too busy to notice it. Game four also portended trouble. After seven innings the score was 5–5. In the eighth Rube walked two, hit two batsmen, and gave up two hits, while the A's fielders committed their sixth error of the day. The Phils scored four runs and won 9–5, sweeping the series.

Rube had often been strong at the start of a season. But in 1907 his balloon went up early. He pitched poorly in his first appearance in relief against Boston. In his first start against New York, he took a 4–2 lead into the ninth. Then he walked the first man. The next batter touched him for a hard single to center. Mack didn't like the looks of it. He sent in Bender, and Rube became angry about not being allowed to win his own game. When Bender failed to hold New York and lost the game, Rube turned sullen. Away he went again. Mack did not see him for over a week. On April 27 Mack announced to the press that the absent Rube was suspended for 30 days. Mack said Rube had, contrary to orders, continued to drink and keep late hours.[1]

Rube read the announcement of his suspension and showed up at Mack's office the next morning. Somehow he convinced Mack that he was at a "Turkish bath," asserting that the suspension was unfair. Mack asked for an affidavit of proof, and Rube produced one. How he did it, no one knows.[2]

Mack brought Rube back. Unlike prior years, he did not immediately throw him out to the mound. The team was winning and had the lead in the young season. On May 2 and May 4 he used Rube in relief in games already decided. In the second week of May, the A's began a trip around the western circuit. Before leaving with the team Rube was arrested. Ex-wife May

Wynne filed non-support charges against him, again, and he had to post $500 bond before he could go on the road trip. Rube was not fazed.[3]

The first stop on the trip was Chicago. Jack Coombs was ill; Plank and Bender were hurt. The A's lost two in a row, so on May 14 Mack turned to Rube to stop the slide. Rube came through. He pitched a one-hitter through eight innings and gave up two meaningless hits in the ninth, winning 9–0. He appeared to have his stuff back, and nothing seemed to be derailing him, not even May Wynne.

Three days later in St. Louis, Rube appeared to have celebrated his Chicago victory a bit too zealously. The Browns killed him, 13–1. Detroit was the next stop. The Tigers looked very tough, with young Ty Cobb playing even better than he had the previous year. Detroit mauled the A's in the first game of the series, 15–8, but Eddie Plank stopped them with a shutout the next day, and Rube did the same the day after. The A's old 1-2 punch was still there. But the frustration was the same too — could Rube be depended upon?

In addition to Rube's inconsistency, Mack had injury problems again. Both Plank and Bender had been out for short spells. Infielders Danny Murphy and Monte Cross were out, and Mack had to cut infielder Jack Knight for making too many errors. Mack needed Rube to help hold the team up until everyone was healthy again. The early lead of April had vanished. By June 1, the A's had fallen to fifth place.

Rube lost a close one in Cleveland to Addie Joss. He did not pitch badly, Joss just pitched better. Rube won in 12 innings in Boston, but he did not pitch well. He failed to strike out a single batter, something he had never done in all his years with the A's in any appearance longer than two innings.[4]

Mack took matters into his own hands to try to collar Rube. Rube had wandered over to Camden, New Jersey, and gotten into a fight at a saloon on Girard Avenue. Mack used his influence to have Rube arrested. Mack staged a hearing to frighten Rube. The "magistrate" was a police lieutenant. With Rube nervously standing before him, other officers brought in a man, supposedly the one Rube had assaulted, virtually mummified in bandages. The lieutenant abruptly shouted: "Get that man to a hospital immediately. He may die!" Mack recalled that Rube turned ashen, as the lieutenant placed him under Mack's $300 bond and a threat of six months in jail if he misbehaved again.[5] The whole thing was a hoax, but it seemed to work. Rube behaved for about a month.

Rube finally started to show some consistency — even brilliance — in June. He beat Washington on the 4th, shutting out the Senators for the last five innings. With only a day's rest he threw a great shutout against Ed Walsh and the White Sox. The A's beat the Sox in the next two games as well. Rube followed the shutout of Chicago with a blanking of St. Louis on June 10. In those three wins he had struck out 30 and pitched 23 consecutive scoreless innings.

As drinking takes its toll on gifted athletes, their peaks diminish in height and duration and the gaps between the flashes of brilliance widen. Cleveland ended Rube's scoreless innings streak on June 13 with a run in the first inning. Rube nevertheless pitched seven shutout innings thereafter. But in the ninth Cleveland touched him for three straight hits. Then Rube walked a batter. A run was in and the bases were loaded with one out. Outfielder Elmer Flick was the next batter. With two strikes he hit a hard liner to center, centerfielder "Rube" Oldering charged it. Rather than taking it on the bounce, he charged it. The ball scooted all the way to the fence. Flick circled the bases with everyone scoring ahead of him. Cleveland won.

The A's steadied themselves and won consistently despite Rube's ups and downs. In two games against Detroit, Rube lasted only a few innings. In late June, he pitched well against Washington and Boston. In the first week of July he lasted but a few innings in two outings against the Yankees. Rube was only 30 years old, but he showed all the signs of an aging player. Alcohol does that, and there was nothing amusing about it.

On July 5, after Rube had lasted only three innings against New York, the team traveled to Detroit. In the sixth inning starter Jimmy Dygert was down 3–2 and appeared to be weakening. Mack called for Rube. They found him sleeping in the clubhouse. Whether in disgust or with a hope of reviving him, Mack sent Rube out anyway. Rube shut down the Tigers' sixth-inning rally. But then the adrenaline must have worn off. He gave up four runs in the seventh and two in the eighth, as the A's lost 9–5. With the loss to Detroit, the Tigers climbed one-half game ahead of Philadelphia into third place, six games back of league-leading Chicago. Cleveland was a game and a half out in second.[6]

Rube was missing practices, and rumors were flying about that Mack was going to unload the big misfit. The team left Detroit for Chicago. Rube lost the opener, as Ed Walsh pitched a three-hit shutout. Reporters asked Mack about the trade rumors. Mack denied them and used the opportunity to goad Rube. "Release Rube? Never," scoffed Mack. "Rube is a little out of condition now, having a bad arm, but he is taking care of himself. He will pitch one of these bright days and give a good account of himself. All these stories about Waddell's not appearing for practice are rot. Rube is too sly a fox not to report. He is working hard, and these reports about his short-comings are *for the most part* [emphasis added], made from whole cloth."[7]

Bender and Plank each beat the Sox in the other games of the series. This underscored the point that the team no longer seemed to need a fading

Rube, particularly not with the race tightening. The team went on to St. Louis. Oddly, though, Mack stayed in Chicago "on business." He had never done that during the regular season.

Mack named Schreck manager in his absence. Schreck had a great head for the game, and he knew how not to mix baseball with his social life. He was also Rube's best friend, and if anyone could revive Rube, it was Schreck. Rube had not pitched in a week. In the first game in St. Louis, the A's were down 4–2 in the seventh. Schreck called in his roommate. Pitching at home often inspired Rube because he usually had friends in the stands. Now he was pitching for his buddy Schreck. Rube came in blazing. The A's perked up and tied the game. By the 12th inning Rube had allowed only three hits and had struck out nine. In the top of the 12th, Schreck made another good move. With a runner on second, he pinch-hit for weak-hitting Rube Oldering with Chief Bender. The Chief was as good a hitting pitcher as there was in his day. He singled the first pitch to right, knocking in a run. Rube took the mound with the lead. Facing the Browns' second, third, and fourth hitters, Rube struck out all three. The team felt good, and Rube once again seemed a part of it. The next day the A's pounded the Browns 9–1.[8]

Mack rejoined the team after the second win in St. Louis. A reporter asked him where he had been. Mack snapped, "You see me here, don't you?" This was unusually curt for Mack, and when the reporter asked if he intended to part with Rube, Mack was quite candid. "I was sore at the Rube," admitted Mack, "in fact very sore when I left the boys in Chicago. Waddell is a great pitcher and should never be anything but a great twirler. However, they tell me that Rube pitched great ball yesterday ... so I guess he'll promise to behave." No one knew the details of the deal Mack had tried to close in Chicago, but it had been close enough to fruition that he had taken time off to negotiate it. It apparently fell through, though, and Rube pitched well for Schreck. Mack returned to St. Louis. Fearing that Rube would celebrate his good day, Mack recalled the magistrate's threat of jailing. He did it deftly, too. Rube noticed an unidentified man watching him in the team's St. Louis hotel. When he wondered to Mack who the man was, Mack calmly replied, "'Must be a detective." Two days later Rube won another over the Browns with a five-hitter. Three days later he beat Cleveland. From the fifth to the ninth in the Cleveland game he retired 15 straight batters and struck out eight. It was his third win in five days.[9]

Rube's next outing was a heartbreaker. He struck out 12 against Detroit. But the A's committed four costly errors, and the team lost 4–3. The question was how would Rube react; he had an idle Sunday to contemplate the matter.

The A's lost another tough one to Detroit in their next outing. The

Tigers were the only team in the league with a winning record against the A's. Sam Crawford and Ty Cobb were especially murderous. The day after Rube's loss they roughed up Eddie Plank, scoring five runs in the eighth with Crawford and Cobb cracking consecutive doubles. Plank had given up no runs in his previous 25 innings, except the RBIs by Crawford and Cobb.[10]

Right after the two tough losses to Detroit, first-place Chicago was due in, with the A's six games out. Mack sent Rube out for the opener. Rube put runners on several times, but always worked out of the jams. Five times he ended innings by striking out a batter with runners in scoring position. With the score tied 1–1 in the seventh, Schreck stepped up with a man on and doubled, putting the A's in front. Rube then stepped in. Mack signaled for a bunt. Rube tried to bunt, but fouled off the first two. He stepped back and lofted a shallow fly which fell in. Schreck scored, and Rube shut down the Sox in the eighth and ninth. Mack hoped that getting such a break could combine with good pitching to impress Rube with the wisdom of maintaining discipline. A lot was at stake.

Four games remained with Chicago. Bender and Dygert won both ends of a doubleheader, Bender's win being a beautiful two-hitter. Plank made it four in a row. Two games now separated first and fourth place in the league. Rube was to start the fifth game with Chicago. Could he complete the sweep?

Twenty-thousand fans turned out in Philadelphia to see if Rube could win again. Rube appeared a little shaky in the first, and the Sox scored a run on a sacrifice fly. The fourth inning saw a classic, virtually hitless rally from the Sox. The Sox began by beating out a slow grounder. The next batter hit another slow one, and the throw to second was late. The next hitter squared to bunt. First baseman Harry Davis charged in. The batter missed Rube's offering. Murphy sneaked over to first behind the aggressive runner, and Schreck tried to pick him off. Murphy dropped the throw, and the lead runner went to third. The bunt sign went off, and the batter grounded one to short. The ball bad hopped over the shortstop's head, scoring a run and leaving runners on first and second. Again, the Sox attempted to bunt. Rube charged the bunt to his right. He fielded it and turned to third. His third baseman had charged, too, and when Rube turned there was no one there — safe all around. The Sox thus had scored a run and loaded the bases, without a clean hit. Rube appeared rattled, but Mack made no move. The next hitter caught Rube's first pitch for a double. Two more scored. After Rube struck out pitcher Ed Walsh, the leadoff hitter singled in yet two more. The five runs held up. The A's scored twice on nine hits. The Sox staved off the sweep, and the A's missed the opportunity to knot up the race. It was a sad way to end a streak for both Rube and the team, and they again had an idle Sunday to think about it.[11]

Mack "rested" Rube for the week. Rube was out on another bender. The A's took two from St. Louis and one from Cleveland that week. Chicago lost a pair in New York. As of Saturday, August 3, the Tigers and White Sox were tied with the A's one game out.

Rube went out on Saturday to face Cleveland. In the first inning the Naps had the bases loaded with one out. Rube struck out the next two, and the fans went crazy. Cleveland could not touch him the next five innings. In the seventh, Cleveland's pitcher led off with a weak single. The next batter bunted. Rube fielded it, but his throw to second pulled the shortstop off the bag. With two on the next batter squared to bunt and popped it gently in front of the plate. Rube ran in and dove for it, trying to snare it on the fly. He missed and landed right on his left elbow. Mack had to take him out. Cleveland would score four that inning, as Jimmy Dygert gave up two straight singles. Detroit won that day, and Chicago won as well. Rube had another idle Sunday and, it seemed, a few more days to contemplate the loss and the fate of his elbow. Some papers began to editorialize that Rube ought be suspended. He had grown entirely unmanageable. People recalled the straw hat incident of 1905 and saw more such damage in the future. Fans tried to convince themselves that pitchers like Dygert could take up the slack. Some honestly resigned themselves to the idea that a comfortable second place without Rube was just fine.[12]

Cleveland and the A's had a doubleheader on Monday. Plank beat Addie Joss in game one. Mack started a youngster Bill Bartley in game two. He didn't last an inning. Elmer Flick doubled and Nap Lajoie singled. Mack put in another new kid named Sam Hope. It was quite a test for the youngster. Three singles and an error later, Hope was out. He never pitched another inning of big league ball. Down 4–0, the A's countered with a single run in the bottom of the first. The fans cheered, though a little nervously, when they saw who Mack had sent out in the second inning. It was Rube, sore elbow and all. Rube had told Mack that the elbow was a little painful but okay. Mack figured this was now a throwaway game, so he gave the Rube an opportunity to test the arm. Rube tested it and then some. Over the next eight innings he struck out six and gave up only five hits. Meanwhile the A's caught fire and scored 11 runs. The throwaway had become a winner. The next day during the final game with Cleveland, Mack sent Rube and Schreck out to warm up on the sidelines. The crowd started to cheer like mad. Mack had not intended to put Rube in, but the reaction showed how closely Rube had returned to the hearts of the fans. Detroit was due in next.

The A's took two of three from Detroit, Bender hurling both victories. Rube's arm did need some rest. Only a stupid running error by Bris Lord gave Detroit their one win. Nevertheless, as of Saturday Chicago had faded. The

A's were in second place, a half game back of the Tigers. By a quirk in the schedule Detroit and Philadelphia left on Sunday and headed straight to Detroit for a series at Bennett Park.

Rube started game one on Monday. He scattered eight hits and struck out seven. He held his old buddy Sam Crawford hitless. Cobb went 2 for 3, but Rube got him when it counted. In the third Cobb came up with two on and two out. He popped to Schreck. Rube's stuff wasn't blazing as it had in mid–July, but he was there when it counted, and he was largely sober too. The A's were now in first place.

Plank won the next game on a three-hitter. Mack thought he would try Rube again on Wednesday. Alas, Detroit jumped all over him for three runs in the first inning. Dygert, Bartley, and Coombs each did little better in relief that day as Detroit won 9–2. Even worse, Danny Murphy was out. He had been spiked in the game, by Ty Cobb, of course.

The A's slipped a bit in Cleveland. After Plank lost on Saturday, three games separated first and fourth place. Rube pitched in only one game that week, a single inning of relief. On Monday, August 19, Rube started the final game with Cleveland. He gave up three runs in the first, and Mack lifted him. The A's rallied and had a lead 6–3 midway through the game, but they lost it 10–8. Chicago and Detroit both won.

It was on to Chicago. Plank started the series and lost 4–1. Detroit and Chicago were now tied, a half game out. Bender held Chicago to four hits in the next game, and he lost, 1–0. Rube came through the next day to stop the slide with one of his great games. The A's scored two in the first and that was it. Rube struck out 13, gave up two meaningless hits, and walked none. Someone printed cards for Sox fans and distributed 15,000 of them in the grandstand. The card had a poem, part of which read: "Rube, Rube, You've been drinking; You cannot see the plate." The crowd began chanting this over and over, but Rube did not flinch. He was on another streak, and no chant was going to derail him. Only he could do that.[13]

NOTES

1. *Philadelphia Inquirer*, April 15, 16, 18, 27, 1907.
2. Ibid., April 28, 1907.
3. Ibid., May 3, 5, 1907; *Sporting News*, May 11, 1907.
4. *Philadelphia Inquirer*, May 15, 17–22, 26, 30, June 1, 1907.
5. Told by Connie Mack in Spink, "Rube Waddell," p. 18; Clippings File, Cooperstown.
6. *Philadelphia Inquirer*, June 14, 19, 22, 25, 30, July 3, 5, 6, 1907.
7. Ibid., July 8, 1907.

8. Ibid., July 13–14, 1907.

9. Ibid., July 14, 17, 1907; Spink, "Rube Waddell," p. 18.

10. *Philadelphia Inquirer*, July 21–22, 1907.

11. Ibid., July 28, 1907.

12. Ibid., August 4, 1907; editorial, August 8, 1907, unidentified newspaper, likely the *Philadelphia Public Ledger*, August 8, 1907, Clippings File, Cooperstown.

13. *Philadelphia Inquirer*, August 6–9, 11, 13-15, 18, 20–23, 1907.

Chapter 42

Oh, That Ty Cobb!

After Rube destroyed Chicago on August 22, it was on to St. Louis. Eddie Plank returned to form and won on Friday. The A's split a doubleheader with the Browns on Saturday, while Detroit, Chicago, and Cleveland all won. At the end of the day the league standings were indeed close:

	W	L
Philadelphia	66	44
Chicago	69	47
Detroit	64	44
Cleveland	66	48

Philadelphia had another doubleheader with the Browns on Sunday. The A's lost the first game, so a win in the afternoon game was a must. The A's scored a run in the top of the first. Out stepped Rube with a one-run lead. That would be all he would get from his hitters that day, and it would be all he would need. As against Chicago, he gave up two hits, though this time he walked one and struck out ten. The A's then had a few days off, and Detroit made the most of it, winning and taking over first place.

After their days off the A's rolled into New York. Plank lost the opener, but Rube came back on Friday to win 6–3. New York's three runs stopped his scoreless inning streak at 19. Bender won the next day, but Detroit kept winning, and they won while the A's were idle on Sunday.

The first week of September gave the A's a great opportunity. Detroit and Chicago had a series with one another, while the A's were to play lowly Washington at home. In a Labor Day doubleheader over 28,000 came to Columbia Park. Jack Coombs started the first game and gave up two runs. Rube relieved him after seven innings. He gave up one more, but the A's could just garner one run all day. It was tough to lose against such a weak opponent at such a critical time. Plank won the afternoon game. Meanwhile, Chicago and Detroit split, and Cleveland split in St. Louis. A victory in game one would have left the A's tied for first. Dygert and Rube picked up the

morale, winning a doubleheader the next day. After Chief Bender beat the
Yankees on September 4, the A's again found themselves in first place by a
half game.[1]

Chicago, Detroit, and the A's kept pace with one another through early
September. Two Rube losses were rumored to have come due to the effects
from a debauched sojourn to Atlantic City in early September. Whether it
was true or not, it was certainly believable, resentment against Rube on the
A's being what it was. Still, no team in the AL bolted ahead. It was as though
the clubs wanted to mark time until they faced each other again. On September 9, Boston came to Philadelphia. Boston had had a bad year. Only
Washington lay lower in the league standings. But the game had meaning,
and not just because the A's were in the pennant race. Rube and Cy Young
were going to face each other once more. Young gave up six hits; Rube four.
Young struck out eight; Rube six. The A's made five errors and put Rube in
some terrible jams, but he pitched out of all of them. (Some said the A's poor
fielding behind Rube was deliberate, in this game and elsewhere, as many
wanted to get back at Rube for the alleged Atlantic City escapade.) Neither
Rube nor Cy walked a batter that day. After 13 innings the score was knotted, 0–0. It had taken only an hour and 53 minutes. From the eighth inning,
both sides had gone 1-2-3 every time. It was almost spooky how the two
greats had put their opponents to sleep. The spookiness grew all the more lit-
eral as the game progressed. It was a damp afternoon and mists began to mix
with smoke from an adjacent railroad yard. The haze blanketed the field, and
the game had to be called with no score. It was a great game for history. But
by ending at 0–0, it meant nothing in the standings. Some continued to
grumble that a dependable Rube would have inspired better play from his
mates and yielded a needed victory.[2]

On September 23, Chicago arrived in Philadelphia for three games. The
A's were even with Detroit and one and a half up on the White Sox. The A's
won two of three from the Sox. Chicago was fading. Detroit was not, and
guess who was due in Philadelphia for the weekend? Detroit.

The first game on Friday was a tough one. Eddie Plank squared off against
Wild Bill Donovan. The A's got 13 hits to the Tigers' nine, but the final score
was 5–4 Detroit. This put the A's out of the league lead for the first time
since September 3. It rained all day Saturday, and since this was still the
Quaker City, come what may, no game was permitted on Sunday. (The law
did not change until 1934.) A doubleheader was slated for Monday the 30th.[3]

Amidst all the excitement, where was Rube? He was off somewhere getting very drunk. "The team fool was away four to five days," noted *The Sporting News*. Fans knew it. Mack knew it. Given the critical juncture of the
season at hand, no one was laughing.[4]

Ticket sales for the Monday twin bill totaled 24,127. Many more tried to crash the gates. Two brass bands paraded about the stands. Other fans came with cowbells, bugles, frying pans, and anything else with which to make noise. Countless fans without tickets climbed over the outfield fences as friends in the bleachers secured ropes to the benches and threw them over the back. The police put a stop to this, but their intervention nearly caused a riot. Fans ringed the outfield and were held back by squads of police. People in buildings with strategic window views were selling entry to their rooms for the unheard-of price of $5. One man sold space on his rooftop at $3.25 a pop, but the demand was so great he quickly raised his price to $5. The last two spots went for $15. City workers pushed trollies to selected spots on the streets, and dozens climbed on top of the cars. A druggist on 29th St. and Columbia Avenue took in 200 people at $3 apiece and had them take turns standing on the soda fountain chairs for a glimpse of the ballfield. Downtown in front of the *Inquirer* office thousands gathered to listen as callers with megaphones relayed the game's events as they were phoned in from the press box.

Jimmy Dygert started for Mack in game one. Detroit countered with Bill Donovan, who had beaten Plank on Friday. Dygert shut down the Tigers in the first. The A's countered with four hits and three runs, batting eight men in their half of the inning. The fans were delirious. In the second inning, the pressure got to Dygert. The first batter singled. The next man grounded to Dygert. He threw to second, but his toss landed wide and in the dirt, pulling Murphy off the bag, leaving all safe. A sacrifice advanced runners to second and third. The next batter chopped back to Dygert. The runner on third had advanced too far and Dygert had him in a rundown. Again, however, Dygert threw wildly. The run scored and the runners advanced. Dygert then yielded a walk, filling the bases full with only one out. Mack decided to make a move.

With the bases loaded and one out, Mack sent for the Rube. He wanted Plank for game two. Bender was ill and Jack Coombs was hurt. Fans were more than a little nervous as Rube took the mound. His phenomenal play of earlier years was a distant memory. As was normal in those days, Rube took no warm-ups; Bang! Rube immediately struck out Detroit's next two hitters, their leadoff and second batters, no less. Detroit left the inning with three runners standing. The crowd roared. Rube seemed to have his stuff and he had a lead, to boot. Confidence grew even more as Rube struck out four in the next two innings, thus fanning six of the first eight he faced. The A's, meanwhile, hit Donovan for two runs in the third and two more in the fifth. Going into the seventh inning the A's lead remained 7–1.

Then came the weird seventh. Donovan led off the inning for Detroit with a pop to center. Rube Oldering was camped under it but, inexplicably,

Rube gained a well-deserved reputation for zaniness and high jinks, but at times it was a trifle distorted. When asked by a photographer to pose, he obliged, goofing a bit as there was no game at stake. The resulting photograph (when the grassy surface was cropped to leave the impression it was actually taken at a game) lent further support to the notion that Rube was a simpleton and a loon even during a ballgame. (National Baseball Hall of Fame Library, Cooperstown, N.Y.)

he flat dropped it. Perhaps a little rattled, Rube walked the next batter, the only man he would walk all day. Then Simon Nichols muffed a grounder at shortstop that could have been a double play. Were it not for the dropped fly and the muff at short, Rube and the A's would have been out of the inning. As it was, the bases were loaded with nobody out. Up stepped Sam Crawford. Crawford was as dangerous a line-drive hitter as ever played the game. He could hit 'em low, high, inside, or out, it didn't matter. A reporter once asked Chicago's Ed Walsh, "Is there any place where you can throw the ball where Crawford won't hit it?" "Yeah," Walsh cracked, "second base."[5] Walsh was not far off: Crawford knocked Rube's first pitch for a double, scoring two. Ty Cobb stepped in. Cobb was leading the league in hitting for the first time that season (he would do it a few more times), but Rube worked him for an infield grounder. Murphy elected to toss it to first, however, and a run scored. Murphy could have gone to Schreck, but he apparently preferred to keep Cobb off the base paths. He didn't want to risk being spiked again. It was one of countless ways that Cobb's terror tactics worked in Detroit's favor. With Crawford now on third and no one on first, the next batter grounded to second. He was thrown out but Crawford scored. It could have been a double play even if Murphy had failed to cut down the lead runner on the previous play. Cobb died on second as Rube struck out the next batter to end the inning. Crawford's double had been the only hit of the inning, yet Detroit had scored four.

The A's got one back in the bottom of the seventh, and Detroit hustled one in the top of the eighth on a double, a steal and a grounder. Going into the ninth, the score was 8–6. Rube again faced Sam Crawford who singled to start the inning and set things up for Ty Cobb. Rube worked Cobb carefully, throwing him three straight curves. Each offering just missed. At 3 and 0 Rube would not yield. He threw two more curves, and each cut the corner. Cobb usually leaned his shoulders toward the plate to hit more for contact than power. This time he pulled slightly away, guessing, with the count full, that Rube's next delivery would be a fastball. He guessed right. Cobb pulled back and connected, knocking the pitch over the crowd and over the fence. In his 24 years in baseball, Cobb never hit more than nine home runs in a season. He hit only one off Rube Waddell, and this was it, one of two home runs Rube yielded all season. The score was now tied. Connie Mack fell off his seat on the bench and landed in the bat rack.[6]

The mess of the seventh inning was not Rube's fault. And there was no disgrace in the ninth, given who had touched Rube for the two runs. Crawford and Cobb were the best one-two punch in the game, as good as any at any time, including Ruth/Gehrig and Maris/Mantle. Sam Crawford was a future Hall of Famer. He would be (and likely always will be) baseball's all time leader in triples. And Ty Cobb was — Ty Cobb. Some wondered how Cobb could hit a pitch so far, particularly since he hit a ball that had been in use since the fifth inning. The answer was in his body motion. With Cobb pulling his shoulders away from the plate, he was connecting with more than just the weight and strength of his arms. Such a swing is not the way to hit for a high average, and Cobb seldom hit that way. But it is one way to jerk the ball a long way. Whatever the reason for Cobb's homer, the fact was that Rube had failed to hold a substantial lead, and people were angry. Whether Rube could have held Detroit from there, we'll never know, for Mack sent in Eddie Plank. No one realized it then, but they had just witnessed Rube Waddell's last appearance for the A's in Columbia Park.

The 8–8 tie held up through the tenth inning. In the 11th each side scored one. In the 12th, Detroit loaded the bases but didn't score. Some real controversy came in the 14th. The outfield was still ringed with people with no barriers but squads of police. The police were supposed to move the crowds back in case a play came their way so there would be no interference. In the top of the 14th, the A's big first baseman Harry Davis led off with a high drive to center field. Sam Crawford was out there. He raced for the ball; it grazed his glove and glanced into the crowd. Normally a ball hit into the crowd under such circumstances is ruled a ground rule double. Davis anticipated this and jogged into second. Plate umpire "Silk" O'Loughlin ruled, however, that a policeman had interfered with Crawford and ruled Davis out. The second umpire of the day had ruled ground rule double, but O'Loughlin over-ruled him. The A's put up a fearsome argument. Even Connie Mack grew red-faced. He would not speak to O'Loughlin for over a decade because of the call.[7]

The Detroit players streamed out and threw their two cents into the discussion. With both teams out, shouting and pushing started. First baseman Claude Rossman and Bill Donovan got into a fight with the A's Monte Cross. Rube jumped into the melee to protect Monte. A policeman was going to arrest Donovan, but a Detroit player appealed to him on the basis that Donovan, like the policeman, was Irish and his family was in the stands. The policeman yielded. Rossman and Monte Cross were tossed out of the game; neither was Irish. Rossman needed a police escort.

Fans began to spill onto the field, and when word of what was going on reached the people on the street beyond the left field bleachers, hundreds more climbed over the fences and streamed onto the field. It was sheer chaos.

The police were able to restore order. The umpire's decision stood. Danny Murphy and Jimmy Collins were the next hitters. Both singled. Murphy's hit caused the crowd to stir again. His hit, as well as Collins's, would have scored Davis. Crawford had simply missed Davis's fly. But the A's had no runs to show for their efforts in the 14th. The game went on. Plank pitched the rest of the way for Philadelphia. Donovan went the distance for Detroit, throwing over 200 pitches. After the 17th inning, O'Loughlin said it was too dark to see the ball. There would be no second game, and in those days teams did not make up ties. An A's victory would have put them on top. Now they were still percentage points behind.

The A's-Tigers game of September 30 was one American League fans talked about for years. It was a critical game, it was well played, it had stars like Crawford, Plank, Cobb, and Waddell, and it was full of excitement and controversy. Fans and reporters second-guessed Connie Mack incessantly. He could have inserted Plank and come back with Dygert for game two. The subtext of such a point was obvious — why had he inserted the undependable Rube? Mack was not too happy about it himself. He "will never forgive himself for giving Waddell one more chance," wrote one reporter.[8] The game was not a loss. Indeed, had it ended in a loss, people other than Rube could have been more blameworthy. The anger at Waddell seemed to derive from other obvious points of frustration about him which had lain dormant. No matter the other factors in the game, no matter Dygert's errors, no matter that Jack Coombs was hurt, no matter that Chief Bender was ill, no matter that O'Loughlin blew a key call, no matter what, Rube had just not come through for the team when it counted.[9]

Like Rube's duel with Cy Young in Boston earlier in the month, the Detroit game was one for history, but it had no effect on the pennant race of 1907. It was as though Rube had evolved, or devolved, to a point where he seemed not to be pitching for Philadelphia anymore.

Detroit left town for Washington and proceeded to beat up on the hapless Senators. Dygert came back the next day for the A's to beat Cleveland. O'Loughlin umpired and the crowd boos were minimal, but then this was Philadelphia. On Wednesday, key errors and untimely hitting threw away a good pitching performance by Eddie Plank. Cleveland won, while the Tigers swept two in Washington.[10]

With the loss to Cleveland, the A's and Tigers each had 56 losses, but the Tigers had 90 wins to the A's 84. Earlier in the month, with Rube drinking and Bender and Coombs out, Mack had bypassed the second game of several home doubleheaders against lower-level teams, and reporters questioned this in hindsight. (Home managers have control over the start of games until they turn in their lineup cards to the head umpire, and back then they could claim things like wet grounds or a late hour.) The A's were not out of the race, but now their chance was merely mathematical. Dygert again blanked Cleveland on Thursday, but Detroit completed their sweep of Washington. The A's went down to Washington for a doubleheader. In the first game Eddie

Plank, on one day's rest, faced a new kid, fresh out of the Idaho farm country, named Walter Johnson. It was 1–1 after nine innings, and in the tenth Washington sneaked a runner following a hit, an error, and two infield grounders. Dygert pitched the second game and won on no days' rest. Bender could not pitch; neither could Rube. Bender was hurt; Rube was drunk.[11]

Saturday, October 5, was the A's final day of the season. They had another pair of games with the Senators. Their chance for a tie for the pennant entailed their winning both games against the Senators and St. Louis sweeping all three games they still had to play with Detroit. Coombs was hurt, so was Bender; Mack decided to try Charlie Fritz, a rookie he had recruited from New Orleans. Fritz pitched three innings of shutout ball. Then in the fourth he walked two and hit a batter. Mack told Harry Vickers to warm up. Vickers had just won 25 with Williamsport, Pennsylvania, that summer. He was so good out there that folks nicknamed him Rube. While the young Rube was getting ready, Mack sent the old Rube out to fill in for Fritz. Rube faced one man and gave up a hit. By that point, Vickers was ready, and Mack put him in. The A's won the game 4–2 in 15 innings. Vickers went the distance, and he came back to pitch the second game, where he hurled a five-inning no-hitter; darkness fell and the game counted. Vickers earned his spot for 1908. Meanwhile, Detroit had beaten St. Louis that afternoon, so the 1907 season was all over.[12] The pennant went to Detroit.

It would be hard to fictionalize any better symbolism than the game in Washington that afternoon. The old Rube was a rum-soaked shadow of the man who had pitched six straight days over Detroit en route to winning the pennant for the A's in 1902. A new Rube had come in and, in Rube-fashion, won both ends of a doubleheader. Meanwhile, his old nick-namesake could not even get out the one batter he faced. Given how he had frittered away his colossal talents, such an ending was somehow appropriate to Rube's 1907 season. Though no one knew it at the time, it turned out to symbolize much more than that. It was the end of Rube's career with Connie Mack and the Philadelphia Athletics.

NOTES

1. *Philadelphia Inquirer*, August 24–26, 29–31, September 1, 3–5, 1907.
2. Ibid., September 10, 1907; see also Harold Seymour, *Baseball: The Golden Age*, p. 106.
3. *Philadelphia Inquirer*, September 24–26, 1907.
4. Ibid., September 28–30, 1907; *The Sporting News*, October 3, 1907.
5. *Philadelphia Inquirer*, November 27, 1907.

6. Ibid., October 1, 1907; see also Irwin M. Howe, "Pennant Winning Plays," syndicated column, quoted in the *Minneapolis Journal*, March 14, 1912.

7. Seymour, *Baseball: The Golden Age*, p. 138.

8. *Sporting Life*, October 5, 1907.

9. *Philadelphia Inquirer*, October 1, 1907; see also John Thorn, *Baseball's 10 Greatest Games* (New York: Four Winds Press, 1981), pp. 7–23.

10. *Philadelphia Inquirer*, October 2–3, 1907.

11. Ibid., October 4–5, 1907; *Sporting News*, October 3, 1907.

12. *Philadelphia Inquirer*, October 6, 1907.

Chapter 43

Divorce, Rube Style

With all the drinking, late hours, leaves, and suspensions, Rube's 1907 record was still 19 and 13. His mediocrity was still pretty good. And he *again* led the league in strikeouts. This was the sixth year in a row he had done that. Only one pitcher, Chicago's Ed Walsh, approached Rube's total of 232. Walsh pitched in an incredible 56 games that season, compiling 422 innings (to Rube's 44 games and 285 innings). With all that work, Walsh struck out 206. Plank was the only other pitcher in the league to top 180. In their five and a half years together, Rube and Plank had combined for 56 percent of all the A's victories. The total was 267 wins; no pair of pitchers had ever done that, nor would any.

Detroit faced the Chicago Cubs in the World Series that fall and lost. While the series was taking place, Rube went on some post-season exhibitions. He again appeared in Hartford, Connecticut, to raise money for a tuberculosis hospital. As he had the previous year, Rube delighted the crowd of 4000. The sensation of Rube pitching such exhibitions, while the World Series was occurring elsewhere, underscored what had changed about, but not within, him. Whether wrestling alligators or turning cartwheels on the mound, Rube was always a sideshow artist. He just happened to have been a sideshow artist who could also play the big top better than anyone. But now, as he deteriorated, he had no clue of what was occurring, and no one could tell him.

After the Hartford game, Rube, Schreck, Chief Bender, Harry Davis, and some of the other A's went on a tour in Pennsylvania. They played all the big towns — Bloomsburg, Reading, Clearfield, Williamsport. Rube's absenteeism wasn't too bad, either. He loved the clowning. Given the way the season had turned out, his teammates were hardly charmed. Still, they had to acknowledge that Rube was the big drawing card that put extra money in their pockets. They all needed the cash. But that underscored the aggravation, as many felt that were it not for Rube's high jinks and boozing the post-season money they would be making in the World Series would be a lot better than the chump change from barnstorming.

The money was coming in, though, and one reason Rube could be depended upon during the tour was the fact that all the players had agreed that no money would be paid out to anybody until the tour was over. Given that Rube was on board, this was a wise move. Rube stuck to the bargain, too, but late in the tour Schreck grew thirsty and he wanted to renegotiate matters. The boys held a meeting. Rube sided with Schreck, but Davis, Bender and the rest would not budge. They knew full well that cash in the hands of Rube and Schreck would spell the end of the tour. No one knows exactly what was said at the meeting, but apparently words were exchanged, particularly between Rube and some of his opposition, words that were not the sort that one can easily take back. Rube was always a braggart who would readily impress his greatness on anyone in such company. Responses to his puffery doubtlessly grew personal, and the *ad hominems* likely escalated from there.

Rube had regularly inquired about the receipts after the games. Harry Davis, Socks Seybold, Topsy Hartsell, and Monte Cross had been keeping the books on the tour, and they always gave Rube the figures of any game whenever he requested them. Rube was no math whiz, however, even when sober. Somehow he got it into his head that the figures didn't add up and that he was being cheated. One problem was that Rube was looking at game receipts and not factoring in costs like transportation and hotels. With his dander up, no one could convince him of his accounting errors. Rube believed he was being cheated, and that was all there was to it. No matter the rancor, though, the original deal stuck: there was to be no money given out until after the tour stuck. Schreck went thirsty. Rube's charges of cheating led the players to drop him after their stop in Williamsport. They finished the tour without him. Telling the fans that Rube would not play disappointed many, but it surprised few. After the tour the players divvied up the receipts. They gave Rube his share and went their separate ways.[1]

Rube went off to Alabama. His parents were spending some of the winter months there. Rube had developed a fondness for the place, never mind that he had been whacked on the head in Montgomery. In Mobile he acquired quite a passion for shark fishing and an even greater passion for the Gulf seafood at the local taverns. His particular favorite was raw oysters. Noting that the oysters were particularly large, a newspaperman reported that Rube could eat a box at a single setting. (A box usually held about six dozen.) Apparently Rube was upset when he learned that another Mobile gastronome could consume more oysters than he at a single sitting.[2]

After his excursion south, Rube headed for Massachusetts. He was still married to May Wynne and may have wanted to spend some time with her, or at least felt he needed to keep up appearances so as not to give her greater leverage in the various suits she had filed against him. How she now felt would soon become clear to him. Other news about his future would await him in Massachusetts as well.

In February 1908, after the barnstorming tour, Harry Davis, Topsy Hartsel, Rube Oldering, and a few others had a meeting with Connie Mack. They laid it on the line. They were sick of Rube's antics and told Mack that if Rube reported for spring training, they would not show up. In early 1907, several of the A's had approached Mack, upset with the Rube's habits and claiming he was bad for the team. At that juncture, the wily Mack had responded with the point that Rube was great for ticket sales. He argued to the players, then, that he could trade Rube but that they would have to take a cut in salary. The players chose not to press the matter. This time was different; they were adamant, and they would actually quit. Some had continued to harbor resentment at how Rube's shenanigans had cost them the 1905 World Series. They felt even more strongly about how Rube's late-season drinking in 1907 had rendered him less effective than he should have been during the pennant fight with Detroit.[3]

Mack had bent over backwards for Rube since he first went out to Kansas City to retrieve him in 1902. He always felt that Rube's ability was worth the effort. As Rube's quality waned, the special treatment grew ever more difficult to justify. An ultimatum from so many players made Mack's recalculations simple. Mack had tried to sell or trade Rube to Chicago during the middle of the 1907 season, but he could not get the deal he wanted. This time he would not demand so high a price.

Mack talked to New York and Washington, but could find no takers. Then on February 7, Mack announced that he had sold Waddell to the St. Louis Browns. The $5000 sale price was kept out of the papers. In 1901, Barney Dreyfuss had sold Rube from Pittsburgh to Chicago. When Rube naively demanded he get some of the selling price Dreyfuss got for him, Dreyfuss offered him the whole cigar, literally. Rube made no such demands this time, and Mack was not about to share any part of the $5000 anyway. Later in 1908, Mack sold Schreck to the White Sox.[4]

Rube had been in Mobile tending bar during much of the winter, but he was with May Wynne when he received the news he had been sold. May and he, though still married, had hardly managed a good life with one another. In 1903, just two months after her wedding day, she had threatened Rube with prosecution for non-support. Rube had reformed his ways with her about as well as he had on the ball field. As with any alcoholic, promises and hints of improvement only underscore the insidiousness of the malady that affects others who are emotionally involved.

Ongoing domestic troubles plagued Rube's marriage. In February 1905, there had been the violent outburst in Peabody, Massachusetts. Grudges from such events are not easily dropped. When the news of the trade came, the family feared Rube might abandon all obligations in regard to back support that was due. They filed charges of non-support, and Rube became a wanted man in the Commonwealth. "We are strongly inclined," quipped the *Boston Post*, "to hand the palmetto to Mr. Waddell. Every time you turn around you see his name in print."[5] Charges relating to assault, support, and divorce would hang over Rube's head for over two years. While playing for the St. Louis Browns in 1908 and 1909, Rube would never travel with the team across the Massachusetts line. Throughout those two seasons, whenever the Browns' train pulled into Boston's South Station, constables waited there for Rube, and Rube would never be there to oblige them.[6]

Rube would not pitch in Boston until one fateful day in May 1910. Until then, Rube gleefully forgot his domestic troubles and headed off to train with his new team. He signed for a mere $1200 ($2400 had been his best with the A's). He left Massachusetts and headed for St. Louis well before the training camp reporting date. Folks in St. Louis smirked and noted that something appeared to be making Rube show quite a high level of eagerness to leave home and begin playing baseball. He sure did love to play ball. Rumor also had it that within days of the trade Rube had already touched up the Browns management for a $50 loan.[7]

NOTES

1. *Sporting News*, February 20, 1908.
2. *St. Louis Globe Democrat*, March 10, 1914; Clippings File, Cooperstown.
3. Clippings File, Cooperstown.
4. *Philadelphia Inquirer*, February 8, 1908.
5. *Boston Post*, February 11, 1908.
6. *St. Louis Globe Democrat*, February 20, 1908; Clippings File, Cooperstown.
7. *Boston Post*, February 13, 1908.

Chapter 44

McAleer's Gamble

Jimmy "Moses" McAleer thought he could make a pennant winner out of the St. Louis Browns. For anyone familiar with the history of the American League, the mere imagining of the Browns as pennant contenders seems ludicrous to most fans of baseball history. The only pennant the Browns ever won was in 1944, when virtually every good player in the game was off fighting World War II. Along with the Washington Senators, the Browns were the perennial doormat of baseball. But that reputation would be earned in subsequent decades. The Browns were actually a solid team for most of the American League's first decade. They had done well in their former existence as the Milwaukee Brewers. They finished second to the A's in 1902. They were only sixth in 1907 but had shown some strong hitting. Their team batting average in 1907 was .253, a meaningless difference with the A's .255. Only the champion Tigers, at .266, hit better. Pitching was the Browns' weakness.

The Browns were in a battle with the NL Cardinals for the hearts (and money) of baseball fans in the city of St. Louis. New York was large enough for three teams. Chicago could support two. But the survival of two teams was not so clear in smaller cities like Boston and Philadelphia, and it was even more uncertain in St. Louis. Because the 16-team, two-league format of baseball which settled in 1903 happened to last for 50 years, it did not mean that baseball folks out in St. Louis in 1907–8 felt secure about their future. They were clawing and scraping to survive, and the way to gain fan support was obvious — win.

For McAleer, building a winner meant improving his pitching. Then as now, there are two ways one can beef up a staff. One is to find new talent out in the bushes. This is hard enough today. In an era of sparse communications and no farm networks, it was even tougher. McAleer had unearthed one prospect out of Texas named Dode Criss. He came with rave reviews but never amounted to much.

Outside of his pitching, McAleer felt he indeed had the talent to make the Browns a contender, but it was talent that could age in the years it could take to develop new pitching prospects, even if they panned out. The other way to build up the Browns' pitching was McAleer's only option — trade for or buy established players. Teams with star pitchers will not readily give them up. What they will do is give up someone they think has passed his peak and trade him to someone willing to gamble that the old boy may still have a few good seasons left in him. This was McAleer's gamble. During the 1907 season, he picked up Bill Dineen from Boston, who had been the Pilgrims' best pitcher during their pennant winning years of 1903–4. It was with the same hope that McAleer nervously bought Rube from Philadelphia. He also picked up two veteran infielders, Hobe Ferris from Boston and Jimmy Williams from New York. Waddell, proclaimed one reporter, is "just as liable to win a pennant as to add some gray hairs to McAleer's head."[1]

McAleer was gearing up for one good shot at the pennant. He was not building for the future. He was shooting for an immediate success. Rube, Dineen, and McAleer's other two starters, Jack Powell and Harry Howell, were all over 30, as were five of his eight starters and four of his substitutes. It was by far the oldest team in baseball, hence more susceptible to injury and inconsistency. If they were going to make a run at the pennant, 1908 had to be the year. "What Detroit did," gleefully reported one newspaper, "surely the Browns can do too."[2]

Rube reported to McAleer at a kind of pre-spring training camp in French Lick, Indiana. McAleer wanted his new veterans to get into top shape. Leaving Massachusetts, Rube was more than willing. McAleer had Rube and others doing calisthenics. They exercised with various pieces of gymnasium equipment and ran ten miles a day. Rube did it all with a smile. It was better than facing alimony and assault hearings in Massachusetts.

McAleer was pleased with what he saw. He obviously wanted to put a positive face on everything with the press, but McAleer was a straightforward man from small-town Ohio who always spoke his mind. So there was something to it when he stroked his chin and told the papers in his Ohio twang: "Waddell, well he pleases me much. He seems in perfect trim and will hardly have to lose more than five pounds. For a man his size that is nothing." When he learned of Rube's oyster feats in Mobile, McAleer would add that he was going to look into whether any of the hotels the team would visit on the road had the European plan available.[3]

About the only trouble Rube raised in French Lick came one evening when McAleer took the team bowling. Rube had never bowled before, but, as always, he was eager to try. He hurled the ball down the alley with such force that the pin boy nearly surrendered his job for fear of being maimed.[4]

Nervously hopeful, McAleer and St. Louis embarked upon a new season

The A's grew sick of Rube's antics, and in late 1907 Connie Mack traded him to the St. Louis Browns. Here Rube is photographed at the outset of the 1908 season. He would pitch well that season, winning 19 and compiling an ERA of 1.89. He would also soundly beat his former Philadelphia teammates on several outings, including one in which he struck out 16, then a major league record. (National Baseball Hall of Fame Library, Cooperstown, N.Y.)

with their volatile new star. When Rube arrived in town, a reporter who met him described what was on the minds of many Browns fans:

> Rube Waddell, as he is today, is what he seems always to have been — inscrutable as a sphinx, unfathomable as infinity, yet simple as a child, … talkative and friendly in certain moods. No one has yet read full the vacillating mentality of George Edward. No one has plumbed the mystery of his moods; yet everyone knows him for a great overgrown boy, friendly and sociable.

Considering all the stories printed and told about Rube, the reporter found

> It is hard to see Rube today and believe that all the indiscretions credited him are true. Lean of face and limb, weighing 196 — less than in 7 years, he seems a carefully cared-for athlete rather than one accustomed to heap vagaries on the altar of pleasure.

This was certainly a testament to the physique and to the natural strength with which Rube had been endowed. No one ever frittered away so many God-given assets. All Browns fans wanted to believe the best would come out of Rube in 1908, and, like everyone, they could easily charm themselves. With all Rube's natural endowments, this was easy to do. But the reporter was wary:

> A mournful glint lurks in his eye at times and a slight pallor lends a conviction that something is awry, whether it may be too many moods or too many underdone roles.

One is left wondering, the reporter concluded, "How long will his gipsy wander-lust keep his uniform hanging in the Browns' clubhouse?" Back in St. Louis, Rube was already doing "some stunts around the refreshment resorts of the city."[5]

McAleer took Rube and the whole team down to Shreveport. Rube was already a great favorite of the fans there from his previous spring trainings with the A's. Some of his pitching stunts showed that this 31-year-old was neither the *kind* nor the *wunder* he had been. In a game in Munroe, Louisiana, he hollered to a batter. "I'm going to put this one straight over." The batter hit it for a single. He told the next batter, "I'm going to strike you out." The result: strike one, strike two, then a single over second base. The next day, up 8–1, Rube yelled to a hitter, "Here's a straight one." The batter knocked it out of the park. He was still a showman in his heart and mind. What was in his arm was another matter.[6]

When the team returned to St. Louis, McAleer was still effusive.

"Waddell," he declared, "certainly looks better than I have ever seen him at the opening of a season." McAleer was complimenting his own training regimen, of course. He declared Waddell "one of the easiest men in the world to handle," predicting, "he is going to pitch good ball for me this year."[7] Fans in St. Louis were keyed up. The first test would be the annual spring series between the Browns and the Cardinals.

The series with the Cardinals was good but not great for Browns fans. Harry Howell lost the first game for the Browns. Rube started game two. He struck out nine but gave up nine hits. Though he walked only two, he had a little control problem, causing him to groove a few too many pitches. The Cardinals won. Howell won the third game. Rube won the fourth, again striking out nine. Howell won the last to clinch the series. Rube wasn't bad, but the dreamy blazing stuff was hardly there.[8]

Rube jolted Browns fans out of their ambivalence in his first start of the regular season. Facing the tough White Sox on April 17, Rube hurled a one-hitter. He struck out five and only one ball left the infield the entire day, and that one came in the ninth inning with the game all but over. Rube could have called off his outfielders that day. The fans were jubilant.[9]

Rube would show some inconsistency that would frustrate those who hoped he had returned to the form of yesteryear. In his next outing on the 20th, he was perfect for five innings. Then in the sixth, after a single, a batter bunted. Rube and his catcher, "Tubby" Spencer, collided while attempting to field it. The next batter bunted as well. Rube fielded it, but his throw to third to cut down the lead runner was late. Then in rapid succession came two hits, a wild pitch, a walk, and a double. Five runs scored. Two more scored the next inning, and McAleer relieved him. Rube's good streaks were shorter now, and slight mishaps would throw him off his game. In baseball the key is not always to avoid mishaps, so much as it is to handle them when they occur. Whatever the combination of aging, alcohol, or temperament, Rube seemed less able to handle the usual bumps of a ball game.

Nevertheless, the Browns did well their first week. By the time of their home opener on April 24 their record was 6 and 2, including two victories in Detroit. They were in first place. The Cardinals, meanwhile, were 1 and 6, in the NL cellar. Rube won the home opener 2–1 over Chicago, and the city was completely with him and with the Browns. Then for ten days Rube inexplicably disappeared. Likely, it was another binge.

When Rube wandered into the St. Louis clubhouse on May 4, McAleer said nothing but, "You're pitching today." Detroit was in town. Rube got the first two batters out. Sam Crawford was next up. He dribbled one at second baseman Jimmy Williams, who was slow to field it. With Crawford on, Ty Cobb stepped up and slammed a double. Crawford scored, and folks started to groan. McAleer stuck with Rube, however, and Rube was up to it. Detroit scored no more after that. Unfortunately, the Browns could not score at all. When rain came in the seventh inning, the 1–0 margin became the final score. Such luck can be part of the game; now it seemed to accentuate any downturn for which Rube seemed sadly ill-prepared. Against Chicago on May 9, Rube didn't finish the first inning. McAleer gave him another try the very next day against Detroit. On that day, as one reporter said, "Rube did everything but run the bases for Detroit." He made an error early in the game, and twice in the sixth inning Rube had to cover first base on grounders. The first time he dropped the ball; the other time he fell over the bag and dropped it again. At the plate Rube had yet to get a hit all season. He could still pitch, inconsistently. His hitting and fielding were atrocious. The edges had long since frayed. The question was how much longer the center could hold.[10]

NOTES

1. *St. Louis Globe Democrat*, February 8, 1908.
2. Ibid., March 2, 1908.
3. Ibid., February 24, March 10, 1908.
4. Ibid., February 24, 1908.
5. Ibid., February 26, March 2, 1908.
6. Ibid., March 14, 1908.
7. Ibid., April 2, 1908.
8. Ibid., April 6, 7, 10, 12–13, 1908.
9. Ibid., April 18, 1908.
10. Ibid., April 21, 24–25, May 5, 10–11, 1908.

Chapter 45

Rube's Gonna Pitch

The Browns headed east. Their first-place standing in April was gone, but they were still well within the leaders' pack. Their first stop on the road was Washington. The Browns won the first two. Rube started game three, facing "Long"(6'8") Tom Hughes. Rube pitched well, but Hughes pitched better, as Washington won 4–0. Even if Rube had a good day, luck, it seemed, would not be on his side. Rube was beginning to appear to be the softest touch on the Browns rotation, quite a switch from being the most feared on a staff that included Chief Bender and Eddie Plank. The question was whether anything could turn things around for him. Just as importantly, if something did reverse his fortune, would he be able to handle it without shooting off into space again? The next stop on the road trip would provide answers, for Rube was due for his first return to Philadelphia.

Jimmy McAleer was a cagey manager and showman. He knew that Rube would be most apt to go out and paint up the town after he had pitched and that he would be more apt to stay in line beforehand. So with four games scheduled with the A's, he held Rube until the third. He may have wanted to wait another day, but by then Rube was virtually bursting a vein in his head in anticipation of his appearance. McAleer never announced his plans, either, so the crowds of Philadelphians turned out each of the first two days in hoping to see their beloved Rube. On Monday, May 19, McAleer made a simple announcement to the press: "Rube's gonna pitch."

Over 20,000 came on Monday afternoon to see the Rube. Thousands more were turned away. The crowds cheered as Rube warmed up. When he came up to bat in the third inning, the game was halted and Rube received a gift of a rifle and gun case in appreciation from the A's fans. (He later pawned the items.[1])

In the game Rube faced Chief Bender. (Schreck did not catch that day.) Bender looked invincible at first. The Browns scored nothing through five innings. As for Rube, the A's jumped on him in the way others had in the past. They bunted, hoping it would rattle him. It did at first, and the A's scored a run in the each of the first two innings. Rube settled in the third, though. Maybe it was from being given the gun, maybe it was from the turn of the events in the inning. Topsy Hartsel had led off the A's third with another bunt. He beat it out and went to second on a sacrifice. It looked like more trouble, but Rube caught Hartsel bluffing a steal of third and picked him off. Rube settled completely. From that point, he pitched a no-hitter.

In the seventh inning the Browns finally got to the Chief with three singles, two doubles, and four runs. The Philadelphia crowd rooted for Rube. Rube's flawless pitching in the seventh and eighth drove the crowd to further heights, and in the ninth he struck out the side 1-2-3. The Rube still had it.[2]

The Browns had one more game in Philadelphia, in which they bested Eddie Plank. Rube did not turn up at the ballpark. He was out celebrating. The team was going on to Boston after the fourth game, so Rube would not make the trip. He stayed in Philadelphia, and all kinds of craziness broke loose.

The evening after his victory, Rube went to McAleer and asked him for a $50 advance on his salary. The Browns were wisely paying Rube in small sums, one and two dollars at a time, fully aware of how Rube handled money. When Rube asked for $50, the cagey McAleer offered him $2, telling him, "You won't be able to buy many automobile rides with that, to be sure, but it will go a long ways in a trolley." Rube took the $2, of course, but he checked out of the hotel and stayed with some friends on Girard Avenue. When the team left for Boston, Rube had an announcement for the press: "I positively will not play again for the Browns. I have been treated meanly by McAleer ever since I reported early this season, and he should never have another chance to belittle me."

There was a new baseball league forming that season — the Union League. They were trying to start a team in Philadelphia. After McAleer had refused Rube the $50, a representative from the Union League club found Rube. He offered Rube $200 to sign with his team, with $35 up front that evening. Rube took the $35, accepted the offer, and apparently signed some sort of contract.[3]

Folks in St. Louis may have been a little shocked at such news, but Connie Mack and all the folks in Philadelphia were just chuckling. "In all likelihood," predicted the *Inquirer*, "Rube will pitch a few games, have a few days fishing, and when the funds run low he will return to the St. Louis team."[4] The paper was not far off in its prediction. When Rube signed with the Union League Philadelphia team, their new manager, Walter Schlichter, immediately resigned. The team owner found Rube fishing in New Jersey. He brought Rube back to Girard Avenue. On Saturday, May 23, the Union Club was to play a game with a team from Paterson, New Jersey. Three thousand people came to the Union Club Grounds to see the Rube pitch with his new team.

Result: no Rube. Rube had actually not forgotten his obligations. He had crawled out of whatever bar he was sleeping under, and gone to the ballpark. It just happened to be the wrong park. To Rube, a game in Philadelphia meant Columbia Park, so that was where he went. Rube logic! When club officials caught up with him on Columbia Avenue, he was wandering about, wondering where everybody was. Paterson beat Philadelphia that day 3–2.[5]

Amidst the shenanigans, the Browns completed their series in Boston and moved on to New York. Connie Mack intervened and induced Rube to rejoin the Browns there. Browns owner Robert Hedges was a man of good sense and humor, and he told McAleer to forget about it all, take Rube back, and get on with the pennant race. As for the contract with the Union Club, it was real but not easily enforced. In anticipation of the Marx Brothers (*A Night at the Opera*), the Browns could likely have argued that an implied sanity clause in any contract nullifies a deal if either party is not in his right frame of mind when the contract was signed. Anyone connected with Rube had to believe in a sanity clause. As for the $35 advance the Union Club had paid, Rube kept it of course.[6]

NOTES

1. Clippings File, Cooperstown.
2. *St. Louis Globe Democrat*, May 20, 1908; *Philadelphia Inquirer*, May 20, 1908.
3. *Philadelphia Inquirer*, May 21, 1908.
4. Ibid.
5. Ibid., May 22, 1908.
6. Clippings File, Cooperstown.

Chapter 46

He Who Laughs Last

Rube rejoined the Browns in New York, and they went off to Cleveland. "There was never a ball player with a lighter sense of responsibility," noted the *Philadelphia Inquirer* upon Rube's departure from Philly, "yet there is not an ounce of malice in his make up. He can't submit himself to discipline and can't understand what his personal delinquencies have to do with the rest of the team." Rube was not going to change, but McAleer and Browns president Robert Hedges figured he was worth it, if only because of the gate receipts.[1]

Rube should have been a boxer, and Jim Jefferies, who had boxed with him out in Los Angeles, said he was good. In the ring Rube would not have been responsible to a team, and his showboating would have been part of the game.

When playing for Connie Mack, Rube's pattern after one of his zany outbursts usually involved promises of good behavior and a spurt of excellent pitching. In his next start against Cleveland on May 31, Rube pitched good ball for six innings. In the first inning he got himself in trouble. He loaded the bases with one out, but went on to strike out two in a row. Rube singled in the top of the seventh. The next batter grounded to second. As Rube slid into second base, Cleveland shortstop Bill Hinchman accidentally kicked him in the head. Rube was safe, and McAleer substituted a pinch runner. The Browns won, and Rube's head was a little sore but OK. He had experienced headaches before, usually the morning-after variety.[2]

As of June 1, St. Louis was in the thick of the race. New York, Detroit, St. Louis, Philadelphia, and Cleveland were the top five teams, and fifth-place Cleveland was a mere game and a half out of first. Sixth-place Chicago was only three back. Rube started against Chicago on June 4. His head was fine. He would have had a shutout but for a disputed call that gave Chicago their only run through nine, but the Browns could score only one run themselves, and the White Sox won it 2–1 in 11 innings. Rube pitched well, striking out 11 that day.[3]

241

Philadelphia was the next team into St. Louis. While it was not as dramatic an occasion as his return to Philadelphia, Rube was up for another chance at his old teammates. He shut them out 10–0, defeating "Rube" Vickers, the man who had replaced him in his final game with the A's. Next time out, he closed a game, blanking Washington from the fifth through the ninth innings. In 41 innings since his return to Philadelphia, Rube had allowed six runs, and put together an ERA of 1.30. He had promised good behavior after his return, and he delivered. The question was how long he could maintain himself on and off the field.[4]

McAleer pushed Rube a little too much. After his five-inning outing against Washington, McAleer started him the very next afternoon, only to lift him after four innings. St. Louis won the game, but Rube was ineffective for the first time in nearly a month. The next outing against Boston was another tough one. Rube pitched well, only giving up five hits, but the Browns committed *nine* errors. Boston started a young pitcher named Eddie Cicotte, in his first full year in the majors. Cicotte yielded six hits, but the Red Sox committed no errors and won.[5]

Chicago was the hot team of the league in the early part of June. They started the month in sixth place. By June 22 they were in first, with St. Louis in second two and a half games back. Then Chicago lost three in a row. If St. Louis could beat Detroit on the 24th they would be in first. Rube started. Throughout the game Detroit players tried to jar him. This time they employed a new tactic. Everyone knew Rube loved animals so Tigers manager Hugh Jennings and several players held up dogs from their dugout, yelling, "Look, Rube!" Jennings even took one dog out to the third base coaching box with him one inning. Ty Cobb yelled to Rube that he was going to kill one of the dogs, and since it was Cobb, he probably meant it. Nothing worked, though. Rube maintained his concentration, and the Browns won 7–1. The Browns were in first place. They won their next two, extending their winning streak to eight and their lead over Chicago to one and a half games.

When the Browns returned home from their trip to Detroit, 15,000 turned out at Union Station to greet them. This was like the high-flying years in Philadelphia, though this time the band played *Dixie*. Rube did not seem to mind. Whatever the song, he would always bellow long, loud, and off-key. Whether it was the music, Rube's singing, or the play of the Cleveland Naps, the Browns began a bit of a slide. They lost two of their next three, and fell to second place. Rube appeared only in relief and was effective. His next start came on July 2 against Chicago. He was pounded for three runs in the first, and McAleer lifted him. Detroit beat Cleveland twice, and the race tightened again. On July 4, the Browns had first, with Cleveland, Detroit, and Chicago right behind them. The AL "West" was totally dominant over the East.[6]

McAleer tried Rube again on July 4, but the result was the same. Rube was out in the first inning. It looked like Rube was down again, as he had been in early May. The team remained in the race. They still needed Rube to sustain them. McAleer sought some sort of revival, and he found an opportunity in the schedule — another trip to Philadelphia.

After the Chicago series, the Browns had to play one game in Cleveland. Knowing he would not be using him, McAleer sent Rube directly to Philadelphia. Teams did that in the early days. It saved a bit of money, and for McAleer it had the added benefit of getting Rube out of his hair. Rube apparently downed a quart of whiskey on the train to Philadelphia. When the rest of the Browns arrived in Philadelphia a day later, Rube's whereabouts were a mystery. McAleer appeared to employ the same trick he had used in May. He appeared to be waiting until the last game in the series to use Rube. McAleer did not let on, but he actually had no choice. Connie Mack, always the patient hustler, appeared to do his best to exploit the situation. The day the Browns arrived in Philadelphia, a local theater owner named Grant Lafferty immediately invited Rube and the Browns to an evening at the Chestnut Street Theater, where a comedy called "Browns in Town" was playing. Rube showed up at the theater in fine spirits. It may have been a coincidence, but Mack clearly knew what a center attraction Rube would be at the theater, and how this could lead to further high jinks. McAleer could have refused the invitation and forbidden any of his players to go. Likely, that would have only driven Rube further into space. McAleer had no choice but to hold his breath and wait. It worked out. Rube showed up for his start and pitched a shutout, striking out nine, including Schreck, who was facing Rube for the first time. McAleer shook his head to a reporter: "Confound him, sober a day, a shampoo and shave, and he is the best pitcher in the world." "There's no denying it," graciously conceded the *Inquirer*, "the Reuben has still got the laugh."[7]

Rube seemed to return to form after the win in Philadelphia. Through the month, the Browns continued to stay in the race. In late July they reeled off four straight wins. On July 28 they tried to make it five in a row. They faced Washington, and Bill Dineen was slated to pitch against young Walter Johnson. The game was a great pitchers' duel. It went 16 innings, with both hurlers going the distance. Washington won it 2–1, with Johnson striking out 15, a new record.[8]

Rube watched this young Johnson kid throw on the 28th. He may have felt his own fame for strikeout artistry a little threatened. If he needed any further inducement, Philadelphia was due in that evening to start a series in St. Louis. McAleer did not need to build up any drama at home against the A's. He started Rube in the first game. As game time approached, Rube did a little strutting in front of his old teammates, telling them he was going to beat them soundly that day. More than anyone else in baseball, the A's knew that when Rube's focus was squarely on the game there was no stopping him. This day would be a magical one. Topsy Hartsel was the first man up. Rube struck him out on three pitches. He did the same to the next man, Eddie Collins. Rube struck out five of the first seven he faced. He struck out the side in the fifth and fanned two in the sixth, seventh, and eighth. Hartsel struck out three times. In all, Rube struck out 16 that day. It was a single-game record that would stand for 30 years.

Two days later Rube entered in relief. He snuffed out an A's rally in the seventh and held them scoreless from there. He had now beaten Connie Mack and his old Quaker mates four times.[9] Rube certainly had the last laugh, at least in August 1908.

NOTES

1. *Philadelphia Inquirer*, May 25, 1908.
2. *St. Louis Globe Democrat*, June 1, 1908.
3. Ibid., June 5, 1908.
4. Ibid., June 7, 9, 12, 1908.
5. Ibid., June 13, 18, 1908.
6. Ibid., June 25–27, June 29–July 4, 1908.
7. Ibid., July 5–10, 1908; *Philadelphia Inquirer*, July 10, 1908.
8. *St. Louis Globe Democrat*, July 29, 1908.
9. Ibid., July 30, August 1, 1908.

Chapter 47

The Browns in a Pennant Race

By late July, Detroit had overtaken the rest of the league. With Ty Cobb leading the way, the Tigers were on a tear. Cobb was once again the league's leading hitter. On August 1, he towered over the league, batting .344, with the next highest average .295. (Rube was dead last, by the way, at .065, with three hits in 46 at bats.) Despite Rube's expectedly poor hitting, the Browns were winning. They were the only team to stay close to Detroit during this stretch. On August 1, St. Louis stood two games out. Third place Chicago was six back. Jimmy McAleer was reasonably content with the play of his veterans. The question was whether they could sustain their play for two more very hot months.

Rube had shut down Philadelphia in relief on August 1. The very next day McAleer gave him another start against Connie Mack's men. It proved to be too soon. Rube gave up two runs in the first two innings. The sharp snap of Rube's curve was always the sign that he had his good stuff. It was just not there that day, and McAleer relieved him after two innings. The Browns came back to win the game 6–5. McAleer gave Rube two days' rest, then started him against New York. Again, the sharpness was not quite there, but McAleer chose to leave him in. One key for a pitcher to survive in the majors concerns his ability to be effective when not at his best. Rube showed such savvy against New York, scattering his hits, with the Browns fielding well behind him. St. Louis won 5–2. Detroit won too, however.

St. Louis finished their home stand against Boston. During this series, Rube won his fifth in a row, scattering five hits and striking out seven. His season record now stood at 12 and 7. Detroit kept on winning, though. On August 12, the Browns headed off on a critical trip around the Eastern circuit, still in second place, still two games back. All the Eastern teams were at the bottom of the league, and McAleer knew that to win the pennant he would have to beat the tailenders.[1]

The Browns' first stop was Philadelphia, and Rube had one more shot at the A's. He squared off against Eddie Plank. It proved to be an excellent pitchers' duel. The only dispute between the St. Louis and Philadelphia reporters was over how well Rube pitched. The *St. Louis Globe Democrat* said Rube pitched a game good enough to beat nine out of ten teams which faced him. The *Philadelphia Inquirer* said he would have won seven out of eight times. However, Plank and the A's shut out the Browns while the A's pushed across three.[2]

The rest of the Eastern trip proved a disaster. The fault did not rest with Rube. Between August 1 and August 26, the Browns' only wins came in games in which Rube pitched. Rube threw several strong wins in Washington and New York, but otherwise the team was losing. Rube was carrying them. When the fences at Sportsman Park needed to be painted that month, Rube took care of that, too. During the Browns' slide, Detroit luckily came back to earth from their late-July streak, so St. Louis didn't lose too much ground. After August 26, when the Browns won a doubleheader from Boston and Detroit lost two in Philadelphia, St. Louis was still only three games out of first.[3]

The Browns returned home and prepared for some games with the tough Western teams, games that could yield major shifts in the league standings. Chicago was the first team due in town. In game one, Rube squared off with Ed Walsh. The spitballing Walsh had been carrying the White Sox almost as much as Rube had the 1902 A's. Walsh would start 66 games for Chicago that year and win 40 of them. But on August 31 against Rube, he would come out second best. Rube took two days off, during which Chicago won two games; Walsh won one of them. Rube came back to win the fourth game.[4]

Rube could still throw well. His reputation wasn't completely a matter of history, and the reputation certainly had a life of its own. Out in Ohio, a Columbus Senators pitcher tossed a no-hitter against Indianapolis. He threw so well that the Giants signed him within a week, and his speed was such that folks complimented him with a new nickname. He never liked the nickname, but it stuck. The pitcher's name was Richard William Marquard. After the no-hitter against Indianapolis, everyone called him Rube.[5]

Still in second place after the Chicago series, the Browns next faced Detroit. St. Louis won the first two games, leaving them one half game out. A victory in game three would put them in first place. Rube got the start against Wild Bill Donovan. Sportsman's Park in St. Louis was like old Columbia Park in Philadelphia. It was a nineteenth-century park trying feebly to accommodate the growing popularity of baseball in the burgeoning American cities of the new century. As in Philadelphia's big games of prior years, St. Louis fans turned out in droves for game three with Detroit. Rube was on the mound, and first place was in the balance. Over 27,000 filled the stands and ringed the field. Thousands more were turned away at the gates, and all the neighborhood rooftops and telephone poles were dotted with spectators. Sam

Crawford would come through for Detroit this day. He went three for five, driving in three runs and propelling Detroit to a 6–4 victory. With Chicago beating Cleveland, St. Louis had not only failed to grab first place that day, they had fallen to third. The next day the Browns traveled to Detroit for two more games with the Tigers. They lost both. As Chicago and Cleveland split, St. Louis fell further in the standings.[6]

As the Browns appeared to be in danger of sliding out of the race, Rube started against Cleveland on September 9. He pitched a masterful shutout for nine innings, giving up just two hits. The Browns could not score, however. In the fourth they had two on, but a good catch in the outfield by Bill Hinchman saved the day for Cleveland. Hinchman was the same man who had kicked Rube in the head back in May. The game went into the tenth inning. A single, a sacrifice, a fielder's choice and another single scratched the winning run across for Cleveland. It was a tough one to lose, but such things tend to occur during a slide.

There is certainly something dispiriting about playing a game for first place and four days later finding oneself barely holding on to third. Such was the fate of the Browns. Cleveland wanted to take over third place, and they had another chance at the Browns on September 11.

Harry Howell started for St. Louis against Cleveland's Addie Joss. After six innings the score was 1–1. In the seventh Cleveland got a run across and had runners on second and third. McAleer sent for the barely rested Rube. Rube came in and killed the rally; McAleer chose to stay with him in the eighth. Rube walked Larry Lajoie then got two quick outs. The next batter doubled, with Lajoie stopping at third. It was all up to outfielder Joe Birmingham, and he came through with a single, scoring two. Joss shut the Browns down in the ninth, and the Browns found themselves just a half game from fourth place. Bill Dineen lost the next day; St. Louis was now in fourth. They went home, and there were no marching bands waiting for them this time, just Ty Cobb and the Detroit Tigers.[7]

Rube had been uneven since August, but he was still McAleer's best bet against Detroit. When Rube gave up a run in the first inning on a triple by Ty Cobb, the fans' eyes began to roll. But Rube shut Detroit out from there. Then in the bottom of the second inning the Browns finally got some offense going. After two singles and a sacrifice, runners stood on second and third. First baseman Tom Jones popped for the second out. With Rube on deck, Detroit elected to walk the next batter. Rube stepped up with the bases loaded and smacked the first pitch to right for a single. One run scored. Cobb cut down the second runner at the plate with a great throw. Rube continued to baffle the Tigers. The 1–1 tie went to the 11th inning. Then Detroit allowed a man on with an error. After a steal and a single, the game belonged to the

Browns. The next day the Browns won again, and as of Tuesday morning, September 15, it was a race again, with the four Western teams all back to within two games of one another.

St. Louis had drawn close, but they gave it back the very next day in a sloppy, badly umpired contest that Detroit won, 8–7. The fans reacted to the shoddy play, to the umpiring, and to the 90-degree heat by tossing lots of empty bottles and jeers. Police had to be summoned to maintain order. As with their season, the Browns and their fans were losing control. The hopes of previous weeks made the disappointments all the more bitter. The Rube had been there to hold the team up in August, and he had his moments in September. There was still time for him and for the Browns, but precious little.

Rube tried to settle the Browns and the fans, starting the final game of the Detroit series. A hit and an error pushed a run across for Detroit in the very first inning. They scored two more in the third. St. Louis's offense was silent all day, and the Detroit lead held. Tuesday's talk of a renewed pennant race now seemed like ancient history.

After the disappointing losses to Detroit, the Browns lost their next four. But they came back to win seven of their next ten. One of those was a great match between Rube and Walter Johnson. It was a 1–1 tie through nine innings, with each side yielding a run on errors. The Browns won it in the tenth; Rube struck out 17 in the extra-inning affair. It was a great win for posterity, but would it have any significance for 1908? Neither Rube nor the Browns were thinking much about posterity at this point. Three days later Rube shut out Boston, and on September 25, a mere two games once again separated the top four teams in the league. No one could accuse the Browns of being quitters.

As the AL race was coming to a close, the NL race was coming down to the wire, too. This year it was the Chicago Cubs, McGraw's Giants, and Fred Clarke's Pirates who battled for the league lead. In mid September the Pirates were in first place. Rube dearly wanted to win a pennant, face Clarke, return to Pittsburgh, and play in the old Exposition Park, particularly since it was the last year the Pirates would play there.

Amidst the dreaming, Bill Dineen was hurt, so on September 26 McAleer turned to Rube on one day's rest to beat Boston and stay in the race. With two out in the second, a little Boston pop-up fell in for a single. Shortstop Bobby Wallace booted a grounder, and there were two on. A single brought in one run, and left runners on first and third. The Red Sox attempted a double steal, the throw to the catcher was in time, but he dropped it. The Browns garnered only three hits all day, and Boston's two unearned runs held up.[8]

With little more than a mathematical possibility remaining, the Browns had a final series in Detroit. Anticipating a pennant, Detroit fans packed the stands of old Bennett Park, and ringed much of the outfield. St. Louis was leading 7–5 going into the bottom of the ninth with darkness quickly approaching. Detroit led off its half of the inning with a single. Sam Crawford doubled and Ty Cobb followed with a single. The next batter, Claude Rossman, hit one down the left field line. The umpire ruled it fair, as it rolled into the crowd lining the field. "Into the crowd" usually meant a ground rule double, just as it was supposed to in the previous year's contest between the Tigers and A's. Rossman's hit, however, had rolled into an exit tunnel. Normally, few people would be there, and the fielder was to do the best he could with it. On this crowded day, and in the bottom of the ninth, the exit tunnel was packed with people. As the ball got lost in the crowd, Cobb scampered home behind Crawford with the winning run. The umpire ruled that Rossman's hit was a double, hence Cobb had to go back to third. Cobb began screaming at the umpire to such a degree that manager Hugh Jennings had to restrain him. (Jennings actually grabbed Cobb and threw him on the plate.) The field umpire weighed into the discussion. He and the plate umpire conferred, and the decision was reversed. Cobb's run counted, the ball game was the Tigers', and just like that, the Browns were out of the pennant race.

McAleer's gamble with Rube came close to paying off. St. Louis had been in the race to the end. Rube could get some satisfaction in the Browns finishing 16 games ahead of Philadelphia. Rube would not have faced Pittsburgh anyway. The Cubs had overtaken the Pirates in late September. The Giants came very close but lost, due in small part to the famous Fred Merkle "boner" play. The Cubs won their third straight pennant, and they beat Detroit in the series.

With veteran players, McAleer faced risks of injuries and inconsistency. This happened with Rube and with others as well. McAleer had feared pitching was his weak link before the season began. This is why he went for some veterans. His 30-year-olds did fairly well, however. Bill Dineen did taper off badly toward the season's end, finishing with a record of 14 and 7. Jack Powell had hurt his ankle, but he ended up 16 and 13. Harry Howell was a casualty of St. Louis's August heat. He broke even at 18 and 18. Rube was the team's top pitcher, with 19 victories and 14 defeats. Several of his defeats were squeakers, a point underscored by his impressive ERA—1.89. The team ERA was 2.15, second in the league. The pitching had generally come through, particularly Rube's. More than anything else, it was the Browns' hitting that had fallen off. The team batting average in 1907 was .253. In 1908 it was .245. Led by Cobb and Crawford, Detroit had batted .264.

Most fans cared little for statistics, however. They knew their Browns had traded for veterans to give them one good shot at the pennant. The team fell a trifle short, and now it seemed that such a roster had nowhere to go but down. Indeed, one statistic spoke to their fears of decline. For the first time in his American League career, Rube Waddell did *not* lead the league in strike-outs. Chicago's 40-game winner Ed Walsh nosed him out with 269, after working a record 464 innings. Rube struck out 232 in 286 innings. It seemed the Browns had staked their lump sum on 1908. Because they failed, fans could hardly be expected to be optimistic about the year ahead.

NOTES

1. *St. Louis Globe Democrat*, August 2–11, 1908.
2. Ibid., August 15, 1908; *Philadelphia Inquirer*, August 15, 1908.
3. *St. Louis Globe Democrat*, August 16–27, 1908.
4. Ibid., September 1–4, 1908.
5. *Ohio State Journal*, September 4, 1908.
6. *St. Louis Globe Democrat*, September 5–8, 1908.
7. Ibid., September 10, 12–13, 1908.
8. Ibid., September 14–17, 21, 25, 27, 1908.

Chapter 48

Winter Games

The Browns' management had several good ideas for the off-season. Owner Robert Hedges got busy boosting the Browns' play. He and McAleer again believed they could put themselves over the top with just a few more trades. As close as they came in 1908, they certainly had reason to think they had a chance. Again, they went after veterans. Boston had had another disappointing year, finishing under .500, in fifth place, 17 back of Detroit, so the Pilgrims went on a youth movement. Hedges tried to pick up 42-year-old Cy Young, but Young went to Cleveland, where he had begun his career. The Browns did pick up catcher Lou Criger from Boston. Catching had been a sore spot for the Browns in '08, in regard both to hitting and to defense. Tubby Spencer had made many critical errors for the Browns in 1908 and had batted a puny .210. Criger was one of the best defensive receivers in the league. Ty Cobb had not been able to steal a single base on him in all of 1908. The question again was whether, at the age of 37, Criger could hold up for a full year, particularly since no ballplayer takes punishment like a catcher. Ossee Schreckengost was available, too. Connie Mack had unloaded him to Chicago in late 1908, but he played in only six games. No one wanted him now. He was nearly 33 and all worn out. Schreck would never play big league ball again. He would never see Rube again, either.

In regard to Rube, Hedges and the Browns knew the boy's many tendencies all too well, and wanted to protect him during the winter. Hedges liked Rube personally. Even more, he liked the gate receipts which had risen so dramatically with Rube's presence on the team. Some thought Rube should be traded after 1908, but Hedges would not part with him. For the winter months, Hedges hired Rube to be the team's "gamesman." Rube had contemplated opening a bar with New York Giant notable Arthur "Bugs" Raymond. Bugs was almost as looney as Rube, and could drink as prolifically. (It was said that Raymond did not have to work to throw a curve ball; he'd just breathe on it, and it would come out woozy.) Everyone knew the bar would draw many customers, but they knew even more that Rube and Bugs would drain all the profits, as well as and everything else out of the place. Robert Hedges' idea was safer. Paying Rube in small bills, as always, the Browns front office had Rube serve as their supplier of fish and game for the winter months. Robert Hedges knew, as did Connie Mack, that hunting and fishing were Rube's least destructive habits. So they sent Rube off to the wilds. No one knew exactly where Rube was staying in the evenings, but all winter long the Browns' office staff enjoyed a steady diet of fresh fish, venison, quail, rabbit, duck, pheasant, and other delicacies. Rube was in earnest about his duties. He protested to the press, "I ain't bughouse!" When Rube was sober, he simply lived in denial about his antics.[1]

Management knew Rube was doing some of his hunting over in Illinois. It was out there that Rube saved a drowning man. Rube was duck hunting at Pittsburgh Lake near East St. Louis, Illinois, using the gun the A's fans had given him back in May. Nearby, two hunters out on the lake capsized their boat. Rube charged into the waters, righted the boat, and saved one hunter who could not swim.[2] Rube was the original baseball pride of St. Louis.

In addition to working the trading block and hiring Rube for work in the wilds, Robert Hedges made one other move. Without Rube, the Browns had lost several key games in Boston, so Hedges put his team's attorneys at work on Rube's divorce situation. They would ultimately get all matters settled, but it would take longer than anyone expected, as Mrs. Waddell first said she would accept Rube's desire for a divorce, then expressed reservations. Rube had to spend another season never stepping across the Massachusetts state line.[3]

Recalling the final winter in Lynn and strapped for cash with which to make support payments, Rube offered the following story, which Connie Mack felt was likely written by a reporter:

> It was Mrs. Waddell who suffered from failing memory not I. Instead of leaving her in hock in hotels [something she claimed Rube had done], she left me to the mercy of the cold and heartless world without a hotel to go in hock to. I had to wash my one pair of socks in a washbowl, when I could borrow the bowl, and go to bed when I sent my shirt to the laundry. I will never forget that terrible winter. It was love alone that kept me from perishing. With all her faults, I am still hers truly.
>
> Mrs. Waddell recovered her lost memory early that spring. She was the first person my eyes beheld on that first salary day, and she has been my porous plaster ever since. If I did not love her so much, I almost wish she would jump to an outlaw league.[4]

The divorce proceedings dragged out, and Rube's posturing caused Mrs. Waddell to grow ever more recalcitrant.

With Rube somewhere out in the woods, Hedges had no idea as to where to send notification about where and when to report for pre-spring training sessions. They were worried when they learned that Rube had taken a blow to the head during a football game on New Year's Day. But Rube continued to be dutiful about his supplying the office with the prizes of his hunting and fishing. When he walked into the office in late January with a mess of birds, uncleaned of course, Rube was told to report to West Baden Springs, Indiana. When the team train pulled into Vincennes, Indiana, a newsboy yelled out, "There's Waddell, see him in the window." Some magic was still there.[5]

NOTES

1. *St. Louis Globe Democrat*, March 3, 16, 19, 1909.
2. Ira Smith, *Baseball's Famous Pitchers* (New York: A. S. Barnes, 1954), p. 45.
3. *St. Louis Globe Democrat*, February 26, 1909.
4. Pete Martin, *Peter Martin Calls On...*, p. 57.
5. *St. Louis Globe Democrat*, February 11, 20–21, 23–24, 1909.

Chapter 49

Disappointment and Pathos

Rube showed up for spring training in good shape. His weight was 199 pounds. He came full of stories about his hunting and fishing exploits. This opened the floodgates for other stories and arguments around the Browns' training camp that could end only with the ringing of the dinner bell. Rube told one story about how he had shot a deer through the heart with a steel bullet and had to chase him three miles before he fell. For that, McAleer ordered Rube onto the rowing machine for 15 minutes.

Rube was his usual crowd-pleasing self at the pre-training camp in Indiana. He accepted a challenge from a local who was the champion at the golf club in nearby French Lick. Rube had never played much golf, but was willing to give any game a try. He halved the match with his host. He had borrowed clubs and shot a 43 on what one newspaperman described as a "rather difficult 9 hole course." The athleticism was apparently still there. When the team left Indiana for the South, a huge crowd turned out to say good-bye to the Rube. "It cannot be denied," noted a reporter, "that George is still the good hearted boy that he has always been."[1]

The Browns headed for Texas. McAleer roomed with Rube throughout the month. He wanted to keep an eye on the boy, and he figured that involving Rube in the thinking and planning of the club would keep him in the best focus. Rube really liked pitching to Lou Criger, the team's new catcher, so his enthusiasm for the new season was high. In spring training, everyone is a hopeful kid. Rube was never anything else, so spring training was always a great time for him.

Some ill fortune hit the team. Danny Hoffman, who had joined the Browns from the A's, suffered the loss of his brother, and suffered emotionally for a long time. Bill Dineen, who had Rube's affinity for drinking and even less tolerance for the stuff, came to camp woefully out of shape. Harry Howell tore a ligament in his throwing arm. Howell and Dineen would win a total of seven games that year. Rube looked good, though not great. He had one good outing against a local Houston team. The Browns played two practice games with Detroit and were completely shut out in both. When the team limped back to St. Louis, McAleer was making noises about how the team needed to get into shape before the season started. Everyone then naturally wondered what all the work in Indiana and Texas had been for.

The Browns started the season with bad breaks and bad play. They lost two of three to Cleveland. Rube opened against Chicago and pitched nine innings of shutout ball. Unfortunately, the Browns could not score anything. With a man on, a Chicago liner to straight center saw Danny Hoffman take a step inward, then casually run back for it. The ball went over his head, and an easy out turned into a triple. Rube then gave up two doubles. With the Browns again doing nothing in the bottom of the inning, Chicago won.

Rube had a disastrous start in his next outing in Cleveland, giving up nine hits and five runs in five innings, while the Browns committed four errors. In a second start against Chicago he pitched a shutout into the ninth inning. Then in the ninth a walk, a sacrifice, and a single gave Chicago one run, and with the Browns getting three hits all day, the one run was all the White Sox needed. Rube had had two good starts, but no wins. Against Cleveland he lost yet another game 1–0. As of May 3, the Browns were in last place. "One sure thing," noted a reporter, "the Browns are not losing games because of any poor pitching." They just couldn't hit.

With a seven-game losing streak, the Browns had to face first-place Detroit. Rube started the first game. He gave up only five hits all day and held Ty Cobb hitless. Catcher Lou Criger made several heady plays. This seemed to spark the Browns, as they played well defensively. The team won 4–2. But the Browns lost the next two to Detroit. The Browns' fortunes tumbled further. Two outfielders, George Stone and Al Schweitzer, were hurt. Worse, catcher Lou Criger was injured as well. They remained in last place, and there was already talk in St. Louis of trying "some of the young blood." Rube, said the *Globe Democrat*, "is the only Brown who is pitching well."

Rube helped rally the team in a series against Washington. He gave up a run in the first inning, then blanked the Senators the rest of the way. On offense the Browns could do nothing until the third inning. Then Rube took up matters of offense himself. After a batter walked, Rube doubled and scored on an error. In the fifth he scored again. The lead held up. The next day the team beat Walter Johnson. This was young Johnson's fifth loss in six starts, and the papers were snickering about last year's "big find" proving to be a mere flash in the pan. (Indeed he would only pitch another 18 years and win 400 games.) For now, though, Johnson was a disappointment to the Senators, and the Browns pushed past Washington and lifted themselves out of the cellar.[2]

The upturn seemed to be continuing for the Browns largely on Rube's arm. He beat New York, and against Boston he won a 1–0 game. Three days later he again shut out the Red Sox, and in his next start against Cleveland he threw his third shutout in a row. A young reporter named Grantland Rice attended that game. Rube was up 1–0 in the ninth. An error, a Texas leaguer, and a walk filled the bases with none out. The heart of the Cleveland order was due up — Larry Lajoie, Bill Bradley, and Elmer Flick. "The Rube," wrote Rice, "had brought two friends to the park who were sitting in a box," Rice noted. "He left the pitcher's mound and walked over to the box, saying: 'Ladies, I'll be with you in about two minutes.' He then struck out Lajoie, Bradley, and Flick on nine pitched balls."[3]

Rube was 5 and 0 from May 13 through the end of the month. In his next start he began with four shutout innings, giving him 34 consecutive scoreless innings. He had yielded just two runs in 49 innings. The Browns were back to playing respectable .500 ball. They were now in fifth place, seven games behind league-leading Detroit, and Lou Criger was coming off the injury list.[4] For the fans in St. Louis, baseball was fun again.

Rube's tear through the league in May would be the last sustained series of unhittable baseball he would ever hurl in the major leagues. As in the past, his drinking would get the better of him. Before a game against New York, third baseman Jimmy Austin and the team were on the way to the game. As they passed a St. Louis tavern, Austin heard someone yell, "Hey look, there's Rube!" It was Rube, all right. He was leaning up against the front door of the saloon with a big mug of beer. He waved at the Highlanders and downed the whole mug. Austin recalled, "Doggone it, though, when game time came, darned if Rube wasn't out there ready to pitch." Rube was ready, and he did fine for a few innings. Then with two on in the fourth inning, Austin caught a Rube fastball for a home run. "As I'm trotting around the bases," Austin remembered,

> Rube is watching me all the way, and as he kept turning around on top of the mound he got dizzy and by golly he fell over on his rear end. That started everybody to laughing so hard we could hardly play. Some guys laughed so hard they practically had a fit.... The St. Louis manager ... came running out and yelled, "Come on out of there. You didn't want to pitch anyhow." Somehow that made everybody laugh all the more.[5]

Austin chuckled heartily at the story and concluded with a sigh: "Good old Rube. In his life he gave a lot of people a lot of enjoyment." Austin made his comments some 55 years later. To McAleer and the 1909 Browns, there was nothing funny about it.

Jimmy McAleer suffered another memorable incident that year when Rube was to start but didn't arrive at the ballpark. McAleer learned that Rube was at the racetrack. For some reason Rube had promised a friend out there that he would help him sell hot dogs. (More than likely, it was a way to work off an unpaid debt or earn a loan.) McAleer went out and collared Rube at the track, but Rube protested that he had promised that he would sell the hot dogs. McAleer asked how many Rube had to sell. Rube told him 24. McAleer promised to buy the 24. They gave away most of the dogs and headed back to the park, with Rube munching on the rest of McAleer's purchases all the way. He pitched, and he lost. Such feats had a delight about them back in the days when the final sentence of such a story involved a Rube shutout. Now there were mainly losses, little humor, and more pathos.

A highlight for Rube in 1909 was a chance to pitch in Philadelphia's new stadium. Shibe Park was certainly a needed addition to the Philadelphia sports scene. (The park actually opened tragically: during the A's home opener that year, catcher Doc Powers crashed into a wall chasing a pop foul and died from the resulting head injury.) The size of the new park filled a great need, however. There had been so many games at old Columbia Park where the spectator demands had completely outstripped the seating capacity. This was part of the inexorable rise of population in the city, as was the case in Chicago, Brooklyn, Boston, Cincinnati, Pittsburgh, and Detroit, where new stadiums were constructed in these years. But the actual talent in the baseball of the era greatly boosted the movement. No one player or team was responsible for the growth of the game's popularity, but Rube was as responsible as any. The new Shibe Park was in many ways "the house that Rube built."

In Rube's first start in the new park, the fans greeted him warmly, as they always had in Philadelphia. Once again he hooked up with Eddie Plank. There was no score until the seventh when the Browns sneaked a run across. In the eighth the A's got a runner on. With two outs, the next batter grounded slowly to second and beat the throw, with the runner advancing from first to third. The crowd started yelling, and Rube began looking about. The runner stole second as Rube just stood there. Everyone began laughing. Flustered, Rube failed to field an Eddie Collins bunt, and the tying run scored. Rube had made a dumb mental error, the kind he seldom made on the field when a younger man. In the 11th inning the score was still tied when Eddie Collins again stepped up. He hit a slow one to first. Tom Jones gloved it, but when he turned to toss it to first, Rube was still standing on the mound. Collins then moved to second on a sacrifice. Harry Davis batted next. With two strikes, Davis fouled off ten straight pitches. He wore Rube down and finally singled to right, with Collins scoring the winning run. Rube was simply losing his edge. A younger Rube would not have erred mentally or yielded to Davis. Rube was now 32, and the boozing had rendered him every day of it and more.[6]

Along with Jack Powell, Lou Criger, Danny Hoffman, and Bill Dineen, Rube spent some of June on the injury list. With all the injuries, the Browns slipped back in the standings. Sloppy play, discouragement, fan abandonment — each began to feed on the other. In June Danny Hoffman was batting .340, and now he was injured. No other Browns batter was hitting above .240. Rube had seven victories, and he had lost five games by one run. No other Brown hurler had even four wins.

The Browns were going downhill, and in late June they had two series slated with first-place Detroit. Detroit was in the midst another hot streak, expanding their league lead. Ty Cobb was actually playing another notch better than he ever had. From early May to late June he raised his average from .309 to .376. He led the league not only in batting average, but also in singles, doubles, triples, home runs, RBIs, and stolen bases. He would win the triple crown that year, and begin a five-year streak during which he would bat over .400.

The Tigers won every game against the Browns. They not only had greater skill, they had luck. Rube was pitching one game with the score 0–0. He faced Sam Crawford with two on and one out. Wishing to give Crawford nothing, and knowing how well Crawford could reach out and hit bad balls, Rube decided to pitch him inside, way inside. On the second pitch, Crawford had to dodge backwards to avoid being hit. As Crawford moved, Rube's pitch struck the exposed bottom end of Crawford's bat. The ball rolled gently between first and second. Crawford was out, but a run scored as though it was a perfect sacrifice. That was Detroit's only run, and the Browns of course scored nothing that day. With Lou Criger out, McAleer's second-string catcher, Jimmy "Little" Stephens, injured himself that day. Now the Browns had no catchers.

During Rube's next start against Detroit, the malady of bad play and bad luck devolved into something even more weird. Robert Hedges was in Detroit that day, the guest of Tigers vice president Tom Yawkey. He could only shake his head with what he saw. It was something that would have made even a Little League coach sigh. In the fourth inning, Detroit loaded the bases with Sam Crawford on third, Ty Cobb on second, and Claude Rossman on first. There were none out. Charley O'Leary batted, and he grounded to first baseman Tom Jones. Jones threw to hastily reactivated catcher Lou Criger. Crawford was called out, and here the zaniness began. After being called out, Crawford inexplicably ran *back* to third base. Seeing this, Ty Cobb stopped and stood between second and third, completely befuddled, and Claude Rossman remained standing like a statue on first base. Forgetting his own mistake, Cobb began screaming at Rossman to head for second, as O'Leary, the only runner behaving sanely, already stood on first. Sam Crawford left third and raced back home where Lou Criger, still with the ball, endeavored to tag the already-out runner. Criger tagged him, but the bemused umpire made no signal, for there was none to make. (How do you signal "out again?") As Criger untangled himself from the sliding Crawford, all the runners advanced safely. Instead of getting out of the inning with a triple play, the Browns had to face bases loaded, one out. Hedges choked on his hot dog. Jimmy McAleer began chewing up his scorecard and mouthing something indecipherable, and in any case unprintable.

Rube stood on the mound watching all this, and even he was shaking his head. He had done far more wacko things off the field, but he had never done or seen such play on the field. Second baseman Germany Schaeffer was up next. Rube threw a fastball, and Schaeffer wacked it for a double. Cobb and Rossman scored easily, and when O'Leary tried to score from first, Danny Hoffman's throw sailed over home plate, over Rube as he backed up Criger, and over a few dozen rows in the grandstand. O'Leary scored, and Schaeffer was awarded third base. Schaeffer scored on a sacrifice fly. Detroit garnered four runs under most bizarre circumstances, and they won 6–2. The Browns' 40-year reputation for inept play began at that moment.[7]

In the early 1960s the New York Mets were playing some of the worst baseball in the modern history of the game. Not in spite of it, but in a perverse way because of it, they cultivated a cadre of loyal fans who took pride in their boys' amazing antics. The inept Mets could endear themselves to insular New Yorkers because the fans had always arrogantly disregarded the sneers of anyone about most anything. Early twentieth-century St. Louis baseball fans had none of the chic with which to delight at lousy play and turn it into something fashionable. Their immigrant and laboring populations were more straightforwardly assimilative and hardworking. They could afford little coddling of the inept. With the Browns' play of 1909, their fans were just mad as hell at what they regarded as a bunch of inept, dispirited, drunken, old-timers. Across town, even the Cardinals were in sixth place.

When he was not pitching, Rube would spend some afternoons working in the coaching box. There he often spent more time entertaining the fans with some of his old antics. Generally, though, he was more subdued. "Rube," noted one reporter, "has changed from an impulsive, original, daring person to a quiet, sober, domestic hurler... [He] has become so blamed proper." His worst escapade in the locker room was to steal some candy from Jack Powell. His most outrageous act that the summer in St. Louis took place at the Chestnut St. Ice Cream Emporium, where he got mad at the waiter because he didn't like a walnut sundae.[8] Rube did a lot more than that, but the press was trying to goad him, likely figuring it could wake up the Browns' play, or at least prompt the one and only to do something interesting for the newspapers.

As it was, on or off the field, the team was just not good copy, and neither was Rube. Since his 5 and 0 streak in May, Rube was just plain lousy. Since May, he had not won a single game except when opposing the lowly Washington Senators. This "streak" did not end till September 10 when he shut out the White Sox 2–0, with both Browns runs unearned. When the play is that bad, no one's jokes work, not even Rube's.

Rube could still have his fun, though. One Chicago reporter, Jim Crusinberry, recalled Rube inviting him up to his room during a rain day in Detroit. Crusinberry had just seen Rube walk through the lobby with two buckets, and figured they were full of beer. When Crusinberry arrived in the room, Rube was sitting next to the bathtub prodding around three large black bass. Rube never liked the hotel food in Detroit, and he and Crusinberry ate well that night.[9]

By September, Washington had the cellar sewn up. They were 50 games behind Detroit. Even the Browns were not that bad, but they had seventh place all to themselves, with sixth-place Cleveland a full ten games ahead of them. After Rube beat the White Sox, the Browns had to play a Sunday doubleheader with Detroit. In the first game, the Browns started out with a 3–0 lead, only to be crushed 11–5. After that dispiriting loss, McAleer asked who would like to pitch the second game. Everyone declined. Then someone yelled, "Let George do it." Rube had just pitched on Friday, and it had been a long time since he had pitched on such short notice. Given that it was a Sunday twin bill and league-leading Detroit was in town, there was a good crowd that day, and Rube always liked to perform before a crowd. So Rube thought he might reingratiate himself with the fans.

It was like old times. Rube faced Wild Bill Donovan. Donovan was the same age as Rube, and he too had seen his better days, and for many of the same reasons as Rube. The Browns jumped on Donovan for two runs in the first. The Tigers got one back in the second when Rube failed to field a bunt with a man on third. Rube gave up one more in the fifth inning. Otherwise the two old guys put on a great show, though between them they walked 13. In the top of the seventh, Sam Crawford singled to right. The Browns outfielder fumbled the ball, and Crawford trotted to second. The next man singled, and Crawford scored easily. After eight innings it was too dark to continue. Rube had been as sharp that day than at any time since May. A few errors let in the runs, so he trotted off the field with nothing to show for his work. That was pretty much what had happened to the Browns' season and to Rube's career.

A week later McAleer announced that he was quitting and would manage the Washington Senators next season. His team had fallen apart around him. Clark Griffith later commented, "had he not taken cast offs and old-timers

instead of developing youngsters he would still be manager of the Browns."
Many newspapers commented on how McAleer's move to Washington put
him on an even more feeble team: "How that fellow must love cellars."[10]

Everything on the Browns was totally limp. After the Detroit outing,
Rube did not pitch another game that year. McAleer did not even show up
the last day of the season. Various AL and NL teams played post-season
series — the White Sox played the Cubs, the Red Sox played the Giants, but
no one in St. Louis had much desire to see the Browns play the Cardinals.
All Rube could do in October was sit back and read about his old friend
Honus Wagner outplaying Ty Cobb to lead Pittsburgh to victory over the
Tigers in the World Series. (Who would have guessed that this would be
Cobb's last appearance in post-season play?)

NOTES

1. *St. Louis Globe Democrat*, February 24, March 3, 1909.
2. Ibid., April 15–18, 25, 28, May 3, 5–7, 15–16, 1909.
3. Clippings File, Cooperstown.
4. *St. Louis Globe Democrat*, May 21, 24, 27, 31, 1909.
5. Quoted in Lawrence Ritter, *The Glory of Their Times*, p. 137. Austin recalled
the St. Louis manager to have been Jack O'Connor, but it was McAleer; O'Connor
came to the Browns in 1910, and Waddell was gone from the team by that time.
6. *St. Louis Globe Democrat*, June 12, 1909.
7. Ibid., June 23, 27, 1909.
8. Ibid., August 14, 1909.
9. Bill Corum, *New York Journal American*, undated, Clippings File, Cooperstown.
10. *St. Louis Globe Democrat*, February 8, 1910, and September 24, 1909.

Chapter 50

A Fateful Day in Boston

Robert Hedges hired Jack O'Connor out of Little Rock, Arkansas, to be the Browns' new manager. Most Browns fans figured there would be a major housecleaning of the veterans, including Rube, but this did not occur. Hedges wanted to keep Rube, especially because of the gate receipts. O'Connor was willing to go along to some extent. Meanwhile, Rube was out in the wilds, spending another winter as the supplier of fish and game to the Browns' front office.

When the Browns assembled for spring training, a large crowd gathered at the train station to see them off. Like any baseball fans, Browns supporters were always optimistic at spring training time. At that point it seemed to make no difference that last year's seventh-place team was year older and largely unchanged. Rube was not at the station, however, though not for reasons of misbehavior. He had gone down to Arkansas to begin training early, as well as to hunt and fish. The St. Louis fans who had gathered at the station at 18th and Market streets were disappointed. "The absence of Rube Waddell robbed the fans of their annual treat. George Edward always has a little comedy on tap for the [fans'] edification. ... He was conspicuous by his absence."[1] That vital need of baseball fans to be optimistic was also an essential ingredient in the affections held for the Rube, much as it was in another generation of fans for Babe Ruth. Baseball and Rube were one on that score.

Rube's appeal was unprecedented in the game. As he was fading the appeal remained no less compelling, and in some ways it actually grew. The new stars like Ty Cobb were anything but appealing in their personalities and off-field activities. When the Browns were training in Arkansas a youngster called out to a group of players jogging. He asked, "Are you running for exercise?" Jack Powell snapped back: "No, you chump. I'm making a balloon ascension in the subway." Ballplayers have to endure the dumbest questions, over and over, from reporters and fans. Many grow impatient. Rube was the opposite. It was not that he was calculatingly cool in his sense of good public relations, he just naturally grasped the idolatry that was present, no matter the silliness of the conversation, and he warmed to it. Others, like Babe Ruth and Mickey Mantle, would possess this trait. The New York Mets of the early '60s seemed to be able to do it collectively, becoming the darlings of New York fans, not in spite of terrible play but because of it. True idols of the game who fans love and not just respect are always able to maintain not just equanimity but some warmth of personality amidst the daily pressures of play and press. Rube could always suffer fools, for obvious reasons; thus he could not understand why others could not accept him.

Hard-boiled baseball types had accepted Rube, often begrudgingly, but only because of the quality of his pitching. The question was beginning to form as to what Rube would do now that his skills were undeniably fading. In 1909 his record had been 11 and 13. Many losses were one-run affairs in which the Browns could not hit or field, and no other pitcher on the team fared much better, but Rube's diminishing talent was apparent. A statistical point that could not be explained away was the fact that Rube's strikeout total had fallen to a mere 141. Such lesser lights in the league as Frank Smith and Heinie Berger had compiled more, as did Chief Bender and Walter Johnson. Fading stars can fall prey to the politics and whims of management, particularly when they seem to cause trouble. That could have affected Rube, but fate had something else in store for him.

Hedges wanted to keep Rube for his fan appeal. New manager Jack O'Connor wanted to develop some young talent, however. He had to keep Rube, but there would be no nonsense. O'Connor ran a military-style training camp. Everyone was up at 7:30. Jogging and practices took place in both the morning and afternoon. Rube behaved himself and did all the drills. He helped the rookies, too. O'Connor divided his team on tours between veterans and rookies, and he often sent Rube off with the rookies. Wherever the team traveled on exhibitions in Arkansas and Texas, fans still turned out to see Rube. He could still turn a few cartwheels and strike out bush leaguers. Hedges and O'Connor's desires appeared compatible.

Rube wrote of his exploits in the wilds of Arkansas and took what he thought to be a little jab at his new manager, penning a little note to the *Sporting News* replete with inimitable Rube logic:

> I have had good luck fishing, so far, and ought to be satisfied, but since I have been associated with that advanced financier, Jack O'Connor, I have developed a hankering for lucre. Jack has drilled it into me that I owe it to myself to go get the money. He may be right, but it is not clear to me how a fellow can owe himself anything in any way.[2]

Owing something to oneself was indeed a concept that never penetrated the skull of George Edward Waddell.

Though the fans held onto their optimism, the team showed little potential for the season. The veterans were all a year to the worse. Catcher Lou
Criger had quit. (He would try again with the Yankees, but he did not stick,
particularly after Ty Cobb viciously spiked him one day.) None of the rookies showed much during the spring. Rube's own play in the exhibition season was inconsistent at best.

One good development for Rube and the Browns was that Rube's mar-
ital troubles were finally resolved. Hedges' attorneys had finally fixed some of
the suits over non-support and alimony. The Browns had earlier advanced
Rube $1223.63 for alimony payments (no word on whether Rube actually
turned it over to May Wynne).[3] Rube got married again, too. His new bride
was a New Orleans native named Madge Maguire. Rube had met her in May
of 1909, just before his final hot streak of shutout pitching. Miss Maguire had
recently moved to St. Louis, and she met Rube at her own birthday party,
hosted by a mutual friend. She was 19; Rube told her he was 31, and he put
it on the wedding license. He was actually 33.

The marriage nearly put a temporary kibosh on the lawyers' divorce
arrangements, as back East the former Mrs. Waddell, now living in Derry,
New Hampshire, reacted with anger. The earlier divorce proceedings had
occurred in May 1908 and December 1909. They had not gone smoothly. May
Wynne had accused Rube of continuing non-support. Rube accused May of
frequenting disreputable sections of several cities they visited and of lying
about calling him a bad name in front of his parents. He summarized his role
in the marriage: "I put in one Hades of a time." Connie Mack had testified
that Mrs. Waddell had used improper language in his presence. May Wynne
was angry enough about these earlier proceedings, but Hedges' lawyers had
secured the divorce arrangements in Missouri. With the marriage, Rube's ex-
wife voiced new protests — she did not recognize the marriage, she would
challenge its legality, and she was considering a further suit for bigamy. She
and her family also threatened to bring back the 1905 charges of assault. It
looked like many more troubles ahead for the Rube, but in a few days the
former Mrs. Waddell and her family relented, figuring it was best for all par-
ties to get on with their lives. Rube was at last free of May Wynne, and she
of him.[4]

The newly married Rube made solemn pledges: "My marriage to Miss
Maguire," he intoned, "will make a man out of me. I have stopped drinking
and am in better condition than I have been in years. ... I think that the happy
part of my life has just begun. I have had a great deal of trouble lately, but it
is all over now." The new Mrs. Waddell voiced strong sentiments against the
gossip that flew over her tender age. "I have admired Mr. Waddell since the
first time I saw him," she stated, "and I am giving him my whole life because

I love him, not because I was hypnotized."[5] Casually, the papers noted that the couple would set up house together after the team returned from their first road trip out East. Rube's life seemed reformed. The team, while not the best, looked forward to a new season. "Rube Waddell looks the same as he did 10 years ago," proclaimed one St. Louis paper. "He has not lost an iota of speed or a dot of confidence. The 'bridegroom' should be in for another good season."[6] April hopes were everywhere. The Browns were bound to improve, and when on the road Rube would no longer have to jump off the train when the team headed for Boston.

As the season began, Rube appeared on good behavior. He had a good relationship with O'Connor, and all seemed smooth. On opening day against Chicago, Rube stepped in to save a lead in the ninth inning. He put down the side 1-2-3, striking out the last man, to the delight of the crowd. O'Connor used Rube in relief on several more occasions, and he was effective. This seemed to be the role for which O'Connor had Rube in mind. The sense that Rube could pitch any time was good for the gate. Others could be developed as starters. Relieving kept Rube from tiring and ineffectiveness, and it kept him on his toes like a fireman; possibly, he would not misbehave so much. Fate would not allow time to test the theory.

O'Connor would let Rube start on special occasions. One start came on May 4 against Cleveland. The day was special because President William Howard Taft was in St. Louis and at the game. All the players lined up before the game out of respect for the president as he entered the park. Rube, naturally, broke ranks and waltzed over and shook the president's hand. Taft seemed amused by it all. "Rube should be caged up whenever there is anything out of the ordinary doing at Sportsman's Park," lamented one reporter. In the game, Rube faced Cy Young, still pitching with Cleveland at age 43. The game ended in a 3–3 tie after 14 innings. Young went the distance; Rube could not. President Taft left the game in the fifth inning. In the interest of impartiality he attended the NL game across town. Besides, the Cardinals were playing Taft's hometown favorite, the Cincinnati Reds. His Reds won.[7]

The game with Cy Young, like so many of Rube's late games, ended inconclusively. It was as though someone wanted to keep him playing but somehow not really be in the game. If so, playing for the Browns was a great route to meaninglessness. By early May the Browns stood at 3 and 12, dead last, behind even the Senators.

After the Cleveland games, the team headed on their first tour of the East, after which Rube was planning to return and set up house with Madge. The first stop on the Browns' road trip was Boston. Rube had not been in Boston since he played for the A's back in 1907. Like all fans, the Boston faithful had an affection for the Rube. They remembered his great duels with

Cy Young, and the local saloon scene had not been quite the same in Rube's absence. Given the happiness of the occasion of Rube's return, O'Connor slated him to start the first game of the series. In the first innings, as Rube walked out to the mound, the crowd gave him great rounds of applause. Rube reacted with a big smile, and he began to pitch well. He struck out three batters in the first three innings and had a shutout going.

In the fourth inning Rube stepped up to bat against the young Red Sox fireballer, Eddie Cicotte. Cicotte was a right-hander with a rising fastball. The very first pitch he threw to Rube was a hard one that tailed. Rube batted right-handed, and as the ball curved into him, he instinctively raised his arms to dodge the bullet. The ball continued to tail toward him, and it struck Rube right on the point of his front elbow. He went down in a heap and stayed down for several minutes. O'Connor lifted him for a pinch runner. Rube was hurt, and as he batted right-handed, the elbow Cicotte had struck was Rube's left. This was serious.

At the hotel after the game, Rube began complaining of severe pains in his left arm. O'Connor took him to a local hospital. There Dr. H. W. Goodall determined that the elbow was fractured. Rube would have to carry his arm in splints for several weeks. The doctor said there was but "a remote chance" he would ever pitch again. Rube had always said that Boston was his unlucky city, his "hoodoo town." First it was his disastrous second marriage, now this. To most baseball people, it looked like Rube was through.[8]

Rube got to go home to his new bride sooner than he expected. Now he had a problem that was more than medical. Early twentieth-century baseball had no such programs as workman's compensation. Rube had no savings. He had never even had a bank account. Whatever money he had ever made he had spent, along with all the money he had borrowed and never paid back. Baseball was the only thing he knew how to do that could earn him a living. In July he took a job driving a St. Louis water delivery wagon for three square meals a day.

His arm did heal. Rube came back and made a start for the hapless Browns on August 1. He won the game 5–4, but he did not look strong, walking one and striking out none. In the ninth inning he hit a batter and threw two wild pitches. O'Connor relieved him that inning. On August 8 O'Connor released him. Even Robert Hedges did not see any more gate value in Rube. The question now was whether anyone would take a chance on an aging player with a bad drinking problem who had just fractured his pitching elbow. Where could he possibly go?[9]

NOTES

1. *St. Louis Globe Democrat*, March 2, 1910.
2. *Sporting News*, March 17, 1910.
3. Harold Seymour, *Baseball: The Golden Age*, p. 192.
4. Clippings File, Cooperstown.
5. *St. Louis Republican*, April 5, 1910.
6. *St. Louis Globe Democrat*, April 16, 1910.
7. Ibid., May 5, 1910.
8. Ibid., May 11, 1910.
9. Ibid., August 2 and 10, 1910.

Chapter 51

New Jersey

By August, Rube's arm seemed to be better. The doctors had pronounced him fit. The question was whether he could throw again with any effectiveness. No doctor could determine that. Rube got out and did some tossing and felt good. When he hurt his shoulder in 1905 he had attempted to come back too soon and reinjured himself. This time he had no World Series on the horizon to rush him, and he appeared not to cause his arm further problems. What he needed now was a ball club to give him a chance to prove he could still play baseball.

In the recovery period, Rube's frustration and depression over the injury began to show themselves. He continued to drink while his young bride tried to keep him on the straight and narrow. As is often the case in such situations, the inability and unwillingness of the depressed to accept a helping hand results in conflict, and in late June, Rube lashed out. He struck Madge. She contacted the police. Rube was taken before a St. Louis magistrate and fined $150. The judge was inclined to be more severe, but Rube signed a pledge to keep a peaceful home and to abstain from all alcohol for a year. Rube wanted to keep a copy of the pledge to give to Browns' owner Robert Hedges to gain reinstatement.[1] He still hoped he could return to the major leagues, but Hedges and all other owners needed more than a piece of paper to be convinced that Rube had both healed his arm and reformed his ways. The mediocre outing on August 1 confirmed Hedges's sense that Rube was not worth it anymore.

In the modern major leagues a team can take a player back and give him some time in the minors to test himself and work out any problems. This arrangement did not exist in 1910. The major teams had informal networks with clubs in the lower leagues, but the teams in the minors were autonomous. They set their own salaries and scratched out a living off their own gate receipts. As no major league club would give Rube a chance, he had to turn to the minors to get a start somewhere on what he hoped would be a road back to the major leagues.

Joe McGinnity had been a great pitcher. He had hurled for a year with the Brooklyn Dodgers and played for many years with John McGraw in New York and Baltimore. Rube had faced McGinnity during his years with Louisville, Pittsburgh, and Chicago, and he would have faced him in the 1905 World Series but for the straw hat. McGinnity retired in 1908 and had a desire to manage. He secured part ownership of the Newark, New Jersey, Bengals of the Eastern League and became their player/manager. The Eastern League was one cut below the majors, akin to the International League of the mid/late twentieth century. In 1910 the Bengals were in a race with Rochester for the Eastern League championship. McGinnity needed to boost his pitching corps to stay in the race, and no one else in management objected to anything that would boost gate receipts. So even though it was Rube who conked him in the head during the World Series of 1900, McGinnity decided to give the big fellow a shot in Newark.

Rube arrived in New Jersey on August 11, and the very next day McGinnity sent him out to start against the Montreal Royals. The results were good. "Rube had everything that he possessed in his palmiest day," reported the *Newark Star.* "His curves had baffling breaks, and his speed was marvelous." The Bengals won that day, 7 to 1. Rube went the distance, and the one Montreal run was a meaningless tally in the ninth inning with the outcome of the game secured. Rube was effective in some tight spots. With two on in the very first inning Rube shut the Royals down. With bases loaded and none out in the eighth, Rube got the next three to hit harmless pop-ups. The crowd of 4000, one of the season's largest, stood and applauded.[2]

Rube continued to pitch effectively. A little revenge of sorts came on August 20. He shut out the Baltimore Orioles 4–0, and the Oriole pitcher he bested that day was Rube Vickers, the pitcher who had replaced him on the A's. That younger Rube had not panned out for Connie Mack.[3]

By September 11, Rube's record was 8 and 2. One loss was by one run in extra innings. In the other, the Bengals failed to score. Attendance grew whenever he pitched, and he worked well with Joe McGinnity. McGinnity's nickname in the big leagues had been "Iron Man" because of the quantity of work he could take on. He once pitched over 480 innings in a single season. But as a manager his "Iron" took on added meaning. He was a very tough leader. There was no nonsense. Players were fined for being out of shape. When one player, Jake Gettman, asked for time off because his wife was ill with pneumonia, McGinnity refused him, claiming the kid was merely showing a "yellow streak." Gettman immediately quit the team.[4] Rube was mature and compliant under McGinnity's leadership. He caused no problems on the team with any off-field antics, and he engaged in no nutty behavior on the field, even when a victory was secure. Clearly, he knew he had to prove not only that his arm was OK but that he was someone on whom a team could depend.

The Bengals fell just short of the Eastern League championship. They stayed within striking distance of Rochester through the season, but they could never overtake them. Rube had done all that was asked of him. The question was whether any big league club now would call him back for the 1911 season. The answer would be: No. The Browns, meanwhile, lost 107 games in 1910. They finished in the cellar, not only 57 games behind the pennant-winning Philadelphia A's but a full 17 games behind seventh-place Washington. The Browns had to rebuild, but they were not going to do it with old problems. Rube's contract rights were returned to St. Louis, and they dumped him.[5]

NOTES

1. Clippings File, Cooperstown, June 27, 1910.
2. *Newark Star*, August 13, 1910.
3. Ibid., August 21, 1910.
4. Ibid., September 14, 1910.
5. *Minneapolis Journal*, November 28, 1910, Clippings File, Cooperstown.

Chapter 52

The Minors

Joe Cantillon was a good ole boy. He had first seen Rube back in 1899 when he umpired in the Western League and Rube was blazing his way to 30 wins with Columbus. Cantillon had also managed the Washington Senators from 1907 to 1909. He was not terribly successful there, but few ever were, and to his credit, it was Cantillon who discovered the young Walter Johnson.

When Jimmy McAleer replaced Cantillon as the manager of the Senators in 1910, Cantillon moved to Minneapolis. He and his brother Mike became the manager and owner of the Minneapolis Millers. The Millers had been part of the old Western League. Ban Johnson had dropped them as he developed the American League and turned the league's focus eastward, where the big money lay.

Though abandoned by Ban Johnson, the people of the Minneapolis area maintained a strong baseball tradition. Through the early and mid twentieth century not only would the Millers thrive, across the river the city of St. Paul also supported their own team, the Saints. People in the Twin Cities commonly referred to the two as the "Big Twins" and the "Little Twins." The fanaticism was strong. Even after the Washington Senators moved to Minneapolis in 1961 and adopted the name "Minnesota Twins" to try to take in the entire region and alienate no one, St. Paul defiantly held onto their Saints.

The Millers and the Saints were part of the American Association, which formed out of the remnants of the Western League. Aside from the Twin Cities, there were teams in Milwaukee, Toledo, Columbus, Indianapolis, Louisville, and Kansas City. By 1911 the Millers were a perennial power in the Association, and they had just won the Association title in 1910. Joe and Mike Cantillon wanted to continue this winning tradition.

Joe Cantillon knew what Rube could do. He had seen it in Columbus and Washington, and he knew what had occurred in Newark. Like Rube, Joe was a country boy. He hailed from rural Kentucky. Back home he had seen plenty of eccentrics like Rube. Most folks in Kentucky took them in stride, so Cantillon never understood all the fuss about Rube's antics. Besides, he liked to hunt and fish as much as Rube, and Joe had a few Rube stunts under his own belt. While manager of the Milwaukee Brewers in 1903, for example, Cantillon saw a dog he liked. The kennel owner wanted $100 for her. Joe did not have the cash. He learned, however, that the kennel owner had a brother who ran a ball club in Springfield, Illinois, so he traded a pitcher from Milwaukee to Springfield for $100 and had the owner transfer the money directly to his brother. Joe got the dog and named her Sue. The Brewers' owner was furious. But Joe kept Sue and still had her when Rube joined the Millers.[1] Cantillon spoke Rube's language and knew he could handle him. He and his brother knew as well that Rube would greatly stimulate ticket sales. So they brought Rube to Minneapolis for the 1911 season. Rube went along happily.

Today's minor league clubs do the bidding of the organization, which is there to serve the big club. They help nurture young talent, or any other talent that needs a little brushing up after a bad patch of play or an injury. Modern minor leagues rarely maintain the employment of anyone deemed washed up in big league circles. Back in 1911, however, this was common practice. A player "on the way down" was indeed part of the lexicon of baseball. A few like Cy Young and Ty Cobb could maintain a big league level of effectiveness throughout their years. The typical player got to the big leagues after a few seasons in the minors and returned to the minors for a few more years after he had spent his talents.

Most ballplayers cherish the fan adulation. "On the way down," the adulation could prove bittersweet. Regardless of this depressing factor, ex–big leaguers also had to seek employment for the simple reason that the vast majority were poorly paid. Continued ball playing, somewhere, was a financial necessity. Back then the team owners were the only baseball people making good money.

The character of the minor leagues was similar to what football fans saw in the early 1960s when the American Football League was in its infancy. While the new football league reached some level of parity with the senior National League by the late 1960s, in the early years it was a clear cut below. Proof lay in the fact that many players who were stars in the new league had either been marginal players or well past their peaks in the senior circuit. The games had a certain excitement, though, and locals were so hungry for a team that they could turn a blind eye to most shortcomings. Back in 1911, people in a city such as Minneapolis could gain similar pleasure out of the Millers. In an age of minimal communications, the local team was the only way to experience decent baseball.

The Millers had a few stars who had had their day in the major league sun. Claude Rossman had played several strong years with Cleveland and

Detroit. In 1908 he was third only to Ty Cobb and Sam Crawford in AL batting. He was the Millers' first baseman. Hobe Ferris had been a steady, though not great, infielder with the Pilgrims and the Browns. He now played for the Millers. Otis Clymer had played in Pittsburgh and Washington with modest success, but he led the American Association in hitting several times while playing outfield for the Millers. He would go back to the majors but flop with the Cubs and Braves. The American Association was the highest point where he could sparkle. The Cantillons hoped Rube would shine once more.

Rube may have entertained the fantasy that a good season with the Millers could spark the interest of someone in the big leagues. In any case, he certainly needed the money. He was broke, as usual. He had spent much of the winter of 1911 in New York pitching in an indoor baseball league. In one indoor game against the same Rochester team that had bested Newark for the Eastern League championship, Rube threw a perfect game and struck out 25 of the 27 who faced him.[2] Rube felt his arm was plenty strong. So in March he headed off to the Millers' spring training camp in Cantillon's hometown of Hickman, Kentucky.

Rube's infamous personality and behavior reemerged as soon as he arrived in Hickman. "Rube," wrote one reporter, "appears not at all serious about anything but his pitching. That he takes very seriously." On the mound, Rube looked sharp indeed. Catcher "Hub" Dawson's glove "boomed like a Salvation Army bass drum." His knuckleball made batters swing twice before the ball crossed the plate. His curves made batters put *both* feet in the bucket. "I don't see but that he has everything he ever had," judged Cantillon. "During my career in the AL," wrote Claude Rossman, "I never saw him one bit better."[3]

Meanwhile, off the field Rube was up to his usual tricks. He joined a marching minstrel band, grabbed a bass drum and attempted to play and conduct simultaneously. He hunted, leading several expeditions out to nearby Reelfoot Lake where Joe Cantillon owned land. Rube and other players' "gross neglect of table culture" became the talk of all the help at the LaClede Hotel. Apparently, Rube and the Millers never sprinted as well on the ball field as they did when the dinner bell rang at the LaClede.[4]

The Hickmanites, who did not like the name "Hicks," took it all in stride, and this was all to the good for someone with the temperament of a Rube Waddell. When the players went jogging, everyone got out of their way and shouted encouragement. All the players got a nickname — "Yip" Owens, "Red" Killifer, "Wib" Smith. Joe Cantillon was known as "Pongo." Rube already had a nickname, of course, and the Hickmanites warmed to it, though they pronounced it with a lingering on the "eu" sound before moving on to the "b." Just as Pongo saw nothing terribly out of the ordinary in Rube, neither did the Hickmanites.

The people in Hickman had a pretty stable life. Theirs was an old river town that had not changed much since the Civil War. The population was 4000 in 1865, and it was the same in 1911. While the other river towns were either growing or dying, Hickman remained as it was, though it did open one theater. The big change in the offing involved a nearby railroad under construction, and the town was pretty much of one mind about it — they did not want it. (The railroads were killing river commerce and thus hurting the economies of river towns.) The presence of a ball team, on the other hand, was not a disruption. Rather, it was a reminder of how the town can serve others while still being itself. They warmed to Pongo's ballplayers out of natural friendliness as well as with a decided determination to show themselves the viability of their established way of life. This defiant provincialism resonated in many, including the Rube. It probably reminded him of Prospect, Pennsylvania. The "Hickmanites," as one Minneapolis reporter put it:

> don't speak to players with the nervous energy of a city folk who wants a player to know that his wife's brother was once pals with a fellow whose sister met Joe McGinnity at a country dance. They talk with a friendly frankness that would make any ball player but Ty Cobb stop and talk.[5]

Rube liked it in Hickman, and of course he joined the fire department. He appeared to be staying sober, and his young wife Madge was there to help him, candid in her desire to get her husband back to the big leagues. Whether or not he would reenter the majors, Rube seemed to be stable and content with Madge and Pongo.

NOTES

1. *Minneapolis Journal*, March 31, 1911.
2. Arthur Baer, "The Rube's Invisible Record," 1947, Clippings File, Cooperstown.
3. *Minneapolis Journal*, March 11, 12, 27, 1911.
4. Ibid., March 12, 1911.
5. Ibid.

Rube on the Mississippi

(The following is based on an account of one of Rube's hunting expeditions, witnessed and recorded by journalist J. H. Ritchie of the *Minneapolis Journal*, March 11, 1911. It nicely encapsulates the joys, the absurdities, and the terrors that came with knowing George Edward Waddell.)

Joe Cantillon canceled practice one day after a rainstorm. With a day to let the ballfield dry out, Rube and some of the Millers decided it would be a good time to go hunting. March was a good month to go after geese, and Rube learned of an island upriver from Hickman that was supposed to be the best place to bag 'em. Cantillon knew Chicago owner Charlie Comiskey, who kept a boat under Joe's care down at Hickman. Rube and the hunting party commandeered Comiskey's boat, the *Whitesox*, and prepared to cast off.

The *Whitesox* was an old flatboat, perfect for hunting and fishing expeditions. It was not in the best of repair, however. When the party reached the boat, Rube inspected it and found one of its propeller tunnels packed with driftwood, rail pieces, dead swine, empty bottles, tin cans, and various other items that flavored the Mississippi. There was symbolism in all that, but Rube and friends paid no heed and tooted off upriver.

Just north of Hickman lay mudflats. With Rube at the wheel, the 200-horsepower engine of the *Whitesox* chugged its way through the flats when a volume of *something* belched its way out the exhaust pipe, making enough noise to be heard down towards Memphis. The noise drowned out a loud snap, which proved to be the tiller cord breaking off the pilot's wheel. The *Sox* suddenly took a nose dive for the Missouri side with the ferocity of one of Ty Cobb's hook slides when Larry Lajoie was perched at the bag. The boat was going down for sure. The only question was whether it would hit soft mud or crash into a submerged tree stump.

The entire hunting party figured the water on the Kentucky side was deeper and prepared to make a dive for safety. Just then Rube took command in much the same way he entered the stage to save the heroine in *The Stain of Guilt*. He grabbed the loose cable, pulling and twisting until the *Sox* headed rightward. With Waddell holding an Atlas pose, the other hunters held an immediate committee meeting, their deliberations interrupted several times by strained shouts from a weakening Rube, insisting that a monkey wrench could capably replace his large and still baseball-worthy digits. Still, the party insisted on continuing its meeting. Meanwhile, the *Sox* was heading for New Orleans sideways.

The earnest committee spied a mud patch on the Missouri side that appeared safe. After proper procedures were observed, they decided to pry Rube from the cable and stuck the nose of the *Sox* into the soft Missouri mud. A broomstick, several button hooks, and some twine effected the necessary repairs, and the party again headed upriver.

Their destination that day was Medley, Kentucky. Nearby, the geese awaited them. Medley got its name because it looked like a medley of items that float off the Mississippi floodplain — one house, two dead trees, a wagon with one wheel leaning against one of the trees, six ducks, one very lean turkey, two mangy mutts, and an even mangier looking couple. Rube felt right at home.

Just below Medley lay Wolf Island and geese. Folks called it Wolf Island, though they said the wolves all swam over to Missouri during the gunboat battles of the Civil War. Now the only hostile varmints on the island were blackbirds and water moccasins. The blackbirds simply made noise and were a waste of ammunition. The cottonmouths made all the boys nervous, so it was good that high-knee running was necessary during spring training.

First things first: When the boys arrived at Wolf Island they had lunch. They had brought along a cook from the LaClede Hotel who used the little *Sox* stove to boil water. The boys sat down to boiled ham, boiled cabbage, boiled onions, and several other things that weren't boiled. It was a good meal, and it proved to be the only thing upon which everybody agreed all day. Even Hobe Ferris, a city boy who had regretted joining the party from the moment they cleared the propeller tunnel, liked the ham.

Full-bellied and ready to hunt, they took the *Sox* up the Wolf Island Chute. There were geese there, all right, and the engine noise scared thousands of them out of the nearby fields. Many of the party were now disheartened, but Rube and a few others figured the geese would come back. After some debate, they made plans for the beasts' return. Rube took out his "tin boosters," decoys fashioned out of tin. They didn't look much like geese, and another argument started over whether they would be of any use, some pointing out that even a goose can't be that dumb. The argument grew and was quelled only when someone pointed out that the geese came from Tennessee.

Rube dug two pits and placed his decoys all about the holes. He put out so many decoys that some said it started to look like a suffragette convention. This promised to inspire another long argument until Hobe won it for the negative, pointing out that the decoys weren't squawking.

The boys manned the pits, three in each. Those who could not fit headed back to the boat. Standing in the holes, the hunters waited, and waited. The temperature started to drop, and the wind blew out of the north. The boys grew uncomfortable. Several boys' boiled cabbage started to disagree with them, and the wind, unfortunately, wasn't all that stiff. A couple of boys got the bright idea to convince the olfactorally offended Hobe that the whole affair had been a snipe-hunt prank. Hobe bought it and was just about to charge out of his hole and shoot Rube when the geese returned.

Rube shot first and crippled one. The others climbed out and chased it all over the island. They must have shot at it a hundred times, but it still escaped. As darkness began to fall, everyone headed back for the *Sox*. On the way, Rube actually bagged a few 12-pounders.

Back at the boat another discussion heated up over whether to tie up for the night. When it was discovered there was not enough food left for breakfast, the decision was easy. Everyone huddled around the engine, and they headed downwind and downstream.

Rube piloted the craft again and barely missed ramming a couple of boats, though he did manage to hit a stump or two. Thankfully, there was soft mud at Hickman that night, and many a willing hand helped tie up the *Sox*, securing her for anyone else foolish enough to again join Rube on the Mississippi.

Chapter 54

Minnesota Rube

Hearing that Rube was about to play for Joe Cantillon and the Millers, Cleveland's star second baseman Larry Lajoie commented, "I know both of them well and, believe me, they make a good combination. Waddell is far from the 'has been' stage. He still possesses the stuff, and it only remains for someone to get it out of him. Joe is the one to do it." Lajoie was not naive. He expected Rube to "pull off a select series of stunts" as usual, but he knew that Cantillon would take it all in stride, as had Connie Mack. Lajoie expected, and Minneapolis hoped, Rube would come through with a strong season.[1]

The hunting travails on the Mississippi River notwithstanding, spring training down in Hickman went well. Rube looked sharp in some exhibitions, and his charisma had not dimmed one whit. First baseman Claude Rossman noted that "it seems puzzling how Rube retains his popularity among the ball fans for he attracts more attention from the spectators than anybody else on the field, not even barring the game itself."[2] On the way to a game in Meridian, Mississippi, Rube spied an eight-ox team and decided to mount the lead one. He rode it for several blocks to the joy of all the locals who lined the streets that afternoon. Rube said the sight of a team of oxen always made him homesick for western Pennsylvania. Attendance at the ball game later that day set a town record for any event ever held in Meridian.[3]

Once back in Minneapolis the team quickly got down to the business of the new season. They had a great start. Rube pitched well. He proved a delight to fans in many of the league towns, especially in Louisville, Columbus, and Milwaukee, where he was returning after many years. They all seemed to think of him as one of their own. When Rube was not pitching he and Madge were staying at a lake near Minneapolis. As in Milwaukee in 1900, Rube was at his most stable when he kept himself fishing. He showed up for practice one afternoon, after being gone for three days, and presented Cantillon with a string of prize fish. Cantillon took one of the fish and slapped Rube square in the face with it. Rube got the message and did not miss a practice the rest of the season. The team was going great. By May 6, Rube's record stood at 6 and 0. Outfielder Otis Clymer had hit safely in every game of the season, and the Millers were in first place at 18 and 6. Baseball historian Bill James once declared that this Millers team was the best minor league team of its time, and they were certainly showing it in early 1911.[4]

Baseball teaches one to expect good and bad streaks over the long life of a season. Having Rube Waddell on one's team provides an added lesson as to how violent these swings can be. In mid May, the Millers' fortunes began to go awry. Rube lost his next six outings. His speed seemed gone. His curves had no snap. His mood worsened when he went to a sporting goods store, bought $38 worth of fishing tackle, and told the storekeeper to box it and send it over to the Millers' baseball office. Mike Cantillon refused delivery, and that day Rube lost to Kansas City, giving up five runs, eight hits, and six walks. He made two errors and had to go fishing later with a cane pole.

Amidst Rube's gloom, the team fell out of first place. By May 30, their record had reversed completely. They stood at 24 and 24, in third place. On June 1, Rube promised not to shave until he won a game. Some of the players joked about what Rube's beard would look like by Labor Day. But Rube came through that afternoon with nine strikeouts and a victory over Milwaukee. He knocked in the winning run himself with a triple in the ninth inning. Madge was in the stands cheering loudly. She did not like beards.

Rube's beard-threatening victory over Milwaukee brought the Millers out of their daze a little. They turned, however, not back to winning but to a decided mediocrity. Through June they played steady .500 ball and hovered around third place. In a game against Toledo, Rube was up 5–4 in the sixth. Then he yielded three straight singles. The next man bunted. Rube charged it, picked it up and then just stood there with it, throwing to no one. He walked off the field before Cantillon had even finished climbing the dugout steps to relieve him.[5]

In early July, there seemed little doubt that the Millers were back in a fog. As of July 4, they were in sixth place with half their victories having come in the month of April. Rube's fogginess was less mysterious. He was drinking again. Madge must have given him some sort of ultimatum. The feistiness she had shown the press at the time of their marriage revealed itself here as well, for when she saw that Rube was drinking to excess, she left for St. Louis. "Rube is too crazy for me," Madge declared. Rube never saw her again.[6]

Rube did not grow despondent with Madge's departure. Quite the contrary; he revived. On July 7, the Millers were down 3–0 to first-place Kansas City. In the eighth inning they rallied for five runs. During the rally, Cantillon had pinch-hit for the pitcher, so in the ninth he decided to send out Rube. After a walk came a quick strikeout and a double play. Just like that it was over. Cantillon liked what he saw, and started Rube the next afternoon.

Rube had the goods. He struck out nine, going the distance and making a key sacrifice bunt during a rally that put the Millers ahead. He struck out two in the ninth, and the crowd was completely his. Rube beat Kansas City again on July 14. The next day the Millers again played Kansas City. Minneapolis was ahead, but Kansas City rallied for three to tie the game 4–4 in the seventh. With two on and one out, Cantillon put Rube in. He threw a no hitter the rest of the way. In the ninth he singled and scored a key run on a head first slide. After puffing his way around the bases in the top of the ninth, Rube went out and struck out the side in the bottom of the inning to win. With the win, the Millers had climbed back to within a game of second place.[7]

While pitching well again, Rube's high jinks continued. After the Kansas City series, the Millers traveled to Milwaukee. Rube pitched four games in five days. During his day off he cavorted about the stands. There he ran into club secretary Ed Dickinson, whom he had known back in 1900. Rube asked Dickinson if there was anything he could do to help since he was not pitching that day. (He was serious.) Noting the big Sunday doubleheader crowd, Dickinson suggested he go to the ticket office and help count receipts. As Dickinson was returning to his office later in the afternoon he heard a huge commotion in the ticket office. He found Rube with three policemen draped over his shoulders and club president James Havenor excitedly shouting to the police that Rube was trying to force his way into the office to steal receipts. Rube was arguing, of course, that he was needed there and that he had been asked to help. Dickinson explained the situation and the scuffle ended.[8]

Starting the fourth game of the series against Milwaukee July 18, Rube incurred the ire of Cantillon in the fourth inning. He broke his bat on a grounder to second. His hands stung, and he simply stopped running. The first baseman dropped the throw from second, and Cantillon became angry at Rube's lack of hustle. Rube made up for it in the seventh. He singled; the next batter grounded into an apparent double play, but the shortstop missed the throw. Rube scampered to third, but he started his slide a full ten feet from the bag. He safely clawed and scraped the rest of the way, packing his face and ears with sand in the process. Rube brushed off the excess but remained covered in grime. Cantillon liked the grittiness of the performance, as Rube retired the Brewers in order the rest of the way.[9]

Cantillon was not the only one inspired by Rube's performance. As had happened in Philadelphia in 1902, Rube's grit caught the poetic muse of one fan, Mique McBride, who published the following:

> They say that a streak of saffron hue
> As broad as a Chinese flag, about
> Slants down his spine; perhaps it's true

But a million fans will dispute the view;
You've seen him at work — or haven't you?
"Strike 1— Strike 2 — Strike 3 — and out!"

They tell of times when he lost his grip;
Was hammered fiercely and put to rout
At a critical pinch; just take a tip
From all the batters he's caused to trip
And fall to the curves of his mighty whip —
"Strike 1— Strike 2 — Strike 3 — you're out!"

Like many another of big league fame,
When he's bad, he's extraordinarily bad, no doubt;
When he's right — oh shucks! What's in a name?
Naps, Tigers, Athletics, Highlanders tame;
Sox, white or red, all look the same —
"Strike 1— Strike 2 — Strike 3 — side out!"

Here's to George Edward "Rube" Waddell —
Oh you Rube of southpaw stout!
Sometimes you're a bum and again you're swell;
What you're going to do no man can tell;
But when you're right, you can pitch like — well
"Strike 1— Strike 2 — Strike 3 — side out!"[10]

The length of a baseball season accommodates natural human hopes for redemption throughout the summer months among fans whose team is lagging. The vagaries of an alcoholic can do the same at any time. As with Babe Ruth and Mickey Mantle, the stories about Rube's zaniness made many pull only harder for him. And, as with the Babe and Mick, when he did come through, the fans' joy was all the sweeter. That elusive quality that drew the attention of all in Columbus, Grand Rapids, and Los Angeles was still there. For those closest to Rube, like Madge, the attraction to that quality was potentially lethal. When one is that close, redemption has to be more substantial than a mere well-pitched series of baseball games. Such deeper redemption was not going to occur, and as soon as Madge realized it she departed. Meanwhile, at their vicarious level of involvement, the fans rejoiced.

Whatever the mixture of baseball, summer heat, beer, and divorce working within Rube, it prompted "The Waddell Renaissance," as the newspapers termed it. Particularly pleasing to Rube was the fact that Madge elected not to contest and drag out the separation proceedings. He did not need another three-year wrangle of the sort he had gone through with May Wynne. Cantillon would not have liked it either, for the marriage had occurred in Missouri, and the team could not have fared well with Rube unable to set foot in Kansas City. The divorce was easy, and Rube won seven in a row.

As Rube regained his top form, so did the Millers. By August 8, they had rallied back to first place. Through August, Columbus and Kansas City stayed right on the Millers' heels, so there could be no letup. Rube was determined to lead the way, perhaps still dreaming that a big league manager would pick him up. In Louisville on August 23, Rube entered in relief in the sixth inning. He hurled a one-hitter from there. He felt good. The next day was a doubleheader, and Cantillon started Rube in the first game. Rube won it, and afterwards he asked Cantillon to let him pitch the second game. It was a very hot day, and even the first-game catcher asked to be relieved, but Rube was willing. Cantillon agreed, and Rube won the second on a five-hitter. Rube had pitched three wins in two days. He was full of beans, full of post-divorce glee, full of hope, and full of everything else.[11]

The Millers' train left Louisville for Columbus. When it pulled into Cincinnati, Rube hoped some major league agent would be there, as had happened when he and Sam Crawford left the Grand Rapids club for the majors. He was disappointed, and headed off to Columbus with the rest of the club. Between Columbus and Cincinnati that day a freight train had needed to go off on a sidetrack. There the switchman had neglected to throw the rail back to give the Millers' train a clear line. The club was hurtling for Columbus when the unchanged switch jostled it rightward. Suddenly the train was lurching straight for the freighter. The engineer threw the engine into reverse and began to hurl sand like a maniac. The wheels screeched like bagpipes, and the train came to a halt three feet from the freighter's cow catcher. There ensued what one newspaperman described as an exchange of "some real Baltimore and Ohio profanity," with railroad men and ballplayers spilling out of both liners. Eventually, the engineer backed the Millers' train out of the siding. The switch was properly thrown, and the team made it to Columbus without further incident. Rube may have hoped his hot pitching and hurling both ends of a doubleheader would spark major league interest. But all he seemed to have accomplished was head off onto sidetracks where slower going was the wiser policy. Maybe he could have been an effective "closer" for a contender that summer, but no one wanted a 34-year-old with a drinking problem.[12]

By September 1, Rube's record stood at 19 and 11. From there he had a few no-decision outings and won three more. When Toledo came to town for an important series, Rube also went off, but this time it was on a useful absence. He took Toledo's best pitcher — Earl Yingling — off fishing with him, causing Yingling to miss a critical start in a game which the Millers won. Rube said the boy loved to fish, though, mysteriously, the Millers' office received a bill for some fish which Rube bought. If Rube and Yingling did not go off to the lakes, no one ever knew what Rube and the Toledo pitcher actually did, but the Cantillons were grateful for the Toledo ace's missed start, and they paid Rube's bill.[13]

The following week, Rube missed a few games in St. Paul. The Saints and Millers had a keen rivalry, and Pongo wanted Rube on hand for the games. One evening Cantillon had arranged to have Rube held in a Minneapolis jail. Rube was kept under polite conditions and won the next afternoon. On this day in St. Paul, Rube disappeared *after* showing up for a game. The Saints played in a park adjoining the property of a wealthy horseman named Commodore Kittson. A gun club had leased the property for a trapshooting tournament. Rube was warming up to pitch against the Saints and could not help but hear the popping of shotguns. He slipped away. Cantillon was furious about Rube's absence, of course. But when Rube finally reappeared several days later at Nicollet Park in Minneapolis he presented Cantillon with a new gun and case. Rube had won the trapshooting contest and gave the prize gun to Joe. Pongo knew a quality gun when he saw it, and his anger subsided.[14]

Rube's last victory that season occurred on September 27 against St. Paul. It clinched the pennant for the Millers.[15] With the close of the season Rube's record stood at 22 and 12. It was a more than solid season for the Rube. He was the best pitcher on the team and in the league. Larry Lajoie's prediction was on the money. Minneapolis baseball people were congratulating themselves on the point that they, especially Joe Cantillon, handled the quixotic Rube so well. The trouble was, no matter how much the locals wished to pretend otherwise, this was minor league ball. Rube now had fully to face the fact that no one above Minneapolis wanted him. The Philadelphia A's squared off against McGraw's Giants once again in the World Series that fall. The A's won it this time, and all of Philadelphia rejoiced. Rube was a distant memory. All he could do was sit and read the articles Ty Cobb wrote covering the series for the papers. When you're "on the way down," the end of the season can bring a most hollow feeling.

NOTES

1. *Minneapolis Journal*, April 11, 1911.

2. *Minneapolis Morning Tribune*, March 30, 1911.

3. *Minneapolis Journal*, March 28, 1911.

4. Bill James, *The Bill James Historical Baseball Abstract* (New York: Villard Books, 1988), pp. 106–7.

5. *Minneapolis Journal*, May 10, June 2, July 1, 1911.

6. Quoted in Harold Seymour, *Baseball: The Golden Age*, p. 102.

7. *Minneapolis Journal*, July 8–9, 15–16, 1911.

8. Ibid., July 17, 1911.

9. Ibid., July 19, 1911.

10. Ibid., July 23, 1911.

11. Ibid., August 24–25, 1911.

12. Ibid., August 25, 1911.

13. Howard Liss, *Baseball's Zaniest Stars*, pp. 51–52; Daniel Okrent and Steve Wulf, *Baseball Anecdotes* (New York: Oxford University Press, 1989), p. 45.

14. George Barton, "Sportographs," May 21, 1937, Clippings File, Cooperstown.

15. *Minneapolis Journal*, September 28, 1911.

Chapter 55

Levees and Whiskey

Joe Cantillon owned a 30-acre farm outside Hickman, Kentucky, where he lived in grand style. It was a great piece of property adjacent to woods and lakes and fully serviced with water, electric, and telephone lines. He built several houses on the property and had lots of guns and fishing equipment. It was a sportsman's dream. Joe liked Rube personally, and because he wished to protect his biggest gate attraction for the 1912 season, he invited Rube to stay at his farm during the off season, slightly docking his 1912 season pay as rent. Rube could not refuse. He had no money and no place to go. Besides, for him Cantillon's spread was heaven. Rube kept the compound well stocked with fish and game, just as he had done for the St. Louis Browns' front office in 1909 and 1910. The only thing that held back his output was the unusual quantity of rain that winter.

After the healthy winter of hunting and fishing, Rube was ready for spring training. He looked to one reporter "hard as iron" and "big as a coalhouse and as clear of eye as a kid." Rube threw really hard that March, and everything appeared to be shaping up for the season. Then on March 28, flood alarms sounded all over Hickman. Ready to a fault in any crisis, Rube was the first one out of Hickman's LaClede Hotel. The ball field was completely inundated, but that was not at issue. The town was imperiled and needed to be saved. All the players lent a hand with the sandbagging. Rube was everywhere on the levee, working several days without sleep. When the field cleared, the players went back for some practice, but Rube would not leave the levee. He sandbagged for four straight days. As one player noted, among the levee workers "the rugged form of Waddell towered above them all."[1]

After the fourth day of sandbagging, forecasts of more rain proved sadly accurate, and on April 1 all the sandbags failed; the levee burst again. The rush could be heard for miles. From Cairo, Illinois, clear down to Memphis the news was the same. The bad winter rains had weakened the levees. The spring thaws and yet more rain burst them up and down the central Mississippi. Between Cape Girardeau, Missouri, and Memphis, 7000 were homeless.

Hickman had it as badly as any. It was under eight feet of water with 2000 left homeless. Kentucky governor James B. McCreary could only send along tents, but nobody knew where to put them.[2]

In addition to worrying about his home town and property, Joe Cantillon still had a baseball team to run. He had had the players pitch in on the levees as best they could, and the local folks were grateful. It was clear that there would be no more ball playing in Hickman that spring. Cantillon made arrangements to take the team out of Hickman and go to another practice site. They had to go by boat. No one in the town begrudged Cantillon. They had all been through such times before, and they would do what had to be done. Rube was beside himself, however. He didn't want to leave. To him, it was like leaving a burning building. He departed with the team, but he certainly was not happy about it.

Cantillon arranged for the team to train in Owensboro, Kentucky. Owensboro was dry, at least in terms of its land conditions. The Millers got in some sorely needed practice. The locals were delighted to have them and endeavored to show them something of the local culture. Owensboro was then home to 14 different rye and bourbon distilleries. Several factory representatives invited the players to tour the various works. Practically everyone accepted the invitations. At every place, the players were presented with complimentary glasses, flasks, quarts, and sometimes full jugs. By the end of the week, team discipline was not good. There was enough booze in the players' hotel to float a steamboat. How reluctantly is unclear, but Rube initially refused the presents at the distilleries, but, as one accompanying reporter sarcastically put it, "Out of respect to the feelings of his hosts he eventually yielded — at every place."[3]

After abandoning Hickman, Rube may have felt less obliged to be on good behavior. Maybe the cause was something less explicit. Whatever the reason, he was off on another bender. Rube began to return to the distilleries like a little kid knowing where to get free candy. He even searched Owensboro for a set of false whiskers, so he could make an extra round of distillery visits posing as someone else. It was more pathetic than funny. Fittingly, all of this occurred as the *Titanic* sank.

The Millers were to open the season in Louisville. They were to play there and go onto Indianapolis, Columbus, and Toledo, before returning to Minneapolis later in April. Rube was in no condition to pitch, and missed every game of the opening trip. The team's lack of practice showed itself, too, but that wasn't Rube's downfall. He was just plain sloshed. He may have been bored at the letdown of leaving Hickman, but the irony was that although Hickman rebounded, Rube did not.

Out of shape and poorly practiced, the Millers began the season in mediocre fashion. By the end of April they were lucky to be at 10 and 5, in second place. It wasn't a bad start, but Cantillon knew his players were capable of better baseball. Throughout April, Rube was still up in the air somewhere. In Toledo on April 20, Rube showed up at the Boody House hotel. He had been out fishing and drinking all night. In the lobby he spied teammate Claude Rossman and playfully punched him right in the back of the head. Rossman staggered about, and Rube thought it all very funny. Rossman was anything but amused, and the pair began to scuffle. Other players separated them, ending the zany, irritating behavior of someone who was rapidly dissipating what little talent he had left.[4]

Rube finally appeared able to start a game on April 30. In the first four innings he gave up five hits and three runs. In the second inning, he fell down fielding a bunt and threw the ball away. In the fourth he booted another bunt, and Cantillon relieved him.[5]

Cantillon decided that the Millers needed practices in the mornings, even on game days. It was a kind of season-long spring training. This proved to be a good solution, and the Millers' play began to live up to their potential. Rube was another matter, however. He was struggling with issues he never understood, problems he used to be able to handle with laughter, adrenaline, and athleticism. Now the athletic skills were ebbing, the adrenaline was not pumping, and no one was laughing. A year before he was dreaming about returning to the majors. Now those who had shared his dream, like Madge, had abandoned him, and the only question was whether he could even hold on to a place in the minors.

With so much else failing him, Rube's teeth began to give out, too, a classic problem for chronic drinkers. Always the child, Rube backed out on two appointments with a dentist. Finally, one of the Millers, W. Darst Gill, intervened. "Doc" Gill had been trained in dentistry, and his credentials were legitimate (but, then, so were "Doc" Holliday's). Another teammate, Danny Sweeney, took Rube by the hand, and they went to Gill, who pulled a couple of Rube's bum teeth.[6]

Rube took his second start on May 9. Here the baseball fates were cruel to him. He pitched "sterling ball." He even fielded several bunts without error. But, perhaps because they were nervous with the quixotic Rube on the mound, the Millers played poorly. They committed three errors and were shut out for the first time in the season. Like anyone climbing out of a problem, Rube could not expect any more than indifference from the real world.

Rube's fall to a minor league level of play was obvious against rival St. Paul on May 13. He had a shutout going into the sixth inning. He looked strong. At the top of the sixth, Rube booted a bunt and walked two to load the bases. Rube then went to work. He struck out the next batter on three pitches. He went up 0 and 2 on the next man and playfully waved to the crowd, just as he used to, telling them it was all over. But the batter connected with Rube's next pitch for a grand slam. Such was the fate into which Rube had dragged himself. He had blunted his athletic strength. The mind and the ego were still there, but his skills were no longer commensurate. "What a waste," people reflected, but they didn't reflect too long. Later in the week the Millers were in Kansas City. Rube blew a relief job one day. The next evening the players of both clubs were invited to a local theater. After they had taken their seats in the stage boxes, Rube decided he was to be the center of attraction. He stood up to deliver a monologue, and players from both sides physically restrained him and convinced him that his speechifying was inappropriate. Rube had nothing to offer them.

Rube kept whining that he had a sore arm. "I don't pretend to say that I have been at my best for several years," he opined. "Still, the way my arm has been feeling ... I am afraid that I have nothing left. The trouble now is something that I have never before experienced, and it is worrying me considerably. Of course, the pain may wear away, but I have a hunch that something is wrong in that elbow and that is something the doctors cannot fix." Rube may not have been right about the elbow being the problem, but he was right about the doctors.

By late May, Rube was close to being out of a job. Cantillon had signed a couple of young left-handed pitchers, and Rube had yet to win a game. On May 26 Rube started a game against Milwaukee with his job possibly in the balance. He came through. He hurled a no-hitter for seven innings, and gave up just four hits thereafter. He struck out nine and singled in a run. Cantillon did not fire him.[7]

Rube finally began to pitch decently in June. He threw a couple of shutouts. There were times when the Millers' good hitting won games for him. But his antics were unwelcome. In several games Rube ran out to coach third base, only to be called back by Cantillon. Cantillon wanted no silliness from the coaching box any more than the players had wanted it from the theater box. Rube asked to pitch both ends of a doubleheader in Milwaukee, and Cantillon flatly told him "No." Rube did knock in the winning run of the second game that day, however. The next week in Kansas City, Rube walked out with a two-run lead in the first inning and hit the first two batters who faced him. Cantillon relieved him immediately.[8]

It was a time for new heroes on the mound. Joe Wood was the greatest pitcher of the day, going 32 and 4 for Boston in 1912. In Washington, Walter Johnson was coming into greatness. Philadelphia fans idolized a new youngster named Herb Pennock. Even in Minneapolis, the best pitcher was Cy Young (not *the* Cy Young). Rube was an afterthought. He did not even seem to be sparking much gate attendance anymore. In early July, Rube was out for two weeks with an attack of indigestion and gallstones. The team did not miss him.

In August the Minneapolis papers printed an article about a local athlete named Louis Sockalexis. He had run marathons and pitched for Cleveland in the big leagues. But he was unmanageable. He drank and quickly burned up his talents. He faded into the minors and broke his ankle falling out of a hotel window. That ended his baseball career, and he was now "ordinary fat and lazy." Few baseball people (save one) in Minneapolis who read the article missed the implication. Several Eastern papers printed reports that Rube had fallen into destitution, that he was forsaken, broke, hungry, and alone. They were not so much wrong as premature.[9]

Rube was like the old dog in a family that now had younger ones. The family remembered the dog in its prime and marveled whenever the old boy showed signs of perkiness. On August 10, Rube lost a game to Indianapolis. His record stood at 6 and 7. On the 24th he shut out Indianapolis in the first game of a doubleheader. Once more he asked Cantillon to let him pitch the second game. Cantillon relented this time. Rube went out and shut down the Indians 1-2-3 in the first, and the crowd shouted its approval. Then he allowed six hits and four runs over the next three innings. Cantillon pulled him. Rube was barely capable of normal pitching feats, let alone something the young Waddell had made famous.[10]

In August the Millers took first place in the league. They widened their lead in September. Rube won four that month, closing his season out at 11 and 8 — not bad, but decidedly average even for the minor leagues. The Millers won their third straight championship by six games over Toledo. In a special series against Western League champion Denver, the Millers lost four games to one. Rube made the trip but was "unable" to appear in a game. Left flat and without optimism for his baseball future, Rube spent another winter in Kentucky.

NOTES

1. *Minneapolis Journal,* March 18, 29, 1912.
2. *Louisville Courier Journal.* April 2–4, 1912.
3. *Minneapolis Journal,* April 9, 1912.
4. Newspaper note, Toledo, Ohio, April 20, 1912, Clippings File, Cooperstown.
5. *Minneapolis Journal,* May 1, 1912.
6. Ibid., May 6, 1912.
7. Ibid., May 10, 15, 17, 27, 1912.
8. Ibid., June 15, 18, 25, 1912.
9. Ibid., August 4–5, 1912.
10. Ibid., August 10, 25, 1912.

Chapter 56

Floods

The winter in Hickman was another rainy one. This time the rains were so strong, nature did not even have to wait for spring thaws to raise the Mississippi to dangerous levels. Because Hickman lay below both the Missouri and the Ohio rivers, excessive rains in either valley, as well as the central Mississippi, could hurt them, and in the winter of 1913, the Ohio Valley was especially hard hit. By January much of Kentucky was imperiled. From Christmas into early January rain fell almost every day. The first floods hit on January 12. Matters stabilized with a late-January cold snap that froze some rivers. But this only served to increase the water buildup, and when the weather warmed in mid February, all hell broke loose.[1]

Hickman was hit hard, and everyone got out to sandbag. Rube became quite a town hero with the Hickmanites for the yeoman work he did during the flooding. He was made a deputy sheriff and chief of the fire department. Unfortunately, as he spent hours on end standing in icy waters, he caught a very bad cold. Pneumonia set in, and Rube was bedridden for over a week. Still, in March when the rest of the Millers came to Hickman to train, Rube was there. He was three pounds under his normal playing weight, but he eagerly claimed the pneumonia had done him no perceptible harm, though he coughed incessantly while out on the ball field.

While Rube was a hero in Hickman for his flood work, his stature dimmed in the eyes of at least one family for the work he did on March 9. While practicing with the Millers that morning, Rube heard a fire siren. Fire Chief Rube immediately ran from the field, stripping off his uniform as he ran. Outside the ballpark, Rube stopped a liveryman and commandeered a pony. He searched for the fire, galloping the pony without a bridle or saddle through the streets of Hickman. Joe Cantillon told Minneapolis reporters that Rube had stripped to his underwear. However, the experiences of the reporters from many a post-game locker-room interview led most to catch on to the fact that Pongo was being charitable. Rube did not wear anything under his baseball uniform, and Cantillon was trying to save Rube the embarrassment of his Lady Godiva act. The galloping Rube must have been quite a sight, but that was mere prologue. When Fire Chief Rube arrived at the fire, he asked no one for the status of matters. He simply saw the smoke, grabbed an ax, and climbed onto the rooftop of the imperiled house. Still "in his underwear," Rube proceeded to chop off the entire roof as everyone stood dumbfounded. When he finally climbed down, beaming with pride, he was informed that the entire fire was contained in the house's chimney. Rube helped rebuild the roof later that week (wearing a pair of overalls).[2]

Rube felt confident about his pitching prospects for the new season. He checked his weight every day to make sure the pneumonia was no longer affecting him, and he claimed he was maintaining his weight. Then flooding hit Hickman again on March 22. One reporter with the *Memphis Commercial Appeal* was in Hickman at the time, and noted how curious it was

> that most of the volunteer workmen were Negroes. Under the lashing commands of whites they sloshed out into the angry waters and threw up a temporary barricade of bags filled with sand....
>
> The Negroes chanted a familiar spiritual as they waded back and forth through the rushing torrent now up above their waist line. This was sheer living drama, unmatched in any book, on any stage. A beleaguered village, a rescue unit of naked Negroes a melodious obbligato of chanting voices.
>
> I saw ... the sudden appearance of a white man among the Negroes; he, too, was stripped, his broad shoulders bent under the weight of a heavy sand bag and his voice raised in song as he staggered forward in the teeth of the lashing stream. It wasn't difficult to recognize him. It was Rube Waddell.... This was an assignment he could measure up to. It required a strong back and a mechanical procedure.[3]

Whether playing ball with Rube Foster, knocking around with the locals in Spartanburg, South Carolina, putting out a fire in Montgomery, or anything else of an emergency or everyday nature, Rube let no mere custom stand in his way. Posterity has judged some of the customs he ignored quite negatively, others positively. Rube simply never judged. His ways — comical, noble, or destructive — simply marched to their own drummer. Amidst his self-destructiveness, there was something endearing at the man's core. At flood times, no one cared if he sang off-key.

From the new round of sandbagging in the cold waters, Rube suffered a relapse. A doctor gave him creosote, a common medicine for lung ailments in those days. Rather than take a teaspoon twice a day, Rube drank an entire pint at once. His stomach began to ache something fierce, and the pains would remain with him for the rest of his life.

In some exhibition games down South, a greatly weakened Rube did not pitch well. In one game he gave up 16 hits in four innings. Some reporters began to speculate that Rube was not going to be able to pitch for the Millers and would have to consign himself to a lesser level of play. The Millers arrived back in Minneapolis on the morning of April 9. It was still cold in the city. Snow remained on the ground, and that very afternoon Rube was seen outside his home on Franklin Avenue building snowmen with the local children. Rube disciplined himself in sickness no better than he did as an athlete. He insisted, as well, on getting out to Nicollet Park to help prepare the field for opening day. With such outdoor activity in cold weather, Rube suffered yet another relapse and found himself in bed during the Millers' opening day on April 12. The doctor diagnosed his condition as pleurisy. On April 13 he suffered a lung hemorrhage. The doctor was concerned, of course, but he predicted Rube's still-impressive physique would pull him through.[4]

A new baseball league — the Northern League — was to begin its first year of play that spring, with teams in places like Grand Forks, North Dakota; Winnipeg, Manitoba; and Superior, Wisconsin. Minneapolis had a team, the Broncos, and their field was the southernmost point of play in the league. Cantillon had determined that Rube was not strong enough to pitch for the Millers. He wanted Rube to have some work, however. The Cantillons had an interest in the Broncos, and they arranged for Rube to play there. After further rest, Rube started for the Broncs against Superior on April 25. Rube admitted that this start hurt him greatly. He was still quite weak and yielded ten hits in four innings. After giving up six runs in the fifth inning, he was relieved. During the game, while running to cover first base on a grounder, Rube was spiked in the leg. This led to infection and blood poisoning, for which doctors actually contemplated amputation.[5]

Despite the bouts with pneumonia, pleurisy, and infection, Rube seemed to rebound by early May. He went to Mike Cantillon and told him he was ready to rejoin the Millers. Cantillon told him he belonged to the Northern League. This made Rube pretty sore. On May 3, he started one more game for the Broncos against Grand Forks. He threw a complete-game shutout, giving up just three hits and striking out 11. Rube may have felt his performance against Grand Forks would change Cantillon's mind. But it had no more impact on Cantillon than his 1910 work for the Millers had had on major league managers. After the game, the Broncos' manager, Robert Unglaub, joked with Rube: "I guess I'll send you back tomorrow against Grand Forks." Rube snapped back: "No you won't." Rube turned in his uniform and quit the team. Unglaub had been the journeyman batter for Boston whom Rube had easily struck out on three pitches at the end of his 20-inning masterpiece over Cy Young in 1905. It must have been galling for Rube to find himself with the Broncos. How could he be playing for such a man as Unglaub? Rube quitting baseball was nothing new, but in his precarious physical condition, people feared the worst for him.

Another baseball league, the Federal League, was growing at this point. Previously, its geographic focus had been the Midwest, but the league's organizers had designs on expanding the enterprise into a third major league. With talk of putting a team in Philadelphia, rumors grew of Rube Waddell's return to the Quaker City. But this was nothing more than gossip. Rube also claimed he was going to play for a semi-pro team in Marshall, Minnesota. He never did. Joe Cantillon still wanted to help Rube, and he secured him a place on the Virginia (Minnesota) Ore Diggers, also of the new Northern League.[6]

The town of Virginia lies in the northeastern corner of Minnesota, north of Duluth, in the iron mining plains above Lake Superior. Rube's career seemed now to have taken the full bell curve. If playing for the Millers was the mirror image of Columbus and Grand Rapids, Virginia was the equivalent of Franklin, Pennsylvania, and they were as poor a team, to boot. On May 17, the Virginia Ore Diggers were playing in Duluth. Rube met them there. Some newspapermen spoke to Rube in the Duluth hotel. Rube seemed chipper. He acknowledged that he had been weakened by the bouts with pneumonia and infection. As for his leg nearly being amputated, Rube nodded, "By George, that was a narrow escape." But, said Rube, in his usual denial-laden confidence: "I am as good as when Connie Mack found me." He went on to spin yarns about the fishing he had planned for that summer.[7]

No sooner had Rube arrived in Duluth than he disappeared for a few days. He had gone for a walk around town and noticed a work crew on Lake Superior breaking the ice, which still lay heavy about the port that cold spring. Like fighting fires and floods, this kind of work attracted Rube. So, bad lungs and all, he signed on to an ice-breaking crew for a few days. This was hardly something a doctor would have prescribed. The Virginia baseball team, meanwhile, had no idea where he had gone. Virginia played several games with Duluth, but there was no Rube. Virginia's next series came just across the state line with Superior, Wisconsin. On May 19, Rube wandered out to the Superior ball park. Virginia was up 5–2 in the ninth, but the Superior Red Sox had just scored their two runs; the bases were loaded with one out. Rube did not report to the manager. He just walked out to the mound. The pitcher yielded the ball, figuring the manager had sent him. Rube reported himself to the umpire who energetically yelled to the crowd: "Now pitching for Virginia, Rube Waddell!" The crowd cheered, and the Virginia manager, former Giant Spike Shannon, learned who had gone in to pitch. Rube struck out the next two batters, and Virginia won. Welcome to the Northern League, Rube! (Welcome to Rube, Northern League.[8])

It was certainly good of Cantillon to secure Rube employment. But if Rube's lungs were to heal, a cold northern climate was not the place for it to occur. Further, it rained a lot that summer all over the upper Midwest. Rube pitched a few good games for Virginia, including one in which he struck out 12. When he faced the Broncos on June 6, he struck out Bob Unglaub, just as he had in Boston eight years before. Rube also pitched a number of bad games. Even when he was effective, it was all rather pathetic, since this was such a low grade of baseball. Virginia was the worst team in the new league. Eight or nine errors a game was not unusual. Crowds two and three times as large as normal still turned out to see Rube wherever the team went. Rube did a little of his on-field and coaching box clowning, too. He also had to play some outfield, just as he had in Los Angeles, and he dropped plenty of fly balls, including three in one game. In disgust with the whole team, Spike Shannon quit in mid-season.[9]

The team was in disarray, and Rube's health grew worse amidst the cold rainy weather of that summer. His coughing was ceaseless, though he never voiced complaints, nor did he ever brag about previous days of glory. Several times he was badly chilled when rains interrupted games. His catcher, Harry Brammell, later wrote of the sight of Rube trying to pitch: It was hard, Brammell recalled, to see "his constitution undermined, leaning over to cough between pitches as if his frame would be torn apart; then bracing, putting all that he had left in him on the ball, only to see his efforts hit to all corners of the field by bushers that would have been unable to get a foul off him when he was in his prime." All this, said Brammell, was exacerbated by the fact that Virginia was, in his opinion, the "poorest [team] in professional baseball." Rube never complained, Brammell noted. "No gamer, bigger hearted man ever lived."[10] On July 9, against Superior, Rube collapsed on the field and had to be carried off. On July 19, Rube lost to the Winona Highbrows, 9–0. He passed out after the game. The doctors diagnosed Rube with another attack of pleurisy. His season record stood at 4 and 6. He would never play ball again.[11]

NOTES

1. *Louisville Courier Journal*, January 10–17, February 15–18, 1913.

2. *Minneapolis Journal*, March 9, 1913.

3. Articles by Joe Williams, *Memphis Commercial Appeal*, undated, Clippings File, Cooperstown.

4. *Minneapolis Journal*, April 3, 10, 13–15, 1913.

5. Ibid., April 26, 1913.

6. Ibid., May 4, 13, 16, 1913.

7. *Duluth News-Tribune*, May 17, 1913.

8. Ibid., May 20, 1913; see also A. H. Tarvin, "More About Waddell," *Baseball Magazine*, LXXXI, July 1948, pp. 270–71.

9. *Duluth News-Tribune*, May 25, June 1, 5, 7, 9–14, 18, 24, 28, July 4, 14, 1913; see also Roy J. Dunlap, "Waddell's Last Game," Clippings File, Cooperstown.

10. Letter from Harry Brammell, Kansas City, Missouri, April 2, 1914, Clippings File, Cooperstown.

11. *Duluth News-Tribune*, July 10, 20, 25, 1913.

Chapter 57

The Crease in His Nose

The Virginia Ore Diggers ended up in last place in 1913, 50 games behind first-place Winona. After he was through pitching, Rube remained in northern Minnesota another month. He had been a member of the Elks, and a wealthy member of the order gave Rube use of his summer cabin. Rube did some fishing, of course. Two men had capsized in a rowboat on a nearby lake that summer. One of them drowned. Searchers could not find the body. Rube dove into the cold waters and retrieved it. Once again it was like the kid diving into a stream after an elusive fish. Rube went straight to the heart of the matter at hand, without the slightest regard for himself. Given the condition of his lungs this was hardly the wisest thing to do, but Rube could not discipline himself.[1]

Up in Virginia, Rube also spent an hour every day at the little zoo in the town's Olcott Park. He would climb into one of the cages and play with the zoo's four black bears. Three of the bears were very playful and loved to wrestle with the Rube. Rube named the playful ones John McGraw, Connie Mack, and "Tilly" Schaefer (a female he named after another zany ballplayer, Herman "Germany" Schaefer). One bear was standoffish and generally refused to play or wrestle. Rube named him Ty Cobb. Rube left Virginia in September, and within a few weeks McGraw, Mack, and Tilly all died.[2]

Rube went back to Minneapolis, just as the weather was starting to turn cold. In the woods he had developed an infected throat and could barely talk above a whisper. His stomach pains continued from the creosote, and, as usual, he had no money. Doctors told him that his health was precarious and that he should get to a warmer climate. He went to Hickman and stayed with Joe Cantillon. Some newspapers began to report that Rube was seriously ill. Rube denied it, claiming but a slight attack of bronchitis from getting his feet wet while hunting.[3]

Sometime after leaving Hickman, Rube ended up in St. Louis. Rube may have been drunk or in some other way incoherent, or he may have imagined he could find his former wife Madge or some other old friends. Whatever the reason, Rube was wandering the streets. On November 17, 1913, the St. Louis police picked him up. He was a vagrant. His health had deteriorated, and he was diagnosed with tuberculosis.

One of Rube's sisters, Margaret, lived in Boerne, Texas, near San Antonio, and Joe Cantillon offered to help him pay for his trip down there. His sister met him and took him to her family's ranch. The hope was that the warm Texas climate would help restore Rube's health. That winter, Rube wrote to "Kid" Taylor, the new manager of the Virginia Ore Diggers, that he would not be able to play with them that spring. "I am sending back the contract unsigned," he lamented. "I would like to play, but never could get in shape. I might as well admit the truth about myself. I am in hopeless shape. I have lost fifty-four pounds since I was up North. I now weigh only 151. I am very weak and cannot walk twenty feet. I am writing this in bed." Rube's sister and her husband did their best to restore Rube, but it was too late. By March, they had to send Rube to a San Antonio sanitarium. Joe Cantillon again helped with the expenses, as did Connie Mack and Ben Shibe. Rube also sent a confessional letter to the young baseball fans of the nation warning them of how destructive was his example of alcohol abuse: "I had my chance, and a good one it was," he confessed. "Many boys may have a better one ahead of them than I had. If they will leave the booze alone they won't have any trouble. I am not a very good preacher, but ... keep away from booze and cigarettes."[4]

Rube's spirit remained strong. Several ex–big leaguers were in the San Antonio area, hoping to start a baseball school in the Texas town of Mineral Wells. Among them were Donie Bush, Otto Williams, and Rube's old Detroit rival, Wild Bill Donovan. They ventured down to the sanitarium to see Rube. They walked into the ward but could not identify their old buddy. Then Bush yelled, "There's Rube!" Others were in disbelief, for this fellow weighed less than 100 pounds. But it was Rube, all right. Williams grinned, "That's Rube, I can tell by the crease in his nose." They all had a good visit. Rube warned them: "I'll be over tomorrow and show you bums how to run. My weight is down to fighting trim now. I'm in shape." They all smiled and then said their good-byes.[5]

It was late March, and all the big leaguers who had come down to Texas for spring training were heading back North to start the new season. What was left for Rube? By his bedside he kept a picture of himself and Schreck. He told his sister he wished to see his first wife Florence. He did not mention Madge, and he certainly never mentioned May Wynne. Rube also said he wanted to see Connie Mack. Remembering Florence, Rube may have thought of his first getting to know her when back in 1899 he was ill in Columbus. He had recovered then, and the subconscious will always look for some sort of miracle.

Rube's sister wrote Connie Mack of her brother's request too see him. Word got to him too late, but Mack was deeply touched.[6]

No miracle recovery was in the offing. Margaret let their parents know that Rube was not going to last much longer. They hurried to the see their son, arriving on March 31. Rube's father was weak and ill, but he and his wife rode out to the sanitarium the very next day. They arrived late in the day; alas, Rube had died earlier that afternoon at 2:30 on April 1. You see, even the Grim Reaper could not fully silence the spirit of the Rube. After all, it was April Fool's Day; Rube had to get in one final jest. April Fool's, Ma!

The day after Rube died, the zookeeper at Olcott Park in Virginia, Minnesota, announced that "Ty Cobb" had also died. He said the children had fed the little bear too much candy and peanuts.[7] Others knew better. Within a month John Waddell, Sr., also passed away. He never could quite keep up with his son. And three months after Rube's passing, Ossee Schreckengost died in a Philadelphia hospital. Schreck was usually just a little behind Rube's curve, too.

TO RUBE WADDELL

— By Harold Skelton

April, 16, 1914[8]

When in praise to the stars of the present day,
Your voices glad you raise,
Think of the one who has gone before,
The star of former days.

When Walter J.[ohnson] was still a youth,
And Russell* was a boy,
The pitching deeds of Rube Waddell,
Thrilled many fans with joy.

They speak of Walter Johnson's speed,
Of Wood's[†] "smoke" ball as well,
Think of the speed of the southpaw king,
The speed of Rube Waddell.

They talk of Bender's mighty curves,
Of Rucker's[‡] famous drop,
But Rube Waddell had everything,
From a slow one to a "hop."

---

*Ewell "Reb" Russell had just won 22 games with the White Sox in 1913, but he never sparkled like that again, winning just 59 games over the next five years.
†Smokey" Joe Wood won 34 games in 1912, but, due to an arm injury, he subsequently faded.
‡George "Nap" Rucker won 22 in 1911 but would never do as well again.

One hears much of the pitcher's skill
And of the hurler's spell,
Just ask the batters Rube has faced
Of the skill of Rube Waddell.

But time has claimed its victim,
And Rube has heard the call,
No more will Waddell toe the slab,
No more will he play ball.

No more will batters fear his skill,
For Rube Waddell is gone,
No more will he mow the batters down
As he has always done.

So when you talk of Johnson,
Wood, Bender and the rest,
Just speak one word for Rube Waddell,
When he was at his best.

NOTES

1. Roy J. Dunlap, "Waddell's Last Game," Clippings File, Cooperstown.
2. *Minneapolis Journal*, April 2, 1914.
3. Clippings File, Cooperstown.
4. Ibid.
5. Robert Miller Smith, *Heroes of the Game* (New York: The World, 1952), p. 184; Pete Martin, *Peter Martin Calls On…*, p. 56.
6. *Philadelphia Inquirer*, April 2, 1914.
7. *Minneapolis Journal*, April 2, 1914.
8. Clippings File, Cooperstown.

Postgame

Baseball has produced many clowns. But, as Connie Mack reflected, in his 60-plus years in the majors he never saw a nutty player who could hold a candle to the Rube. Rube was not just the looniest man who ever played the game, he was also the first player *celebrated* for his looniness. He invented a pattern many others followed consciously. Most loons were run-of-the-mill players. Others were more cunning than cracked, knowing they could trade well on a Rube-like reputation for eccentricity. Some of more recent vintage who were not mere image cultivators, like Jimmy Piersall, were psychiatrically diagnosed and treated. Rube neither cultivated his lunacy at the bank, nor can he be fully captured by psychological nomenclature. He was the genuine article, a wacko babe in the woods, who also happened to be one of the best players of all time.

Some may think Rube was just a simpleton, a dumb amiable clod, the likes for which baseball no longer has room. But Rube was a more complex character than that. Yogi Berra and Casey Stengel are, of course, richly famous for their many aphorisms that appear a little cockeyed. Yet neither could ever be considered dumb. Rube had a bit of this uniquely American quality, born of smarts which developed on the baseball field yet did not flourish elsewhere. Rube's mound savvy was terrific, too great for him to have been plain stupid.

Never, indeed, has baseball since seen such a combination of wackiness and greatness, nor do the game's magnates really care to. Rube defied all the categories, and as the game has grown ever more corporate, such zany defiance elicits ever more affection from fans while management seeks to exclude it. What the little black bears knew in the zoo up in the tiny town of Virginia, Minnesota, still strikes at the souls of baseball fans.

For all his contributions, the game of baseball gave Rube his just due, but it took a while. When Rube died on April Fool's Day, 1914, newspapers around the country noted his passing, of course. The *Philadelphia Inquirer* made it a front page story. Several papers commented upon the appropriateness of Rube's death on April Fool's. *Baseball Magazine* noted, for example,

"He burned his life away when he should have been in his prime, a cruel April jest."[1] Most papers, however, printed reverent articles befitting the passing of a beloved ballplayer. Stories abounded of his greatness, of his good-heartedness, of how his eccentricities adversely affected few but himself. There was nothing insincere in the pieces penned about Waddell, and, as is the case with the passing of any such celebrity, the world noted the moment and quickly moved on. Three weeks later, the A's played their 1914 home opener at Shibe Park; there was no moment of silence.

Given the nature of Rube's life, it was no surprise that he died penniless. He had never saved a dime, living off his measly paychecks and off the money others gave or "loaned" him. Because Rube had been a member of the Elks Club, when he died in San Antonio local Elks took care of the funeral. Their pastor, Rabbi Samuel Marks, presided, and other local members served as pallbearers. Not one major league ball player could attend the funeral. Players were not intentionally staying away, as they did in 1961 when Ty Cobb died. It was simply due to the fact that it was early April, and everyone was preparing for the start of a new season. Rube would have understood. His grave was a simple one with but a little wooden marker. The laments appeared in the papers; the new season got underway. Stars like Walter Johnson and rookies like Babe Ruth quickly grabbed the headlines. When Ossee Schreckengost died that July he barely got a paragraph. "The Rube is gone, and I am all in," he lamented. "I might as well join him."[2]

In sports, as in music, acting, and other celebrity fields, this sort of rush into anonymity is often the sad fate of stars who burn out from lives of excess and eccentricity. Some considered Rube's rapid fall to anonymity a shame, however, and in March 1921, someone did something about it. That spring, the New York Giants trained in San Antonio. H. J. Benson, a former owner of a local baseball club, hosted a party for various Giant officials, including John McGraw. There he announced: "Gentlemen, I would like to report a condition of which baseball cannot be proud. Rube Waddell's remains are down here, with nothing but a weather-beaten board over his grave. Even the name is almost obliterated."[3] McGraw put the word out. Connie Mack, McGraw, the offices of both major leagues and of the *Sporting News* began pooling cash. They raised sufficient funds ($570) to secure a larger gravesite. Rube's remains were then disinterred, along with those of his father, who rested nearby. At a larger site at San Antonio's Mission Burial Park, Rube was again laid to rest, and this time beneath a large granite monument. The monument stood just over six feet in height, the same as Rube. As in life, the state of Rube's affairs always needed to be corrected. It was only in death that he sat still long enough for things to become organized. Rube deserved better, and thanks to the good sense of others he eventually received it.

When the Baseball Hall of Fame opened in 1939, Rube was not among the charter members. As in burial, he would have to wait. Four pitchers were admitted to the Hall straight away — Cy Young, Christy Mathewson, Grover Alexander, and Walter Johnson. Rube was not selected until 1946. There was no real injustice in the delay. Rube had not had the lengthy career of any of those four. Rube's won/loss record was actually not that great — 191 and 145. During the balloting between 1939 and 1946 those who also entered the Hall ahead of Rube were such highly deserving baseball figures as Judge Kenesaw Mountain Landis, Clark Griffith, and Albert Spalding, managers Connie Mack and Fred Clarke, and top players like Eddie Collins and Rogers Hornsby. The vexing quality of Rube lies in the point that compared to the Hall's four charter pitchers (and he faced three of them), Rube, at his best, was the superior hurler, as Walter Johnson himself had reflected about Rube in 1924: "More sheer pitching ability than any man I ever saw."

The phrase "at his best" gets at the heart of the frustrations with Rube that every fan in his day felt so keenly. Rube could blow away any team, but how could he be kept at his best? The answer was simple: he couldn't. Efforts at control, such as those Fred Clarke attempted in Pittsburgh, had had the opposite effect. Connie Mack was always wise. Rube had to be given his way. He could be manipulated a bit, but that was tricky and could readily backfire. One simply had to hope. Such a state of hope can be poisonous with a man like Waddell, if the relationship involves more than mere baseball. The sufferings of Rube's three wives illustrate this poignantly. Those who could maintain their own calm sense of self, like Connie Mack and Tom Loftus, would get a few more gray hairs, but that was all.* They got the best mound work out of Rube, and that was some phenomenal pitching indeed.

There was no real injustice in Rube not making the Hall of Fame until 1946, and some could argue that several pitchers, notably Lefty Grove, should have entered before him.[4] But Rube's overall record, particularly his strikeouts, was utterly phenomenal. Even more, part of Rube's appeal was unashamedly sentimental. Other members of the Hall of Fame, like Judge Landis, gained entry for contributions to the game that were exclusively off-field. Some, like Boston's Mike "King" Kelly, were admitted because of intangible qualities on the field. Rube had such intangibles, as well as a magnificent on-field record. He made the Hall, and the timing was about right.

With the "intangibles" in mind, the repairing of Rube's gravesite corrected

---

*Mack's own non-obsessive patience that made him so successful a baseball man is born out in the fact that his various reminiscences about Rube, to Peter Martin, to J. G. Taylor Spink and elsewhere, often changed factually. Mack was not trying intentionally to confuse the record. His nature was simply such that it was not important to remember all past details precisely. Fred Clarke remembered everything perfectly, and he had no success with Rube.

a wrong. Mack, McGraw and others were keenly aware of what Rube had contributed to the early popularity of major league baseball. The building of an appropriate gravesite in San Antonio involved much more than mere humanitarianism. Though not the only cause of baseball's early growth, Rube was as responsible as any single player of his era. He was among the game's first real drawing cards, among its first honest-to-goodness celebrities, and the first player to have teams of newspaper reporters following him, and the first to have a mass following of idol-worshipping kids yelling out his nickname like he was their buddy.

Rube's games were among the first to build such popularity that the crowds burst the capacities of the little stadiums which had stood the game well up to that point. The drawing power of Rube helped prompt an era of ballpark construction which left a great mark on the game. So many of the parks that housed the major league teams through the 20th century were built in the wake of the popularity which Rube and others brought to baseball. Shibe Park in Philadelphia was the first, in 1909. Another Philadelphia park, the Baker Bowl, opened in 1912, where the Phillies played until 1938. Outside Philadelphia came Ebbets Field in Brooklyn, Wrigley Field and Comiskey Park in Chicago, Redland Field (later named Crosley Field) in Cincinnati, Braves Field and Fenway Park in Boston, Forbes Field in Pittsburgh, and Briggs (later Tiger) Stadium in Detroit, all opening between 1909 and 1916 in the wake of Rube's heyday.

With the popularity of Rube, baseball became a bigger business. He was so good and so outrageous that the old-time game could not accommodate him. With the growth, baseball became more corporate, ironically in part to protect itself from any more such challenges that were so lethal yet so profitable. Fans turned out, and owners made lots more money. Here the $570 Mack and McGraw raised for a proper resting place for Rube was a pittance, like Rube's salary, which never topped $2500 a year.

It is a bit too easy and fashionable, though not entirely incorrect, then, to cast Rube as an early example of how greedy sports owners exploited a talent and tossed it aside when it ceased to be of use. Without question, Rube deserved a higher salary. Whatever raise Connie Mack or Robert Hedges would have granted Rube, however, there is no doubt he would have simply spent it and still died penniless. Rube's eccentricities ran more deeply than the levels to which the positives and negatives of capitalism could penetrate. One of the charms of Rube's incorrigible childishness was indeed the fact that his character, like sandlot baseball, lay beyond economic strictures.

A fondly held part of America's self-image is that our society has somehow escaped the bounds of class consciousness. Whether valid or essentially a pipe dream, that belief makes a figure like Waddell appealing in both his naiveté and his self-destructiveness. His greatness and his decline were never really the consequence of economics. He was a child who happened to be the very best at throwing a baseball, and his appeal lay in the combination of his character and ability. Indeed, the baseball ability likely began forming in Rube before many of the eccentricities of his character were manifest. This is why he could be so brilliant on the field and so freakish, though lovable, elsewhere. Baseball ran that deeply within him. Both his ability and zaniness comprised his contribution to the game, and both earned him a place in the Hall of Fame.

Rube's appeal, involving both his on-field greatness and his weaknesses of character, touches Americans who give their greatest affection to heroes who are "flawed men." Babe Ruth and Mickey Mantle, superb as they were, always prompted laments from fans about how much better they could have been had they lived with more mature discipline. Ruth was not the player he could have been; Mantle certainly was not, and Mantle's contemporary, Henry Aaron, compiled a better record. But there was always the sense with Ruth and Mantle that just around the bend, like the perfect land supposedly just over the horizon, lay the true greatness of the man, if only he could get to it. Rube Waddell elicited the same feelings. He even inspired poetry.

Hank Aaron, Ty Cobb, Lou Gehrig, and Joe DiMaggio, each arguably the "perfect" player of his era, were ballplayers who never gained quite the same love from fans as did people like Rube, Babe, and Mick. With stars like Aaron, Cobb, Gehrig, and DiMaggio people always knew they were seeing perfection. Day in day out, each could be depended upon to perform at his very best. This engendered enormous respect, which came in Cobb's case despite deep hatred. Fan admiration was genuine, but it was not quite the same as the love given to the Mick, Babe, and Rube. The nicknames for Aaron, Gehrig and DiMaggio illustrated this contrast. "Hammerin' Hank," "the Iron Horse," "Joltin' Joe" (or "the Yankee Clipper")— these nicknames accurately reflected the power and strength of the men, as well as the limits to the affection people felt for them. One cannot warm to a hammer, to iron, or to an electric jolt the way one can to a Babe, a Mick, or a Rube. And the sight of a majestic clipper ship makes one simply stand in awe from afar. (Ty Cobb may have been dubbed "The Georgia Peach," but no one referred to him that way in his presence, and no one ever found anything fuzzy about him.) Ruth's and Waddell's nicknames were so ensconced in their baseball personae that many fans were unfamiliar with their real names. Other than perhaps Dizzy Dean, no other star had a nickname which so affectionately overwhelmed his identity. Affection did grow for Aaron, Gehrig, and DiMaggio, but it emerged mainly as each man's career waned, particularly so for Gehrig, who became beloved when he fell terribly ill. Ty Cobb never gained the slightest bit of affection, even in his later years, though the respect in which he was held never wavered, any more than did the hatred.

When Ty Cobb retired from baseball, he spent many years in the San Francisco area, where his vile fits of temper succeeded in getting him banned from every public golf course in the region. The detestable personality of the man ultimately proved itself greater than his remarkable athleticism. With Joe DiMaggio and Hank Aaron, the stable, great man people knew on the field remained ever the same. The balance of character and athleticism never wavered. They were great guys on the field and off. Everyone respected that. Baseball fans, however, seem to hold their love for men more complex and more flawed. What Rube and Babe were to a fault, DiMaggio and Aaron never were: men of excess.

For Babe Ruth and Mickey Mantle, the fans' love not only never ceased, in certain respects it actually grew after each retired, in Mantle's case even with tarnishing stories about his gambling and drinking. Babe's and Mick's personalities proved a greater asset than either of their great athleticisms. Rube did not live to see how this balance would reveal itself with him. He may have proved such a lout that people could have grown as sick of him as had some of his former teammates and all his former wives. That would have occurred largely among people close to him, as it had in his life. Elsewhere, he would doubtlessly have continued to have lots of kids yelling, "Hey, Rube!" and asking him to play marbles or baseball with them. And he would have done it, of course. The affection was always there for Rube, and that ran deeper than the irritation over his eccentricities, deeper even than the cut of his curveball. Still, the heritage of Rube, as with the nature of his accomplishments, leaves one guessing.

Some facts of Rube's legacy are indisputable, however. And they are as important as any matter of on-field statistics. The Rube was one of just a few ballplayers to have had a comic book published about him. It takes a character like Rube to have kids warm to an image in which they can invest themselves while reading illustrated fiction (and do so long after their hero is dead). A successful comic book character has to penetrate the imagination of children. To do that he or she has to have a believability and a vulnerability in addition to undeniably admirable qualities. This is a rare combination.

Only Rube can claim so many players inheriting his nickname. Granted, "Rube" had long been a part of the lexicon of American slang, but so had "Babe." And while Ruth's "Babe" may have been passed on to Babe Didrickson, "Rube" went everywhere, not always but often in conscious hope that the one so dubbed would take on some of that greatness. It was as though the huge talent that Waddell wasted had to lie somewhere out in spiritual limbo, waiting to reinhabit another. Richard Marquard was the most famous such "Rube." When he showed promise in the minors he was consciously named after Waddell. He won a record 19 in a row one season and later made the Hall of Fame. Arnold "Rube" Foster was another Waddell progeny. He may have been able to surpass Marquard's accomplishments but he was black and never got the chance. Of lesser ability, John Calhoun Benton, Ray Bressler, George Walberg, Henry Vickers, Ray Caldwell, Weldon Ehrhardt, Floyd Kroh, George Ellis, and Walter Lutzke were all big leaguers who played with the name Rube. Waddell's greatness never rubbed off on any of them, but the way people longed for the spirit to reappear speaks to the legacy left by the one and only Rube. No other player bequeathed this sort of legacy to the game.

A question any student asks about great people concerns whether they are born or made. The answer of course varies with each figure. Americans seem to make the greatest heroes out of those who are born with colossal talent, and who defy their maker by breaking convention and forcing a recalcitrant world to reckon with them and their ways. As with Babe Ruth, part of Rube's appeal lay in the fact that people wanted to watch someone who had apparently tied one on the night before and yet was out there performing brilliantly the next day. Americans admired political figures like Henry Clay and Jack Kennedy for such ways, though now the culture prefers to mask the admiration a bit. But behind the mask lies the true character people want to touch. It is risky business, to be sure, because such characters often prove lethal in their self-destructiveness and narcissism. But there is just as much danger either in pretending the appeal is not there or in truculently, and no less narcissistically, asserting a political line that it should simply be shunned. The defying of conventions is an appealing aspect of a culture which has always celebrated the testing of limits.

The appeal of those who challenge authority and restriction has always been at work in the popularity of sports figures. Henry Aaron may have been better than Mickey Mantle. But Aaron didn't have the Mick's box office appeal. In part this was due to race and to the fact that Mantle played in the nation's media capital. However politically appealing, such points are a trifle simple. In many sports mere excellence proves to be boring and yields less financial reward. The "bad" gets the headlines and the dollars. We have seen similar patterns in other sports, such as tennis (John McEnroe) and basketball (Dennis Rodman).

"Playing it close to the edge" has a special appeal in American culture. In lore and literature characters like Br'er Rabbit and Huck Finn have appealed on this basis, as well as on the basis of their primitivism, which was part of Rube's appeal too. He was a primitive even in his own times, and his era of playing is one of apparent simplicity to which ball fans hearken with affection.

Unlike a primitive who tests every limit, the specter of safety and predictability in an athlete seems to imply one not fully pushing the limits, one who has found a comfortable level and is content with it. That may win some minds, but Americans' hearts always want the sense that the frontiers are being tested, even, perhaps especially, to the point of self-destructiveness. Within this appeal lies many beliefs among fans that they could solve the player's problems if they had the opportunity. (The appeal of deeply flawed movie stars, notably Marilyn Monroe, has much of this element too.) A Rube or a Babe thus draws fans into the game at a level other players do not. When fans see Hank Aaron or the Yankee Clipper, a very clear message is conveyed: "Just watch; I don't need any help, thank you." There lies the difference between love and respect.

Rube was really the first American athlete who was known for breaking all the conventions and had people loving him for it. This occurred aplenty with regard to his antics on and off the field. But it also occurred with his mound artistry, too. Before Rube there were other "fireballers." But none of them had Rube's control. As a result, before Waddell's day pitchers were generally discouraged from throwing too hard, lest they walk too many. Rube threw harder than any, yet he never walked 100 batters in a season. He broke all the rules, and he triumphed. A classic statistical measure of a pitcher concerns his ratio of strikeouts to walks. Anything to the favor of the strikeout side is considered good. Rube's ratio of 2316 strikeouts to 803 walks is good to the extreme. (Sandy Koufax's was similar: 2396/817.) And Rube pitched in a day when hitters did not swing for the fences, seeking instead just to make contact. Strikeouts were then more rare, but Rube was breaking 300 a season while few others could even reach 150.

When one looks at the great strikeout artists measured by such figures as strikeouts per year, per game, and per inning, Rube is a leader in all categories, and he is one of the few who pitched in baseball's early years. Aside from Walter Johnson and Rube, all the game's strikeout kings pitched after 1945. Later pitchers gave up more home runs, but with batters swinging for the fences, they could log more strikeouts. Pitching to batters who were not swinging for distance, Rube compiled the strikeouts without the walks and without the homers. He was a marvel. Fans witnessed all this skill and artistry from someone who simultaneously "wised it up" like no other—joking, turning cartwheels, running to fires, wrestling alligators, and, of course, drinking like crazy. Even his escapades with his wives, lamentable though they were, caught the public's imagination. (Rube's one antic that really disturbed people when he was in top form was his playing ball with blacks.) Here was a man who was out beyond the customary edges of his craft and of his society. And out there he was not only surviving, he was triumphing, and doing it all with a big, broad smile. Whatever the mixture of inherited character and circumstance, Rube was one of a kind. Everyone knew it, and they could not help but want to get close. Because the appeal was a mass one, the people generally could not get too close, and this was to the fans' own good. Since they did not have to know this, the mystique could grow and the vicarious image/reality amalgam became the nation's first big media phenomenon in sports.

If the appeal of Rube was mere substanceless hype, it would not have lasted. But there was content. When Rube pitched in little Chatham, Ontario, back in 1898, before much media attention, he left such an impression that one Canadian fan said only Tecumseh had made a bigger mark in the region. Like Tecumseh, Rube was indeed one of those sorts of people who comes out of nowhere, defies all norms, and leaves the world a very different place. Granted Rube's "world" was that of a mere game, but he left it quite different — a big business, with a mass following, fireball pitching, big ballparks and lots of money.

The ballparks that Rube built are fading. Fenway and Wrigley stand defiantly, but baseball may seem to be closing the book on Rube and the era in which he played. And yet, the "retro" parks of the 1990s in places like Baltimore and Cleveland hearken back to an "old time" baseball that Rube helped produce. Rube's world of baseball in wooden grandstands is long gone, but baseball's late twentieth-century nostalgia tries hard to evoke that era.

The baseball world that Rube helped usher in remains the world the game wants to hold on to. The banal and now-reviled polyester-era parks of Pittsburgh, Philadelphia, and Cincinnati proved this, and no one builds ball yards like those anymore. The contrasting character Rube had in excess is something baseball needs, though in more controlled doses. Like Rube's cemetery marker, the "old-fashioned" new parks build upon a memory that grew after Rube and because of him. The essential Rube, like the true old days of baseball, remains elusive, just as he did to the many who played with him and tried to manage him.

The America in which Rube played baseball was entering a new century. It was obviously going to be a time of bigger cities and more concentrated, interdependent populations where certain levels of government or corporate control would emerge. A certain nostalgia then naturally grew for older, yeoman times, which appeared to be passing from the scene. Some of the resulting nostalgia involved concerns about forgotten histories. Mass marketed forms of the nostalgia invent a past that never really was. Popular show people like Buffalo Bill Cody and Annie Oakley, and countless Western stories and movies gave people a Western frontier that never really existed. But it was fun for people to think it was once that way, and the early twentieth-century image of the Old West has largely displaced the region's actual history in the public mind.

Various figures have come forth in American lore and literature that present similarly pleasing, albeit historically inaccurate imagery and hearken back to the same sentiments on which Buffalo Bill and others capitalized. Davy Crockett, Mike Fink, Huck Finn, John Henry and Paul Bunyan all enjoyed a place in the hearts of Americans amidst the nostalgia over a fictionalized nineteenth-century America. In the urban twentieth century, men could no longer be the men as they imagined they had had to be in the frontier days. They began to invent rituals and imagery to fortify their psychological need for a masculinity the everyday world was telling them was not only unnecessary but dangerous. As they invented rituals and found heroes, a figure like Rube grew popular since he embodied the timely imagery in reality. John Henry was fiction, but Rube was neither a pre-modern nor a post-modern construct. He was real, and he was real in a game which itself strikes at the heart of American culture.

One of baseball's appeal has always lain in its ability to combine dualisms, a key one being the ideals of collective team work versus the virtues of individualism. The game requires both, but with a decided recognition of the individual, more than most others. No other team sport has permitted the existence of loonies as has baseball. In other sports zany people are summarily tossed out, or marginalized as mere show business, like the Harlem Globetrotters *vis à vis* the rest of professional basketball. In baseball, team skills are necessary, yet the hitter and the pitcher stand out there alone. While any domination by the individual side of the game can result in chaos, a different diminution occurs if the team concept is too pervasive. Americans have always held a soft spot for the individuals who risk chaos and eclipse the Orwellian power of groups, not merely by running off to the woods but by holding their place in the field and winning. Rube did this grandly. The team aspects of the game were beyond him. Indeed, he became a poor fielder, largely because he could pitch but not field while hung over. He was also a mediocre hitter, often at the bottom of the league in batting average, particularly as his drinking wore him down. But no one could stand out on the mound and single-handedly destroy an entire team like the Rube. When he did so his zaniness stood in defiance of the game's establishment, and for that, more than for everything else, the fans gave Rube their love.

The fact that Rube actually called his teammates off the field during some exhibition games and struck out hitters with no defense behind him illustrates just how his mound artistry could transcend baseball's team aspect. Here Rube eclipsed the game as much as his personal and financial irresolution defied all management strictures. He destroyed his own life with his bad habits, but at his best his pitching could not only beat an opponent, it could beat the actual rules and balance of the national pastime. In top form Rube did not need a team, and fittingly when one of his "call off the fielders" stunts nearly backfired on him, the rest of the team sat back and loved every minute of it. For if a man shows such hubris, he has to be willing to accept any consequence. Rube did. He shouldered all responsibility on himself, and he usually won. No pitcher on a sandlot can imagine any baseball feat more audacious than what Rube actually did. It is the epitome of baseball arrogance. How then could people not love someone who actually lived out the most extravagant fantasy of any boy who ever pitched a baseball? Americans likely have a softer spot in their hearts for Alcibiades than do the Greeks. Like Rube, he was great and a non–team player to a fault.

When Rube called off the fielders and struck out the side, the fans celebrated. The ensuing celebrations swallowed Rube, and ultimately killed him. Rube could otherwise have been so good that he may have diminished the very game he played. He could have rendered baseball boring. Rube with the self-management of a Lefty Grove or a Bob Feller — that very thought made Connie Mack look skyward and wonder aloud, "My, my, my, my." Is there, indeed, any reason why the rules prevent a pitcher from calling his fielders off the diamond while he intentionally walks three and then strikes out the next three batters? Rube challenged such restrictions on the individual. He proved he did not need the help, but the game would not recognize such individualism. It never has; a pitcher still cannot dismiss his fielders.

In modern baseball, individualism comes forth most during salary negotiations. Rube was terribly inept here. This had nothing to do with the game as far as he could grasp it. Such naiveté has always been a key element in baseball's national appeal. The fact that this spirit has been crushed explains many of the difficulties late twentieth-century baseball has had in maintaining its standing in popular hearts and minds. The troublesome Albert Belle and the blandly dedicated Frank Thomas may be great players, but there is not a shred of Rube in either of them.

Some have speculated that a colossal stage talent like Richard Burton needed alcohol to calm a spirit that would otherwise have overwhelmed his tasks. Whatever the links are between certain people's greatness and their propensity toward narcissistic destructiveness, students of the mind will likely never explain them. But the links are certainly there among great figures in many fields, from music to art to sports. In a nation which has apotheosized the lack of constraint and which holds resources to be best regarded as limitless, the image of stars who burn out their talents feeds both the nation's self-image as well as its critics. Even accepting the critics' obvious point that such fancies can be lethal in the everyday world, the fancy finds no health in repression but can be more appropriately vented in the instrumentation of a mere game. The problem here is that the audience usually knows where the game ends; the particular player may not, unless his or her self-destructiveness is merely a clever ruse. Unlike other zanies, Rube was no posturer. He was the real article. His intensity was invaluable in a flood or a fire and marvelous in a ball game. In such places he could laugh at danger and swallow it whole. Elsewhere, it was the dangers that swallowed him and left others to laugh and lament and laugh.

NOTES

1. *Baseball Magazine*, April 9, 1914; quoted in Stephen Fox, *Big Leagues: Professional Baseball, Football, and Basketball in National Memory* (New York: William Morrow, 1994), p. 139.

2. *Philadelphia Inquirer*, July 10, 1914.

3. Clippings File, Cooperstown.

4. Bill James, *The Politics of Glory: How Baseball's Hall of Fame Really Works* (New York: Macmillan, 1994), p. 47.

RUBE WADDELL'S LIFETIME STATISTICS*

Year	Team	W	L	PCT	G	GS	CG	SH	SV	IP	H	HR	BB	SO	RAT	ERA	†ERA+	OAV	OOB	BH	AVG
1897	Lou-N	0	1	.000	2	1	1	0	0	14	17	0	6	5	15.4	3.21	133	.297	.374	0	.000
1899	Lou-N	7	2	.778	10	9	9	1	1	79	69	4	14	44	10.4	3.08	125	.235	.288	8	.235
1900	Pit-N	8	13	.381	29	22	16	2	0	208	176	3	55	130	10.5	2.37	153	.229	.291	14	.173
1901	Pit-N	0	2	.000	2	2	0	0	0	7	10	0	9	4	23.5	9.39	35	.313	.476	0	.000
	Chi-N	14	14	.500	29	28	26	0	0	243	239	5	66	168	11.6	2.81	115	.255	.310	25	.255
	Yr	14	16	.467	31	30	26	0	0	251	249	5	75	172	11.9	3.01	108	.257	.316	25	.248
1902	Phi-A	24	7	.774	33	27	26	3	0	276	224	7	64	210	9.7	2.05	179	.222	.276	32	.286
1903	Phi-A	21	16	.568	39	38	34	4	0	324	274	3	85	302	10.2	2.44	125	.229	.284	14	.122
1904	Phi-A	25	19	.568	46	46	39	8	0	383	307	5	91	349	9.7	1.62	165	.221	.275	17	.122
1905	Phi-A	27‡	10	*.730*	*46*	34	27	7	0	*328*	231	5	90	*287*	9.1	*1.48*	*180*	*.199*	.263	20	.172
1906	Phi-A	15	17	.469	43	34	22	8	0	272	221	1	92	*196*	10.7	2.21	123	.225	.298	14	.163
1907	Phi-A	19	13	.594	44	33	20	7	0	284	234	2	73	232	10.2	2.15	121	.226	.287	12	.119
1908	StL-A	19	14	.576	43	36	25	5	3	285	223	0	90	232	10.1	1.89	127	.213	.281	10	.110
1909	StL-A	11	14	.440	31	28	16	5	0	220	204	1	57	141	10.9	2.37	102	.267	.323	5	.067
1910	StL-A	3	1	.750	10	2	0	0	1	33	31	1	11	16	11.7	3.55	70	.242	.307	1	.111
Total	**13**	**193**	**143**	**.574**	**407**	**340**	**261**	**50**	**5**	**2961**	**2460**	**37**	**803**	**2316**	**10.3**	**2.16**	**135**	**.228**	**.288**	**172**	**.161**

*John Thomas & Pete Palmer, eds. Total Baseball: The Ultimate Encyclopedia of Baseball, 3d ed. (New York: HarperPerennial, 1993), p 1885.

†Adjusted Earned Run Average. This value relates the pitcher's ERA to the leage ERA — thereby accounting for the fluctuating value of runs that accompanies so-called "hitters' years" and "pitchers' years" — and factors the possible influence of a pitcher's home park, which may be deemed either "hitter-friendly" or "pitcher-friendly."

‡ Italics figures indicate league leading totals.

Bibliography

Books

Acocella, Nick. *The Book of Baseball Lineups*. Seacaucus, NJ: Carol Publishing Group, 1996.

Alexander, Charles C. *John McGraw*. New York: Viking, 1988.

_____. *Our Game: An American Baseball History*. New York: Henry Holt, 1991.

_____. *Ty Cobb*. New York: Oxford University Press, 1984.

Allen, Lee, and Tom Meany. *Kings of the Diamond*. New York: G.P. Putnam's Sons, 1965.

Appel, Martin, and Burt Goldblatt. *Baseball's Best: The Hall of Fame Gallery*. New York: McGraw Hill, 1980.

Astor, Gerald. *The Baseball Hall of Fame 50th Anniversary Book*. New York: Prentice Hall, 1988.

Barrow, Edward Grant, with James M. Kahn. *My Fifty Years in Baseball*. New York: Coward-McCann, 1951.

Benson, Michael. *Ballparks of North America*. Jefferson, NC: McFarland, 1989.

Broeg, Bob. *Super Stars of Baseball*. St. Louis: The Sporting News, 1971.

Burkholder, Ed. *Baseball Immortals*. Boston: The Christopher Publishing House, 1955.

Cataneo, David. *Peanuts and Crackerjack*. Nashville, TN: Rutledge Hill Press, 1991.

Cobb, Ty, with Al Stump. *My Life in Baseball—The True Record*. Garden City, NY: Doubleday, 1961.

Cohen, Marvin. *Baseball the Beautiful: Decoding the Diamond*. New York: Links, 1974.

Curran, William. *Strikeout: A Celebration of the Art of Pitching*. New York: Crown, 1995.

Daley, Arthur. *Inside Baseball*. New York: Grosset and Dunlap, 1950.

_____. *Sport of the Times*. New York: Dutton, 1959.

_____. *Times at Bat: A Half Century of Baseball*. New York: Random House, 1950.

Danzig, Allison, and Joe Reichler. *The History of Baseball: Its Great Players, Teams, and Managers*. Englewood Cliffs, NJ: Prentice Hall, 1959.

DeValeria, Dennis. *Honus Wagner: A Biography*. New York: H. Holt, 1996.

Durso, Joseph. *The Days of Mr. McGraw*. Englewood Cliffs, NJ: Prentice Hall, 1969.

Einstein, Charles, ed. *The Fireside Book of Baseball*, 4th ed. New York: Simon and Schuster, 1987.

BIBLIOGRAPHY

Fox, Stephen. *Big Leagues: Professional Baseball, Football, and Basketball in National Memory.* New York: William Morrow, 1994.

Gilbert, Thomas. *Elysian Fields: The Birth of Baseball.* New York: Franklin Watts, 1995.

Goodman, Michael E. *Baseball's Best.* Racine, WI: Western, 1989.

Grayson, Harry. *They Played the Game.* New York: A.S. Barnes, 1944.

Hittner, Arthur D. *Honus Wagner: The Life of Baseball's Flying Dutchman.* Jefferson, NC: McFarland, 1996.

Honig, Donald. *The American League.* New York: Crown, 1987.

_____. *Baseball America.* New York: Macmillan, 1985.

_____. *Baseball When the Grass Was Real.* New York: Coward, McCann and Geoghegan, 1975.

_____. *A Donald Honig Reader.* New York: Simon and Schuster, 1988.

_____. *The Greatest Pitchers of All Time.* New York: Crown, 1988.

James, Bill. *The Bill James Historical Baseball Abstract.* New York: Villard Books, 1988.

_____. *The Politics of Glory: How Baseball's Hall of Fame Really Works.* New York: Macmillan, 1994.

Kavanaugh, Jack. *Honus Wagner.* New York: Chelsea House, 1994.

Kramer, Sydelle. *Baseball's Greatest Pitchers.* New York: Random House, 1992.

Lee, Allen. *Kings of the Diamond: The Immortals in Baseball's Hall of Fame.* New York: Putnam, 1965.

Lieb, Frederick B. *Baseball As I Have Known It.* New York: Coward, McCann and Geoghegan, 1977.

Liss, Howard. *Baseball's Zaniest Stars.* New York: Random House, 1971.

Martin, Thornton. *Peter Martin Calls On...* New York: Simon and Schuster, 1962.

Mathewson, Christy, with John Wheeler. *Pitching in a Pinch.* Lincoln: University of Nebraska Press, 1994.

McCallum, John D. *Ty Cobb.* New York: Praeger, 1975.

McGillicuddy, Cornelius. *My 66 Years in the Big Leagues.* Philadelphia: John Winston, 1950.

McGraw, John. *My Thirty Years in Baseball.* New York: Boni and Liveright, 1923.

Meany, Tom. *Baseball's Best: The All-Time Major League Baseball Team.* New York: F. Watts, 1964.

_____. *Baseball's Greatest Pitchers.* New York: A.S. Barnes, 1951.

_____. *Baseball's Greatest Players.* New York: Grosset and Dunlap, 1953.

Moreland, George. *Balldom: The Britannica of Baseball.* New York: Balldom, 1914.

Mueller, Lavonne. *Baseball Monologues.* Portsmouth, NH: Heinemann, 1996.

Murdock, Eugene C. *Ban Johnson: Czar of Baseball.* Westport, Conn.: Greenwood Press, 1982.

Newcomb, Jack. *Fireballers.* New York: Putnam, 1964.

Okkonen, Marc. *Baseball Memories: 1900–1909.* New York: Sterling, 1992.

Okrent, Daniel, and Steve Wulf. *Baseball Anecdotes.* New York: Oxford University Press, 1989.

Patten, William, and M. Walker McSpadden. *The Book of Baseball.* New York: P.F. Collier and Son, 1911.

Pietrusza, David. *Major Leagues.* Jefferson, NC: McFarland, 1991.

Pope, Edwin. *Baseball's Greatest Managers.* Garden City, NY: Doubleday, 1960.

Porter, David L., ed. *Biographical Dictionary of American Sports: Baseball.* Westport, CT: Greenwood Press, 1987.

Powers, Jimmy. *Baseball Personalities.* New York: Rudolph Field, 1949.

Rader, Benjamin. *Baseball: A History of America's Game.* Urbana, IL: University of Illinois Press.

The Reach Official Baseball Guide. Philadelphia: A.J. Reach, annual editions, 1897–1913.

Reichler, Joseph. *Baseball Encyclopedia,* 7th edition. New York: Macmillan, 1988.

_____. *The Baseball Trade Register.* New York: Macmillan, 1984.

_____. *The Great All-Time Baseball Record Book.* New York: Macmillan, 1969.

Reidenbaugh, Lowell. *Cooperstown: Where Baseball's Legends Live Forever.* St. Louis: The Sporting News, 1983.

Reiss, Steven A. *City Games: The Evolution of American Urban Society and the Rise of Sports.* Urbana, IL: University of Illinois Press, 1989.

_____. *Touching Base: Professional Baseball and American Culture in the Progressive Era.* Westport, CT: Greenwood Press, 1980.

Ritter, Lawrence. *The Glory of Their Times,* enlarged edition. New York: W. Morrow, 1984.

_____. *Lost Ballparks.* New York: Viking Studio Books, 1992.

_____ *The 100 Greatest Baseball Players of All Time.* New York: Crown, 1986.

_____, and Donald Honig. *The Image of Their Greatness.* New York: Crown Trade Paperbacks, 1992.

Seymour, Harold. *Baseball: The Early Years.* New York: Oxford University Press, 1960.

_____. *Baseball: The Golden Age.* New York: Oxford University Press, 1971.

Shapiro, Milton J. *Baseball's Greatest Pitchers.* New York: Julian Messner, 1969.

_____. *Laughs from the Dugout.* New York: Julian Messner, 1966.

Shatzkin, Mike., ed. *The Ballplayers.* New York: Arbor House/William Morrow, 1990.

Smith, Ira. *Baseball's Famous Pitchers.* New York: A.S. Barnes, 1954.

Smith, Kenneth. *Baseball's Hall of Fame.* New York: Grosset and Dunlap, 1970.

Smith, Myron J. *Baseball: A Complete Bibliography.* Jefferson, NC: McFarland, 1986.

Smith, Robert Miller. *Heroes of Baseball.* Cleveland: World, 1952.

Stearns, Peter. *American Cool: Constructing a Twentieth-Century Emotional Style.* New York: New York University Press, 1994.

_____. *Be a Man: Males in Modern Society.* New York: Holmes and Meier, 1990.

Sullivan, George. *Baseball's Wacky Players.* New York: Dodd, Mead, 1984.

Thorn, John. *A Century of Baseball Lore.* New York: Hart, 1974.

_____, and Bob Carroll, eds. *The Whole Baseball Catalogue.* New York: Simon and Schuster, 1990.

_____, and Pete Palmer, eds. *Total Baseball.* New York: Harper Collins, third edition, 1993.

Voigt, D. Quenton. *American Baseball, Vol. II: From Commissioners to Continental Expansion.* University Park: Pennsylvania State University Press, 1983.

Newspapers and Periodicals
(located in Library of Congress, unless noted otherwise)

Baseball Digest
The Baseball Magazine
Baseball Research Journal
Boston Globe
Boston Post
Butler [Pa.] *Eagle* (Slippery Rock University Library, Pennsylvania)
Chicago Daily News
Chicago Daily Tribune
Chicago Inter-Ocean
Chicago Record-Herald
Detroit Free Press
Detroit News
Duluth [Minn.] *News Tribune*
Grand Rapids [Mich.] *Journal*
The "Little Red Book": Spalding's Official Baseball Record
Los Angeles Herald
Los Angeles Times
Louisville Commercial
Louisville Courier
Louisville Journal
Milwaukee Journal
Milwaukee Sentinel
Minneapolis Journal
Minneapolis Morning Tribune
Montgomery Advertiser
The National Pastime
New Orleans Picayune
New Orleans Times Democrat
Newark [NJ] *Evening News*
Newark Star
Ohio State Journal [Columbus]
Philadelphia Inquirer
Philadelphia Press
Philadelphia Public Ledger
Philadelphia Record
Pittsburgh Dispatch
Pittsburgh Post
Pittsburgh Press
St. Louis Globe Democrat
St. Louis Post Dispatch
St. Louis Republican
St. Paul [Minn.] *Appeal*
St. Paul Pioneer Press
Sporting Life
The Sporting News
Youngstown [Ohio] *Telegram*

Numerous articles and pieces, not always noted as to original source, in Clippings File, National Baseball Hall of Fame and Museum, Cooperstown, NY.

Index